I0828257

ACLS History E-Book Project
Reprint Series

The ACLS History E-Book Project (www.historyebook.org) collaborates with constituent societies of the American Council of Learned Societies, publishers, librarians and historians to create an electronic collection of works of high quality in the field of history. This volume is produced from digital images created for the Project by the Scholarly Publishing Office and the Digital Library Production Service at the University of Michigan, Ann Arbor. The digital reformatting process results in an electronic version of the text that can be both accessed online and used to create new print copies. This book and hundreds of others are available online in the History E-Book Project through subscription.

Many of the works in the History E-Book Project are available in print and can be ordered either directly from their publishers or as part of this series. For information refer to the online Title Record page for each book. Inquiries regarding this series can be directed to info@hebook.org.

ACLS
HISTORY E-BOOK

http://www.historyebook.org

SQUATTER, SELECTOR, AND STOREKEEPER

The jacket illustration is from a coloured engraving of Warwick about 1874 by an unknown artist. It is in the possession of the La Trobe Library, Melbourne and is reproduced by kind permission of the Trustees.

To my wife

Squatter, Selector, and Storekeeper

A HISTORY OF THE DARLING DOWNS 1859–93

D. B. Waterson

SYDNEY UNIVERSITY PRESS

SYDNEY UNIVERSITY PRESS
Press Building, University of Sydney

NEW ZEALAND Price Milburn and Company Limited
GREAT BRITAIN Methuen and Company Limited, London
and their agents overseas

First published 1968
National Library of Australia registry number AUS 67-1486
Library of Congress Catalog Card Number 68-27805
SBN 424 05740 9
This book is supported by money from
THE ELEANOR SOPHIA WOOD BEQUEST
Printed in Australia by Halstead Press, Sydney
and registered in Australia for transmission by post as a book

Contents

Contents

List of Illustrations

PLATES

between pages 94 and 95

MAPS

Acknowledgements

This book is based on a doctoral thesis written between 1961 and 1964 at the Institute of Advanced Studies, Australian National University. For the University's generous assistance, I am deeply grateful. I would also like to thank several of my teachers and friends for their liberal contributions of time and energy. Professor G. C. Bolton first introduced me to the fascinating and rewarding study of Queensland, Mr L. F. Fitzhardinge gave much sage counsel and Dr M. J. E. Steven helped me to clarify and revise the preliminary drafts. Dr B. D. Graham gave invaluable help with the political chapters and my colleagues of the Australian National University and Monash History Departments offered many valuable suggestions. Dr Leon Atkinson, in particular, was most generous with aid and comfort. Needless to say, the mistakes and omissions are mine.

The staffs of the Institute of Advanced Studies Library, Australian National University, the Australian National University, the Mitchell Library, the Queensland Parliamentary Library, the library of the University of Queensland and the Oxley Memorial Library gave freely of their time and energy. Mr R. C. Sharman and his staff of the Queensland State Archives, Brisbane, also assisted in many ways as did Miss Patricia Quinn of the Bank of New South Wales' Archives Section in Sydney.

Acknowledgement is due also to the following who kindly gave permission for extracts from copyright works to be included: Angus & Robertson Ltd, for *Landtakers* by Brian Penton, and for verses from 'Reconstruction' by A. B. Paterson from his *Collected Verse*; Hutchinson Publishing Group Ltd for *Pages from the Journal of a Queensland Squatter* by O. de Satgé; Whitcombe & Tombs Pty Ltd for *The Pastoral Age in Australasia* by J. Collier; Mrs Olga O. Schlunke for *Rosenthal* by E. O. Schlunke; and Mr E. D. Davis for *On Our Selection* and *Green Grey Homestead* by Steele Rudd (A. H. Davis).

To the many people who helped to make my visits to the Downs so fruitful and enjoyable I express my warmest thanks. The list is long and the debts great but I particularly wish to acknowledge the help given by the proprietors of the *Warwick Daily News* and the *Toowoomba Chronicle*. Mr W. Bolton, Mr J. Donges and Mrs T. Walker of Toowoomba and Mrs W. K. Gunderson of Warwick also gave me especial help.

I wish to thank Mrs J. Thompson and Mrs S. Stephens for their patience and efficiency in typing a difficult manuscript and my geographer colleagues for their technical help with the maps and graphs. Finally, I wish to thank my wife for her indispensable counsel, sacrifices and encouragement.

Monash University D. B. WATERSON

Abbreviations

1 OFFICIAL

QGG	Queensland Government Gazettes
QPD	Queensland Parliamentary Debates
QSA	Queensland State Archives Holdings
QVP	Votes and Proceedings of the Legislative Assembly of Queensland
SR	Queensland Statistical Register (also Statistics of Queensland)

2 OTHER

BC	Brisbane Courier
DDG	Darling Downs Gazette
TC	Toowoomba Chronicle
WA	Warwick Argus
WE&T	Warwick Examiner and Times
AIBR	Australasian Insurance and Banking Record
AJSB	Australian Joint Stock Bank
BNSW	Bank of New South Wales
DDWLC	The Darling Downs and Western Lands Company
JRQHS	Journal of the Royal Historical Society of Queensland
Pugh	Pugh's Queensland Almanac
QAJ	Queensland Agricultural Journal
QNB	Queensland National Bank

Introduction

Queensland history has not yet attracted the attention it deserves. Certain aspects have been analysed and discussed, but, in general, it is only the spectacular incidents or unusual developments that have captured the gaze of the southern historians. Far too often, Queensland has been relegated to the footnotes while New South Wales and Victoria have monopolized the text.

The Darling Downs, the Queensland portion of the great inland 'fertile crescent' of Australia was, in the nineteenth century, a microcosm of that neglected colony. Although the region's importance relatively declined as other sectional and local interests arose in the expanding colony, the striking economic, social and political diversity within its geographical borders still made it one of the most interesting, illuminating and picturesque areas in Queensland. Downs conflicts and problems provided many of the basic issues of Queensland politics for over a decade after Separation. Nowhere else were the squatters stronger, the storekeepers more hostile, and the selectors more significant. For the region was not only the pioneer pastoral 'base' of the colony but the only large area in Queensland considered suitable for commercial grain growing by yeomen farmers. Its unique character immediately attracted attention. Here, it was eventually realized, were many of the problems of agricultural settlement in the white colonies writ large.

Every regional historian soon realizes that, however small his own original research, colonial and even local history is much less simple and the paramount issues much more open to discussion, re-interpretation and expansion than some of the many closed-circuit practitioners would have us believe. Australian 'Whig historians' have seen in the evolution of areas such as the Darling Downs, an inevitable, pre-ordained and laudable transition—some called it progress—from one form of Australian colonization, extensive pastoralism, to another and higher aspect of civilization, small-scale commercial agriculture. Once farmer has succeeded squatter, the great story has ended and only the secondary themes of adjusting the needs of the new, seemingly static, society to external change remain to be considered. In writing this history, I have been compelled to take a more pessimistic view. Everything except the soil itself seemed to conspire to defeat the honest agrarians.

Those hardy yeomen were small in number, their products insignificant entries in colonial yearbooks, and their relative importance shrank as investigation proceeded. Yet these very limitations, far from engendering the feeling that a study of 40,000 people rather haphazardly, wastefully and even sometimes pathetically settling an area of nearly seven million acres was a futile undertaking, led rather to the opposite conclusion. Not only did significant differences emerge between experiences on the Downs and in the more southerly portions of the 'fertile crescent' but, even more important, a study of the area convinced me that in some of the answers to the questions posed, particularly those concerning the basic dichotomy between myth and reality, lay partial solutions to problems of examining land settlement in other areas and, ultimately, Australia as a whole.

The main theme that emerges is a familiar one: the problems encountered when one section of western colonial society and its allies decided to replace a whole way of life, based on extensive pastoralism, by another and more diverse social system underpinned by a group of numerous small agriculturalists. For too long the clash of man and man—between squatter, lawyer, storekeeper and selector—has obscured the equally if not even more important and dramatic struggle that occurred when the selector attempted to realize the agrarian dream by mastering an alien and at times hostile environment.

There are our themes. What then, are our findings? After Queensland separated from New South Wales in 1859 a minute, but powerful squatting oligarchy on the Darling Downs which had previously established dominance over Queensland's affairs, was challenged by other groups, with different visions and programmes. While these Pure Merinos were not the altogether closed society that has been assumed, and while material possessions and not social origins determined the composition of the group, they closed their ranks whenever their basic interest in the land was challenged.

Queensland agitation for legislation which would demolish the stranglehold imposed by the squatters on Queensland society came not from would-be farmers and 'honest working men' so much as from a formidable combination: Brisbane merchants, artisans and professional men; western squatters who were jealous of the Downs pastoralists' pre-eminence, economic success and exploitation; and an all-important faction on the Downs led by storekeepers and newspaper proprietors who desired wider political and social opportunities as well as the chance to advance their own material interests. These elements were reinforced by a group that could almost be termed professional politicians: men avid for a paid office with its power and perquisites. The Selection Acts did not have one father but many progenitors, each of which had something to gain from a legislative defeat of the Pure Merinos.

But 'liberal' legislation failed to destroy the squatters' monopoly of the best land. Building on a firm foundation of pre-emptive privilege, they succeeded, using a combination of capital, administrative sympathy, political expediency and deliberate evasion, in preserving much of their original interest. The first Selection Acts produced a chain of freehold pastoral estates that gave the Settled District, between 1870 and 1893, much of its unique character. But for the squatters this was a pyrrhic victory. Many were secretly horrified at the disastrous financial consequences which resulted from their ostensibly successful attempt at self-preservation. The very economic arguments which they had used to support their circumvention of the loosely-framed land acts eventually encompassed their defeat. For them, wholesale selection meant an increase in unproductive capital debt that, no matter what expedients were adopted, could never be overcome. By 1893, most freehold pastoralists, however well-developed their estates, were suffering from the cruel combination of chronic over-capitalization and falling export prices.

Those who wished to see the pastoral interests destroyed on the eastern Downs adopted the old ideal of the yeoman farmer as the basis of the new selection legislation. The Darling Downs was the only area where grain growing—the only supreme and natural way of life—was possible. These agrarians, attempting to blend myth with reality, were reinforced by significant numbers of Irish and German immigrants with complementary ideals. In fact, the striking initial success of the Germans appeared to confirm the validity of much agrarian thought.

It was difficult for the farmer to survive, let alone prosper, unless he had good, well-watered land, and adequate and cheap communications to nearby markets which would pay cash for his produce. Commercial farming was the only possibility which would improve his lot. But the failure of the Downs agriculturalists to produce the grain that was central to the agrarian mystique impaired the whole economic basis of the experiment and postponed the golden future that the sponsors of the selectors were confidently expecting. This failure of agriculture to keep pace with developments in other parts of Queensland led to political frustration and the feeling that the best elements of the colony were being swamped by other sections with antagonistic aims and interests.

Most Downs farmers were quick to realize that mixed farming on relatively large selections was the key to commercial success. What the Pure Merinos had predicted and feared had come to pass. Numerous small graziers replaced a few large squatters. But the legislature was slow to make the necessary adjustments to the Selection Acts. This reluctance reinforces the thesis that many elements of the urban middle-class were content to break the power of the squatters and then leave the selectors to fend for themselves in a harsh and unique physical and economic environment. Yet for many farmers, men of property as they were, there was just enough material progress until the 'nineties to prevent any questioning of the agrarian ideals which, in practice, they had repudiated. Those who survived were essentially small business men bitterly opposed to any tampering with private property.

But in spite of their existence as an impotent section in a dependent capitalistic economy, the farmers were still plagued with the problems of seasons and soils rather than those of money and markets. Downs selectors commenced farming with certain advantages lacked by their brethren in North America. They were not really pioneers in the American sense. The despised squatters were the ones who had established the basis of western civilization and its expanding technology on the Downs. Furthermore, as in New Zealand, it was this increasingly efficient and diverse technology which saved the farmers from a life of hopeless subsistence and even economic extinction. Lastly, some farmers tilled the soils in Australia most suited to continuous wheat production.

By accident rather than design the Downs avoided some of the perils associated with the New South Wales blunder of unrestricted free selection. The western boundary of the Settled District roughly corresponded with existing climatic, soil, and vegetation controls. Unfortunately, the unique summer rainfall pattern, to which the crops of the Old World were not yet adjusted, crippled the attempts of the agriculturalists to produce increasing quantities of profitable cash crops. Unpaid family labour and outside work were the solutions most adopted to bridge the gap between returns and expenditure and insure some margin for further development.

Cheap credit was necessary for any considerable expansion of rural productivity. Few farmers could provide adequate security and could not borrow from the existing financial institutions. The practice of the storekeeper-millers, who played a key role in furnishing short-term and uncertain credit at high interest rates was accepted but detested. The operations of the Downs milling monopoly, whose operators claimed to represent the farmers, reinforced a submerged streak of rural radicalism which was inclined to seek a new solution in the extension of the powers and functions of the State. Increasingly dependent upon markets whose prices were fluctuating more and more in accord with world wide commodity movements which the farmers could not control, they, like the pastoralists, sought for the answer in the reduction of processing and marketing costs. The railway rates controversy on the Downs in the early 'nineties was the crystallizing factor which brought the new rural radicalism to a stage where it was prepared to intervene in Queensland politics.

For thirty years selectors failed to organize for political action. They lagged well behind squatter, storekeeper, and even bush worker. Rural politics were incoherent and characterized by parochial competition for roads and bridges, isolationism, and fragmentation. The very nature of pioneering and the presence of a large alien group frustrated all attempts to mobilize the Downs farmers. 'Individualism' inhibited co-operation but, by 1893, most farmers were prepared to concede that hard work was no longer the sole key to success. By then, a new radical minority of moderately successful farmers had arisen to lead a new and temporarily effective movement whose origins and remedies paralleled other developments in the southern colonies and in North America. In 1891 the farmers took the decisive step when they demanded that in the future their political representatives should be drawn solely from their own ranks.

Downs politics reflected Queensland's politics as a whole. The conflicts, between squatter and storekeeper, selector and miller, locality and locality, and town and town, reflected the region's social diversity. Representation, however, was controlled by a small number of property-conscious factions each of which manipulated the electoral mechanism to serve its own ends. Nevertheless, these groups displayed an initial solidarity on developmental issues when the material needs of the Downs were under consideration in Brisbane. Politics were a matter of personalities rather than parties, the main requirement for a successful representative being his ability to extract loan money for developmental works. This was a natural and inevitable result of colonial conditions and the agrarian policies of closer settlement. Yet it is a mistake to assume that fundamental issues played little part in Downs politics. On questions of land policy and electoral reform, for example, rudimentary polarization did occur.

By 1893 Downs politics were in a state of flux which reflected the rapid growth of new sectional interests. No one group was in complete control. The storekeepers, who had so successfully challenged the squatters, were themselves threatened by the emergence of two new varieties of rural radicalism and the growing political consciousness of the urban working-classes in the country towns. Now that their old and limited radicalism had evaporated and now that the old public works panaceas were useless and impracticable the old groups had little to offer. It was time to refashion old myths and adopt new.

PART ONE

SQUATTERS AND STOREKEEPERS

All else . . . has grown out of this root. The goldfields, and all the transformations they wrought, are only an episode in comparison, tending to aggrandise the pastoral and central life of Australian communities. Other interests rise up by the side of it, like the mechanical industries, or spring up out of it by natural growth, as agriculture and horticulture; but, at the heart of everything the pastoral interest remains, narrowed in area, but deepened in intensity, and destined to an unlimited duration. The history of Australia for fifty or sixty years is the history of that interest; its political history is predominantly pastoral, and the men who figure most prominently in that history were pastoralists.

J. Collier
The Pastoral Age in Australasia
London 1911, p. 5

If I could piece together the picture of that epoch as I had inherited it from him—the savage deeds, the crude life, the hatred between men and women and country, the homesickness, the loneliness, the despair of inescapable exile in the bush; the strange forms of madness and cruelty; the brooding, inturned characters; and, joined with this, an almost fanatic idealism which repudiated the past and the tyranny of the past and looked to the future in a new country for a new heaven and earth, a new justice; on the one hand the social outcasts, men broken by degradation and suffering, on the other the adventurers: blackest pessimism balancing the most radiant optimism—If I could only *see* all this, then I would understand.

B. Penton, *Landtakers*, Sydney 1934, p. 29

CHAPTER 1

THE HOME OF THE PURE MERINO

> The Pure Merinos of the Darling Downs . . . 'leave little to be desired in the way of reputation for industry, courage, honesty of purpose, and absolute good faith; their word being their bond; their agreements seldom written, their servants well used, their animals cared for, and their homesteads open to the most ungrudging hospitality, and what can a country desire more in the founders of her early history?'
>
> O. de Satgé
> *Pages from the Journal of a Queensland Squatter*
> London 1901, p. 202

Twenty years after the Leslies had established the first permanent station on the Darling Downs, the region had become the domain of a unique and powerful squatting oligarchy which dominated every phase of human endeavour. Although many of the 1840 'originals' had disappeared, their initial impact on the environment and their role in establishing a tightly-knit, exclusive society were still very powerful and pervasive. The landscape, however, had changed little. Apart from the few small wooden towns—Dalby, Condamine, Drayton and Warwick—which catered for the immediate needs of the squatters and their servants, and the hundred or so isolated homesteads and out-stations, the countryside was still much the same as when Cunningham had discovered the area. No fences, railways or formed roads intruded on the savannah-like appearance of the inner Downs, with its thousands of acres of rolling grassland, distinctive, isolated volcanic cones and numerous watercourses flowing west through black and red loams to join the Condamine River.

If, at first sight, man himself was almost invisible—and there were only 7,000 human beings scattered over three million acres in 1860—his flocks and herds were not. That year 1,500,000 sheep and 140,000 cattle grazed on the blue-grass plains of the Condamine and the brigalow-belah scrubs of the Western Downs. Over the entire pastoral district—stretching from Jandowae and Killarney in the east to Yuleba and Goondiwindi in the west—European man was firmly in control. Allan Cunningham had discovered the Darling Downs in 1827. After a delay of thirteen years caused by inaccessibility, distance from Sydney, official obstruction and

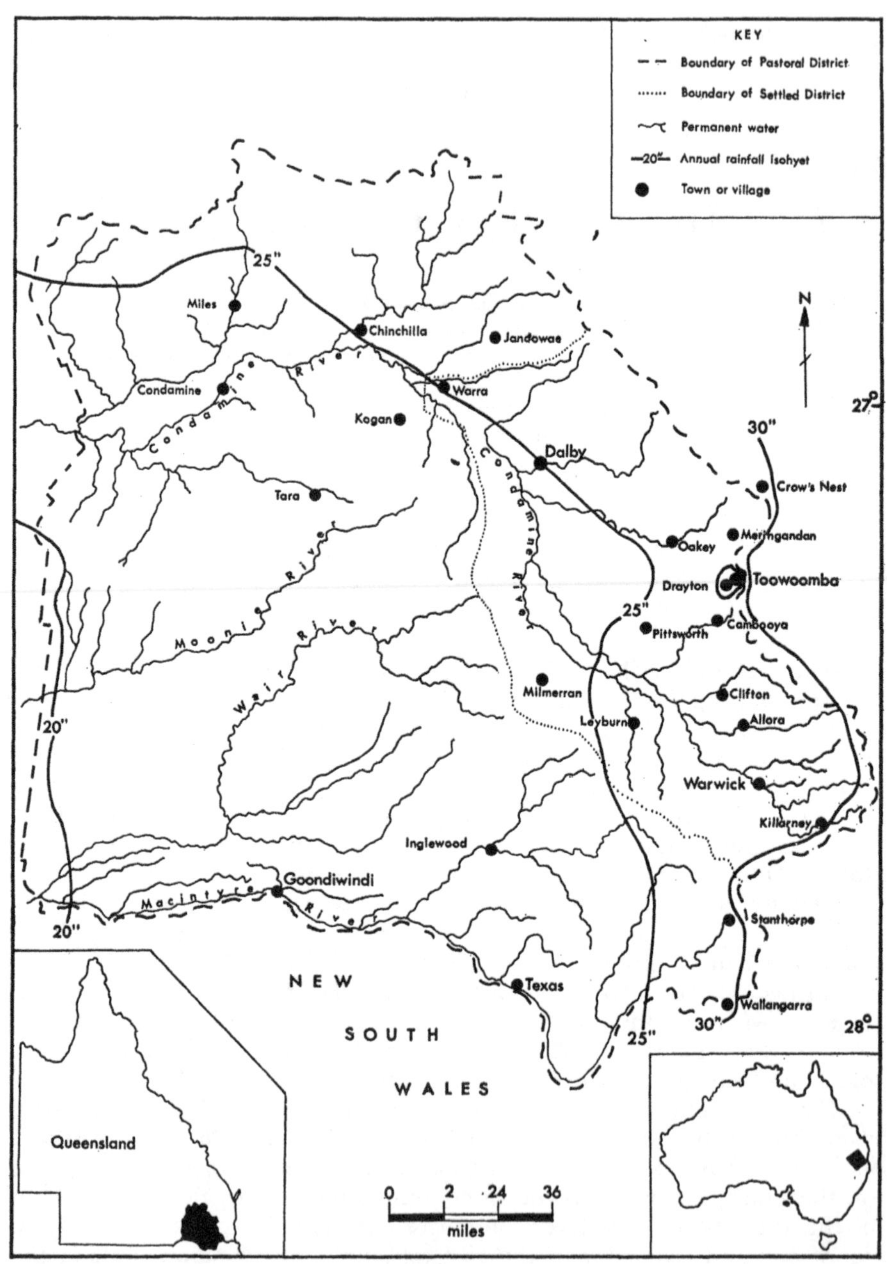

Map 1 Locality map of the Darling Downs

the counter-attractions of Victoria, the first squatters with their stock had arrived in January and March 1840. These were John Campbell and Patrick Leslie. By 1853, nearly all the land in the entire pastoral district—an area nearly as large as the states of Illinois and Missouri combined—had been taken up.[1] The speed with which the pastoralists had established their ascendancy, however, did not mean that their hold over the area was destined to be correspondingly brief and easily destroyed. For the majority their future fate was not as quickly decided as that of many ranchers on the Great Plains of the United States whose position was soon stormed by the advancing homesteaders.[2]

Nor did the Pure Merinos[3] and their contemporaries of the pastoral frontier deliberately attempt to create a new way of life seeking expression in distinctive political and social forms. To them the 'mateship' and dreams of their ex-convict or immigrant employees were unreal, uncivilized and incomprehensible; the Pure Merinos were not Australians but transplanted Britishers who had come to the Downs to make money. Many did so and, like John Watts of Eton Vale, returned 'home' to draw their profits or live on their interest. Others regarded their properties only as a base from which they could sally forth to a colonial metropolis or to Europe. The strong Scottish contingent, shrewd, practical and successful, displayed this economic motivation to a marked degree. This did not, however, prevent the *émigrés* from using their early experience as a basis for the creation of a romantic myth of pioneering settlement. Then the Downs was a true Eden, a virgin land unspoiled by exploitation and human conflict.

But pastoral settlement on the Downs was merely a minor incident in the expansion of Europe, and this idea is reinforced by the real actions and ideals of the first pioneers. The pastoral frontier was never a slowly advancing movement but rather a series of quick forays and slower consolidations which soon remained only a memory as settlement petered out in the deserts of the interior. The effects of the frontier in the United States have been critically examined by scores of historians since Turner's compelling essay: but any attempt to apply every aspect of this 'penetrating', but in many ways misleading, theory with all its implications and ramifications to Downs development is a stimulating but possibly irrelevant academic exercise. This is not to suggest that comparisons with

[1] A. Morgan, 'Discovery and Early Development of the Darling Downs', *Proceedings and Trans., R.Geog.Soc.Aust.* (Queensland), Vol. XVII, Brisbane, n.d. (1902).

[2] W. P. Webb, *The Great Plains*, Boston 1931.

[3] First noted in 1826 by Cunningham in his *Two Years in New South Wales* the term 'Pure Merino' originally referred to a free settler. By the time that the Downs were settled, the scope of the expression had narrowed to describe a group of aristocratic pastoralists of excellent family connections. In this work it is used in its distinctive regional connotation. Until the 'seventies a 'Pure Merino' was a large Downs squatter of family and wealth who had firmly established himself on a vast estate within the Settled District. Later on, the ranks of this group were enlarged to include men whose financial standing compensated for their lack of breeding and social distinction. But by then the phrase had largely lost its significant political and social associations.

areas of contemporary European settlement are valueless. On the contrary they are essential to any understanding of the development of rural Australia. But on the Downs free land—the key-factor in Turner's analysis—was never conceded and the area was first settled by pastoralists, not small homesteaders. Some aspects of Turner's thesis might prove to be applicable to other parts of Australia, although even this approach has recently come under fire, but the evidence certainly demolishes any endeavour to transfer American synthesis to Darling Downs history.[4]

On the Downs the 'Australian Legend' never found even partial response among the squatters. The Pure Merinos soon created, or, rather, attempted to re-create, a society as similar as possible to that in the Old World they had left. Those who had never known or had escaped from this confining and partly illusory class-structure quickly assimilated the mores of their 'betters'. Some—like James Taylor of Cecil Plains—eventually outdid even the purest of the pure in their attempt to re-create a way of life which even in the Mother Country was dying and which now existed largely in the imaginations of those who had emigrated. Indeed it is arguable whether the first generation ever desired, let alone managed, to accept and come to terms with the new environment, favourable as it was for white settlement and rewarding exploitation. In fact the Pure Merinos were to insulate themselves as much as possible from the novel environment. True, they participated in pioneering and performed the monotonous and stark, earthy tasks inseparable from pastoral life, and they could not avoid the impact of a new landscape and the vagaries of an uncertain climate, but most relegated this aspect of their lives to a compartment of their mind labelled 'necessity'. Rigorous self-examination was practised by very few colonists and if it was doubts and hesitations were carefully concealed.

On the Downs such sublimation was not difficult. Economically tied to London or Scotland by bonds stronger than upbringing or sentiment—interest and markets—literate, and in control of the destinies of the new colony, the squatters had the whole apparatus of an expanding western technology at their disposal. And steam, banks, telegraphs and postal facilities were only one aspect of European settlement. Political, judicial and social institutions were transferred and adapted to meet the needs of those who controlled the destinies of the area. Law and order was soon established on the Downs, and rights, duties and obligations were defined to meet the needs of those who operated the mechanism.[5] Once

[4] H. C. Allen, *Bush and Backwoods. A Comparison of the Frontier in Australia and the United States*, Michigan 1959, pp. 110-15; Fred Alexander, *Moving Frontiers: An American Theme and Its Application to Australian History*, Melbourne 1947; N. D. Harper, 'The Rural-Urban Frontier', *Historical Studies*, Vol. 10, No. 40, May 1963, pp. 401-21.

[5] Of the 62 Justices of the Peace on the Downs in 1861, all except 9 were Crown lessees. T. Pugh (ed.), *Pugh's Queensland Almanac*, Brisbane 1862, pp. 46-52. *See also* the lists in the *QGG*. The squatters also controlled the appointments and actions of the Police Magistrates, many of whom were drawn from their ranks. *See* the controversy over the removal of the Warwick PM, J. C. White, who had fallen foul of the Clarks of Talgai. *QPD*, Vol. 3, (1866), pp. 323-7.

they had consolidated their hold on the region it was not difficult for the Pure Merinos to establish ascendancy over the remainder of southern Queensland. Historical, geographic and economic facts encouraged this development which gave the Downs pre-eminence in the first years of Queensland's existence as a separate colony. Brisbane had been a notorious penal station but the Downs, although many of the first shepherds were ticket-of-leave men, was officially free from the 'convict taint' and, moreover, was the first site of genuine 'settlement' in the colony. Adjoining areas were occupied from the Downs rather than from Brisbane. An extension of New South Wales which at first looked to Sydney for markets and capital, the area was an isolated pastoral outpost during the formative years until 'town and Down' were drawn together as Brisbane and Ipswich expanded and communications improved. Initially part of the far frontier of pastoral expansion, yet manning a base for further 'pushes' into the interior of western Queensland, the Downs squatters had twenty years in which to evolve a closely-knit society before they could be confronted by men from the eastern seaboards with different visions and backgrounds.[6] Their model was eighteenth-century English rural society but the same economic and social forces which had destroyed that establishment paradoxically made the creation of a landed colonial gentry virtually impossible.

Extensions of industrial Britain, they could exploit but not consolidate, establish but not mature. The mechanism was certainly constructed but the first operators, on the Downs at least, were soon replaced. Other men, other groups, also sought economic opportunity.

After a short period of depression, drought and aborigine troubles in the 'forties the 'Downs squatters coined money until the crash of 1866'. Wethers sent to the Port Phillip and goldfields markets fetched 12s. to 14s. a head and maiden ewes sent north to stock new runs £1 each. Well-washed wool reached 2s. 6d. per pound and tallow brought 40s. to 50s. per cwt.[7] Most new runs to the north and west of the region were stocked from the Downs, and the New South Wales and Victorian gold discoveries created tremendous demands for fat-stock which the Downs was able to fulfil. Wool prices were also high and the area exuded prosperity—1856 to 1866 was the golden age of the Pure Merinos. During this period financial reserves were accumulated which some put to good use when the Selection Acts presented the squatters with their first human challenge. Indeed, between 1859 and 1875 only six runs in the settled district changed hands as the result of financial disaster, and J. C. White, one-time manager of Jondaryan, estimated that the proprietors netted

[6] On the Downs in 1880, 23 individuals or partnerships controlled 53 stations. From the late 'fifties squatters such as Bell, Taylor and Miles acquired many runs on the Western Downs. Later in the century these properties were integrated with the economy of the freehold of the settled district. Store-sheep and cattle, reared in the west, were railed or driven to the east for fattening before they were sent to the Brisbane market. Furthermore, 22 Downs squatters held at least 40 other stations in various parts of Queensland. *QGG*, 'Pastoral Rent List', 1866-93.

[7] Oscar de Satgé, *Pages from the Journal of a Queensland Squatter*, London 1901, p. 156.

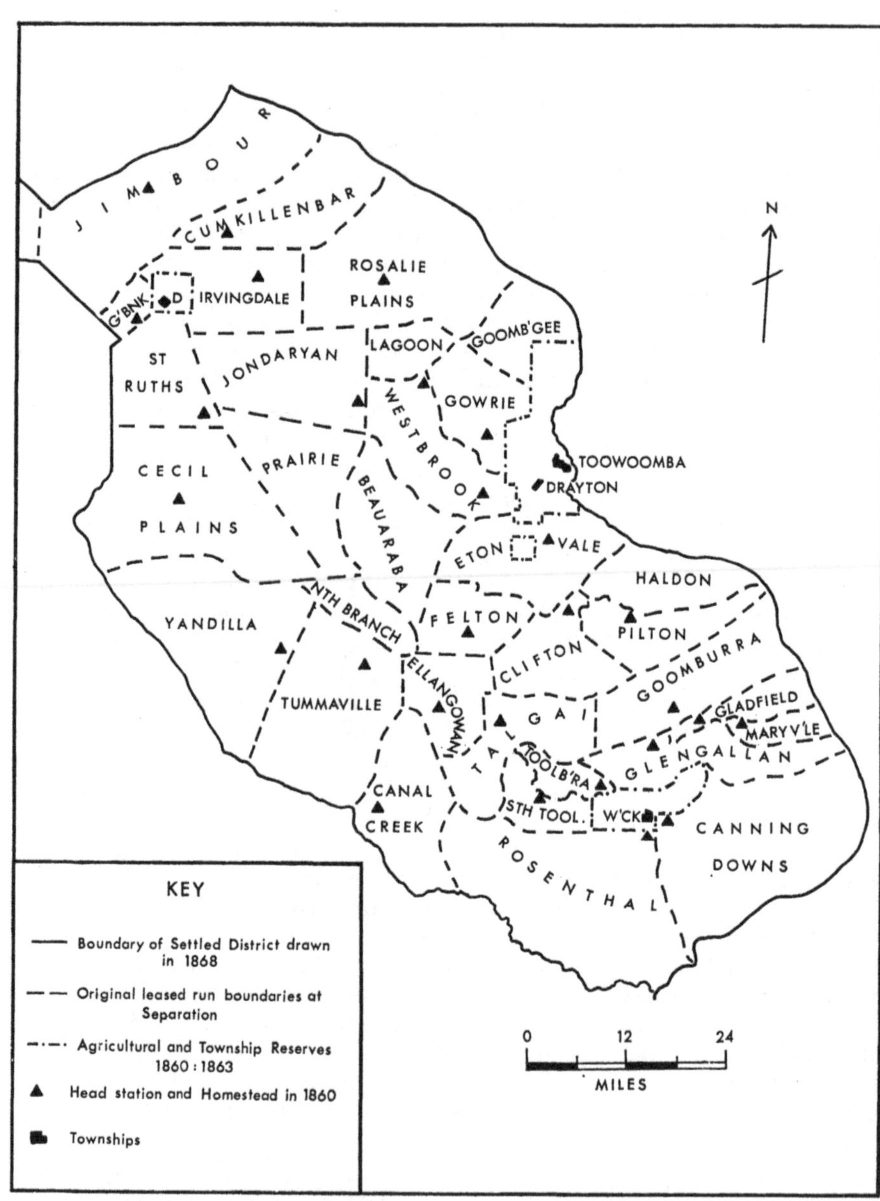

MAP 2 Settled District runs, 1860 (after Buxton's Squatting Map, 1864)

£80,000 in three years during the early 'sixties.[8] But it would be misleading to accept uncritically the 'pastoral legend' of a solid oligarchy, united by breeding, education, taste and social custom. A Pure Merino himself, Oscar de Satgé lauded his fellows and concluded that their rule had on the whole benefited Queensland. His version had just enough truth to make it plausible and acceptable to later generations:

> [They] . . . were a fine set of men; generally men of education and mostly of refinement, who had brought . . . the habits and ways of gentlemen; so that if the Darling Downs did . . . rule Queensland and legislate possibly for somewhat selfish ends, this . . . power might certainly have fallen into far less scrupulous and more dangerous hands.[9]

The Gores of Yandilla with their aristocratic Irish connections, the Ramsays of Eton Vale and the Wienholts of Jondaryan certainly gave the area a distinctive stamp—but such men were not in the majority.[10] Not all 'always wore evening dress for dinner' and held elegant boating-parties as did Ralph Gore.[11] A James Taylor or a Matthew Goggs had at first little in common—beyond the practical and political problems of the pastoral industry—with 'gentry' such as Sir Arthur Hodgson who retired to play the squire in England as soon as they could afford to depart. Most Western Downs squatters, before the advent of pastoral company, bank and manager, lacked 'aristocratic connections' and were resident lessees shackled to their runs and closely concerned with every aspect of pastoral production. Certainly, gentleman-squatters of 'education and culture' were present, particularly in the settled district, in possibly relatively greater numbers than in most other pastoral areas but even there their number was small compared with the Scots, the adventurers and the later managerial group.

The first squatter to settle in Queensland, John ('Tinker') Campbell of Beebo, was a Scot, and Aberdonian capital financed the Leslies, Gammies and Dalrymple when they squatted on the black soil.[12] Later arrivals such as William Miles and William Graham preserved the Scottish connection. Northern capital financed several stations, and northern pastoral companies (particularly the North British Australasian Company and the Scottish Australian Investment Company) invested heavily on the Downs during the 'seventies. Scots squatters were shrewd, hard-working and successful pastoralists, most of whom had risen from the ranks of the pastoral employees. William Miles, for example, graduated progressively from 'general useful' on the Mackay River to overseer and later manager.

8 *TC*, 21 April 1869, p. 3, c. 1-3.

9 de Satgé, *Journal*, p. 157.

10 The hard-core of Pure Merino 'exclusiveness' was made up of the Kings, Wienholts, Clarks, Coxens, Bells, Gores, Isaac, Hodgson, and Watts.

11 de Satgé, *Journal*, p. 62. The best description of the Pure Merinos is in H. S. Russell, *The Genesis of Queensland*, Sydney 1888. Russell himself was a 'genuine' member of the group from 1841 to 1856 (Cecil Plains).

12 L. J. Jay, 'Pioneer Settlement on the Darling Downs: A Scottish Contribution to Australian Colonization', *Scottish Geographical Magazine*, Vol. 73, No. 1, April 1957, pp. 35-49.

After pioneering new country on the Dawson he purchased Dulacca on the Western Downs and eventually constructed a freehold station in the Dalby area. A few Downs squatters had even more humble origins than Miles. James Taylor rose from stockman on Cecil Plains to be one of the wealthiest men on the Downs through a combination of personal ruthlessness, technical ability, political acumen and sheer good fortune in choosing ideal pastoral country. Such men aroused the scorn and enmity of the well-bred failures they replaced and were never completely accepted by the 'gentlemen' of the Downs. Unsuccessful educated gentry such as Charles Coxen, however, could always find a Government billet while the poorer men without connections drifted back to the ranks of the bush-workers or the alcoholics after they had failed.

Until the 'seventies it was not impossible for men to work their way up through the ranks of the Australian pastoral hierarchy by 'indomitable perseverance and a fixed determination to succeed'.[13] Later in the century such advancement became more and more difficult. On the Downs the over-capitalized freeholds of the east and the mortgaged leaseholds of the west offered little opportunity for those with personal initiative and capacity for hard work rather than capital resources. The new men after Separation fell into four groups. Firstly, capitalists or their agents such as Davenport, Loughlin and Simpson arrived from the southern colonies confident that a lavish application of money and improvements, together with better techniques, would yield handsome dividends. This section was heartily detested by the old 'establishment' not only for their presumption in invading an area that had already been 'claimed' and 'settled' but also for their determination to accelerate the old pastoral rhythms. Secondly, Sydney and Brisbane mercantile and industrial capital invested heavily in the Western Downs—the Morts and their partners controlled fifteen runs there in 1874—and the Tooths of Clifton and Jondaryan were first financed by their uncles' profits from the Kent brewery. A decade later in 1885-6 Australian banks nominally held sixty-five pastoral leases on the outer Downs alone.[14] Wealthy Pure Merino, pastoral-company capitalist and bank all required competent managers, and it was this new managerial group represented by such men as Daniel Williams and L. E. Lester who were the 'typical' Downs squatters of the 'eighties and 'nineties. Sometimes sons of the absentee proprietors, but more often men whom the contracting of opportunities had placed in the ranks of salary-earners, the managers were usually native-born, skilled technicians who lived in much the same style as the absent proprietors or bankrupt squatters they had replaced.[15] Lastly the Land Act of 1884, designed to encourage on the Western Downs the new element of small graziers who had arisen in the Settled District as a by-product of the Selection Acts, gave opportunities for frustrated managers, and successful farmers' and squatters' sons to acquire runs of their own.

13 The quotation is from Miles's obituary: *TC*, 25 August 1887, p. 2, c. 5.

14 Map 12 illustrates the extent of company 'ownership' on the Western Downs in 1885-6.

15 James Collier, *The Pastoral Age in Australia*, London 1911, p. 199.

This group, eventual successor to Pure Merino and pastoral company alike, suffered from drought, declining prices and shortage of capital until the turn of the century. Many of the new leases of the Western Downs were too small to return the higher standard of living these graziers expected and, apart from the dubious comfort of social prestige (pastoralism was and is 'superior' to agriculture in the Australian rural hierarchy), their problems were but more immediate, acute and personal versions of the problems of those they had replaced.

Except for the graziers, however, all groups eventually came to subscribe to the ideals of the Pure Merinos and to imitate their way of life as far as their means would allow. This cultural absorption was rapid and thorough, giving this diverse group a solidity and confidence on basic political issues that little could shake. In aims and attitudes squatters such as Fitz of Pilton and Taylor and Tooth of Clifton were soon virtually indistinguishable from the old 'aristocrats'. In fact, Fitz with his reactionary views and political obstructionism, Tooth with his liveried servants and his pathological fear and hatred of selectors, and Taylor with his town mansion and his social aspirations, in some ways excelled the original 'grass dukes' at their own game. This coalescing of small groups with diverse backgrounds but identical political and economic interests was the most significant feature of the pastoral 'establishment' of the Settled District. Concealing the very real differences between squatter and squatter, this surface integration gave outsiders the impression of a monolithic interest, without exploitable flaws, determined to conserve a special way of life and the investments which sustained it. The success of this alliance—eventually cemented by inter-marriage, wealth and social polish—concealed original differences of upbringing, character and attitude and distorted and frustrated later attempts to reconstruct an accurate picture of the lauded or condemned Pure Merinos.[16]

The squatters of the Western Downs pursued a way of life that differed little from pastoral activity in other parts of Australia. On the downlands of the Upper Condamine, though, the Pure Merinos and their satellites evolved a social system which was at once more complex and more artificial than its earthly progenitor. On the surface—as Trollope discovered in 1871—it was a 'plentiful easy life, full of material comfort, informal, abundant, careless, and most unlike life in England'.[17] Hospitality was never stinted at the 'great houses' and nobody, whatever his social standing, was turned away thirsty or hungry from stations such as Jimbour or Yandilla.[18] The arrival of the manager and the impersonal pastoral company, though, abraded the old relationships in both east and west. In the Settled District this development was accen-

16 The headquarters of the Downs oligarchy was the exclusive Queensland Club, founded in Brisbane in 1859. It succeeded the even more restrictive North Australian Club at Ipswich which admitted only Pure Merinos. C. B. Fletcher, 'The Queensland Club', article in the *Australasian*, 17 October 1896, pp. 752-3.

17 A. Trollope, *Australia and New Zealand*, London 1873, Vol. I, p. 116.

18 N. Bartley, *Australian Pioneers and Reminiscences*, Brisbane 1896, p. 219.

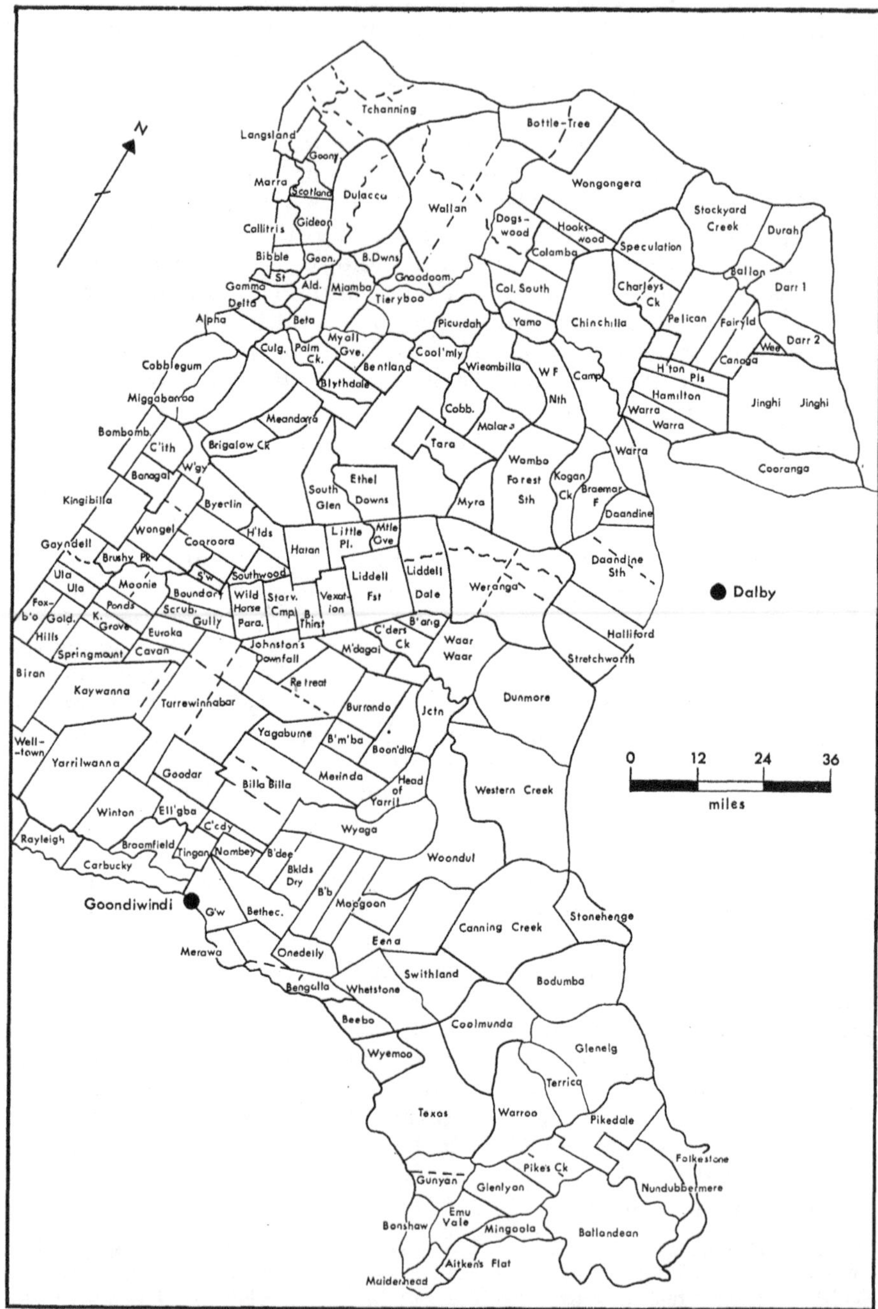

MAP 3 Unsettled District leaseholds, 1884 (after Lands Dept. Run Map, 1884)

tuated by the transformation of extensive pastoral properties into highly-developed freeholds, run on strict business lines by owners or managers who were attempting to counteract over-capitalization and falling prices by specialization and cultivation. By 1893 the free-and-easy days were gone for ever.

Some Pure Merinos lived in almost feudal splendour. Head stations—such as Cecil Plains, Yandilla, Jimbour and Jondaryan—were virtually self-contained villages, with cottages, stores, stables, workshops, post-offices—even schools and chapels. Many resident squatters gradually constructed long, low, rambling, verandah-ed homesteads to replace the original huts and cottages. Talgai, Jondaryan and Canning Downs, with their spacious lawns, orchards, gardens and English trees, were small oases in an empty, brown and dusty summer landscape. As if anticipating Parkinson's law, however, the golden age of pastoral building, which reached its climax in the magnificent freestone mansions of Glengallan and Jimbour, was also a time of declining power and profits for their inhabitants. These costly edifices, complete with ballrooms, billiard-rooms, salons and dining-halls, were symbols of aspirations that were realized for only a few short years before events beyond the squatters' control dissolved the visions and destroyed the reality.[19]

On the Western Downs, homesteads were utilitarian and simple rather than ornamental and elaborate. Tieryboo head station, for example, was in 1881 little more than a small brick-and-wood house with detached kitchen, store, three huts and a couple of sheds.[20] Some of the larger stations such as Welltown and Callandoon resembled the villages of the Settled District but as a rule less capital was invested in these basically unproductive improvements in the west than on the black-soil plains.

Living in a leisurely world of their own creation (or so it seemed to them), undisputed rulers of small communities which they regarded as their personal property, and shuttling between station and metropolis, many squatters lived lives which seemed satisfying and self-sufficient. Trollope observed that:

> The sense of ownership and mastery, the conviction that he is the head and chief of what was going on around; the absence of any necessity of asking leave or of submitting to others—these things in themselves add a great charm to life. The squatter owes obedience to none, and allegiance only to the merchant.[21]

His conclusions were certainly valid in 1871 but twenty years later the environment had undergone such profound political, economic and social changes as to transform the old pastoral nuclei from centres of

19 For description of the great homesteads *see* G. E. Evans, *The Garden of Queensland*, Toowoomba 1899 (Jimbour House cost over £30,000 when it was completed in 1876); C. W. Russell, *Jimbour: Its History and Development, 1840-1953*, Brisbane 1955; D. C. Murray, 'Work and Sport on the Darling Downs', article in *Sydney Daily Telegraph*, 26 October 1889, p. 6.

20 *Australasian*, 5 December 1881, p. 580. Undullah (Palmy Creek, Blythesdale, Culgara, Tara and Woolanguil Runs) was little different twenty years earlier. *DDG*, 8 May 1862, p. 2, c. 4.

21 Trollope, *Australia and New Zealand*, p. 99.

settlement to islands in hitherto friendly but now alien and hostile seas. Significant changes on the Downs has passed the majority of the squatters by; at the turn of the century the remaining Pure Merinos were observers of, rather than participants in, the evolution of the area.

The pastoral employees enjoyed—or, rather, tolerated—conditions that were strikingly different from and inferior to those of their superiors. Once again the distinction between master and man was much sharper in the east than in the west where lessee and manager worked side by side with their labourers and faced much the same difficulties and hardships. Men such as the younger Gores acknowledged, even if they did not approve, the colonial adage that 'a man is not only as good as his master but he's a damn' sight better'—still, there was little social intercourse between the Pure Merino and his servant beyond the paddock, the woolshed or the drafting-yards. The gap between pub and club was very wide and seldom bridged.

In 1844, 259 stockmen and shepherds worked on the Downs, representing over half the total male population over fourteen. Nearly fifty years later there were 1,051 pastoral employees permanently working in the area. Thus, although the number of workmen increased at a greater rate than owners, lessees or managers, their relative strength declined as those of other occupations—particularly urban artisans, farmers and transport workers—rose.[22] In the Settled District, where the 'pastoral village' was well established by the 'seventies, some Pure Merinos conceded that they had 'duties as well as rights' and treated their men accordingly. Old-world practices such as the harvest-home festivals at Eton Vale, responsibility for the aged worker, and a paternalistic interest in education and religious instruction, were maintained by some squatters, but living and working conditions were abominable on several stations. A German and his wife employed as shepherds on Lagoon Station died of scurvy and deficiency diseases in 1860 after being left alone in their hut for several weeks. Single workers were crowded together in corrugated-iron huts in which they ate and slept, and even married couples had sometimes to share their quarters with other employees.[23] Wages were comparatively high during the 'sixties but remained unaltered for the following thirty years.[24] By 1890 many bushworkers worked for rations alone. Cheap labour was always sought by the Downs pastoralists. Chinese were employed on many stations in the 'fifties and early 'sixties to counteract the effects of the southern goldrushes, kanakas were dragged off to die of pneumonia at Westbrook and Callandoon, and many Germans laboured as hut-keepers or shepherds before selecting land.[25]

22 *BC*, 26 June 1869, p. 7, c. 2. *Census of Queensland*, 1891, pp. 1090-1. The latter figure does not include 154 overseers and managers.

23 *DDG*, 15 November 1860, p. 3, c. 4, and 18 January 1861, p. 3, c. 5.

24 Shearers, for example, received 3s. 6d. per score on the Downs in 1860. During the 'seventies the rate was 3s. 3d.-3s. 6d., but by 1888 only 3s. per score was being offered by the pastoralists. *DDG*, 20 September 1860, p. 2, c. 5, and *WA*, 30 March 1889, p. 3, c. 1.

25 *TC*, 26 February 1876, p. 3, c. 5 and *QPD*, Vol. 13, (1871-2), pp. 40, 57.

After freeholding, however, conditions improved in the Settled District. Fencing ended the vile hut-keeping system, houses improved, and closer settlement and its 'civilizing institutions' ended the isolation which was perhaps the greatest hardship the pastoral workers were forced to endure. Also, the type of labour available in the Settled District changed. Ex-convicts, 'nomads' and poor Germans were replaced by selectors' sons and those intent on accumulating enough capital to enable them to take up a small selection. Much of the work was now carried out by contractors who, like their employers, had a 'stake in the country'.[26] This change in the character of pastoral employees, a result of the economic and social diversification of the region, was responsible for the reluctance of many Downs shearers and labourers to accept the new gospel of resistance preached by the radical agitators in the woolsheds of the west. True, the squatters were first challenged at Jondaryan and the other mammoth sheds of the settled district in 1889, and the right to organize and exclude non-Union labour was first conceded as a partial consequence of events on the Downs during the following year, but the great strike of 1891 was not popular with many of the area's shearers. The Downs pastoralists deliberately provoked the strike of 1891 when they repudiated the Pittsworth Agreement and insisted upon 'freedom of contract.' Several sheds—St Ruths, Cecil Plains and Glengallan—struck at the beginning of the strike but free-selector 'blacklegs' repudiated the Union and worked under the pastoralists' rules. There was little trouble on the Downs once the cockies intervened.[27] The signing of the Pittsworth Agreement left the Downs shearers satisfied and reluctant to follow their colleagues of the central west along paths which many thought would lead to the destruction of all private property. Most of them had too much to lose—or so they thought. It was the Darling Downs squatters who then forced the pace: reacting with vigour and decision, the remnants of the Pure Merinos made their last decisive intervention in Queensland affairs. The Darling Downs Pastoralists' Association which had grown out of the Toowoomba social clubs and stock associations was the progenitor of the great Australian organization which eventually challenged and defeated the shearers in 1894.[28] It was a fitting end for a small regional group whose political power had been destroyed, its economic basis undermined and its social system lampooned and rejected.

But—however dramatic and significant the struggles of the pastoral employees—it was the 'storekeepers' of the three major country-towns,

26 *TC*, 3 September 1889, p. 3, and 12 September 1889, p. 3, c. 7. The evidence indicates that most Downs shearers supported the Union in 1889.

27 *DDG*, 27 March 1891, p. 4, c. 4, and *TC*, 22 January 1891, p. 3, c. 3.

28 The Pittsworth Agreement between the Queensland Shearers' Union and the Darling Downs Pastoralists' Association (August 1890) was reluctantly endorsed by the Labour Federation as a temporary truce. *TC*, 16 August 1890, p. 3, c. 2. The Pastoralists' Association had been formed after a meeting at Toowoomba on 15 May 1890. *WA*, 3 June 1890, p. 2, c. 6. For the full text of the Pittsworth Agreement guaranteeing 4s. per score and the exclusive employment of Union shearers, *see TC*, 17 June 1890, p. 3, c. 3-4.

Dalby, Toowoomba and Warwick who, together with their associates the small farmers, contested and finally broke the squatters' stranglehold. Ironically these villages, established at strategic locations, were the creation and the servants of the pastoral interest. So too were the trunk railways which, while lowering the squatters' marketing costs, stimulated the towns and encouraged the attempts of a group of their inhabitants to realize the agrarian dream. Only with closer settlement and the additional number of producers and consumers it would bring could trade and industry expand. Almost all the squatters' needs were supplied from Brisbane and Sydney and the small local villages were merely useful distribution-points for goods and services. Stegner, the American novelist, depicted the squatters' tragedy in another setting:

> They had been counting on the railroad and had helped to promote it. Like other pioneers, they would have believed in Progress, and would have realized no better than others how surely Progress destroys what makes a frontier satisfying.[29]

The supersession of the pastoral 'capital', Drayton, with its hotels, stores, court-house, post-office and stockyards, by the younger, but more vigorous, Toowoomba—intent on becoming a true regional centre—also marked the shift in the balance of power from country to town. Toowoomba had only 1,528 residents in 1864 but by 1891 7,007 persons lived in the town.[30] While pastoralism underpinned the municipality's progress and prosperity, administrative, service, processing and even manufacturing functions expanded at a faster rate, particularly during the late 'sixties and throughout the 'seventies. The Selection Acts had an immediate and beneficial impact on urban growth and profits, thereby justifying in part the hopes of one section at least of their sponsors. Warwick, surrounded by pastoral estates, had a less spectacular rise after Separation and relatively declined for a time after the exhaustion of the alluvial-tin deposits at Stanthorpe. Nevertheless Warwick—together with Allora, a purely 'selector-town'—attracted an increasingly diversified population and became more dependent on the 'bold peasantry' of the adjoining agricultural reserves than upon the pastoral freeholds and the trade of the south-west Downs.[31] Dalby, however, remained a pastoral town—although more sober pioneer grazing farmers were to be seen along its streets in 1893 than aloof Pure Merinos, riotous stockmen, and shearers intent on knocking-down their cheques at the fifteen hotels lining its wide, treeless and dusty main-street.[32] Only towns such as Condamine and Leyburn retained their original character. Condamine—'in need of a good fire' in 1875—with its three hotels, store, two blacksmiths' shops, post-office, school, police-station and court-house, was a typical Western Downs bush-town whose stagnation and decline after

29 W. Stegner, *Wolf Willow*, London 1962, p. 6.

30 *SR*, 1864-91.

31 *Town and Country Journal*, 6 February 1875, p. 334, c. 4, and *WA*, 1 January 1889, p. 2, c. 7.

32 Dalby's population declined and then stagnated after the railhead moved west.

1875 reflected its failure to attract the western railway and also the area it served.[33] The future lay with the new agricultural towns of the east—Pittsworth, Oakey and Crow's Nest—which, established in the 'seventies, owed little allegiance to the old order and almost everything to the new. From the country towns of the Downs came the new men—the storekeepers, millers, artisans, doctors, lawyers, teachers, civil servants and clerks—whose ideas, aims, organizations, entertainments and essentially urban way of life were the complete antithesis of the old concepts and patterns of all rural participants in the pastoral age. The new urban hierarchy had little in common with the representatives of the old order.

Pastoralism appeared to be blocking economic opportunity, political change and social advancement. In fact 'civilization', as the colonial *bourgeoisie* rather narrowly conceived it, could never be properly attained and advanced while a few men, considered to be absentee exploiters rather than true 'settlers', monopolized the basic resources of the region. Using every weapon at their disposal the storekeepers attacked the Pure Merinos on every front. Careful to stress that they were attempting to force only a limited redistribution of property and profits within the existing system, the townsmen attacked the pastoralists with the only effective tool they possessed—the franchise. After securing their home-bases they then attempted—with considerable success—to mobilize the opinions and ultimately the votes of those whom they had helped to obtain land. Once the selectors were established and the power of the squatters was broken, however, the storekeepers' radicalism waned and died. By 1893 they, as well as the surviving squatters, were the economic conservatives of the Downs.

Yet the role of the storekeepers in promoting economic and social change on the Downs can be exaggerated. While they organized and led the elements on the Downs which helped to break the squatters' political power, their great contribution—the Selection Acts—was not immediately decisive. Few pastoralists lost either their runs or their social position; in fact, the pastoral freeholders of the 'seventies appeared to be in a better position than ever before. But in victory lay defeat: world price movements, advancing technology and political trends were all on the side of the storekeepers. The squatter was doomed as soon as he was forced to purchase large quantities of land, and this he failed to comprehend. The country towns' mills might have ground slowly but they ground exceedingly small.

[33] *DDG*, 2 August 1860, p. 3, c. 6 and *Town and Country Journal*, 10 July, 1875, p. 683, c. 4.

CHAPTER 2

RENTS, RESUMPTIONS AND RACKETS

> . . . a great deal of dummying had taken place, but he did not think there was much wrong in it; if he had not been a member of Parliament he would have dummied himself. It was a bad thing that laws should be framed in a way that forced people to do what was seemingly dishonest.
>
> *QPD,* Vol. 5, 1867, p. 459, speech of Clark, MLA for Warwick

THE CREATION OF THE FREEHOLD ESTATES

The outstanding feature of the Downs pastoral industry between 1860 and 1875 was the creation of a score or so of giant freehold estates from the leased runs of the Settled District. To the squatters the selection legislation presented both a menace and a challenge. In the event this challenge was met and the fear that the small selectors would destroy the integrity of the runs was removed by money, influence and evasion. Such a final result was a pyrrhic victory. For many pastoralists, purchased acres meant poorer profits.

From the first, the squatters denied that the agrarians had a monopoly of moral virtues or even of economic progress. The Darling Downs pastoralists in their isolated, yet strategically placed and potentially rich environment, had twenty years in which to evolve and maintain a set of values and assumptions which endured when they were finally attacked and questioned. These tenets were common to most pastoralists in Australia but they flowered more luxuriously on the Downs and in the Western District of Victoria than in all other regions of the Australasian colonies. Never modified, but rather an unspoken portion of their group-consciousness, the narrow creed of the Pure Merino was powerful, logical and compelling, especially when buttressed by education, social custom, economic power and political authority. To conserve these advantages—and they could be preserved only by confronting and defeating the attempt to strip them of the landed resource—all means short of armed violence were considered justifiable. The new theory of the survival of the fittest had already been tacitly accepted by the Black Soilers years before Darwin's name was common currency. After all, 'as far as the squatters were concerned, self-preservation was the first law of nature'.[1]

W. F. Gore of Yandilla pleaded the squatters' case on 18 November 1872 when he protested against the arbitrary resumption of the ten-years leases. After thirty years of hard pioneering, he cried despairingly, all their work and capital were to be swept away. Were these investments to count for nothing? Was not the true pioneer entitled to special consideration? Not a single acre had been or could be cultivated on his run and the men who carried the burdens and endured the hardships 'have been dispossessed to make room for a few other sheep men who are doing neither better or worse than [we] were'. 'No man', lamented Gore, 'could be given back his youth', but the Downs squatters were morally entitled to compensation, not only for improvements but for disturbance.[2] Such concessions were totally out of the question if agricultural selectors were to receive land at reasonable long-term rates.[3]

These claims—so far as most inner Downs squatters were concerned—were untrue, although they had a considerable capacity for self-deception. Only a handful of the men who followed the Leslies remained and most runs were now held by new lessees or absentees, propped up by banks and mortgage institutions.[4] Nevertheless the myth of the perpetual pastoral frontiersman died hard in the Settled District, championed as it was by new and old squatter alike. 'Sentiment and sympathy', may have been 'out of place in such hard-faced company' but they were one weapon, albeit an obsolete one, in the squatters' armoury.[5] Agriculture, in the eyes of the squatters, was no more a pathway to glory than pastoralism. 'Men', declared Wood, 'don't get to heaven any sooner at the tail of a plough than on the back of a sheep.'[6] The true test was the ability of the tenant or freeholder to use the land most profitably and to invest as much as possible in it. Let all, advised Watts, follow the path of Adam Smith and concentrate on producing wool and meat, the only exportable products which could be profitably produced on the Downs.[7] This economic argument had something to recommend it—but mixed farming, not extensive pastoralism, was the key to future development.

Capital, declared those who had access to it, should reign supreme. 'The land of the colony belonged to those who had paid the best price for it, and those who paid for it had the best right to it.'[8] Furthermore

1 *QPD*, Vol. 3, (1866), p. 704.

2 *WE&T*, 30 November 1872, p. 4, c. 1-3 and *BC*, 22 November 1872, p. 3, c. 6-7.

3 *QPD*, Vol. 21, (1876), pp. 168-9, 945, 1043-6, 1293-305, 1339-40.

4 *See* Appendix I. The whole pastoral industry now rested on financial credit supplied by banks, woolbrokers and mortgage companies. If the run was fragmented by small settlement, the vital security was impaired. Many squatters were forced by their creditors to purchase in order to secure the latters' advances. *QPD*, Vol. 14, (1872), p. 978; Vol. 5, (1867), p. 438 and Vol. 3, (1866), p. 346.

5 *BC*, 11 September 1872, p. 2, c. 3-4.

6 ibid., 14 August 1872, p. 2, c. 2.

7 *QPD*, Vol. 3, (1866), pp. 342-6.

8 *QPD*, Vol. 5, (1867), p. 8.

freeholders were more valuable to the State than leaseholders, and the great financial, economic and political successes of the Pure Merinos should not serve to disqualify them from further participation in development and profits.

> If they [the squatters] had run a race and won it, that was no reason why they should be prevented from running any more.[9]

Hence the arguments of those thinly-disguised 'liberal squatters' who were:

> . . . prepared to throw open the land to all classes, taking care that the man of small means shall have equal chance with the capitalist.[10]

The result was always the same. Whatever the conditions imposed capital and the lawyers always found a way, and the early Land Acts were no real impediment to the freeholding of the great estates. The squatters thus wanted things all ways. Secure in the knowledge that they could circumvent any legislation devised by political man, they desired immense acreages at little cost and with few onerous conditions. These, most obtained.

Shrewdly, the squatters examined certain agrarian arguments and stood them on their heads. Classical agrarian theory was modified by patriarchal Old Testament and Latin-American examples underpinned by a recurrent streak of hard economic fact.[11] The idea that the colony was one large common for the use of all was a 'lawless attitude conducive to . . . [that] disrespect for private property common in the bush'. The sooner lands became freehold the sooner would people recognize the 'true principles of civilization and respect the property of others'.[12] Selectors by implication were nothing but a 'horde of thieves and robbers', incapable of the higher civilization so painstakingly created in the lonely pastoral homesteads and urbane, exclusive clubs. Not only did the colony depend on the sales of land for steady revenue but the whole colony rode on the sheep's back and those on the Downs had the broadest backs of all. Every activity in town, port and village depended on the squatter.[13] Accurately guessing that much of the 'class legislation' and the hostile feelings were the products of urban politicians advancing their own causes when all that the country required 'was a simple business directory', the Pure Merinos genuinely felt that these men were harming the infant colony by disorganizing a proved, efficient and vital export industry in order to establish a group of shiftless and improvident selectors whose fate was hopeless subsistence or utter defeat and who had neither the capital nor the technical experience and equipment needed to make up the economic loss to the State.[14] 'Just as much

[9] ibid., Vol. 3, (1866), p. 369.

[10] *WA*, 4 June 1867, p. 3, c. 2. Manifesto of C. H. Green of Goomburra.

[11] Trollope, *Australia and New Zealand*, Vol. 1, p. 176 and *QPD*, Vol. 5, (1867), p. 317.

[12] *QPD*, Vol. 3, (1866), p. 366. Speech of J. D. McLean of Westbrook.

[13] ibid., pp. 367-9, 820. For a later expression of this view, *see Australasian Pastoralists' Review*, Vol. 2, No. 8, 15 October 1892, p. 859.

[14] *DDG*, 7 February 1861, p. 2, c. 6 and *WA*, 11 June 1874, p. 2, c. 2.

credit', they considered, 'was due to the man who could run an extra sheep or bullock per acre than was due to the agriculturalist who made two more blades of grass grow.'[15] Such feelings were intensified by the speedy failure of many selectors, their addiction to land speculation and their indulgence in new forms of polite blackmail.

Whatever their public idealization of their struggle to retain exclusive possession of the soil—which they had never been granted but always assumed would be perpetual—the squatters retained few private illusions. From first to last they correctly diagnosed the battle for the Downs as a naked class-struggle between run-holder, country-town agrarian, urban merchant-lawyer and some would-be selectors.[16] In regard to the extent of concessions, which political change made inevitable and to which most Pure Merinos were reconciled by 1868, they differed amongst themselves according to temperament, likely personal losses and financial position. Superficial differences existed between those in the Legislative Council and those in the Assembly. The former '. . . were not influenced or bound by the opinions of constituents; they were in an independent position . . .' and were less likely to guard their tongues and 'pander to the prejudices of the popular Chamber'.[17] On the key issues, however, —free selection before survey, auction sales, liberal conditions and land administration—all were united.

Safe from the influx of small selectors, the outside squatters of the Western Downs and North Queensland were jealous of the social and political superiority of the 'inner circle'. The Land Act of 1868, however much it broke down when operated, was as much a victory for the 'outers' over the old ruling group as it was for the urban agrarians and lawyers.[18] Beyond the Condamine Plains pastoral life was harsher and returns more uncertain. Lacking the traditional exclusiveness of the Pure Merinos, the 'outsiders' never forgot that the Black Soilers had ruthlessly used their initial advantages to monopolize the supply of breeding stock for new runs, had made tremendous profits out of the southern gold-rushes and, by their domination of the political scene after Separation, had compromised the cause of other more deserving pastoralists.[19] The refusal until 1869 of the Downs squatters to grant others the pre-emptive right was also resented.

By 1860 most squatters privately regarded fixed leasehold tenures and low rentals as their sacred right. As security they were little inferior to freehold and any attempts to tamper with them were a step towards the repudiation of contracts and a dangerous and radical departure which might serve as a precedent for the destruction of all property.[20] The

15 *QPD*, Vol. 3, (1866), p. 703.

16 ibid.

17 *QPD*, Vol. 15, (1872), p. 959. Speech of J. F. McDougall (Rosalie Plains).

18 *QPD*, Vol. 6, (1867-8), p. 776. Views of H. B. Fitz (Pilton).

19 *QPD*, Vol. 2, (1865), pp. 372-3. Speech of R. R. Mackenzie (Burnett). *WE&T*, 30 November 1872, p. 2, c. 1.

20 *QPD*, Vol. 14, (1872), p. 906.

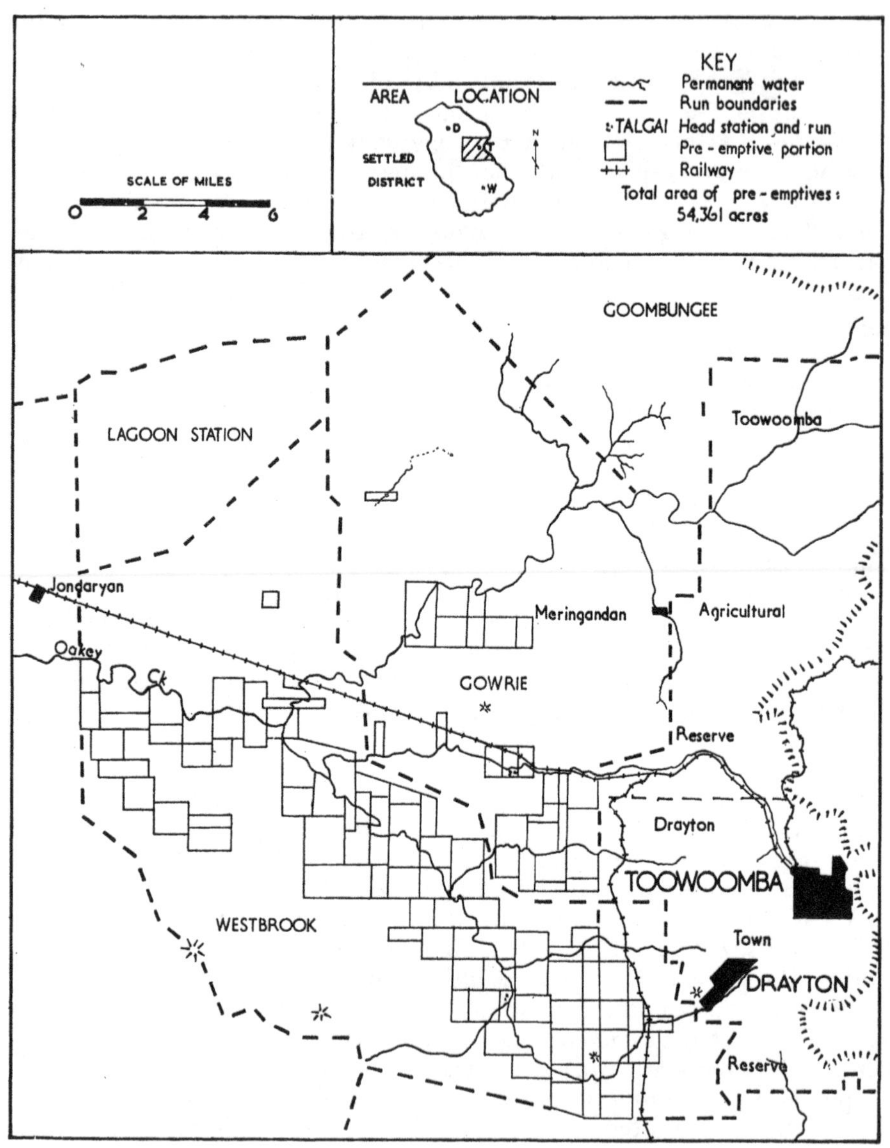

MAP 4 Toowoomba area pre-emptive purchases, 1860-75 (after Buxton's Squatting Map, 1864; Parish maps and *QVP*, Vol. 2, (1874), p. 562)

notorious 'George Street Resolutions' formulated at Brisbane on 25 April 1866 embodied all the demands of the Southern Land League, a political organization of extreme squatters dominated by the Downs pastoralists. These resolutions recommended that Crown lands should only be sold by auction and that 'while reserves sufficient for the public requirements should be made in each district', the approval of both Houses of Parliament should be necessary before they were proclaimed. In addition the Crown lessee should have the power to purchase at auction any portion of his run in lots of 640 acres or more. The upset price was not to exceed five shillings per acre for country lands. All expiring leases, the extremists demanded, were to be renewed for a period of fourteen years.[21] Needless to say Parliamentary acceptance of these resolutions would have granted the squatters a complete monopoly, far beyond the wildest dreams of 1847, over the land on the Downs.

The squatters already enjoyed tremendous advantages derived from the famous Orders-in-Council of 9 March 1847 which had given them undisturbed possession of the Downs almost since it was first settled. Rentals were ridiculously low and runs were usually under-assessed.[22] The main feature of the 1847 regulations, however, was the grant to the squatters of a pre-emptive right conceding a monopoly of all alienation by the Crown. Pre-emption at £1 per acre was the curse of the Downs. Before the right expired 323,658 acres of the finest land in the Settled District had been freeholded by the Pure Merinos.[23] 132,572 acres were pre-empted in 1865 when the right expired. The Pure Merinos exercised this privilege ruthlessly and intelligently. Some freeholded almost half their area in this way. Nearly all the creek frontages were pre-empted, together with the vital water-holes, the best potential agricultural land and those areas strategically guarding leased acres in remote portions of the run.[24]

Pre-emption, unwisely continued in 1868 as a concession in lieu of compensation for improvements, was also extended to the Unsettled District but the acreages were limited and the squatters were never permitted to run riot as they had on the Eastern Downs. The squatters could pre-empt one acre for every 10s. worth of improvements on any part of the resumed portion. A 2,560-acre limit was imposed on the leased part but pre-emption could occur at any time during the currency of the lease.[25] Pre-emption gave the squatters the necessary base, including their improvements, on which to build and expand but the result was disastrous for the agrarians. Their reaction produced the damaging wholesale resumptions of 1868-76. Charles Clark of Talgai placed the

21 *QPD*, Vol. 3, (1867), pp. 95-7.

22 For many years after 1847, the Pure Merinos only paid a £10 p.a. licence fee and a small stock assessment for police protection. In 1867 Clifton carried 80,000-100,000 sheep but was assessed for a mere 16,000-18,000. *QPD*, Vol. 6, (1867-8), p. 773.

23 *See* Appendix III for a detailed list of pre-emptives between 1860 and 1874.

24 Maps 4, 5 and 6 illustrate the extent and location of all pre-emptives in the Toowoomba-Allora-Warwick area.

25 *QVP*, Vol. 1, (1867), (JLA), p. 539 and *QPD*, Vol. 6, (1867-8), pp. 703-34.

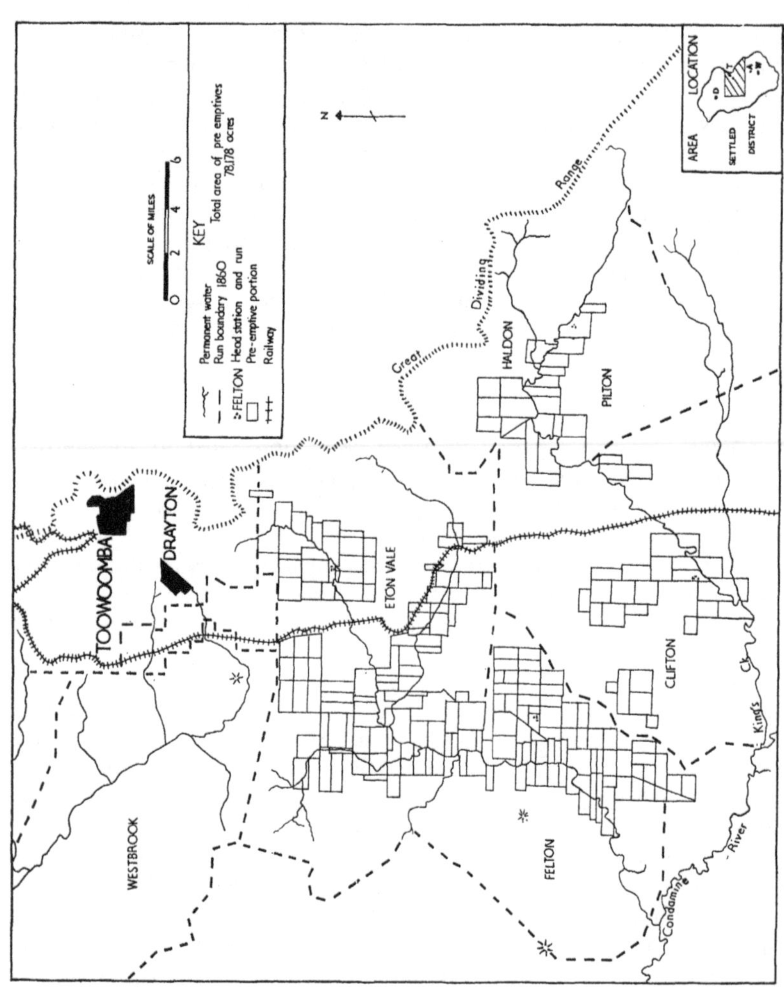

Map 5 Central Downs pre-emptive purchases, 1860-75 (after Buxton's Squatting Map, 1864; Parish maps and *QVP*, Vol. 2, (1874), p. 562)

blame for much of the 'reckless land agitation' on those squatters who had abused their great privilege:

They had never been a wise class, and had never known what were their true interests. Why, at the very time that they were actually enjoying the pre-emptive right, they were sowing the seeds of a vast amount of discord.[26]

Leases within the Settled District expired in 1868 but were renewed for a further ten years and the rents raised to a minimum of £1 per square mile. In 1878 they were extended for another five years and the rental doubled.[27] Lessees in the Unsettled District were more fortunate. The security of tenure sought by all was granted in 1869 when twenty-one-year leases were conceded at low but slowly rising rentals.[28] During the debates on this measure [the Pastoral Leases Bill], the question arose as to whether members who were squatters and were thus personally affected by the proposed legislation could discuss and vote upon it. All agreed that the Bill would increase the value of pastoral property—longer leases meant greater security and higher premiums. The Speaker ruled that 'a direct pecuniary interest must be proven' and that this Bill was a matter of State policy and not of group interest. This decision was yet another victory for the squatters, reinforcing their contention that they were perfectly entitled to legislate for their own benefit.[29]

RESUMPTION IN THE SETTLED DISTRICT, 1868-76[30]

Year	No. of runs	Acres resumed
1868	33	*c.* 1,500,000
1872	33	218,000
1874	30	1,147,340
1875	14	108,280
1876	23	749,298
		TOTAL ACRES: 3,722,918

Dutton's revolutionary 1884 Land Act evenly divided all remaining leaseholds on the entire Downs and issued new leases on a sliding-scale which provided for the eventual subdivision of all runs into moderately-sized grazing farms appraised by local Land Boards.[31] In the Settled

26 *QPD*, Vol. 14, (1872), p. 801. *See also* the identical views of Gore: ibid., Vol. 5, (1867), pp. 11-12.

27 W. Epps, *Land Systems of Australasia*, London 1895, pp. 87-97 and S. H. Roberts, *History of Australian Land Settlement*, Melbourne 1924.

28 *QPD*, Vol. 5, (1867), pp. 503-21 and Vol. 6, (1867-8), pp. 1009-19.

29 ibid., p. 822.

30 *DDG* for relevant years. *QPD*, Vol. 14, (1872), p. 852; Vol. 17, (1874), p. 1020; Vol. 18, (1875), p. 88 and Vol. 21, (1876), pp. 965-84, 1293-305; *QVP*, Vol. 3, (1876), pp. 278-82.

31 *QPD*, Vol. 43, (1884), pp. 251-65, 314-84 *et seq.*

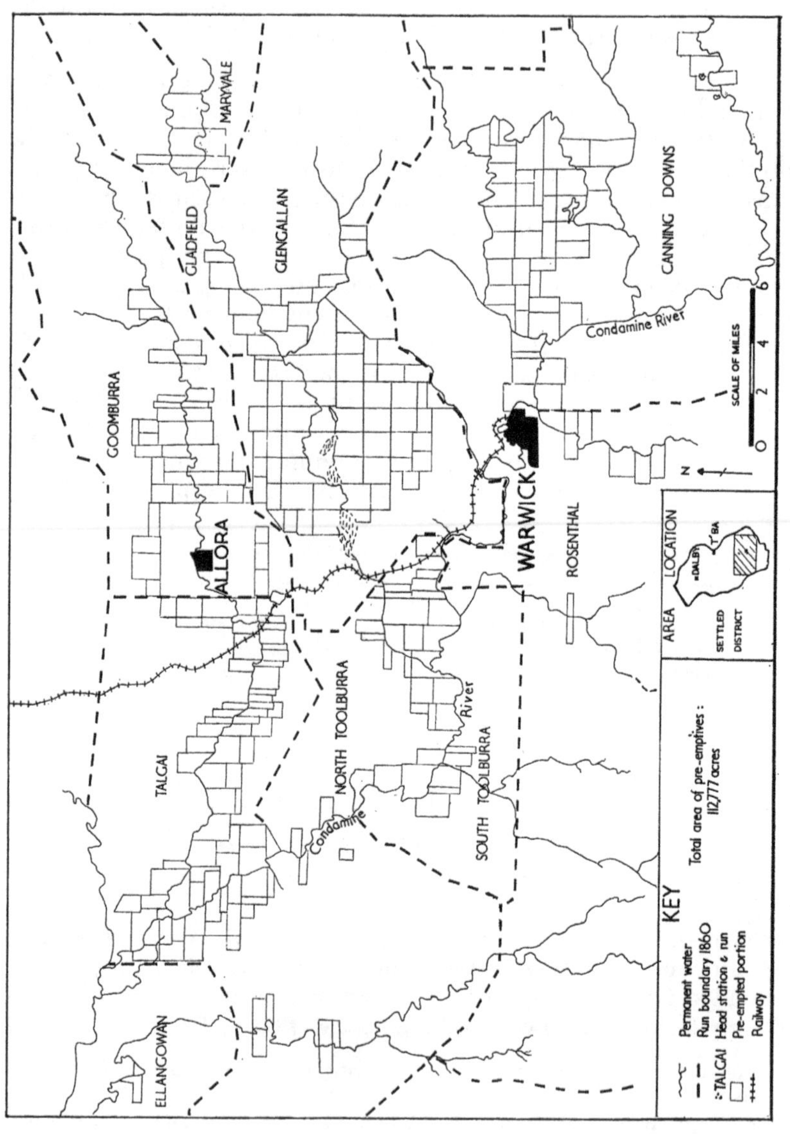

MAP 6 Warwick-Allora area pre-emptive purchases, 1860-75 (after Buxton's Squatting Map, 1864; Parish maps and *QVP*, Vol. 2, (1874), p. 562)

District, however, long leases were poor securities as the Agricultural Reserves Act of 1863 set a precedent for resumption that was enthusiastically maintained by later Parliaments. The Act of 1868 stipulated that all runs were to be divided by the lessees into equal halves, the regional Lands Commissioner then selecting the half to be resumed for settlement. Tenants were given a ten-years lease of the remainder but this could be broken at any time by resolutions for resumption passed by both Assembly and Council. In addition three-mile strips on either side of the new railways were resumed as Railway Reserves.[32] Further resumptions in 1872 were bitterly contested, run by run, by the Pure Merinos but they later accepted the inevitable and put up only a half-hearted resistance during the following years.[33] By 1876, however, little good land was left and most tenants had already freeholded as much as they required or could afford.

Until 1866 all Crown lands were alienated by either pre-emption or auction. Auctions with a high upset price were favoured by pastoralist and Treasurer alike.[34] With their capital resources the squatters had little difficulty in securing as much land as they wanted when the Jondaryan, Jimbour, Clifton, Westbrook and Cecil Plains lands in particular were all put up for disposal.[35] During periods of financial stringency—as in 1866, 1870, 1876 and 1879—thousands of acres were surveyed and thrown on to the market where they were quickly acquired by pastoralists without competition.[36] Throughout the 'seventies roughly 25 per cent of Queensland's entire revenue was derived from land, although the proportion fell during the following two decades. The Selection Acts failed to raise as much revenue as their sponsors had anticipated but, on the other hand, agricultural settlement was hindered by auction-sales. This dilemma was never resolved during the period.

While 1865 was admittedly an abnormal year due to the vast sum poured into the Treasury for pre-emptive purchases, land revenue, while slowly rising in absolute terms, relatively declined as a contributor to the finances of the colony. With an interest bill which had already reached £732,175 by 1884-5 this was a serious problem, and the chief fault of the 1884 Act was seen by many to be not so much its practical failure to settle quickly a numerous grazing class on the Western Downs but its disastrous effect as a revenue producer. Thousands of acres were disposed of by auction in the outer Downs until pastoralists could no longer afford to purchase.

The administration of the Land Acts was a critical factor in the squatters' success. Divided control between the Survey Office and the Lands Department, administrative confusion, political influence and, above all, the associations, inclinations and actions of the permanent

32 *QPD*, Vol. 6, (1867-8), pp. 703-34.

33 *QPD*, Vol. 14, (1872), p. 852.

34 *QPD*, Vol. 23, (1877), pp. 310-13.

35 *TC*, 16 December 1874, p. 3, c. 1-2. 21 selections on Westbrook (2,854 acres) were purchased by the proprietors of the station at an uncontested sale on 3 December 1874.

36 *QPD*, Vol. 20, (1876), pp. 22-41. It was usual for squatters to 'spot' and 'gridiron'.

LAND REVENUE: QUEENSLAND, 1865-95[37]

Category	Years			
	1865	1875	1885	1895
	£	£	£	£
Auction	112,789	29,826	43,138	193,967
Selection	—	1,390	10,319	6,239
Pre-emption	218,231	—	14,976	—
Selectors' rents	561	119,099	236,549	78,459
TOTAL*	331,581	150,315	304,982	278,665
Run rents and licence fees	97,875	13,687	258,908	335,853
GRAND TOTAL*	429,456	164,002	563,890	614,518
% TOTAL REVENUE	68	31	22	19

* Includes survey and transfer fees and small returns not enumerated.

officials, were almost as important in affecting the ultimate fate of the resumed lands as the Acts themselves. Nearly all involved in disposing of Crown lands were prejudiced participants overwhelmed by the intricacies and magnitude of the problems they faced. Most pursued no long-term policy but adapted themselves to day-to-day political, financial and administrative exigencies. Those who took the administrative steps necessary to interpret legislation, which was often ambiguous and confused, frequently yielded to temptation. Direct bribery and corruption were apparently rare and insignificant; the real processes—the blatant favouring of one group and certain individuals within that group—were more subtle and oblique, nearly impossible to prove and politically defensible.[38] But the final result was the same as if money had changed hands. Nearly all, politicians and officials, were playing the same game and only when personal animosities flamed and factions disintegrated, did what was common gossip on the Downs become public property.[39]

'Political expediency', in Gregory's phrase, was always a motivating factor affecting the disposition of Crown lands. Here there was no

37 *QPD*, Vol. 18, (1875), pp. 143, 175; *QVP*, Vol. 3, (1884), p. 143 and Vol. 2, (1881), pp. 167-9. *Statistics of Queensland*, 1865-94.

38 '. . . it was natural', declared Hope, 'that, as administration was conducted in Queensland, Government supporters should meet with, sometimes, perhaps, partial consideration'. *QPD*, Vol. 21, (1876), p. 941.

39 Even J. Morgan, the dummies' scourge, used his influence to save the best land on Pikedale (his friend Donald Gunn's run) from resumption. *WE&T*, 10 July 1875, p. 2, c. 2-3.

appreciable difference between so-called 'liberal' and 'conservative' factions. If anything the former were more dangerous and culpable, as their actions at the desk were at total variance with their speeches in the Assembly. Macalister cynically purchased A. Wienholt's vote in 1863 by condoning the transference of the Gladfield Agricultural Reserve on the latter's run to a site which was hopeless for small settlement.[40] Lilley's Ministry was the most disastrous of all from the point of view of those who wished to see a more equitable distribution of excellent land on the Downs. It issued the crucial instruction not to alienate the pastoral supporters of the Government by forfeiting their leases even when it was well known that they had not complied with the conditions. Taylor, the Lands Minister, who had merely 'taken office to see what he could get' auctioned huge areas of Cecil Plains 'choice Condamine frontages' when the market was saturated, and gazetted resumptions to suit himself and his friends.[41]

J. P. Bell of Jimbour, 'honest, amiable and popular', secured 7,000 acres, denied to others, when Minister of Lands and was openly favoured by the 1872 resumptions which were judiciously surveyed to preserve the integrity of his run.[42] Even the 'spotless' Gores of Yandilla, who 'never dummied' and had hardly ever pre-empted, secured 17,000 acres by auction in 1882 as a reward for their support of Allan at the 1878 election.[43] The final example of this kind was the Jimbour and Cooranga auctions of 1881 in which several members of the McIlwraith Ministry had a direct interest—'like the sale of steel rails'. The formation of the Darling Downs and Western Land Company coincided exactly with these auctions.[44]

Ministerial intervention of this sort, however, was spasmodic and confined to a limited number of specific cases. As Governments rose and fell, Minister rapidly succeeded Minister. Between 1860 and 1875—the decisive years—all Queensland land administration and practical policy were virtually in the hands of one man, A. C. Gregory, and his tame officials. Combining, until 1866, the offices of Surveyor-General and Under-Secretary for Lands, this most talented explorer and scientist was by nature and upbringing not an impartial career civil servant on the new British model but one whose sympathies and decisions openly favoured the Downs run-holders.[45] Accepting their hospitality, a member of the same clubs and social institutions, a strong freemason, and the possessor of inflexible private views which he did not hesitate to translate into administrative action, Gregory was, from the squatters' viewpoint,

40 *BC*, 9 September 1863, p. 2, c. 2-3.

41 *QVP*, Second Session, Vol. 2, (1879), p. 1449; *BC*, 28 March 1870, p. 2, c. 3 and 26 May 1870, p. 2, c. 4; *QPD*, Vol. 9, (1869), pp. 755-6. 35,351 acres were sold to Gore and Taylor on 17 February 1870. *BC*, 21 February 1870, p. 3, c. 4.

42 *QPD*, Vol. 14, (1872), pp. 852-3, 866, 1004.

43 *TC*, 24 May 1882, p. 3, c. 1. For F. A. Gore's weak defence that the 'land was so poor and liable to flooding that nobody would take it up', *see* ibid., 30 May 1882, p. 2, c. 7.

44 *TC*, 17 May 1881, p. 3, c. 2; 16 July 1881, p. 2, c. 1-2 and 21 July 1881, p. 3, c. 1-2.

45 *BC*, 1 July 1905, p. 12; P. Mennell, *Dictionary*, pp. 196-7; Burke, *Colonial Gentry*, Vol. 1, (1891), p. 45.

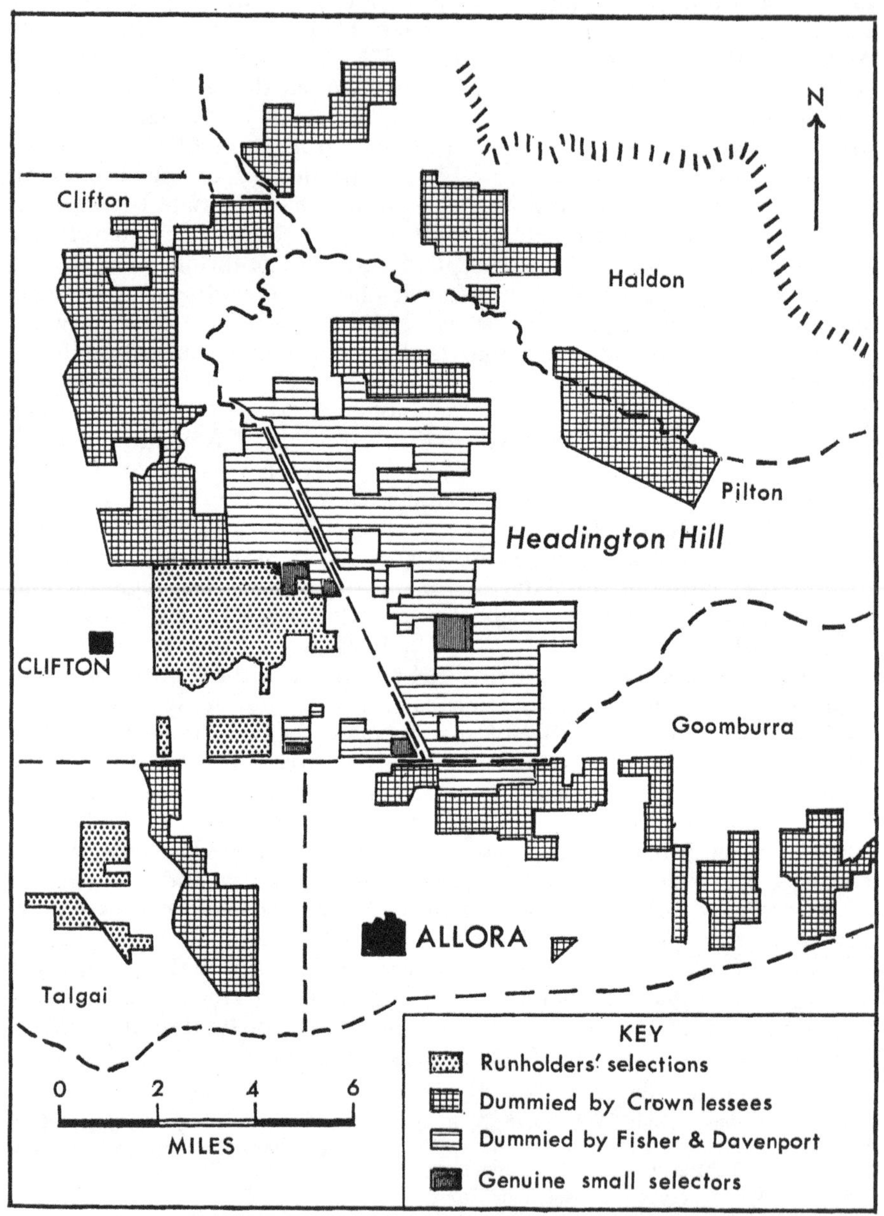

MAP 7 Dummied selections, 1866-8 (after *QVP*, Vol. 2, (1875), p. 867 and Vol. 3, (1877), p. 107)

the perfect occupant of 'this position of colossal power'.[46] Few Downs lessees could have promoted their group's interests more successfully.

Gregory, with all his 'masterly inactivity', power over Ministers, and pro-squatting sentiments, could never have deserted his principles and supplied the cutting-edge to destroy both a social system he was part of and those individuals he counted as friends and equals.[47] In his own eyes he was perfectly entitled to attempt to preserve a system he felt to be inherently superior to one others felt should replace it. The fault lay not so much with the man but—if blame can be apportioned and if the agrarians' concepts were logical and attainable within the context of Queensland's political and economic development—with his pliant, often ignorant, masters and the prevailing mental climate of the era in which he lived.

Acknowledged even by his opponents to be personally incorruptible and 'a highly competent, trustworthy and deserving officer', Gregory did more for the Pure Merinos by default and by turning a blind eye than by actual intervention.[48] Only once did he openly express his views. During the debate on the 1868 Land Bill Gregory was called by the 'ultra' faction to the Bar of the Council to bolster their case. His carefully prepared analytical statement disclosed that he had no confidence in the main principles of agricultural selection; that he was anxious to retain complete control over all land administration; was opposed to any system of classification; and denigrated all attempts to impose any conditions whatever. Gregory's opinions, favouring 'the free flow of capital' and the auction system, were indistinguishable from those of the Pure Merinos of the Fitz, Wienholt and Taylor stamp.[49] This was the man responsible for planting the yeoman on the soil and loosening the grip of the pastoral tenants.

Gregory condoned abuses of which he had ample proof and in this respect must be held culpable. He failed to provide the technical facilities—maps, instructions and an official atmosphere of helpfulness which would place poor men on an equal footing with the rich—and he invariably interpreted the regulations to favour the squatter.[50] For instance, in reply to a letter from a conscience-stricken and unhappy Warwick land agent who felt that in accepting applications from men he knew to be dummies ('I am . . . identifying myself with a false and dishonourable act'), Gregory blandly and insensitively stated that the onus of

[46] *WA*, 29 October 1874, p. 2, c. 2. The intimation 'that Mr Gregory stayed the night with the squatter' was always an occasion for cynical comment.

[47] *BC*, 22 September 1863, p. 2, c. 5. Gregory immediately joined the ultra-squatting rearguard on his elevation to the Council in 1883.

[48] *QPD*, Vol. 6, (1867-8), p. 712 and Vol. 2, (1870), pp. 36-7. *BC*, 16 March 1875, p. 2, c. 3-4. This issue contains a masterly analysis of Gregory's position.

[49] *QPD*, Vol. 6, (1867-8), pp. 877-84. 'Examination of A. C. Gregory, 17/1/68'.

[50] No proper maps were provided for intending farmers and application forms made no provision for the date of selection. Selections accepted at Warwick were refused by Gregory after Wildash's Brisbane agent had lodged later applications. Books of blank forms were provided for Crown lessees. *QVP*, Vol. 2, (1867), pp. 781, 921, 950.

proof of a selector's bona fides rested with the officer and *not* the applicant.[51] As his instruction read:

It is not the business of the department to inquire as to who individuals are who select land . . . so long as they select land and pay their money.[52]

Much of the trouble with the 1866 deeds was due to his deliberate laxness, secretiveness and failure to confer with the Under-Secretary for Lands.[53] Justification can be pleaded for the Surveyor-General. His technical skills were indispensable to the raw politicians oblivious of the practical consequence of their actions. The men and the means they provided him with were wanting alike in quality and quantity. No sooner had one measure been implemented than another was gazetted. Gregory was expected to perform the impossible: he had simultaneously to create two departments, cope with an explosive pastoral expansion and operate the confused and often contradictory legislation emerging from Parliament House. The Downs agrarians' charge that he neglected and subverted their interests is true. Outweighing this partiality, however, are his great services to a new colony struggling with the problems of administration and the sectional conflicts over the allocation and regulation of its major resource. Queensland was fortunate in the quality of its first public officials and Gregory was not the least of this group.

The subordinate officials, the men who actually classified the land, divided the runs and handled the mechanics of selection, were also closely identified with the Downs pastoralists. The key-figure was Gregory's brother, F. T. Gregory, Commissioner of Crown Lands in the Darling Downs between 1862 and 1869 and also a subsequent member of the Council.[54] His peculiar classifications, personal selections near Gowrie, and strange resumptions gave him a reputation for performing his duties 'with an earnestness and success that could not be too highly commended—by the squatters'.[55] Some even claimed that Gregory had personally 'in 1868 entirely ruined settlement of the Darling Downs'.[56] His

51 *QVP*, Vol. 2, (1867), p. 949. 'Report of the Select Committee on Selection in Agricultural Reserves . . .' C. F. Cumming to Gregory, 11 September 1867; Gregory to Cumming, 25 September 1867.

52 ibid., p. 935.

53 *See* the inconclusive inquiry into the conduct of G. N. Geary, Chief Clerk in the Lands Department, who had released some deeds of dummied lands without authorization. Geary was cleared as there was no proof of corruption or collusion but the evidence was limited, the right questions were neglected and the real responsibility was never fixed. Davenport's alleged statement that they knew every man's price in the Lands Department was not investigated. *QVP*, First Session, (1873), pp. 1003-21.

54 F. T. Gregory left an estate of £18,000 and had been a trustee of the Beit estate (Westbrook) and financial manager of the Clifton property, much of which had been dummied while he was the local Commissioner. Burke, *Colonial Gentry*, Vol. 1, p. 45.

55 *WA*, 16 July 1874, p. 2, c. 1-2. Gore alleged that South Toolburra was divided into three portions, thus allowing the North Brit. Aust. Company to retain the choice central core while the inferior margins were resumed for small settlement. *QPD*, Vol. 2, (1870), pp. 37, 215-17.

56 *WA*, 16 July 1874, p. 2, c. 1-2. *See also* Gregory's choice of the Jimbour resumption in 1868 which 'was a very fortunate one for the lessees'. [Bell]. *BC*, 15 August 1874, p. 5, c. 7 and *WA*, 13 August 1874, p. 2, c. 1.

successors, Archibald McDowall (1869-75) and W. C. Hume (1875-85) were more popular and respected by the lower orders. Both, however, had strong pastoral affiliations and personal prejudices which occasionally affected their judgement. McDowall was a son of the Chief Magistrate of Tasmania, twice married to daughters of Thomas Coutts of Toolburra and a member of the 'best clubs'. His 'sympathies always lay with the Downs'. In spite of his social affiliations he 'enjoyed the full confidence of the small selectors' and their country-town supporters.[57] Hume, connected by marriage to the Gregory brothers, was a realistic administrator who nevertheless 'has been known to pass over selections in which the conditions were not fulfilled [where] . . . the parties interested were wealthy gentlemen or in whose houses Hume enjoyed the rights of hospitality'. Thus Gore received certificates for 12,000 acres of dubious selections, while Tyson of Felton was thoroughly investigated. Tyson's reactions can best be imagined.[58] But with increasing Ministerial supervision, the accession of the able and impartial W. A. Tully to the control of the Lands Department, and the decline of the squatting power, the opportunity for favouritism and malpractice on a large scale no longer existed. By then the inaugural administrators had saved the interests of their pastoral confederates and there was now no need for further bureaucratic intervention.

Pre-emptions tore the heart out of the Settled District. Land which remained was supposedly reserved for small settlement. Resident pastoralists could select on their runs only on the same terms and in the same limited quantities as anyone else.[59] The 'liberal land legislation' between 1863 and 1872, however, proved to be no barrier to those with capital. Evasion and fraud completed the process of aggregation begun by pre-emption and auctions.[60] Apart from 'spotting', 'peacocking' and 'triangulating', the main devices used by the run-holders to circumvent the Settlement Acts were family selection, dummying and deliberate evasion of residence and improvement conditions. Special facilities were offered by Gregory's surveyors to those pastoralists intent on selecting the strategic portions near water-holes, along creeks and near the railways. When the Toowoomba, Drayton and Warwick Agricultural Reserves were proclaimed in 1860, the adjacent lessees pounced, using their children to take up contiguous 40-320 acre selections.[61] As only fencing was required, this suited the purchasers whose leases were accepted by the Government.[62] The result was satisfactory for the Toowoomba lessees (*see* table p. 40).

Some dummying took place under the Acts of 1860 and 1863 but the acreages were insignificant. The Leasing Act of 1866, however, passed at

[57] *BC*, 14 June 1876, p. 3, c. 5 and Burke, *Colonial Gentry*, Vol. 2, p. 506.

[58] *TC*, 29 July 1879, p. 2, c. 2-4.

[59] The tables in Part Two, Chapter 7, set out the acreages and conditions imposed by the major Selection Acts.

[60] *WA*, 13 May 1868, p. 2, c. 1-2.

[61] *QVP*, Second Session, (1863), pp. 635-43.

[62] ibid., p. 647.

Agricultural Reserves Selections, 1861-3[63]

Reserve	Total portions 1861-3	Total acres	Squatters' portions	Squatters' acres
Drayton	62	3,776	32	2,250
Toowoomba	88	4,802	30	1,710
Warwick	101	5,536	16	788
TOTAL	251	14,114	78	4,748

a time of political readjustment and confusion and economic depression, and when two Pure Merinos had just entered the Ministry, produced dummying on a scale which was unique in the colony.[64] The price Macalister paid for Downs pastoral support was too heavy. Under this Act 635 selections totalling 101,465 acres were taken up in barely two years.[65] Much of the choice land near the new Toowoomba-Warwick railway was selected by scores of dummiers and agents.[66] Initial agrarian delight at the new Act with its revolutionary provisions evaporated overnight on 17 August 1867 when the incoming Mackenzie Ministry instructed Gregory to issue new regulations.[67] Gregory's memorandum was the greatest single concession to the squatters since the 1847 Orders-in-Council and the stroke which paralysed agrarian endeavour on the Eastern Downs.[68] The regulations permitted free selection in Agricultural Reserves before survey in areas of 80-320 acres at an annual rental of 2s. 6d. per acre for seven years. The only condition imposed was that one-sixth of the land should be cultivated within one year of selection.[69]

Receiving advance warning, the squatters acted with amazing speed. 14,878 acres were selected near Warwick in less than two weeks.[70] Time-payment, unenforceable conditions and wholesale disposal gave them 'their great opportunity to close the Darling Downs against the plough'. This was their final chance: such concessions were too great ever to be

[63] ibid.

[64] *QPD*, Vol. 3, (1866), pp. 678-89, 709-22. An earlier Bill had been rejected after the Pure Merinos and their allies in the Council had mutilated it. ibid., Vol. 2, (1865), pp. 37-43, 367-78, 633-5. 630 selections totalling 97,245 acres were taken up in the Warwick and Toowoomba areas alone. *QVP*, (1871-2), p. 625.

[65] Map 5 depicts the operation of the Leasing Act on the Central Downs along the Warwick railway.

[66] These Regulations are reproduced in Appendix IV. For agrarian approval of the 1866 Act, *see WA*, 1 February 1867, p. 2, c. 1-2.

[67] ibid., 23 August 1867, p. 2, c. 1-2. No conditions were imposed on land outside agricultural reserves and even within them; no declarations or oaths were required. The agreement to observe the condition was a simple statement, carrying no penalty for non-compliance, which the lessee could evade if he thought fit.

[68] *BC*, 9 May 1874, p. 5, c. 3-5.

[69] The use of discounted land-orders reduced the actual cost per acre to about 12s. *QVP*, Vol. 2, (1867), p. 784.

[70] *WA*, 3 September 1867, p. 2, c. 1-2.

repeated. Dummies became as common as wallabies, as 'Queensland became a liar's paradise' and magistrates—'preaching morality from the Bench at poor wretches'—accepted declarations all knew to be false.[71] Clark, the Warwick magistrate and Member, was stigmatized as:

> . . . a corrupter of public morals, a violater of the law and public decency, and . . . [one who has] prostituted justice for the paltry purpose of personal aggrandisement.[72]

Except for a few courageous individuals such as James Morgan of Warwick, most Downsmen—bank managers, lawyers, doctors, storekeepers, shepherds and labourers—sold themselves or their consciences to the pastoral lessees.[73] 'Land stealing'—and this mode of acquiring the Downs' basic resource *was* thievery—'became one of the leading fashions and appeared more profitable than gold digging . . . visions of stone breaking on the roads were only seen in the remote perspective, if seen at all'.[74] False declarations, blank powers-of-attorney and transfer forms were as abundant as confetti. Men made a jest of the swindle, connived at by Ministry, Lands Office and populace alike.

Two examples of the process will suffice. G. H. Davenport, acting with C. B. Fisher, the great Victorian and South Australian pastoralist, came to Queensland specifically to select a freehold estate. With 'excellent legal advice' and great capital resources he created Headington Hill out of a myriad of small selections whose normal holders had never been near the Downs and who had sold their immigrants' non-transferable land-orders at a considerable discount to Barnett, Davenport's Brisbane agent.[75] Captain Charles Blick was a Brisbane marine agent who 'selected 320 acres on the Warwick Agricultural Reserve but had never been on the Reserve or seen the Darling Downs' and could not identify his selection on the chart, and was simply a tool of Wildash who had approached him and conducted all negotiations. Other transactions were carried on by bank managers who played a key role in all these proceedings.[76]

Pure Merino and capitalist both defended their actions; the former regarded dummying as an act of necessity, and the latter pleaded that the capital invested and the new mixed-farming techniques to be practised at Headington Hill were an example well worth a minor technical infringement of laws which could not be enforced as they lacked any basis of popular consent.[77] Bankers were forced to save their outstanding advances by helping squatters preserve their land. This was not a time

71 ibid. and 10 September 1867, p. 2, c. 1-2.

72 ibid., 18 December 1867, p. 2, c. 1-2. This was confirmed by evidence offered to the Select Committee. *QVP*, Vol. 2, (1867), p. 917.

73 *See* a list of dummies including the 'wealth and respectability of the Downs' reproduced in *QVP*, Vol. 3, (1877), pp. 103-21, 'Transfer of Lands Taken Up Within the Settled District of Darling Downs'.

74 *WA*, 10 December 1874, p. 2, c. 1-2.

75 *QVP*, Vol. 2, (1867), p. 965. 'Evidence of George Henry Davenport'.

76 ibid., pp. 940, 975-6.

77 *BC*, 20 October 1873, p. 3, c. 4.

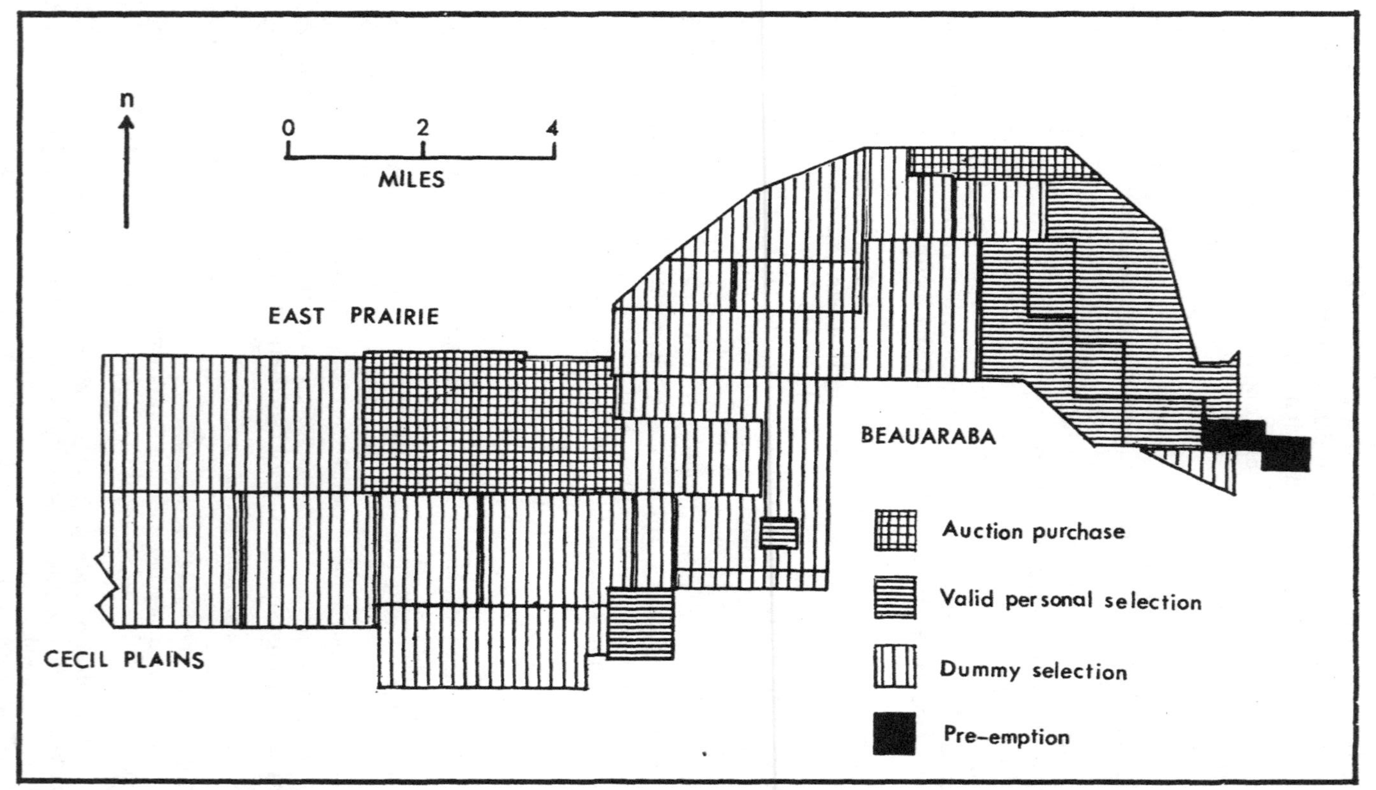

MAP 8 The selection of a freehold pastoral property, 1868: Mount Russell, James Tyson (after *QVP*, Vol. 3, (1877), p. 113 and Vol. 4, (1901), p. 73)

for inconvenient 'moral scruples' to intrude on what to them and their directors was simply a matter of common-sense business procedure. Apart from the damage to the agrarian cause—if such a crusade was indeed 'progress'—dummying and evasion of conditions had the same effects on the Downs as Grant's Act in Victoria. Nearly all participated and nearly all must be held responsible for abusing their official positions, abandoning their private convictions or selling their birthright for a glass of whisky or a golden sovereign. The administration never investigated the wholesale frauds. They could not be proved in a court of law, as the technical machinery was non-existent, reliable witnesses were lacking and men were not prepared to incriminate themselves.[78] Long before the 'Fifth Amendment' gained its mid-twentieth-century notoriety, such a defence was already a commonplace on the Downs.

Although the 1868 Act contained much more stringent conditions, including penalty clauses for fraud and misrepresentation, dummying did not cease. Near Dalby, new freehold estates were pieced together by Simpson, Miles and Nelson, while Bell of Jimbour brought the prefabricated hut, the walking fence and the skimming plough to a fine art.[79] Between Bowenville and Dalby a strip ten miles long and ten miles wide along the railway was dummied by Kent and Wienholt, while James Tyson of Felton and Mount Russell followed Davenport's path.[80] By 1880 Felton had been reconstituted with 111 different freehold titles.[81] Altogether 72,796 acres of conditional purchases, representing 5.89 per cent of all land selected on the Downs under the 1868 Act, were unquestionably dummied and the real total was probably twice as large.[82] Stephens' instructions of 1874 and 1875, however, effectively controlled dummying by introducing a more rigorous examination of selectors' bona fides.[83] Furthermore the case of Bright versus Attorney-General decided that, although a selector might apparently comply with all conditions of the Act, this gave him only the right to *ask* the Minister for his title. For the first time the responsible Minister instructed officials that 'the completeness of the documentary evidence does not justify you acting on it in the absence of a thorough knowledge of the facts'.[84]

78 *BC*, 30 April 1873, p. 2, c. 3-4 and 20 May 1873, p. 2, c. 3-4.

79 *Dalby Herald*, 25 February 1871, p. 2. For a selection-by-selection account of these dummied lands, *see* the remarkable series of articles in the *Courier* which focused attention on the problem and did much to check abuses. *BC*, 15 June 1874, p. 3, c. 3-5 and 16 June 1874, p. 3, c. 3-4.

80 ibid., 23 May 1874, p. 5, c. 2-5. Map 8 illustrates Tyson's dummying on Beauaraba and East Prairie. His violations were the subject of special reports and Cabinet memoranda: *QVP*, Vol. 2, (1874), pp. 473-80; *DDG*, 5 July 1876, p. 3, c. 4 and *TC*, 21 March 1874, p. 2, c. 5.

81 *BC*, 15 April 1913, p. 13, c. 1-7.

82 *QVP*, Vol. 2, (1879), pp. 220-1. 'Report of the Under-Secretary for Lands'.

83 *BC*, 10 March 1874, p. 4, c. 3-4 and 28 March 1874, p. 4, c. 5-6. Appendix V reproduces part of Stephens' regulation setting up properly constituted courts to deal with applications for certificates of fulfilment of conditions on conditional purchases.

84 *QVP*, Vol. 2, (1874), p. 479.

A series of remarkable cases—three of which reached the Privy Council—decided the fate of the lands openly dummied under the Acts of 1866 and 1868. After the Ministry—suddenly discovering that they had the power to withhold titles—had refused to issue the deeds to thousands of acres of Downs land, Hurtle Fisher sued the Under-Secretary for Lands for them. This suit was delayed and in 1874 Macalister, under strong urban 'liberal' pressure, determined to press for a decisive answer. The result of the test cases, tried by the Judicial Committee of the Privy Council, was a great victory for the dummiers. The Palmer Ministry had deliberately accepted the rents from the lessees, knowing that the conditions had not been fulfilled and that the land had been obtained by fraud.[85] Regina versus Davenport was decisive. Taylor had accepted the rent as 'we could not afford' to forfeit revenue and the Privy Council concluded that Davenport was entitled to succeed *without* the certificate of fulfilment, as

> . . . where money is paid and received as rent under a lease, a mere protest that is accepted conditionally and without prejudice to the right to insist upon a prior forfeiture cannot counteract the effect of such receipt.[86]

In addition the New South Wales case of Barton versus Muir decided that selection by agents was not illegal, whether the employer was previously a lessee of the maximum 320 acres or not.[87] There was thus no legal impediment to lease transfers provided that the total did not exceed 2,560 acres in any one year.

The second case referred to London—Regina versus Simpson and Another—settled the fate of the dummied lands selected under the Act of 1868. One Smith had selected two portions in East Prairie for Simpson and, after obtaining his certificate, had abandoned his first selection. Under Section 55 of the Act the Government refused the deeds for the second selection as the residence conditions had not been observed. The Privy Council—reversing the decision of the Full Court of Queensland—decided that Smith was exempt from fulfilling residential conditions on his second selection, that he had been refused a fair trial in a properly constituted court and that the actions of the Darling Downs Land Commissioner and the Minister were both illegal.[88]

The only minor victory for the Crown was the decision in the case of Fisher versus Tully which forfeited Fisher's selections at Headington Hill on the basis of his non-residence in Queensland. Fisher's declaration 'was untrue and Fisher must have known that this was so when he made it'.[89]

85 *See* Griffith's analysis of the Privy Council's decisions given on 20 April 1878. *QVP*, Vol. 2, (1878), pp. 79-82. This opinion clarified the whole tangled affair and resulted in the issue of all the disputed deeds.

86 *BC*, 3 August 1878, p. 6, c. 1-2.

87 *QVP*, Vol. 2, (1878), p. 80.

88 *BC*, 2 October 1878, p. 4, c. 2-3. The Supreme Court's proceedings are reported in: ibid., 9 April 1878, p. 3, c. 4-5 and 20 April 1878, p. 6, c. 4-5. Smith (or, rather, Simpson) eventually received titles to all his selections. ibid., 4 June 1880, p. 3, c. 3.

89 ibid.

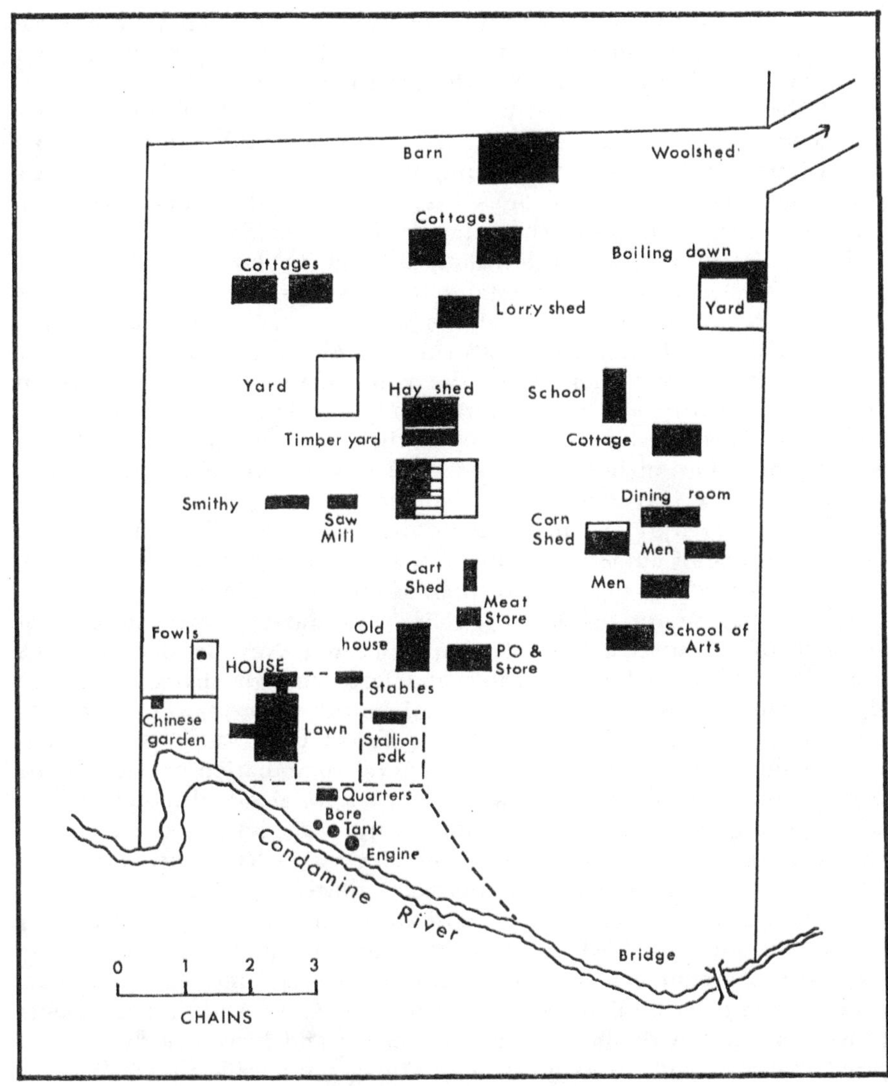

MAP 9 Cecil Plains Estate homestead, 1916 (after *QVP*, Vol. 2, (1917), p. 613)

For once, capital and interest had failed to prevail but the Privy Council decisions were on the whole a triumph of money and 'the big men' over the agrarians and their protégés.[90]

90 For contemporary Downs opinion, *see TC*, 16 February 1878, p. 2, c. 6-7. The *Chronicle* accepted the inevitable. Morgan's *Argus* bitterly concluded that '. . . all fraud is legalized which may be perpetrated by a man worth £50,000 or over . . . it would not do to place the limit too low or the Commune would be with us . . . a licence to commit roguery with impudence must be guarded with a good, high property qualification'. *WA*, 3 January 1878, p. 2, c. 1-2.

The consequences of pre-emption, selection and evasion were obvious by 1875. Odd bits and pieces of land were acquired by pastoralists after that date (mainly by auction) but the great battle was over and the gains and losses could be calculated by the survivors. From Warra to Killarney stretched a chain of huge freehold estates, interspersed with a few small agricultural settlements and grazing farms. Few runs had totally disintegrated and pastoralists such as Tyson, Taylor and Wienholt had even increased their holdings at the expense of their neighbours.

Fisher, Davenport, Miles and Simpson had, by lavish application of capital, selected considerable estates from the pre-existing runs. These outsiders—who had not observed the unwritten covenant maintaining the inviolability of one pastoralist's run against the onslaught of another—were detested even more than the rising class of small graziers on Rosenthal, Cecil Plains, North Branch and Greenbank who had managed to acquire 5,000-15,000 acre farms of their own.[91] The squatters had security of tenure at last. But for several this security was fictional and disastrous. Hope had stated that 'the object of good government was that people should enjoy the investments they had made' but the ensuing period was one of anxiety and financial servitude for several pastoralists, rather than a serene digestion of their riotous freeholding.[92]

While the resumptions of 1863, 1868, 1872 and 1875 avoided some of the evils of unrestricted free selection which rent New South Wales, the areas involved were both desirable and large enough virtually to force the pastoral lessees into illegal actions in order to preserve their equity and security. Many squatters were horrified at their vast capital investment which had overturned the old pastoral combination of cheap rents and borrowed money. Some, however, saw the wholesale disposal of land by the Crown as an opportunity for future profit and soon passed the dividing line between what others thought was a 'cruel necessity' and naked greed. Even these 'cormorants' were glutted by 1876.

Selected at £1 per acre or less, most runs were top-heavy with capital investment which yielded no increase in production but benefited only the bank shareholders and mortgagees in Sydney and London. This capital might have financed a vigorous breeding and improvements programme but with fluctuating wool prices and heavy mortgages the profit margin could no longer support further intensification.[93] Surplus lands could not be sold for cash without infringing the security of the whole and in any case the pastoralist or bank could not offer the liberal terms to the farmer that the Government could afford. The Agricultural Lands Purchase Act of 1894 was a relief to many pastoralists, some of

[91] Appendix VII lists the major freehold estates.

[92] *QPD*, Vol. 14, (1872), p. 863.

[93] The reverse was true in the Unsettled District where the growth of mortgagee control 'was a price to be paid by individuals . . . to provide the financial means for greatly expanded pastoral assets which in turn laid the basis for increased incomes . . .' N. G. Butlin, 'Company Ownership of NSW Pastoral Stations, 1865-1900', *Historical Studies*, Vol. 4, No. 14, May 1950, p. 110.

whom had tried to subdivide, and indeed much of the initiative for it came from them.

The story of two estates, Clifton and Canning Downs, illustrates these contentions. After W. B. Tooth of Clifton died in 1876, it was disclosed that the property was indebted to the Bank of New South Wales for £90,000 which, coupled with compound interest, was increasing faster than grazing profits from the 40,000 acres of freehold. The bank had already compelled the sale of 10,000 acres to C. B. Fisher. In addition the Tooth family owed their London woolbrokers £12,000. The great proportion of this debt had been incurred between 1866 and 1874 precisely when the great Selection Acts were operative.[94] Although a special Enabling Act of 1879 broke the will and allowed dispersal, the whole estate eventually passed into the hands of the reluctant bank.[95]

The other property, Canning Downs, purchased by F. J. C. Wildash in 1865 from Gilbert Davidson, had a more complex and interesting history. On 31 October 1865 the original lease expired but the prospective purchaser evidently secured the promise of the Lands Minister that a new lease would be issued.[96] Wildash then bought the run of 27,000 acres of pre-empted freeholds and 250 square miles of leasehold for £100,000, although Davidson retained a second mortgage of £50,000 and McDonald, Smith and Company, the Sydney mercantile firm, advanced the remainder on first mortgage.[97] In the event, the promised lease was not issued and all Crown land was declared an Agricultural Reserve in 1866, thus ensuring 'the practical destruction of the pastoral lease'.[98] To restore the value of his run Wildash resorted to dummying and slid deeper into debt. '. . . The expenditure of large sums on those selections prevented my reducing the debt, but rather caused its increase.'[99] Under the 1866 Act 21,291 acres were acquired and 15,000 acres under the 1868 Act.[100] Unfortunately for Wildash and his partners, the disputed titles affair stopped the issue of the deeds of grant, and they were unable to preserve their equity, the mortgagees hastily selling the station over their heads before the Privy Council decisions gave them the coveted titles. Wildash, the self-confessed dummier who had 'yet to learn that there is anything wrong in a person having the means of acquiring land doing so, notwithstanding laws passed hedging around the mode of acquisition with all sorts of obstacles and restrictions', had the temerity

94 *QVP*, Vol. 2, (1879), pp. 1087-97.

95 *QPD*, Vol. 28, (1879), pp. 151, 683-4.

96 *QVP*, Vol. 2, (1879), pp. 1225-6, 1434-52 and *WA*, 9 November 1876, p. 2, c. 7. The evidence, however, indicates that Wildash was determined to purchase before he obtained Macalister's assurance.

97 ibid., Davidson's mortgage was later taken over by McDonald and Smith. Wildash had only £5,000 in cash when he 'purchased' but was a distant relation of the Leslies and Davidson.

98 *QVP*, Vol. 2, (1879), p. 1435.

99 *WA*, 9 November 1876, p. 2, c. 7. His current account for 1 July-December 1874 revealed a credit of £25,952 and a debit balance of £94,831. Wildash was then paying interest at the rate of £8,000 per annum. *QVP*, Vol. 2, (1879), p. 1446.

100 ibid., p. 1442.

to petition Parliament for compensation as the withholding of the deeds had ruined him.[101] He aroused the ire of many, including McIlwraith and Griffith, the latter declaring in tones of a future Chief Justice, echoing his religious upbringing, that '. . . [he] must be considered the prototype of dummying . . . the arch-dummier of the colony. Less consideration was due to Wildash than to any other person'. Others supported him, alleging personal vendettas and persecutions.[102] The whole matter—as with all the great land transactions on the Downs—was clouded by extraordinary personality clashes, conflicting evidence and the usual scarcely-veiled political and administrative chicanery on the part of Ministers and administrators in Brisbane.

Parliament narrowly rejected Wildash's impudent—though desperate—claim and the unfortunate gentleman, reduced to seedy drunkenness and the promotion of hopeless speculations, suicided in 1882.[103] This was a classic pastoral tragedy. Seen by some as divine retribution for past misdeeds, Wildash's collapse posed several questions which the pragmatists of the Downs neglected to answer or even probe. Hundreds had dummied —yet Wildash, through a unique combination of circumstances, had lost everything. Much of the fault lay with the man himself, but the Government, mortgagees and urban agrarians—in fact the whole fabric of colonial life—made such disasters inescapable and partly comprehensible.

In Wildash's case the creation of a superb pastoral freehold, whose next owner, Macansh, was in turn technically bankrupt by 1896, meant the destruction not only of his social and financial position but the eventual disintegration of his entire personality. J. F. McDougall of Rosalie Plains or the ill-fated directors of the Darling Downs and Western Land Company were not quite as unfortunate.[104] Those who survived the transition either had great liquid financial resources, such as Tyson and Taylor, and could absorb the sterile capital expenditure or else, like Hodgson and Ramsay, or Kent and Wienholt, had had a long period of occupancy at cheap rentals to cushion the financial blow.[105] Some, such as Marshall of Glengallan, acquired new partners with skill, knowledge and enthusiasm to manage their properties and gradually intensified and diversified until by 1893 squatting on some estates bore little resemblance to life and work in 1860. Others sold out or remained lethargic spectators of a changing scene, attempting to carry on a way of life which bore little relation to economic and social reality.

101 ibid.

102 *QPD*, Vol. 25, (1881), p. 879. Groom strongly supported Wildash's case. ibid., p. 801. The voting was close, Wildash failing by 21 to 19.

103 *WA*, 2 May 1882, p. 2, c. 2 and *BC*, 16 April 1881, p. 1; *Australasian*, 6 April 1881, p. 507, c. 3. His successor on Canning Downs, J. D. Macansh, was really not solvent when he died in 1896. *QVP*, Second Session, Vol. 3, (1910), p. 1062.

104 By 1896 the DD and WLC owed the Queensland National Bank £323,173. *The Worker*, 12 September 1896, p. 2, c. 4.

105 Pre-emption, selection, depression and ostentation ruined John Deuchar, Marshall's earlier partner. W. B. Slade, his successor, was one of the most successful of the new managerial group on the Downs. *WE&T*, 14 September 1872, p. 2, c. 5 and *Australasian Pastoralists' Review*, Vol. 16, No. 3, 15 May 1906, p. 175.

But freeholding not only transformed the majority of the stations from patriarchal seats to business enterprises managed by absentees or 'aliens' but also destroyed the whole basis of Pure Merino faith. No longer could they pretend to be morally superior, incorruptible, local father-figures, impartially guiding the destinies of the region. Twenty years of romantic myth disappeared overnight, as they were revealed to be 'men, not centaurs'. The wildest ravings of the genuine agrarians appeared to have been justified and the fat acres along the creeks mockingly reminded them and their practical farmers of their failure to win the first round in the contest for the soil.

CHAPTER 3

INSIDE AND OUT

> This concentration on fodder conservation in a pastoral district is unique in Australia. There is more hay on a couple of Downs properties than in all the Western District properties in Victoria.
>
> 'Bruni' in *Australasian,* 2 July 1887, p. 11

Professor N. G. Butlin has suggested that the 'objective of a history of the pastoral industry is not merely to describe but to explain the growth and distribution of sheep'.[1] Only by regional analysis, he asserted, could some of the key questions—the evolution of specialized pastoralism, the intensification of land use, the differing regional problems and the attempts to solve them—be answered.

The Darling Downs, between 1859 and 1893, presented a unique and complex picture of pastoral development. Beyond the western boundary of the Settled District the squatters, safe from selectors, contended with much the same problems—and applied similar expedients or solutions—as did their fellows on the Warrego, Balonne, Mitchell or Leichhardt country. Superior natural advantages, better communications and, most of all, the creation of pastoral freeholds, however, compelled them to experiment, diversify, intensify and invest even more heavily in improvements and the novel products of an expanding technology. De Satgé, reviewing his pastoral experiences, summed up the pre-requisites for successful pastoral enterprise. An adequate and reliable rainfall was the first essential, followed by nutritious natural pastures and handy cheap carriage to markets and urban centres.[2] Characteristically, however, he neglected to add the twin essentials of profitable prices and adequate capital and credit. The Downs was extremely well-favoured by nature, its unique combination of physical advantages making it one of the most attractive (and lucrative) areas for wool production in Australasia.

All the Downs received an average annual rainfall of over twenty inches, the Settled District annual precipitation being twenty-five inches. Although the winters were relatively dry, this was of minor concern to

1 N. G. Butlin, 'The Distribution of Sheep Population: Preliminary Statistical Picture, 1860-1956', *unpublished seminar paper,* ANU, 7 October 1958, p. 8.

2 Oscar de Satgé, *Queensland Squatter,* p. 225.

the pastoralist who cared little about how and when rain fell so long as it maintained pasture growth and did not result in flooding. Nevertheless, severe droughts, felt more in the west than in the east, occasionally struck the Downs, causing considerable stock losses. Between 1865 and 1868 drought struck the area, causing heavy losses in the Warwick and Dalby areas. This catastrophe was repeated in 1871, 1876-8, 1881-6 and 1888-9.[3] The short, sharp drought of 1871 was typical:

> For miles around Dalby the country . . . is as bare as the road, and almost entirely devoid of water . . . about the creeks . . . carcasses may be seen in hundreds. The lambs are perishing in immense numbers, the ewes through weakness being unable to rear them . . . public prayers for rain have been offered at Dalby.[4]

James Taylor of Cecil Plains lost 40,000 sheep in 1881 but disasters on this scale—at least in the Settled District—were rare.[5] The numerous creeks seldom dried up completely and improvements after 1870 minimized the effects of water deficiencies. Sudden floods, especially along the banks of the Condamine, Weir, Macintyre and Moonie river systems occasionally caused loss of life, stock and property to western pastoralists but the elements on the whole were much kinder to the Downs pastoralists than to others further south and west.[6]

The pioneer squatters on the inner Downs depastured their stock on natural grasses that 'reached as high as a horse's belly'.[7] These blue-grass downlands (the main species were blue-grass, *Dichanthium sericeum*, satin-top, *Bothriochloa erianthoides*, and shot-grass, *Paspalidium globaidium*) seemed capable of supporting a large and growing sheep population almost indefinitely, but the introduction of exotic grazing animals was sufficient to alter the composition of the plant communities. Defoliation, manuring and trampling eliminated the more valuable species which were replaced by nutritiously inferior grasses. Fencing accelerated the decline of the Downs pastures by concentrating flocks and herds and encouraging over-stocking.[8] At the same time, the Selection Acts removed the margin between rough adjustment and over-grazing by removing the rough 'run-offs' and burdening properties with an unproductive capital investment that could only be countered by maintaining or increasing past stock numbers on static acreages.

The squatters of the Western Downs were less fortunate than the Pure Merinos. From Inglewood to Miles stretched a belt of sandy alkaline

[3] *WA*, 30 August 1877, p. 2, c. 1-2 and 31 August 1881, p. 2, c. 1; *BC*, 14 January 1878, p. 5, c. 1.

[4] *Town and Country Journal*, 23 September 1871, p. 405. At Glengallan only 100 sheep survived out of 1,500 in one paddock alone. ibid., 28 October 1871, p. 562.

[5] *Australasian*, 17 December 1881, p. 792.

[6] Callandoon Station on the Macintyre lost 30,000 sheep from a flood in 1864.

[7] *See* the description in H. S. Russell, *Genesis of Queensland*, p. 24.

[8] *WE&T*, 13 May 1882, p. 4, c. 6-7. *See also* R. M. Moore, 'Effects of the sheep industry on Australian vegetation', in A. Barnard, (ed.), *The Simple Fleece*, Melbourne 1962, pp. 170-83. R. Roe and G. H. Allen, 'Studies on the Mitchell Grass Association in South-western Queensland', *CSIRO Bulletin No. 185*, Melbourne 1945.

soils supporting a close-growing cypress-bull oak-box variety of forest, difficult and expensive to clear and discouraging the growth of the rather inferior Mitchell grasses (*Astrebla lappacea* and *Astrebla pectinata*). North of Jandowae, along the north-east fringe of the region, the open eucalyptus forest on the granite hills had also a low stock-carrying capacity. Further west the brigalow belt (*Acacia harpophylla* and *Casuarina lepidophloia*), developed on deep clay or clay-loam surfaced soils, could only be cleared by ringbarking and burning—arduous and costly jobs which—as the proprietors of Welltown discovered—often failed to yield sufficient short-term returns on the labour and capital expended. The parklands in the south-west of the region between the Macintyre and Weir Rivers and in the north-west around Coomrith, however, were covered by an almost continuous carpet of Mitchell and blue grasses and were some of the best grazing country on the Downs.[9] The carrying capacity of the country varied from run to run, from time to time and from owner to owner. Some pastoralists, particularly in the early years, deliberately overstocked, hoping for high returns and a quick sale before Nemesis in the shape of drought, disease or pasture exhaustion, overtook them. The unfortunate purchaser frequently paid the penalty and relinquished the run to his mortgagees.

In 1844 there were a mere 133,054 sheep on the Downs. By 1864 this had risen to 1,871,398—a fourteenfold increase in twenty years. The Dalby (531,047), Toowoomba (565,218) and Warwick (450,676) Police Districts then accounted for 78 per cent of all the sheep in the area. Sheep numbers continued to rise until they reached their peak of 3,410,812 in 1868. Thereafter, compared with other regions of Queensland, sheep numbers were relatively stable, fluctuating between two and two-and-a-half millions. The 1876-8, 1885 and 1888-9 droughts, however, reduced the sheep population by 300,000-500,000 in each of these years.[10] This stability is quite remarkable in view of the disruptive effect on the pastoral industry the Selection Acts created. Even the distribution of sheep on the Downs did not undergo any significant change between 1864 and 1890. Runs within the Settled District or on its western margin carried over 70 per cent of the sheep population in 1893. Far from declining, the Toowoomba and Warwick-Allora areas maintained their position, and numbers in the former district even increased. An analysis of sheep ownership on the Downs in 1892 reveals that the great stations of the Settled District had, despite selection legislation, maintained their lead. Ten runs depastured 950,967 sheep between them—38 per cent of all sheep in the entire Pastoral District. On a mere twenty-seven properties grazed 68 per cent of the region's sheep. The 221 small graziers, or

[9] Contemporary descriptions of the area are rare, but the picture can be reconstructed by reference to advertisements for station sales in local and colonial newspapers. E. Hirschfeld and R. S. Hirschfeld, 'Concerning the Brigalow', *QAJ*, Vol. 49, Part 4, 1 April 1938, pp. 334-45 and R. F. Isbell, 'The Soils of the Inglewood-Talwood-Tara-Glenmorgan Region, Queensland', *Bureau of Investigation*, Technical Bulletin No. 5, Brisbane 1957.

[10] *SR*, 1861-93.

55 per cent of the Downs sheepmen, held only 24,460 sheep. It was the big men—Kent and Wienholt, James Tyson, James Taylor, the Gores, Shanahan and Jennings, C. B. Fisher and Hodgson and Ramsay—who still dominated the region's great export industry.[11]

The Downs had 32 per cent of all cattle in the colony in 1860. By 1863, 205,158 cattle were grazing in the area but the change-over to sheep on Cecil Plains in 1865 symbolized the failing attractions of meat *vis-à-vis* wool in the best areas. Between 1864 and 1865 cattle numbers were halved in the Warwick Police District and declined by a third in the Toowoomba area. A continuous fall to 99,359 in 1870 was not arrested until the early 'seventies when numbers slowly rose again once more. In 1870 only 10 per cent of the colony's cattle grazed on the Downs and although there were 150,694 in 1874, 203,371 in 1887 and 231,124 in 1890 the region's percentage of the Queensland total remained a constant 4 per cent.[12]

While the differences between the squatting-round on freehold and leasehold widened between 1870 and 1893, certain tasks were common to both zones. Innovations, however, were usually first introduced in the Settled District and spread west to the larger stations and then to the smaller runs of the pastoral 'strugglers'. Lambing took place in August and September, washing began late in September, and shearing a few days later after the sheep had dried. Some shore as early as August by 1892. Expensive and complicated plants, with washpool, boilers, spouts, troughs and yards, first came into general use in the early 'sixties.[13] The main argument for washing was that the shorn wool was about 45 per cent lighter and much cleaner with the black-soil stains removed. Consequently it was cheaper to transport, but the coming of railways to the Downs in the late 'sixties and 'seventies made the difference negligible. It was costly in time, labour (ten men were usually required), and sheep mortality.[14] A few squatters—either too poor or too perceptive to introduce the process—rejected washing and shore in the grease. But washing was more than a pastoral task; until it was abandoned in the early 'eighties a station's efficiency and its lessee's success were popularly measured by the extent of his washpool and the size of his woolshed rather than by the confidential entries on his merchant's statements.

Vast wooden woolsheds were also built during the prosperous years. Jondaryan woolshed, completed in September 1861 at a cost of £3,300, was 'the finest in the colony'. Three hundred feet long, with cover for 3,000 sheep at a time when summer rains often soaked Downs sheep waiting to be shorn, this shed had a tramway for fleeces and bales along

[11] Appendix VII examines sheep ownership in 1892 in greater detail.

[12] *SR*, 1861-93.

[13] *WE&T*, 4 October 1873, p. 2, c. 1-2. For a description of the famous Pikedale Washing-plant, *see* D. Gunn, *Links with the past*, Brisbane 1937, pp. 201-4.

[14] Canning Downs' plant cost £3,000. In 1873 workers were paid 3s. 9d. per day plus rations for 'dry' work and 4s. 9d. for 'wet'. *WE&T*, 11 October 1873, p. 2, c. 6 and 12 December 1874, p. 2, c. 5; *WA*, 3 December 1868, p. 2, c. 4.

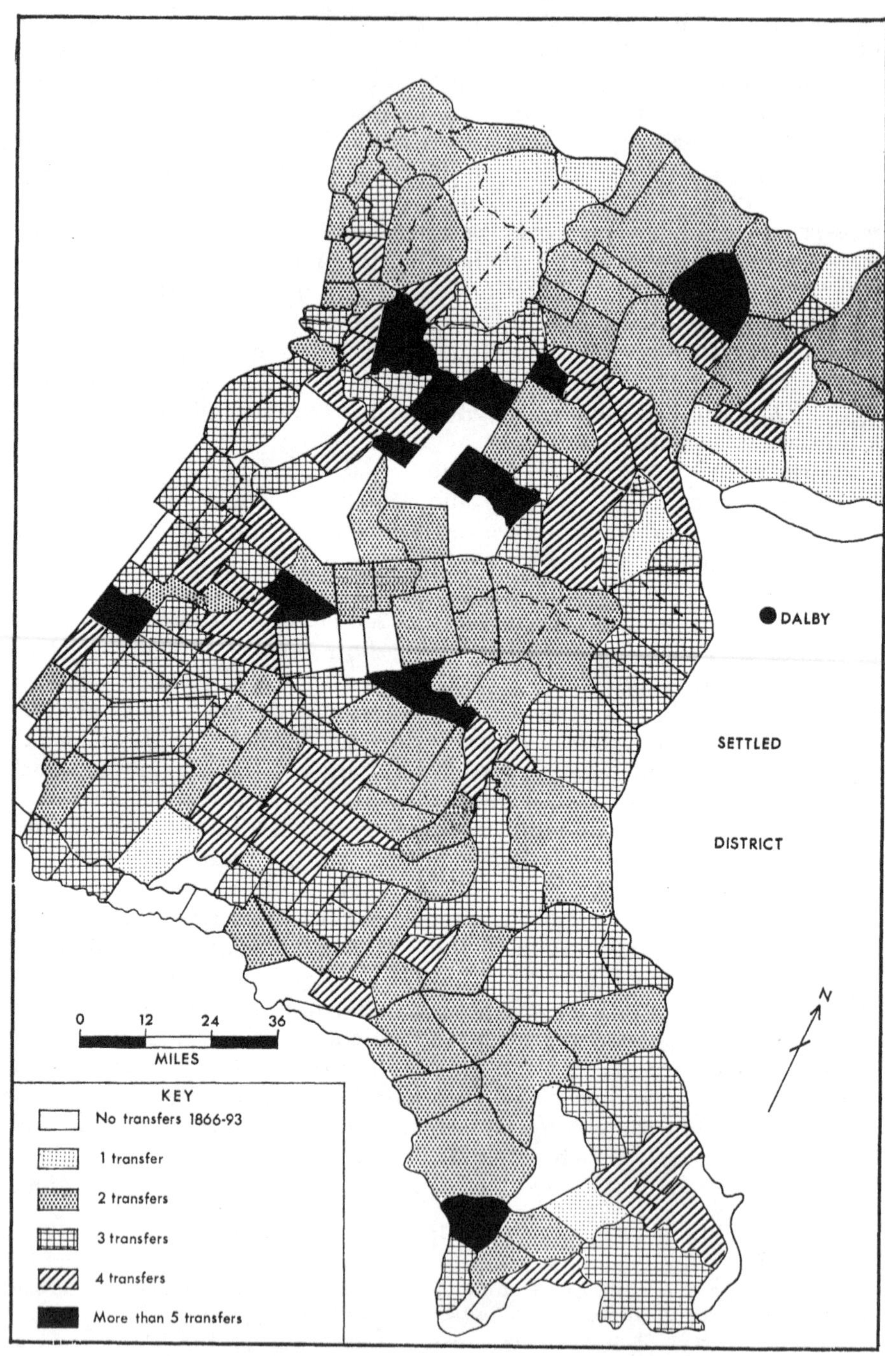

MAP 10 Leaseholds rate of transfer, 1866-93 (after *QGG*, 1866-93, 'Rent Lists')

its centre.[15] It was still the largest on the Darling Downs in 1892, with 52 stands, approached only by Welltown, Callandoon and Yandilla which each had 49.[16] The scale on which the industry operated is indicated by the fact that in 1870 Jimbour employed 54 shearers to shear 210,000 sheep—1,409 bales were filled in 15 weeks.[17] Shearing machines were first demonstrated at Toowoomba on 10 August 1887 and Gowrie was the first shed to install them. The Wolseleys saved labour, removed more wool from the sheep and took off the finest skin-wool, thus reducing the injury rate and enabling some squatters to shear twice in the same season.[18]

Few could afford and fewer wanted to purchase a Downs estate after 1875. Even with the security of freehold land the dividends on the capital outlay were never large. Consequently—apart from sales resulting from death, dissolution of partnership or bankruptcy—very few stations in the Settled District changed hands during the period.[19] The situation was much more fluid on the Western Downs where a large run such as Pikedale, with 30,899 acres of freehold and 75 square miles of Crown lease, together with 13,000 sheep and 300 cattle, could be bought for as little as £35,000 in 1889. Umbercollie, with 12,600 sheep, was sold for only £10,000 in 1875.[20]

An examination of the Pastoral Rent Lists in the *Queensland Government Gazettes* confirms two suspicions. Firstly, that there was a high turnover rate of leases even when temporary transfers to financial institutions are excluded and, secondly, that only a few squatters held the same blocks for any considerable length of time. Maps 10 and 11 illustrate these contentions by portraying the transfer and length-of-ownership histories of each block on the Western Downs.[21] Actual 'ownership' was a different matter. Butlin's techniques have been used to give a more precise picture of changing ownership patterns between 1870 and 1893. The percentages are even more illuminating. Non-banking institutions were never particularly prominent on the Downs although those that held leases in the areas, such as the Scottish Australian Investment Company (Texas) and the New Zealand and Australian Land Company (Wongongera), retained their investments for relatively long periods. In 1885 only 9 per cent of the leases were held by land-mortgage or pastoral companies compared with 5 per cent in 1870 and 7 per cent in 1890. With the growing investment by the banks in pastoral mortgages, however, the number of leases transferred to the banks rose sharply after

15 *DDG*, 19 December 1861, p. 3, c. 2-3.

16 *Pastoralists' Review*, Vol. 2, No. 6, 15 August 1892, p. 762.

17 *Dalby Herald*, 29 January 1870, p. 2.

18 *Pastoralists' Review*, Vol. 1, No. 2, 15 January 1892, p. 452 and Vol. 2, No. 3, 15 March 1892, p. 538.

19 Appendix I gives a list of the owners of the great stations 1860-93.

20 *Australasian*, 30 March 1889, p. 680 and *Town and Country Journal*, 5 June 1875, p. 912.

21 The actual tables on which these maps are based have not been inserted but Appendix II gives the changing ownership of ten Western Downs runs selected as representative of both localities and trends.

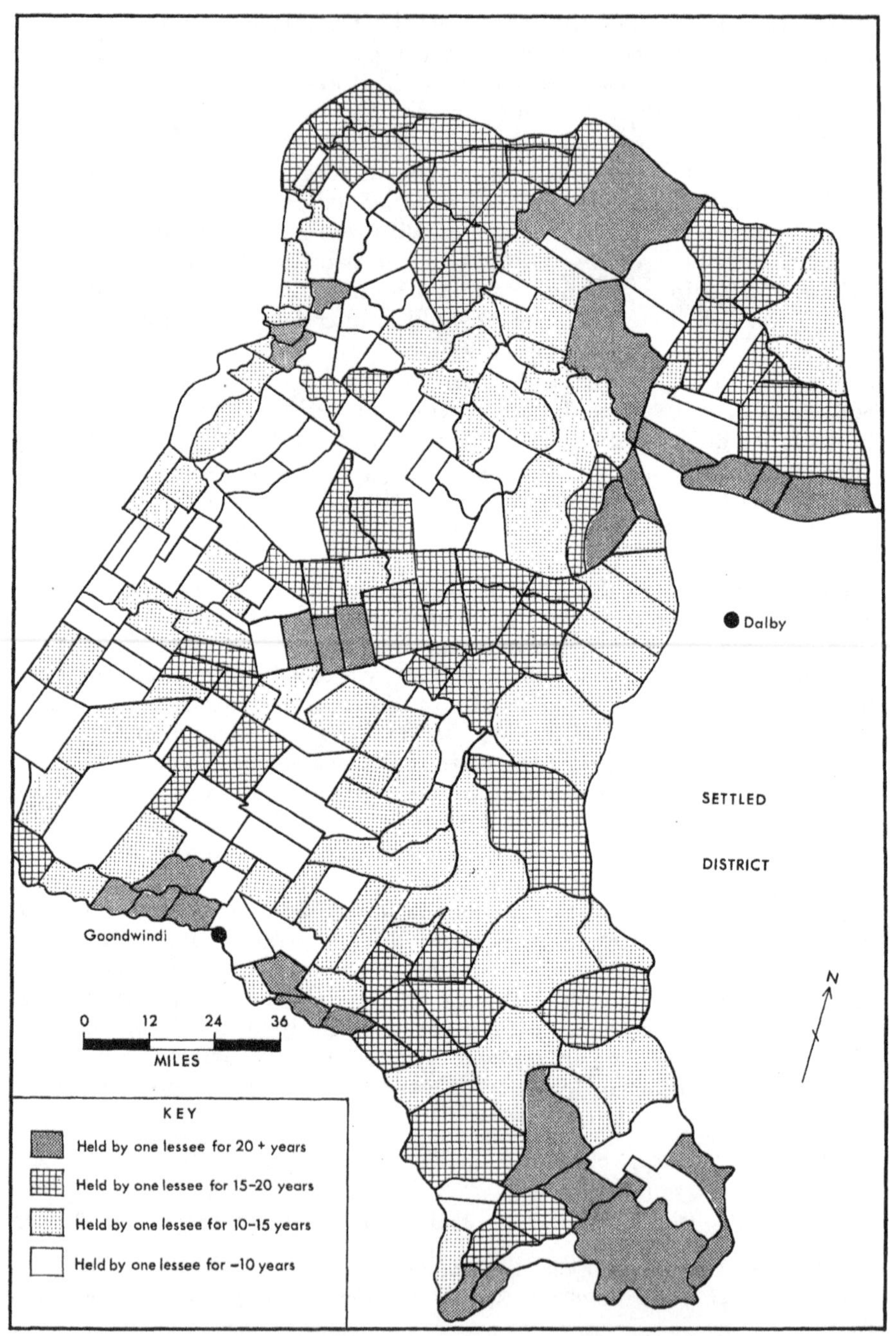

MAP 11 Turnover of run leases, 1866-93 (after *QGG*, 1866-93, 'Run Rent Lists')

1877. In 1875 only 13 per cent of the leases were held by the banks, mainly as collateral security under mortgage. Five years later during droughts and falling prices the banks held 33 per cent of all titles. This figure is higher than that for comparable areas in New South Wales. By 1885 the banks still held 28 per cent of the titles, reflecting the inability of many run-holders to return to the old days of freedom and security. While the ratio fell after 1886, 17 per cent of all run leases were still held by the banks in 1890 and 1893.

REGISTERED LEASEHOLDERS: DARLING DOWNS UNSETTLED DISTRICT, 1870-93[22]

Year	Banks	Non-banking companies	Partnerships	Individuals	Total
1870	10	9	30	116	165
1875	26	5	32	122	185
1880	58	4	16	87	165
1885	65	22	31	107	225
1890	18	8	8	62	96
1893	13	5	10	48	76

Many Crown lessees were in a parlous condition by 1893. Several runs, particularly the smaller blocks, had been abandoned and some were without stock. Few could afford to invest in improvements, and second growth and the regeneration of the brigalow had forced a reduction in carrying capacity. Run-holders alleged that the value of their leases had fallen by 30 per cent during the previous five years and that their properties were virtually unsaleable. H. K. Alford, the lessee of Tieryboo, summed everything up when he testified that '. . . drought and depression have brought added financial burdens . . . land and bank finance companies were moving in'.[23] Prospects for future development on the Western Downs looked very black indeed in 1893.

Trollope predicted (in 1871) that squatting on the Downs would never bear the cost of purchased land. For twenty years the pastoral freeholders endeavoured to prove him wrong. Their success in postponing the evil day when their lands would be subdivided and sold to the 'cockatoos' was undeniable but most were delighted to sell when the State made wholesale disposal possible. At last they could escape with their equity and sometimes even a little more besides. Now it was their turn to receive interest-bearing debenture stocks financed by British investors. The latter did very well out of the Downs even if 1893 shook their confidence. Not only had they financed through colonial banks and mortgage houses

22 *QGG*, 1870-93, 'Pastoral Rent Lists'. N. G. Butlin, 'Company Ownership of NSW Pastoral Stations', *unpublished seminar paper*, ANU, 7 October 1958. Map 12 illustrates the extent of 'Company Ownership' on the Downs during 1885-6.

23 'Proceedings of the Land Board Court' printed in: *WE&T*, 21 October 1893, p. 3, c. 5 and 25 October 1893, p. 3, c. 6; *TC*, 2 March 1893, p. 4, c. 2.

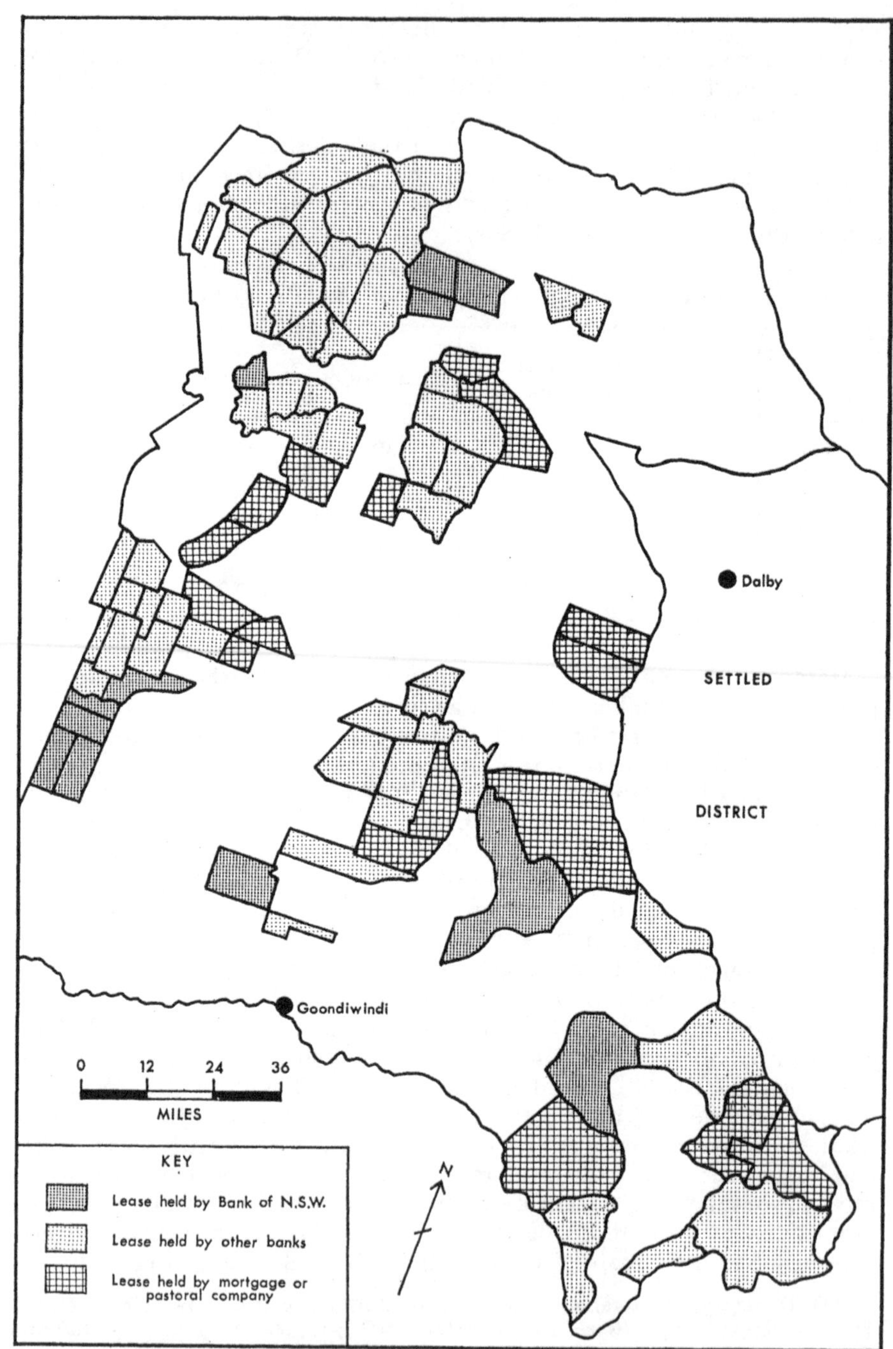

MAP 12 Unsettled District leaseholders, 1885-6 (after *QGG*, 1885-6, 'Rent Lists')

many Downs pastoralists, but re-purchase gave them yet another opportunity to draw their steady four to six per cent from colonial investments.

Butlin maintains that it was not fencing but pastoral capital formation with its accompanying changes in technique 'that was the central factor in the growth of rural productivity'. He goes on to conclude that:

> Pastoral investment . . . was based on the inflow of British capital into Australian private institutions . . . [it] eventually provided a rationale of a powerful real estate interest in pastoral activity . . . it was a primary reason for a rising interest commitment in the still unstable industry, a commitment translated . . . into a growing private interest bill in the Australian balance of payments. The outcome . . . was collapse, foreclosure, and pastoral and financial reconstruction, and the end of a major experimental phase in the utilization of the Australian continent.[24]

All this is indisputable but on the Downs at least politics rather than economics were responsible for a large part of the total investment. So favoured was the Settled District that it is possible that improvements might have been financed from accumulated and current earnings had not the State intervened and attempted to redistribute the land. This argument assumes that speculation and the transfer-rate would not advance and radically distort the rough balance between outlay and return. The pastoralists attacked the problem of maintaining and increasing net returns from relatively highly capitalized land (£2-3 per acre is an average figure) from several different directions.

It was obvious by the 'seventies that the slow decline in carrying capacity would have to be checked. Every acre if possible would have to maintain its sheep. To do this required even greater capital investment. The cycle was a vicious and never-ending one; after saving their land, a process which had cost anything from twenty to over a hundred thousand pounds, further vast sums had to be raised to finance improvements so that the original investment would not be lost. If prices fell, however—as on the whole they did during the boom and slump years of the 'eighties and 'nineties—the gap between wool and stock receipts would narrow and might eventually disappear. A disastrous season or two and total ruin might result although the magnitude and nature of the improvements made such an occurrence the exception rather than the rule in the Settled District. Downs squatters were not in the main the 'avid and reckless borrowers' the banks feared.[25] A few of them were but most, such as Slade of Glengallan, borrowed only from necessity while others, particularly the new Victorian capitalists, were convinced that their superior techniques and plans for massive improvements would yield good dividends. Nearly every pastoralist, moreover, carried an annual interest bill on his current account but the nature of the industry was such that this could not be avoided.[26]

24 N. G. Butlin, 'The Growth of Rural Capital, 1860-1890', in A. Barnard (ed.), *The Simple Fleece*, p. 323.

25 S. J. Butlin, *Australia and New Zealand Bank*, Melbourne 1961, p. 213.

26 Slade held a mortgage with the Scottish Widows' Fund for £25,000 during the 'nineties. *Glengallan Papers*, GP 78/C, *QSA*.

The Downs squatters were fortunate in that the years 1871-7, when funds for improvements were most required, were 'the most profitable period of pastoral enterprise ever encountered in Australia'.[27] After 1877 there was a sharp slump followed by a short boom and slump period in 1880-2. Good prices and bad then alternated until 1891 when the long depression first began to make itself really felt in the station offices and city board rooms. A contemporary estimate of Australian returns illustrates the decline:

WOOL PRICES, 1873-92[28]

Season	Return per bale: (£)	Production index	Value index
1873–4	19¼	100	100
1882–3	16	161	134
1891–2	12¼	298	189

In some ways the Downs estate owners were more fortunate than their brethren in northern and western districts. Their best combing wool frequently brought prices from 3d.-6d. above the colonial average and approached those of the Western District of Victoria. There is some evidence that prices for the finest greasy Downs wool fell relatively less than those for average fleeces.[29] Overall, however, these were minor considerations. When prices fell by 2d. per pound in 1869, the twenty Warwick stations lost £20,000 between them.[30] Stock prices also declined over the period although once again there were considerable variations between stud and run, Downs market and Brisbane yard, and the month-by-month breeder requirements of the Western stations:

STOCK PRICES: WARWICK AND TOOWOOMBA, 1862-93[31]

Animal	Years		
	1862	1882	1893
Shorn wethers	10s.	7s.	4s. 6d.
Maiden ewes	15s.	10s. 6d.	5s. 6d.
Old ewes	9–14s.	6s.	2–3s.
Bullocks	50s.	77s. 6d.	42s. 6d.

27 Butlin, 'Growth of Rural Capital' in *The Simple Fleece*, p. 325.

28 *AIBR*, Vol. 17, No. 9, 19 September 1893, pp. 849-50 and *Pastoralists' Review*, Vol. 2, No. 12, 15 February 1893, p. 1082.

29 *WA*, 14 May 1874, p. 2, c. 1; *WE&T*, 24 January 1874, p. 2, c. 6 and *Glengallan Papers*, GP/32, pp. 17-39 'Wool Book', *QSA*.

30 *WA*, 26 May 1869, p. 2, c. 1.

31 *DDG*, 10 April 1862, p. 3, c. 4; *WE&T*, 4 November 1882, p. 3, c. 3 and *WA*, 10 June 1893, p. 3, c. 7.

The reports of the directors of the North British Australasian Company, owners of St Ruth and Rosenthal between 1860 and 1893, give some indication of the development and vicissitudes of the Downs pastoral industry after Separation. When wool and cattle prices fell in the 'sixties the company was nearly forced into bankruptcy. Nevertheless by 1871 it had more than doubled its sheep numbers (1864: 50,000; 1868: 120,000), purchased 10,000 acres of land, invested £14,000 in 252 miles of fencing and raised the average fleece-weight by nearly half a pound. During 1872 lucerne was sown for the first time and Haran on the Western Downs was purchased for £250 as a rough grazing run for the surplus sheep. By 1875, 22,400 acres had been freeholded and two more runs on the Western Downs acquired to breed store sheep for fattening at St Ruth and Rosenthal. Net profits had risen—'in spite of the extravagance at the head station'—from £3,367 in 1871 to £15,316 in 1875. By 1884, however, the company was in difficulties again. Further land purchases had absorbed all the capital, there was a bank overdraft of £10,000, and a debenture issue of £30,000 was required to finance further freeholding and replenish reserves. The net profit of the company was only £6,975, owing to drought and falling wool prices. St Ruth and Rosenthal returned only a meagre £1,475 and £1,623 net profit respectively. However, 1888 saw the concern in a better position. A capital loss of £20,000 had been eliminated, profits had trebled to £18,256 in 1887 and new perpetual debentures cancelled reliance on bank finance.[32]

The capital investment in another station controlled by a pastoral company whose directors were busily engaged in applying the savings of the English depositors as soon as they were tapped indicates the scale and composition of investment in the Settled District (*see* table p. 62).

Apart from the comparatively large investment in buildings and washing-plants during the 'seventies, fencing was the most expensive item and 'probably as valuable as all the rest of the resources put together'.[33] The decision to fence was generally a result of a combination of factors: scab, dingoes and boundary disputes and—most important of all—gradual changes in shepherding methods. On the Downs, resumption and closer settlement made the erection of adequate fences essential and the resulting need to diversify and intensify—to breed, fatten and cultivate—stimulated still further subdivision. George Clark of East Talgai had by 1873 fenced all his 32,000 acres of freehold, divided it into forty paddocks and was carrying one sheep to the acre. So far he had spent £16,000 on improvements alone.[34] There were few paddocks over 1,000 acres in extent on the inner Downs after 1875. Once subdivision had proceeded, each paddock had to have a permanent water-supply. Pre-emption had safeguarded the natural water but expensive earth-dams and reservoirs were constructed where streams did not flow and waterholes dried up.

32 *WA*, 5 May 1869, p. 4, c. 4; *WE&T*, 6 January 1872, p. 3, c. 1; 28 December 1872, p. 2, c. 5; 4 March 1876, p. 2, c. 5; 9 February 1884, p. 3, c. 1; 14 January 1885, p. 2, c. 6 and 7 February 1888, p. 2, c. 6.

33 Butlin, 'Growth of Rural Capital' in *The Simple Fleece*, p. 324.

34 *WE&T*, 30 August 1873, p. 2, c. 6.

CAPITAL INVESTMENT: JIMBOUR, 1884[35]

Darling Downs and Western Land Company		
		£
	125,859 acres @ £2.10s.	314,648
	115,501 sheep @ 10s.	57,750
	952 rams @ £5.5s.	4,998
	2,500 stud sheep @ £2.2s.	5,250
	177 draught horses @ £20	3,540
	483 saddle horses, 8 entires	6,383
Plant		5,000
Stores		1,500
Cattle		613
	TOTAL:	£399,682

NOTE: This excludes the £40,000 invested in Jimbour House and the village at the head station.

After the mid-'seventies all pastoralists were tapping the sub-artesian reservoir which lay from 40 to 100 feet under the soil. The American geared windmill, constantly pumping into an iron tank, was a familiar sight by 1880. Jimbour by 1884 had 22 dams, 26 reservoirs and 20 wells, while Yandilla alone had 24 windmills.[36]

The indigenous grasses comfortably supported one and a half sheep to the acre during the 'sixties, but unless the now smaller paddocks could be rested deterioration was bound to occur once the pastoralist attempted to maintain his sheep and cattle numbers. The solution to this problem and to that of increasing carrying capacity apparently lay in the cultivation of introduced grasses and fodder crops.

Agricultural experiments were conducted by the squatters during the late 'forties and early 'fifties but the agrarian threat suspended these unwise ventures. Others might have drawn the wrong conclusions at a time when the Pure Merinos were trumpeting that commercial agriculture was impossible on the Downs. To cultivate in the 'sixties was to be a traitor to one's group during its fight for survival. Profits were high and easily earned during the fifteen years before 1866 and there was no economic compulsion to experiment in this direction. Davenport and Fisher had no such inhibitions. At Headington Hill they introduced a completely new system of large-scale mixed farming. £30,000 was invested in improvements between 1868 and 1873 and fifty men, the most modern American implements and 'farm buildings unequalled in Queensland' were placed on the property. In 1873, 731 acres were under cultivation, with lucerne (250 acres), wheat (300 acres) and maize (172 acres) as

35 *Darling Downs and Western Land Company*, 'Particulars and descriptions of its various properties . . .' Brisbane 1884, p. 6.

36 *Australasian*, 6 August 1887, p. 251.

the main crops. Six years later the proprietors had doubled their acreage by increasing their lucerne pastures to 800 acres. Upon these bright green paddocks grazed 3,000 sheep fattening for the Brisbane market.[37]

The Headington Hill venture failed to fulfil expectations as far as cash-cropping was concerned; its over-capitalization contributed to Fisher's financial collapse in the early 'nineties. Original notions of development, however, were sound. Store sheep driven or railed from western stations were fattened and high-quality replacements bred on the exotic pastures. Refrigeration might have made the whole venture a great financial success and saved the pastoral freeholders from 'working all night on their accounts' but it came twenty years too late. By 1893 even the promise of a profitable and reliable export outlet for surplus stock could not erase the red entries in the ledgers of the banks and mortgage companies. Headington Hill's improved pastures of lucerne and prairie grass, while not profitable, were soon copied by those who had once scoffed and condemned. Of the 50,000 acres under cultivation on the Downs in 1887 at least 20 per cent had been ploughed on pastoral freeholds:

CULTIVATION ON SIX FREEHOLD ESTATES, 1887[38]

Estate	Lucerne (acres)	Total area cultivated (acres)
Yandilla	1,300	1,600
Glengallan	1,300	1,600
East Talgai	1,000	1,100
Eton Vale	900	1,000
Jondaryan	900	1,000
Gowrie	700	1,000
TOTAL	6,100	7,300

Paradoxically, then, it was the Downs pastoralists who were once more the innovators. Steam-ploughs, giant steel harrows, hay-rakes, stackers—all the newest tools of nineteenth-century commercial agriculture—were introduced by these men with their access to credit, thousands of acres of black soil, and an income from wool and meat to rely on for a time if things went wrong and drought or financial collapse intervened. The Kings of Gowrie even commenced commercial wheat and maize cultivations in the early 'nineties and for a few short years it seemed as though the bonanza grain-farms of the Canterbury Plains of New Zealand or the American Dakotas might make a belated appearance in

37 *WE&T*, 3 January 1874, p. 2, c. 5 and 16 May 1874, p. 2, c. 1-2; A. J. Boyd, *Queensland*, London 1886, p. 80. Excellent contemporary accounts exist in the *Brisbane Courier* for June 1874 and September 1876: 'Agriculture on the Darling Downs, by our Special Reporter'.

38 These figures are taken from a series of articles by G. A. Brown in *Australasian*, July-August 1887.

Queensland.[39] This development, however, was the sunset which ended the pastoralists' Indian summer on the Downs. Mixed farming was certainly the key to the future but they were not to reap its benefits. For them, new solutions had come too late.

The need to maintain and improve carrying capacity has already been stressed. Almost all Downs pastoralists achieved this between 1870 and 1890 although in the end even this triumph was not enough to avert subdivision and extinction. On Jondaryan 147,857 sheep and 290 cattle were run on 155,000 acres in 1893 while Glengallan, a smaller property of some 41,000 acres, supported 30,000 fattening sheep, 10,000 merino ewes, 1,000 stud cows and 200 horses. These figures had not changed appreciably over the previous decade.[40] The quality and type of stock, however, underwent tremendous changes between 1860 and 1893. In 1874 Canning Downs produced the first cross-bred sheep for the Warwick and Stanthorpe butchers. Big-framed and heavy, the offspring of merino ewes and Leicester rams fattened quickly on lucerne and were most profitable if markets were near and the seasons favourable. Cross-breeding for meat rather than wool was at first heresy on the Downs: had not the squatters themselves been labelled 'Pure Merinos'? Prejudice soon gave way to economic fact. Even Eton Vale, the very tabernacle of the pure, began crossing Lincoln rams with merino ewes for the Brisbane and Toowoomba fat-stock markets in 1886.[41] By 1893 the sight of cross-bred wethers grazing on the apparently indestructible lucerne was no longer a novelty. Horse-breeding, especially on Maryvale and Canning Downs, also expanded in the 'eighties.

The merino breed itself underwent continual modifications. By 1893 the Downs boasted the greatest merino studs in Queensland and some of the best in Australasia. Breeders such as Bracker, Deuchar, Clark and Slade, working with excellent sheep of pure Saxon and Spanish ancestry, eventually produced an animal which was ideally suited to the novel conditions of southern Queensland. Each stud tended to specialize and produce a slightly different type of animal. A selective success meant high profits for a few years but variants which failed to thrive or whose favourable characteristics did not persist could prove very costly indeed to the stud-master. Each estate concentrated on producing a merino with a sound constitution capable of coping with semi-tropical conditions and carrying a well-covered, dense fleece of even consistency, soft and of good length. All—except William Hogarth of Balgownie—tried to lengthen the staple and produce the fine combing wool that on the Downs was replacing the older and coarser clothing types.[42]

39 *Pastoralists' Review*, Vol. 3, No. 7, 15 September 1893, p. 325 and G. E. Evans, *Garden of Queensland*, Toowoomba 1899, p. 82.

40 *Pastoralists' Review*, Vol. 3, No. 7, 15 September 1893, p. 326.

41 *Australasian*, 2 July 1887, pp. 11-12; *WE&T*, 23 June 1883, p. 2, c. 5; *WA*, 13 June 1885, p. 3, c. 1 and 10 July 1880, p. 2, c. 4; *Pastoralists' Review*, Vol. 3, No. 7, 15 September 1893, p. 325.

42 E. W. Cox, *The Evolution of the Australian Merino*, Sydney 1936, pp. 100-10. *See also* G. A. Brown's articles in *Australasian*, July-August 1887.

The most successful stud in Queensland was probably George Clark's East Talgai venture, founded in 1867 with Victorian merinos from Woorowyrite and Ercildoune. This attempt failed as the sheep fell off in staple and covering. In 1870 Clark re-formed his stud on the basis of thirty ewes and three rams from the Mona Vale and St Johnstone studs in Tasmania. These descendants of the great Saxon merino 'Sir Thomas' were an immediate success on the Downs and by 1884 Clark was able to close the stud to outside imports and breed from within. His first consignment of four rams yielded an average price of £268 in 1883 and he even exported to Tasmania, the original Australian home of the best merinos. Clark's achievement is summed up by the statement that 'in 1868 his average fleece weighed three and a half pounds; in 1886 each animal yielded seven and a half pounds.'[43] Glengallan stud, founded as early as 1841 by Frederick Bracker with sheep from Brindley Park in New South Wales and reinforced by German blood, was the first—and for many years the most famous—stud in Queensland. Deuchar's great ram 'Billy', a selected progeny of a picked Brindley Park ewe and a German sire, stamped his characteristics on nearly every pure-bred flock in the colony. 'Billy' was the pastoralists' delight, far more attractive than a storekeeper or a selector, with his 'massive head, regular spiral horns of fine texture, no tail-wrinkles and fleece of the true Negretti type—two inches in length, dense, even, and with a good whitish yolk'.[44] After further importations, Glengallan had 'more Negretti [original Spanish merino] blood than any other stud in Australia'. Other noted studs on the Downs, whose progeny were sought all over Queensland and in other colonies as well, were established at Jimbour (1864), Eton Vale (1850), Welltown (1866), Pikedale (1871), Bon Accord (1870), Canning Downs (1867) and Headington Hill (1871).[45]

Throughout the second half of the nineteenth century and especially during the halcyon years of the freehold estates the Downs pastoralists made a great contribution to the squatting industry of not only the colony but the continent. Their valiant, but in the end unsuccessful, attempt to perpetuate large-scale pastoralism in the region can, in retrospect, be seen as a valuable contribution to the region's development. Whether or not the area would have expanded at the same rate if the squatters had not acquired most of the best land and whether or not commercial agriculture on much smaller farms would have given better returns may be doubted. By 1893, however, the issue was really beyond all argument. Graingrowers could succeed on the Downs, refrigeration had opened up new fields, and all conditions—economic, political and social—favoured the small man. On the Condamine Plains the squatters had run their race—and lost.

43 ibid.

44 E. W. Cox, *Evolution of the Australian Merino*, p. 102.

45 ibid., p. 103 and *Australasian*, 9 July 1887, p. 59.

CHAPTER 4

TOWN AND DOWN

> Elegant persons are to be found in Paris; the provinces may possibly contain people of character.
>
> Siéyès

The attack on the squatters was led by the storekeepers, publicans, newspaper proprietors, and other small entrepreneurs of the country towns. Led into battle by the metropolitan middle-class of Brisbane, they were indispensably allied with discontented outside squatters and other opportunist urban politicians. It was, then, the rising *bourgeoisie* of Toowoomba, Warwick, Allora and Dalby who provided the leaders, money and political basis for radical change on the Downs.

This group was a colonial by-product of the Industrial Revolution. Some of its members had emigrated to the colonies to better themselves while others had failed in the British Isles and now sought material success, willingly or reluctantly, in a new environment. Both elements, whether they succeeded or failed, imitated and reflected Victorian England's essentially middle-class emotional and intellectual values. First and foremost they believed in the Enlightenment and its dominating belief that by rational human control and mastery of the environment the quality of life could be vastly improved. True pioneer society had little need of the sophisticated arguments of the new rationalism. Utilitarian tests and concepts when related to politics, education, and environmental change, were the mainsprings of infant society on the Downs. Optimists all, they had an over-riding faith in novel mechanical contrivances, products of the Age of Reason and the Industrial Revolution. In the space of a generation such devices had made possible the transformation of an area as large as several English counties from an uninhabited wilderness to a civilized commercial farming province of a self-governing colony. They had also provided the shopkeepers with enhanced opportunties for comfort, satisfaction, and upward social mobility. No wonder the steam-engine's child, the railway locomotive, was the earthly God of the *bourgeoisie*. The successful naturally equated force, physical speed and spatial movement, with personal, economic and social improvement.

Nineteenth-century European conquests of time and space reinforced ideas that the historical process was one of inevitable progress. Moreover this progress was plainly an economic form of the new Darwinism. On the Downs a struggle for existence with the forces of Nature was fought by a group who believed that in subduing the environment, removing the Aborigines, and building hotels, churches, and schools, they were demonstrating superior adaptability and human development. In time, by the exercise of human reason, not only would recalcitrant geographical characteristics of the area prove amenable to scientific exploitation but the remaining laws of man's behaviour would be discovered and the new neo-rational society further improved.

And which pioneer, which storekeeper, coming to the Downs in 1860 and surveying the scene again in 1890, would deny this? Surely this new portion of an expanding Empire, this new granary farmed by yeomen supplied by respectable storekeepers, represented the very vanguard of Progress? Each material advance—from one stalk of wheat to two, from wooden store to sandstone bank and from fluttering candle to municipal gasworks—confirmed this view of the inevitability of Progress and the implication that this new form of human advance was predestined if not by God then by evolutionary advantages now monopolized by the Anglo-Saxons, the great colonizers of the world. For if some of the farmers' ideals included German and Celtic components, those of the country-town *bourgeoisie* were urban-English derived from the England of the great Victorian industrial cities of the Midlands, South-east Lancashire and the West Riding of Yorkshire. And, as we shall see, it was this group which provided, in their own interests, the ideology, material framework and political structure into which the selector was expected to fit. Yet behind the palings and wrought-iron lingered doubts and private hells. Above all, the storekeepers feared political revolution; good conformists all, they recognized that as they had destroyed the paramountcy of the squatters, so might the bush-workers and the urban proletariat destroy them. They trembled for their property, the successful acquisition of which had given their lives meaning and satisfaction. When the opportunities for material advance contracted in the late 1880s so did their radicalism. By 1891 the strike-breaking Darling Downs Mounted Infantry, officered by graziers and manned by storekeepers' sons, was as much a weapon of the regional shopkeepers as it was of the old Queensland Establishment.

Few colonists struggling to establish themselves in an alien environment could afford the luxury of religious doubt. In an age when orthodox religious belief was the great prop of moral and social order, of the civilization that they were attempting to build, only a handful were willing to question the assumptions behind, and the necessity for, Christian salvation and observance. To do so would have impaired the storekeepers' faith in the colonial trinity: settlement, improvement, and progress. Metaphysical speculation was never relevant to the harsh physical world of the pioneer colonist, be he farmer, clerk, or auctioneer. The man who could concentrate his attentions on day-to-day reality was the one who survived and prospered in a colonial society where the struggle for uplift was severe and the emotional and material penalties for failure great. When secular dogma did break down, however, as it did with a thunder-clap in the 1890s, the results for the *bourgeois* society were temporarily crippling and long enduring.

But for those establishing new stores, offices, or factories in Toowoomba, Warwick, Allora and Dalby in the 1860s and 1870s, such traumas lay far away. For these men—the Alfords, Robinsons, Godsalls, Kingsfords, Spiros and Kennedys—material comfort and the respect which money alone could command in the new colony were the driving-springs. Wealth was thus equated with that great Victorian commercial objective, respectability. Not landed wealth, based on sheep and leased acres, but brick-and-mortar assets, stocks and shares, a gold watch-chain, and dark-suited respectability, based on urban enterprise and shrewd speculation. In short, wealth earned directly from other men by one's own unaided (unless God be included) efforts. These men ridiculed poverty. Not only was it shameful but it was—on the Downs, with its manifold opportunities for hard-working, sober, earnest, and enterprising immigrants—totally unnecessary.

Certainly, many of the squatters shared these views. This identity of values made their absorption in Downs *bourgeois* society much easier once their political and economic power had been destroyed. In the 1860s what to the Grooms and the Morgans of the country towns was the very real threat of an oligarchic caste system based on eighteenth-century British landed society was vanquished by men who believed in a combination of American egalitarianism and opportunism and the English middle-class virtues of respectability and self-improvement. Man's duty in the new *bourgeois* spirit of Toowoomba and Warwick was not that of the Pure Merino—'to do his duty in the state of life to which it had pleased God to call him'—but to create a new community through a programme of personal and collective financial, social, political, and moral improvement. Once the individual by his own efforts improved himself, then a new society based on superior principles to that of the Old World would follow. Kates' flour-mill, Palethorpe's drapery and Glennie's churches were milestones, then, on the road to a new society based on the middle-class freedoms of 1776, 1791 and 1832.

Obviously, then, the chief idol was monetary success. In a supposedly 'topped-and-tailed' colonial pioneer society, social aspirations were not hindered by caste barriers. But if the God failed, if economic decline—registered by public bankruptcy—assailed the contractor, storekeeper or commission agent, then the results were frequently psychologically destructive. At first men who failed in business were assumed to have done so because of defects in their character, not because of economic cycles or the peculiar difficulties of the Downs environment. When wholesale group failure, however, could no longer be disregarded at the end of the 1880s, other rationalizations were made to account for a situation in which most were unwilling either to recognize a group or to challenge basic assumptions.

Salvation—monetary success—rested on one foundation, hard physical labour. Intellectual strivings and sophistication were discouraged in a colonial society occupied with the scaffolding for society, not the contents of the new erection. Mechanics' Institutes, an accent on 'useful arts' and cultural mediocrity, all testified to the pursuit of the practical. How the land speculators of Toowoomba in 1865 and the Warwick commission agents of the 1870s fitted into the simple equation between work, success, and virtue, however was not clear. But hard physical work, providing the bricks, mortar and wheatfields of the new society, held a tremendous, valid meaning for the men of the towns.

Downs urban society, then, was derivative, a by-product of Victorian England and the American experience, but lacking the depth and contrast extant in those older and more complex societies. Furthermore, it was neither a speculative nor a stimulating society for those who refused or were unable to conform to its values. For, as in English society, respectable conformity was elevated above all else. But on the Downs there was no escape, as perhaps, there was for some in more varied, richer and populous portions of the western world. Restless spirits moved east. Religious observance, the cult of improvement, earnestness, and temperate enthusiasm for the mechanical toys of man's scientific brain, reigned supreme. Deliberately destroying human and animal obstacles to change, adapting the environment to his own communal needs, and ignoring both the flaws in his new creations and the trail of wreckage he left in his wake, commercial man on the Downs created a society largely in his own image. But what if the image itself was flawed and had deeper, less amenable and presentable faces? By 1893 fewer and fewer mirrors were reflecting the confident features they had displayed in earlier years.

To an outsider the urban middle-class society which existed on the Downs in the nineteenth century must have appeared remarkably small and homogeneous. Merely 1,500 males, plus their wives and children, made up this group in 1876. Of these, perhaps 500 were shopkeepers of one kind or another, a further 500 were publicans or involved in other service activities, and the rest were employed in a motley collection of other occupations ranging from lawyers—the bane of colonial society—to doctors, ministers, teachers, newspaper proprietors, clerks, and Government officials.[1]

Furthermore this microcosm of colonial life was further fragmented by an ill-defined hierarchical order based on four criteria: origin, occupation, financial success and—the final accolade—ownership of rural landed property. Bank balances finally overcame all social objections, but, on the whole, the *bourgeoisie* were of Protestant English, Scots or Irish descent. Nevertheless, Toowoomba, as its cemetery bears witness, boasted a considerable Jewish mercantile community in the 'seventies while Hebrew names such as Horwitz, Benjamin and Spiro were household words on the Downs. The ranks of the brewers and publicans were filled with Catholic Irishmen but most tradesmen were colonial replicas of their

[1] *SR*, 1876, 'Occupations'.

counterparts in British provincial cities. Many were Freemasons, almost all were 'joiners' of one organization or another, ranging from cemetery trusts to Progress Associations, benefit societies and sporting clubs.[2]

These people, in reluctant conjunction with surviving squatters and graziers, controlled the framework of life on the Downs. Their urge towards physical improvement was reflected in the gasworks, hospitals, town-halls, waterworks and gravelled streets of their towns, while their materialistic, anti-intellectual and shopkeeper values were expressed in the *Toowoomba Chronicle*, the *Warwick Argus*, and the other five newspapers established in the region. Their pragmatism reinforced a primary educational system devoted to producing literate clerks and farmers, while the two secondary schools provided advanced training for those shopkeepers' sons with conventional intelligence, ambition and financial resources.

Moreover after initial struggle with the squatters the administration of social and legal justice, through police magistrates and justices of the peace, fell completely into urban hands.

The same was true of the churches. Once establishments teaching social subservience or Christian salvation, some became monuments to the material progress and personal advance of their adherents. Shopkeeping Anglicans in Toowoomba, denied access to offices and influence in the mother-church of St James, even constructed an edifice of their own, St Luke's, where they could pursue that social distinction and display they so detested when practised by their social betters.

The shopkeepers, then, controlled urban local government through a property franchise, quarrelled bitterly amongst themselves about roads, rates, and personalities, and battled for status and recognition in the subtle social distinctions that had emerged by the late 1870s. At the apex of the pyramid were the few Pure Merinos—Nelson and Taylor at Toowoomba who had retired to town houses in Toowoomba. Below them were the successful professional men, the rich business entrepreneurs and the clergy—the latter graded according to church, origin and theology.

Then, in descending order, the minor shopkeepers (drapers, chemists, shoemakers, commission agents), clerks, artisans, schoolteachers, and labourers. This is not to suggest that a rigid system of occupational, let alone group, discrimination and easily-defined social attitudes existed on the Downs. It is obvious that they did not. Until the 1880s there was a great deal of social mobility, although less than has commonly been supposed. Compared with the rigid class- and caste-lines of the Old World, however, opportunities for those willing to conform and possessing the commercial talents of the nineteenth century seemed plentiful and rewarding.

But behind the material opportunities in the towns lurked discomfort and the possibility of sudden death. Country-town progress could be classified by the number of hotels supported but these material improvements for a masculine society produced harmful human side-effects.

[2] Details of organizations, clubs, and occupations are to be found in *Pugh*, 1865-94.

There were 31 licensed hotels on the Downs by 1860, double that number by 1875, and well over 120 hostelries in 1893. After the Toowoomba and Warwick breweries were established their light beer eventually replaced whisky and rum, of dubious quality and strength, as the universal beverage. The old colonial practices of 'knocking-down' wage cheques, drinking until intoxicated, and consuming large quantities of inferior or semi-poisonous spirits, however, lasted the century. Afterwards nonconformity and a combination of feminine numbers, segregation and good works began the great prohibitionist struggle. Intemperance, then, was rife: a seemingly inevitable concomitant of a frontier society taking a large toll of life and—more importantly—of property. Within three weeks of September 1873 four young men died from alcoholic poisoning in Toowoomba Hospital alone and many others left their bones near a shanty or were drowned or killed by their uncontrolled horses while returning home intoxicated. Scarcely a week went by at Warwick in the 1870s when the Condamine did not yield the body of a drunk who had missed his footing and drowned in the river.[3]

Drunkenness—like the larrikinism which appeared in Toowoomba during the late 1870s when 'young lads, semi-intoxicated, prowled about the streets at night making use of disgusting language and preparing themselves for a life of crime'—was considered to be an individual failing for which Downs society was in no way blameworthy.[4]

Other hazards of urban life, however, were accepted with less equanimity. A high infant and maternity death-rate was probably unavoidable—dysentery and typhoid fever was preventable. Between 1874 and 1878 an average of ten people died every year from typhoid in Toowoomba alone.[5] Cesspits even drained into the brewery wells, perhaps accounting for the novel flavour of Toowoomba beer. At Warwick, residents complained that raw sewerage and hospital waste were pumped into the Condamine and returned to the people through the waterworks pump, situated a few yards downstream from the sewer outfall. In 1880, and again in 1885, Warwick—once the healthiest town in Queensland—became the most dangerous to live in, with a death-rate of 26.57 per 1,000 people. Hospital services completely broke down and fever patients during the hot summer of 1880 were isolated in an unlined corrugated-iron annexe. Two men died from heat affection when inside temperatures rose to over 120°F.[6]

Government and subsidies eventually enabled hospital services at Toowoomba, Warwick, Dalby and Stanthorpe to be improved, pumps and reservoirs reduced the dependence on wells and streams, and night-soil men and dry-earth closets replaced the old cesspits. Finally the number of doctors increased from seven in 1863 to twelve in 1893 and their qualifications rose from doubtful Continental and Irish certificates to the finest British and colonial degrees. On 11 March 1893 Dr H. Russell

[3] *TC*, 4 October 1873, p. 2, c. 6 and *QPD*, Vol. 1, (1866), pp. 1162-6.

[4] *TC*, 6 May 1879, p. 2, c. 3 and 5 September 1885, p. 2, c. 6.

[5] ibid., 11 May 1878, p. 3, c. 1.

[6] *WE&T*, 25 November 1880, p. 2, c. 6-7.

Nolan performed the first deliberate appendectomy in Australia, adding knowledge and skill to the hard-riding and -drinking abilities, charity and adaptability of such early Downs medical identities as Drs G. W. Aldred, Otto Sachse, Jacob Meade Swift and G. E. Stacey.

But life, although hazardous for the very young, the disillusioned, the drunkards and the physically weak, was not all hard work, respectability, lessons and sermons. Cultural standards were low or non-existent but popular culture prevented total boredom and brought colour and variety to town and country people. For those who had money, inclination and liberty, Warwick during 1887 was the venue for over twenty separate performances covering a wide range of sporting, artistic and charitable activities. These commenced with the Eastern Downs Show in February and concluded with Herbert and Fitzgerald's Great Circus near Christmas. Athletic sports, cricket, race meetings, soirées and shooting, excursions graded by social status, balls by religion, and concerts by local and visiting professional artists, were common. Professor Anderson, 'the Great Magical Wizard of the North', attracted the children in October as the revelations of Edith O'Gorman, 'the Escaped Nun', had drawn their fathers two months before.[7]

For the more serious or those earnest clerks or aspiring Grooms avid for self-improvement, there were the Literary and Debating Clubs, Mutual Improvement Societies and the colonial-Gothic façades, empty libraries and plaster busts of the eight Downs Schools of Arts.

Most men, however, lacking access to the private clubs of Warwick and Toowoomba, the Members' Stand of the Jockey Club, and the billiard-rooms of 'Gabbinar' and 'Clifford House', retreated to the hotels. Slowly emerging from bark grog-shanties to two-storied cast-iron balconied establishments, many hotels—through peculiar combinations of clientele, political affiliations, and hosts—acquired individual characteristics and reputations. Establishments such as the 'European', 'Free Selectors', 'Horse and Jockey', 'Harp of Erin' and 'Freemasons' which were part of Ruthven Street, the main thoroughfare of Toowoomba in 1873, not only tended to separate the sheep from the wheat and the office from the counter and bench but also differentiated between ethnic groups, inclinations and religion.[8]

But Toowoomba and Warwick business life was not all shop counters, account books and printer's ink. The Australian country towns of the nineteenth century represented—particularly on the Downs—miniature examples of balanced urban development. From the engineering works at Toowoomba to the flour-mills of Allora, the Downs supported a range of manufacturing and service industries that, since the turn of the century, has, certainly relatively, and probably absolutely, contracted in both number and diversity. These provided not only local markets, employment and capital but were a source of pride and tangible evidence of material improvement and progress. For the small entrepreneur, as yet

[7] ibid., 1887.

[8] *QGG*, 'Licensing Lists', 1873.

unconcerned with or able to defend himself from metropolitan competition, these were halcyon days. Not that survival in manufacturing businesses was more certain than in farming or shopkeeping. It was not. But success was generally faster and more rewarding. Small-scale financial speculation in country-town land was usually superior to agricultural investment. A farm or grazing property would, of course, come later as one of the distinguishing marks of the successful storekeeper, brewer or miller.

The first industries were concerned with supplying the raw materials of civilization—shelter, transport and food—and treating a small range of pastoral products. As the region diversified its economic base, new industries sprang up to process new crops and recently discovered minerals.

Pit-sawing the pine and hardwoods of the Main Range near Toowoomba, along the Goomburra Valley and around the original pastoral homesteads, was the first factory industry. Prices were high and the sawyers were independent men of the bush, working on their own account and supplying timber to the stations and storekeepers on contract. By Separation, however, all had changed. In 1856 Gilbert Davidson of Canning Downs financed the first water-powered mill on the Downs at Acacia Creek, Killarney. Here the Affleck brothers were able to reduce prices by 25 per cent during their first year. Two years later the ubiquitous James Taylor built the first steam sawmill on the Downs at Drayton, an event which so incensed the Range sawyers that they threatened to punch holes in the boilers.[9]

Responding to a growing urban market, cheap and accessible raw materials and plentiful and expendable labour, steam sawmilling in the major towns and along the ridges north-west of Toowoomba grew apace in the 'sixties. Mills were large and efficient. Before it was burnt down on 17 October 1865 Peter Degen's Victorian Steam Mill at Highfields employed 100 men, worked day and night producing 30,000 feet of timber every week and represented a capital investment of £2,000 in buildings and machinery.[10]

By 1875 there were fifteen mills on the Downs, a number which remained constant until the turn of the century. Of these, six were on the Southern Downs, at Farm Creek (two), Killarney, Emu Vale, Donkey Flat and Warwick, while four cut at Toowoomba and three at Highfields. The others were near Dalby and Leyburn.[11]

The character of the industry changed little over the half-century although mills tended to grow larger and the efficient planing, moulding and joinery mills of Broadfoot and Filshie and E. W. Pechey in Toowoomba acquired a large share of the lucrative urban market. The Warwick Saw Mill Company of A. Robertson, Hazard and Phillips was typical of these larger mills, having a plant at Swan Creek producing

[9] J. H. Allsopp, in *Darling Downs Centenary Souvenir, 1840-1940*, Toowoomba 1940, p. 17.

[10] *DDG*, 6 May 1865, p. 3, c. 4 and 18 October 1865, p. 3, c. 1.

[11] *WA*, 15 August 1878, p. 2, c. 3.

rough timber for the planing and joinery mill at Warwick. Both mills cut 48,000 feet of timber every week and the enterprise returned a net profit of close to £96 per week, timber being sent by railway to Stanthorpe, Brisbane, Toowoomba and Tenterfield.[12]

Profits were high in the 'eighties but low in the 'nineties when the virtual collapse of urban investment forced many Downs mills into liquidation. Even the largest and most efficient mills were hard-pressed to survive as prices tumbled to as low as 10s. per 100 feet, less than half of what they had been twenty years earlier.[13]

When the industry revived after 1896 only the big integrated units in the towns and the small low-cost jobbing mills hidden amid the pine and gum of the Main Range and Bunya Mountains had survived to provide the timber for the fresh wave of farmers and townspeople.

Timber-mills were followed by brick and tile-works near Warwick in 1874 and Toowoomba ten years later. Bricks had, of course, been made as required much earlier than this but the replacement of the old wooden town-centres with fire-resistant buildings created a demand for cheap and plentiful bricks. By 1887 the Toowoomba Brick and Tile Company at Kleinton was producing 60,000 bricks per week, employed twenty men and was starting to make good profits. Its rival, James Renwick at Murphy Creek, employed even more men and had an even larger capacity.[14]

Associated with these building industries were the small joinery, plumbing and furniture factories of the towns, founded by an entrepreneur artisan and employing at most five or ten additional hands. Other small plants such as the Pioneer Coach Works and the Abbott Buggy Factory at Warwick built a large variety of horse-drawn vehicles.[15]

In every town and village the ubiquitous blacksmith's shop provided the crude iron-ware and wooden wheels for farmers and carriers, while saddlers provided the harness.

From bricks, mortar and leather to food, drink and clothing, the first industries to assuage the thirst were the aerated-water factories producing lemonade, soda-water and other flavoured cordials. P. Fleming of Toowoomba and G. L. Ross of Warwick built the first works as early as 1860. By 1893 there were twelve small factories on the Downs, half of them in Toowoomba.[16]

Breweries and maltings quickly followed. Patrick and Thomas Perkins brewed their first commercial hogshead of light ale in Queensland at the Downs Brewery, Toowoomba, on 14 December 1869. Perkins' was an immediate success. Encouraged by preferential railway rates, the Brewery soon penetrated the Brisbane market and by 1882 a subsidiary plant had been established in the metropolis, the concern transformed into a pub-

[12] ibid., 8 January 1884, p. 3, c. 2.

[13] ibid., 21 January 1890, p. 1, c. 1 and *TC*, 4 June 1890, p. 1, c. 3.

[14] ibid., 3 November 1887, p. 3, c. 6.

[15] *WA*, 3 January 1878, p. 1.

[16] *DDG*, 13 December 1860, p. 1, c. 3 and *Pugh*, 1893.

lic company with a capital of £125,000, and production doubled. Unfortunately the new Victorian shareholders lost half of their capital owing to the usual Queensland combination of over-valuation, incompetent management, speculation and depression, but the Brewery survived to linger on as the subsidiary concern of the Perkins Company.[17]

The Warwick Brewery, established in August 1873 by G. J. Wilson, was less fortunate. Although it prospered, serving the demands of the Stanthorpe miners and railway-workers, it did not survive its owner who died on 28 August 1895.[18]

Like all country breweries, Warwick, and even Toowoomba, found it difficult to compete with the large, efficient plants of the metropolis. Unable to supply credit, or to create a network of tied houses, or to maintain a strict uniformity of taste and colour and compete in terms of price and volume with the new lager breweries of Brisbane with their skills, capital and advertising, most country plants were doomed by 1893. Only distance could delay their end.

The six flour-mills grinding on the Downs in 1893 were menaced by similar centripetal tendencies. These early mills were all uncomplicated steam or water mills of limited capacity, capital and staff.

Until the opening of the first large dairy factories in the early 'nineties, the flour-mill was indubitably the most important material creation of the agrarians in a country town. The presence of a mill building standing tall, in all its brick or corrugated-iron glory, above the gently rolling wheatfields and pastures, meant that the town was on the map; that it had risen from the stage where size and status were determined solely by the number of hotel bars it maintained.

Most mills were the same. Small steam-engines drove pairs of burr stones or, after 1885, Hungarian roller machinery. Capital was poured into the modernization of Downs flour-mills when it was realized that the local mills had a local and western market which the new seaboard mills with their imported wheat and higher freight charges could not yet penetrate.

And what of the millers, those prophets of agrarian myths and advocates of all the economic virtues of the country-town businessman? They were on the whole not the jolly personalities of Chaucerian tradition but shrewd, cosmopolitan, hard-eyed entrepreneurs, the vanguard of the new, self-made miniature Queensland colonial society. They resented their squatter betters and were convinced that the processing of wheat into flour was not only a more valuable economic task than fattening sheep or growing wool, but that it was a task of moral and social importance without which the new civilization of an industrious Downs yeomanry could not succeed.

Other improving entrepreneur-crusaders saw the creation of new industries in much the same light. If colonial societies went even further

[17] *TC*, 2 February 1870, p. 2, c. 3; 7 May 1870, p. 2, c. 5-6 and *WA*, 31 January 1882, p. 3, c. 2.

[18] *WE&T*, 23 August 1873, p. 2, c. 2 and 28 August 1895, p. 3, c. 6.

Darling Downs Flour-Mills, 1861-98

Mill	Owners	Site	Notes
I. TOOWOOMBA			
Cocks', 1864	Chas. Cocks, 1864-84 Gisler Bros, 1884-6 Henry Arnold, 1890	Ruthven St	Burnt 1908
Neden, *c.* 1868	Thomas Neden	North St	Burnt 1871
Darlington, 1872	Thomas Neden	Russell St	Closed 1879-81 Closed 1890
Union, 1879	Hartnett & Aland (water mill)	Klein St	Burnt 1883
Dominion, 1890	Creaser & Coy Barnes & Archibald, 1891-3 Dominion Milling Coy, 1893-	Russell St	—
Defiance, 1896	Crisp & O'Brien	Ruthven St	—
II. ALLORA			
Pioneer, 1872	Dougall, Kates, Cooke, 1872-86 F. Kates, 1886-7 Gisler Bros, 1887-92	Drayton St	Burnt 1892
Allora, 'White Rose', 1882	T. & J. Kennedy, 1882-1912	Drayton St	Dismantled 1912
Allora	F. Kates, 1897-1906	Railway St	To Clifton 1906
III. WARWICK			
Ellenthorpe, 1861	Clark & McKeachie, 1861-74 J. Horwitz, 1874-86 F. Kates, 1886-8 Barnes, Archibald & Co., 1888	Wantley St	—
Farmers' Mill (Queensland Steam) Flour Mill, 1873 Operated 1877	Warwick Farmers' Asscn, 1873 F. Kates, 1876-7 W. & C. Hayes, 1877-91 Farmers' Milling Coy, 1891-	Railway St	—

than the English in equating cleanliness with godliness, then Henry Spiro, C. Hampson and F. Hooper of Toowoomba and T. Mogridge of Warwick—all of whom established soap-works based on local tallow—to wash first sheep-fleeces and then human bodies—served the designs of God and the economic and hygienic needs of man equally well.[19]

[19] *TC*, 22 August 1876, p. 2, c. 7; 3 January 1891, p. 4, c. 7 and 10 December 1891, p. 3, c. 5.

But however worthy the motives, however lofty the aspirations, all did not prosper. Green's Toowoomba Steam Confectionery (1873-9), Craven's Cold Storage and Ice Works (1889) and Corteau's Excelsior Tobacco Works (1881-6) failed after a few months. The reasons for financial failure were complex but usually individually explicable. Cyclical booms and slumps in conjunction with, or independent of, droughts and rust wiped out the imprudent and the earnest and thrifty alike. The majority were under-capitalized, one-man-and-a-boy concerns, depending on still imperfect techniques, relying on a very small regional market generally short of ready cash and subject to wild variations in the price, quantity and quality of their raw materials. No wonder most, like W. H. Davis of the Warwick Bacon Factory, failed. Davis, a Victorian, established his business in 1890 to take advantage of the new Queensland Tariff, refrigeration and the growing number of pigs being kept on Downs mixed farms. Two years later he was bankrupt, destroyed, like many of his suppliers and customers, by the great crash.[20]

A few industrial plants survived the holocaust of the 'nineties. Of these, the most prominent was the Toowoomba Foundry, founded in 1871 by G. W. Griffiths and converted to a public company with a capital of £20,000 in 1886. Commencing as a small general engineering establishment, the works built the Downs' first steam-engine and employed fifty men by 1889. The concern, by 1893, while hard-hit by the depression, was ready to take advantage of the great expansion of settlement on the Downs which was to follow resumption and refrigeration. While the foundry produced locomotives and rolling-stock for the Queensland Railways, as well as a large range of boilers, steam-engines and saw-milling machinery, the squatters and selectors were the real backbone of the concern. The prosperity—indeed the survival—of the foundry was based on the manufacture of cheap wood-and-steel 'Simplex' windmills which were necessary on the Downs to raise water from the sub-artesian reservoirs. These devices, costing between £15 and £20 each, were sold in their hundreds to farmers all over the Downs.[21]

Because of the enterprise of its founder, the ingenuity of its engineers, the lobbying of Toowoomba politicians for Government contracts, its capital resources and an expanding market, the Toowoomba Foundry Company survived. William Porritt's Reliance Foundry, established in 1882, was less fortunate and in 1891 was absorbed by the older company. The Reliance Foundry had a meteoric rise based on railway rolling-stock contracts and wrought-iron for the verandahs of the Toowoomba *bourgeoisie*. Foreign, Brisbane and Ipswich competition, high transport costs and an inability to compete with its nearby rival forced amalgamation.[22]

Less ambitious concerns—the Warwick Foundry of Frame and Com-

[20] ibid., 14 July 1877, p. 3; 16 November 1889, p. 3, c. 5 and *WA*, 2 August 1890, p. 2, c. 1.

[21] *TC*, 19 February 1876, p. 3, c. 3; 22 May 1884, p. 3, c. 7; 24 May 1886, Supplement, and *QPD*, Vol. 62, (1890), pp. 1409-15.

[22] *TC*, 7 May 1891, p. 3, c. 2.

pany and the Endeavour Ironworks of Townson, Eastgate and Company —did however survive, although Archibald McKeachie's successful Warwick wagon-and-plough works was forced to close in 1891.

Manufactories based on the processing of pastoral products, however, had on the whole a less eventful and more rewarding history. Raw materials were generally cheap and plentiful, abundant seasonal labour was available, transport costs were low and the relatively simple processes required little capital investment.

The depression of the 'sixties produced the first boiling-down works to convert surplus stock into tallow. These were the original large plants processing primary products. Most squatters, before E. J. Blaxland established his Alderley Boiling Down Works at Toowoomba, managed their own reduction but Blaxland could offer a fixed price of 8d. a head for sheep and nine shillings for bullocks. His large plant at Three Mile Scrub near Dalby could boil-down nearly 1,000 sheep at once, using high-pressure steam and cheap labour on piece-work. Each sheep, purchased for one shilling per head, yielded 5s. 6d. when its tallow was railed to Ipswich for export to Britain.[23]

At Oakey Creek the first and last meat-works on the Downs was established in 1868 to boil-down surplus sheep and cattle. By April 1871 the company—the Hogarth Meat Preserving Company, employing Polynesian labour—was producing over 1,500 tins of preserved mutton and beef a day. The company even marketed a tinned extract of wallaby in England under the trade name 'Australian Game'. This exotic foodstuff failed to sell.

The fortunes of this concern fluctuated with the price of stock. When prices were high the plant was idle; when prices fell over a hundred men were employed. Six months after the plant re-opened in 1892 it had preserved 61,786 sheep and boiled-down a further 13,362. But such wasteful processes had only a limited future. Freezing-works at Brisbane and Tenterfield eventually replaced the Oakey works as the destination of store sheep and cattle. Once again the middlemen of the deep water metropolis had captured the products of the Downs.[24]

As stock prices rose less primitive and wasteful industries began to be developed. Already in 1860 T. G. Robinson had established the first successful tannery on the Downs at Toowoomba, while J. C. Isambert erected the Warwick Tannery during the same year. Both these concerns lasted out the century and were supplemented by other small fellmongeries and wool-scouring plants. The decline of sheep-washing in the late 'seventies stimulated the development of wool-scouring works at Gowrie Junction, Black Gully and Harlaxton near Toowoomba. By 1888 these three concerns employed over sixty men on a wide variety of tasks ranging from scouring to tanning, shoe-making, and harness and saddle manufacture.[25]

[23] *TC*, 19 October 1867, p. 1, c. 5.

[24] ibid., 1 April 1871, p. 3, c. 5 and *Town and Country Journal*, 29 July 1871, p. 138.

[25] *TC*, 2 January 1888, Supplement.

During 1887 Peter Field, a successful Toowoomba boot and shoe merchant, purchased S. H. Whichello's Black Gully plant and established a large factory employing 63 hands to turn out 2,500 pairs of boots and shoes every month. Unable to cope with the failing demand, pressed by his creditors and at the mercy of dumped foreign and Brisbane shoes, Field was swept out of business in 1891.[26]

The Downs was not yet ready for large-scale consumer industries based on local raw materials. Furthermore with the end of inter-colonial tariffs after Federation it was doubtful if it ever would be. Except in a few isolated and individually explicable instances, Toowoomba and Warwick simply could not compete with the metropolis. This is a familiar Australian story. Their markets were too small, their labour supply limited, their transport costs too high and their capital resources too constricted. For most industrial entrepreneurs failure, if not inevitable, could be expected. Only specialist industries based on the particular needs and advantages of the region and the semi-processing of farm-products had a hope of survival and development. But if the towns failed to retain manufacturing industry other factors ensured their survival and expansion. Situation, functions, accident and human interference gave each town on the Downs a distinct pattern of development and some measure of individuality.

Toowoomba was the brash upstart of the Downs, the living symbol of the storekeepers' triumph over the squatter. Settlement actually commenced at Drayton, then 'The Springs', three miles to the west, late in 1843 after the Tollbar Road over the Range to Brisbane was discovered by Lt. Arthur Gorman. Thomas Alford shifted the first general store on the Darling Downs from Cambooya to Drayton and Patrick Flanagan built a blacksmith's shop to service the teams using the track to Ipswich. Settlers on the Downs and further west met the bullock-teams at Drayton, obtained supplies and stores and camped near the fresh water. William Horton built the first hotel on the Downs—the Bull's Head—in 1848 and gradually a group of slab-and-bark huts grew up in the hollow. By 1849 G. C. Burnett has surveyed a township and the following year the first urban land sales on the Downs were held, town lots fetching up to £8 a half-acre.

Cambooya, ten miles south, had originally been surveyed as the administrative centre for the Downs but the police-station, court-house and land offices were transferred to Drayton after 1850. By separation Drayton had achieved a notable list of Downs 'firsts'—the first newspaper, Police Magistrate, Municipality, Circuit Court (12 October 1859), churches (St Matthew's Church of England, 1851; Roman Catholic, 1863), doctor and race meeting. The population of the small town was then nearly 500.[27]

But this progress did not last. Between 1855 and 1860 Drayton was completely eclipsed by Toowoomba, situated—unlike Drayton—in a

26 *DDG*, 3 October 1891, p. 3, c. 5.

27 T. L. Adamson in *Darling Downs Centenary Souvenir*, pp. 36-41.

swamp which had become the great camping- and assembly-ground for the Ipswich-bound teamsters. Other influences too destroyed Drayton's chances of remaining the capital of the Downs. Much of the land was tied up by speculators, a continual feud over impounding rights between townspeople and the neighbouring squatters hindered development—and Toowoomba was well-served by squatter-investors such as J. C. White and James Taylor and more lowly characters of vigour and drive such as W. H. Groom.[28]

Four final occurrences finished Drayton's hopes. It lost its court hearings, the first municipal council split into violent factions and disgraced itself, even by Queensland standards, with a series of outrageous and ludicrous meetings, the first pastoral shows were held in Toowoomba and, the final humiliation, on 1 May 1867 the railway from Ipswich reached Toowoomba's heart and subsequent branches bypassed Drayton altogether.[29]

Thereafter Drayton remained an irritating boil on Toowoomba's neck, feeling neglected by its neighbour's representatives, recalling the glories of pre-Separation days, agitating for a railway deviation (which they secured in 1906 when it was too late to enable the town to survive as an independent entity) and gradually declining into a sleepy two-pub nucleus for numerous smallholders until their little farms were swallowed up by the advancing suburbs of the larger city.[30]

Toowoomba's history is one of almost uninterrupted progress, one of the great urban *bourgeois* success stories of Queensland. Perched on the west of the Main Range, the town had the most commanding and attractive site in Queensland, although the urban centre was built along the swampy valleys instead of on the red-soil ridges.

Toowoomba owed its phenomenal progress to a combination of natural advantages and commercial and political shrewdness. Astride the natural gateway to Brisbane, Toowoomba was the logical channel for the produce of the Downs, the Maranoa and even the border country. Between 26 September and 19 October 1860, thirty-three teams and wagons passed up the Tollbar Road and seventeen returned to Ipswich. Over a thousand working bullocks and 150 drays were parked at the back of the Royal Hotel alone during that week. It was this pastoral carrying trade, together with the distribution of stores for the west, which gave Toowoomba its initial impetus.[31]

The Selection Acts and the conterminous coming of the railway from Ipswich inaugurated Toowoomba's first period of rapid expansion. In 1863, before agricultural selection, only 1,500 persons inhabited the town. Five years later the population had exactly doubled and by 1876 it had reached 4,695. By 1891, 7,007 people—or nearly 20 per cent of all Downs people—lived in Toowoomba. A vigorous programme of

[28] *Queenslander*, 29 January 1898, p. 215, 'Reminiscences of Thomas Davis'.

[29] *DDG*, 11 October 1860, p. 3, c. 2 and 1 November 1860, p. 3, c. 3.

[30] *TC*, 6 March 1869, p. 3, c. 4-5.

[31] *DDG*, 12 December 1861, p. 3, c. 5.

branch railway activity throughout the Downs, considerable investment in the erection of both public and private buildings and utilities and the diversification of the regional economy had all contributed to this result.

Like most other country towns, Toowoomba's beginnings were prosaic and haphazard. In 1849 William Horton, the ex-convict publican, sent two men, Gurney and Shuttlewood, to cut reeds growing in a swamp four miles north-west of Drayton. They found a bush-worker's tent on the site which, in 1850, was auctioned as twenty-acre suburban farms. During 1854 Horton built the first house and hotel, the 'Separation', following the first land-sales of town land the preceding year. By Separation, the town had a population of 700 souls and land that had been auctioned for £4 per acre five years earlier now sold for £120. So rapid was Toowoomba's growth that on 24 November 1860 the town was proclaimed a municipality, having rejected in 1858 a proposal to combine with Drayton into the one administration.[32]

Guided by energetic storekeepers and influential squatters, the town kept ahead, being checked only for a short time in 1866-8 by drought and the great financial crisis. Toowoomba lost population to the goldfields and an observer in 1868 noted that many storekeepers had failed and that much property had passed into the hands of the banks by foreclosure.[33]

Such disasters were only temporary. After the Selection Act of 1868 Toowoomba embarked on a fantastic period of public and private expansion, firmly based on the new selector group, the improvements on the freehold estates of the Settled District, and the reviving trade with the western areas. Already the town had established a School of Arts (1861), the first of six banks (Bank of New South Wales, 1860), a newspaper, the *Toowoomba Chronicle* (6 July 1861), an agricultural and pastoral society (1860) and a benevolent home for the sick and needy. Herbert, in 1862, had even laid the foundation-stone for the first town-hall ever built in Queensland. By 1872 interstate visitors were describing Toowoomba as 'rather a considerable place . . . with a healthy and thriving appearance'. During the next three years buildings went up in all directions. The most imposing railway-station in Queensland was built at a cost of £6,000, a new School of Arts was erected, a Grammar School founded with considerable amenities and new industries in the shape of flour-mills, tanneries, a brewery, sawmills, and an iron foundry added to the market and service facilities.[34]

Overlooking this 'very moral town' in the conventional idiom of the colonial *bourgeoisie*, was 'St. James' Palace', or Clifford House, an old club house of the Pure Merinos and then the residence of the local squire, James Taylor of Cecil Plains, who established the practice where-

[32] T. Thompson in *Darling Downs Centenary Souvenir*, pp. 136-7.

[33] *TC*, 1 February 1868, p. 2, c. 4 and 28 March 1868, p. 2, c. 6.

[34] *Town and Country Journal*, 19 October 1872, p. 498; 19 December 1874, p. 981 and 10 July 1875, p. 52.

by the Governor, Downs squatters and Brisbane merchants, made cool Toowoomba a fashionable summer resort of the wealthier classes.

This urban boom continued into the 'eighties. In 1881 a new 70-bed hospital and a large town hall were completed as well as several groups of brick and stone shops. At Newtown Toowoomba was creating its first working-class suburb from Thorn's paddock and speculators were busy extending shopkeepers' residential areas to the north-east of Ruthven, Russell and Margaret Streets, the commercial core of the town. Eight churches and the Downs' first and last synagogue provided consolation, salvation and social satisfaction, nine schools provided varying quantities and qualities of education, a water supply had been constructed, the large Queens Park laid out, a gas works built and numerous small industrial plants established.[35]

Toowoomba in 1893 was, for most of its people, a comfortable if rather smug and 'respectable' place to live in. Certainly its amenities, both physical and human, compared more than favourably with any other town of similar size in Australia. There was a small, rather grating social price to pay. An observer noted that Toowoomba had become the city of a wealthy leisured class, and, as a natural sequence, more of the niceties and refinement of society were apparent in Toowoomba than in any other city in Queensland. Not all would agree that this refinement was a development to be applauded.[36]

But most people were relatively well-housed and fed, there was a wide range of municipal and private services, cultural interest, soon to flower for a brief time with the Austral Society, was growing and even 1893, 'that year that old Toowoomba hands often spoke of with a shudder', failed to check the material progress of the borough for very long.[37]

Radiating from the railway-station, the hub of the town where idlers, pickpockets, cabmen and carriers waited for the arrival of the daily mail train from Brisbane was the administrative, marketing, processing, banking, retailing, educational and religious capital of the Darling Downs. Its gravelled streets, lined with wooden, stone and brick shops, were filled with horse-drawn wagons, drays, spring carts, dray and station buckboards. Eight stock, station and produce agents controlled the largest saleyards outside Brisbane and numerous small industrial plants processed the products of the hinterland. Two shows every year, racedays, and a host of sporting clubs provided outdoor entertainment, the two newspapers, information, the hospital and asylum, refuge.[38]

Life on the Range was comfortable, tolerable and, for most, satisfying.

Fifty-five miles south of Toowoomba 'on the banks of the Condamine' where the tree-lined river swept round in the form of a horseshoe, was Warwick, a town which never really lived up to the expectations of its founders. Until the mid-'sixties, Warwick was the largest town on the

35 *TC*, 4 February 1886, p. 3, c. 6.

36 A. L. Holze (ed.), *Toowoomba, 1860-1910*, Brisbane 1911, p. 25.

37 J. Donges, 'Toowoomba in the Mid-Early Days', *TC*, 19 June 1964.

38 *Australian Handbook* (compilation), London 1894, pp. 421, 439.

Downs but, after the Selection Acts, Toowoomba forged ahead and, by 1885 was double the size of its old rival. Warwick storekeepers felt that this supersession was bad enough but, between 1881 and 1888, the town actually lost over 500 people. Between 1864 and 1891, the population of the municipality barely doubled, from 1,756 to 3,402, while that of the Downs as a whole rose three and a half times.[39]

Warwick's relative decline and temporary population loss reflected its inferior geographical and political advantages to Toowoomba once the inner Downs was thrown open to agricultural selection. Founded by Patrick Leslie himself in 1847, gazetted a township by the New South Wales Government in 1847, laid out and auctioned on 31 July 1850 for £4 a quarter acre Warwick was incorporated as a municipality on 25 May 1861. The sprawling settlement was always the local haunt for the Pure Merinos of the Southern Downs. Governor Bowen himself first visited Warwick in March 1860 and found an admirably laid out town with spacious and extensive streets but with few permanent buildings. Ten years later, however, the old slab-and-bark humpies, with 'their filth, discomfort and two-gallon kegs', had been replaced by brick, stone and timber buildings. By the 'eighties Warwick had acquired its unique character of being perhaps the neatest and cleanest town in Queensland and the place 'where living is cheaper and better for people who have their own homes'.[40]

Two large public squares, planted with lawns, trees, shrubs and flowers were a unique haven from the unpaved, dusty streets, while the durable and attractively patterned yellow Warwick sandstone was used for a series of attractive public buildings; the Town Hall, Masonic Hall, Police Station and Court House and, perhaps the Downs' best example of functional architecture, the offices and goods shed of the railway-station. Warwick's progress, then, if slow and disheartening to those members of the Progress League was also solid and materially substantial.[41]

Like Toowoomba, Warwick emerged at a strategic location at a time when pastoralists, having settled the Southern Downs, were pushing into south-west Queensland and the Maranoa country. Centrally situated near a ford on a reliable river on or adjacent to the sites of the first pastoral properties in Queensland and near the division of tracks to the border, Brisbane (via Cunningham's Gap) and the Central and Northern Downs, Warwick naturally attracted the hotels, blacksmiths' shops, stores and artisans necessary to service both station and team.

The rich black-soil plains which surrounded the town were also the cradle of agriculture on the Downs and the focus of the great battles for the land waged between squatter and agrarian during the 'sixties and 'seventies. Here the conflict was more fierce and bitter than in any other part of the Downs. Here too, the failure of agriculture to achieve the results of which its sponsored dream rebounded in like measure. The

39 *SR*, 1864-91.

40 *Weekly Herald*, 7 July 1866, p. 12.

41 *Town and Country Journal*, 27 February 1875, p. 334.

storekeepers won the political battle, the squatters retained the estates around the town; both were disappointed, most failed to make the profits they anticipated. After 1875 Warwick was no longer distinguished by the quality and vigour of ideological debate in its two lively newspapers but by the squabbles of social and economic frustrates.

A correspondent in the *Examiner and Times* shrewdly noted this feeling, a bare three years after the completion of the railway had started to drain attention, business and enterprise to the rising Toowoomba. Warwick people, observed 'Old Hand', were divided into little 'cliques' and 'sets' hamstringing public action and hindering the development of a town which had had the chance to make great strides. Everyone 'was on his own hook' and the town was slipping back.[42]

These accurate observations were followed on 3 August 1876 by the great Warwick Council fight when Beresford Hudson, defied and taunted by Alderman Crombie's personal abuse, seized an ink stand, hurled it at his tormentor, missed, and spattered an innocent reporter. An inconclusive sparring match then occurred and the meeting was adjourned in complete confusion. Crombie subsequently resigned: he was financially in debt to the Mayor, Jacob Horwitz, and had no alternative when pressure was exerted.[43]

The economic conditions of which these entertaining but paltry incidents were partly a symptom were repeated after the brief depression and drought of 1879-81 and the poor seasons of the mid-'eighties. Although agricultural development expanded the town lagged behind although, by 1888 a new Court House, Town Hall, Queensland National Bank and two new flour-mills had been built.[44]

The town itself had fulfilled its early promise of attractiveness and solidity. It had failed to overcome Toowoomba's challenge but its wide streets, grid-iron planning, substantial buildings and 800 wooden and stone houses with bright gardens gave it an air of prosperity and comfort that was lacking in most Queensland towns. In 1893 all four churches were of stone, as were most of the five banks and many of the numerous shops and offices. Six schools, two private secondary academies and one Catholic primary school foreshadowed the town's development as the educational centre of the Southern Downs and the town also supported a flourishing School of Arts, Jockey Club, Show Society, Cricket Club. There still remained eighteen hotels and a brewery for the thirsty, a hospital for the sick and six lodges for the charitable and gregarious. Warwick was not a boom town but it had survived and even expanded during the decade of uncertainty in the 'eighties and could look forward to increasing growth and prosperity as land resumptions, technical advances and rising prices strengthened its role as an administrative, transport, marketing and service centre for the farmers and graziers of the Southern Downs.

42 *WE&T*, 6 June 1874, p. 2, c. 4.

43 ibid., 5 August 1876, p. 2, c. 4.

44 *WA*, 24 December 1881, p. 2, c. 1 and 1 September 1884, p. 2, c. 2-3.

Dalby, near the confluence of Myall Creek and the Condamine, fifty-four miles north-west of Toowoomba, scarcely benefited from or was influenced by, agricultural selection. Founded as 'The Crossing' in 1842, it remained until the turn of the century, almost exclusively a pastoral town. Teamsters converging from the new runs of Maranoa and the Warrego originally camped on its site for water before fording the creek and continuing to Toowoomba. After its proclamation as a township in 1854, it matured into the service and administrative centre for the great stations and smaller pastoral freeholds of the Northern and Western Downs.

Hard-hit by depression, disappointed by the failure of agricultural selection in its hinterland, and ignored by the expanding communities of the south, Dalby in 1893 eagerly awaited the coming of fresh selectors to the Jimbour and Warra plains. Its storekeepers by then had realized that only a massive injection of men and capital could shock the stagnant town out of the twenty years of apathy and contraction induced by the end, on 6 June 1876, of its role as the terminal of the south-western railway. Indeed, the years between the coming of the line on 16 April 1863 and its extension to Miles were generally agreed to have been a premature 'Golden Age' of what was to be, when the city was proclaimed a municipality on 31 August 1863, the first great 'city of the western plains'.[45]

In fact, the 'city' turned out to be yet another Queensland pastoral town, trembling between survival and extinction. Situated on the lightly-timbered, rather monotonous plains bordering Myall Creek and astride a barren ironstone ridge, it suffered, as did all Downs towns, from the activities of squatters and speculators. R. F. Tooth and Coy, after requesting that the town be surveyed, purchased most of the choice allotments in 1861, and unfortunate boosters acquired many of the remainder. Furthermore Dalby politically was for long a pocket borough of J. P. Bell of neighbouring Jimbour. When he died in 1881 Dalby's chance of stimulation by paternal public works investment seemed to have passed with him.[46] All this retarded progress, although, with the great western pastoral expansion of the early 'sixties, the 1861 population of 685 almost doubled itself in three years. Thereafter, in spite of the railway for which Dalby was the constructors' depot, progress was slower. Indeed, by 1891, there were only 1,378 people in the municipality, 269 fewer than in 1876.

Dalby, however, in spite of its economic stagnation was occasionally a lively town, reflecting the colour and diversity of the pastoral industry which surrounded it and from which it drew its sustenance. Both masters and servants congregated here: 'wild bushmen, men with strange oaths and bearded like a part [while] . . . the squatter topped his malt and chandon in the swell hotel, while the unpretentious rouseabout and monopathic shepherd buried their sad remembrances . . . in the humble

[45] *Queenslander*, 21 February 1903, p. 4, c. 1.

[46] *Moreton Bay Courier*, 26 January 1861, p. 3, c. 3.

Nepenthean rum'.[47] Thirteen long-verandahed wooden hotels, one for every 100 inhabitants in 1880, catered for this trade. Each hotel had its own clientele, not only of 'regulars' but frequently of occupational groups. A squatter would no more think of deserting the saloon of Wallace's 'Royal' for a nobbler or drinking bout than would his employee consider leaving Dan Lynch's 'Woolpack', Pat Hallinan's 'Hibernian' or Ted Ryan's 'Carriers' Arms'. Others catered for the shopkeepers, clerks and respectable travellers. Yet apart from the dust, lack of trees and contour and inadequate water supply, Dalby, with its 300 houses scattered over two and a half square miles, differed little in essentials from other Downs towns. It too, by the 'seventies, had the same government instrumentalities, schools, banks, churches, hospital, racecourse and School of Arts. Only the fact that saddlers, blacksmiths, bootmakers and western storekeepers and commission agents were comparatively more numerous than in the southern agricultural towns testified to its exclusive dependence on the sheep walks which surrounded it. Dalby, then, was still raw and very, very new.

Unlike Dalby, Allora continued to grow steadily after the Selection Acts of the 'sixties opened up the rich black-soil lands surrounding the pleasant, sprawling settlement on Dalrymple Creek, thirty-five miles south of Toowoomba. Allora's population, boosted in 1879 by the auction of the exchange lands, grew steadily from 292 persons in 1868 to 477 in 1876 and 994 in 1891. Nevertheless, in 1871 the town received a blow which crippled its development and prevented it from superseding Warwick, only sixteen miles to the south, as the agricultural capital of the Southern Downs. The Toowoomba-Warwick railway, through the machinations of squatters and the blunders of officials, passed not through the town but four miles to the west. In an era of bad and costly communications, this was catastrophic. Not until 1897 was a branch from Hendon completed but by then it was too late for supremacy or even modest growth.[48]

Nevertheless, the village made considerable progress during the selection years. Its genesis was Neil Ross' Goomburra out-station, the site of the only suitable ford over Dalrymple Creek on the Tollbar Road. After the first commercial building, the Dalrymple Hotel, was erected by Donald Clark in 1857 the infant village, surveyed in 1859 and auctioned a year later, slowly expanded although it was not until the middle 'sixties that cottages and general stores replaced the bark huts of the small selectors and the shanties of the tradesmen. On 21 July 1869 Allora was proclaimed a municipality having already acquired a post-office, police-station, court-house and enough shopkeepers to staff a council, wrangle about expenditure and provide an urban backbone of ponderous dignity and respectability.

Progress then slowed as the sleepy town below the eroded brown slopes of Mount Allan was confined by the great estates which surrounded it

[47] A. Meston, *Queensland, Railway and Tourists' Guide*, Brisbane, n.d. [1891], p. 41.
[48] B. M. Sims, *Allora's Past*, Allora 1930.

on three sides. Nevertheless, in 1893 Allora boasted two banks, five hotels, two boarding-houses, four churches, two large halls, a School of Arts, a vigorous radical newspaper, the *Allora Guardian*, eight service tradesmen, six general stores and half a dozen minor specialized artisans.[49]

But Allora did not entirely rely on the provision of services to agriculturalists. For its size, it supported more small processing industries than any other Downs town. During the 'seventies and 'eighties, the smoke from the chimneys of its saw- and flour-mills gave an impression of activity and progress that seemed to guarantee expansion and to fortify the hopes of those who looked forward to the day when it would challenge its southern rival Warwick for the trade and produce of the farmers of the Southern Downs. But this dream blew away with the smoke.[50]

As the pine and cedar stands of the Goomburra Valley retreated before the loggers of Adam Rickert, the Hall Brothers and Cameron and Hebbel their mills were forced to close or follow the source of their raw material. By 1883 only one small mill was left in the town.

The history of the other industry, flour-milling, is similar. In 1872 a group of Allora tradesmen, James Dougall, Francis Kates and Robert Cooke erected what was to become the focus of Allora's business enterprise, the Allora Steam Flour Mills. The three-storied galvanized iron mill, standing out above the plain, with its twelve h.p. steam engine driven by coal from the Allora open cut mines and producing three tons of flour every day seemed to be the guarantee of continued expansion. Furthermore, in 1882, Thomas and James Kennedy both, like Kates, prosperous Allora general storekeepers, commenced production at their larger 'White Rose' roller mills. Costing £3,000 when built, of a daily capacity of four tons of flour, this mill, rebuilt and converted to rollers in 1893, worked until dismantled in 1912. Kates' mill, sold to the Gisler Brothers in 1887, was closed in 1892 and burnt down by an incendiary a few months later. The arsonists' spectacular enterprise only anticipated the end of village industry.[51] Although Kates operated a small mill at the railway station between 1898 and 1906 this was never the success its predecessors had been. The flour-mills of Allora, by the outbreak of World War I, had disappeared with the hundreds of other small plants in country towns all over Australia. Allora had lost, partly through inexorable centralization, partly through the problems of the Downs wheat farmers, its sole chance of becoming a sizable, balanced town. Even the coming of the Central Downs butter factory in 1894 could not compensate for Allora's failure to secure the processing of its farmers' grain as well as the satisfaction of their immediate material needs.

But if the railway killed Allora's chances of becoming something more than an agricultural village, it was also responsible for the creation

[49] ibid.

[50] *BC*, 21 October 1871, p. 2, c. 3.

[51] *WA*, 9 November 1876, p. 2, c. 6 and 9 December 1882, p. 2, c. 5; *Allora Guardian*, 8 October 1892, p. 3, c. 1-2.

of several flourishing towns scattered amid the agrarian pockets of the Downs and on the western slopes of the Range where timber-milling flourished after 1870.

Clifton and Pittsworth both owed their progress to the Agricultural Selection Acts of 1868 and 1876 which opened up the rich lands surrounding them to grain-growers and mixed farmers. Clifton, thirty miles south of Toowoomba, grew from a railway hamlet of 48 people in 1876 to a small town of 278 in 1891. By then it was the fifth largest town on the Downs.

This town was never a pastoral settlement but the virtual creation of an astute storekeeper and publican, James Mowen, who settled in the area in 1869, prospered with his twin enterprises and speculated so successfully in township land that he was able to retire in 1883. By 1893 Clifton supported three stores, a similar number of hotels, a bank branch, four churches, a State school, post-office, School of Arts, and fourteen small tradesmen ranging from bakers, butchers and saddlers to William Burgess, the town's solitary (and unsuccessful) undertaker.[52]

Like Clifton, Pittsworth's growth was firmly based on loan money, speculation, wheat and lucerne. In 1876 J. Tyson Doneley, a nephew of the Felton squatter James Tyson and a man who, like his uncle, 'made money out of everything he touched in the district', built the Beauaraba Hotel to serve the pastoral employees of the surrounding freehold estates and the scrub farmers of the Umbiram, Beauaraba, Broxburn and Southbrook Resumptions.[53]

After the railway from Toowoomba arrived in 1887 the town made rapid progress. Within three years three more hotels, four stores, two butchers, a bank, two churches and two blacksmiths had been established. Coaches ran over the black-soil roads to the small agricultural settlements at Domville (Milmerran), Bark Creek and Leyburn. Wool from the south-western Downs stations was also carted to the railhead at Pittsworth.

Reflecting its strategic position in the heart of the best part of the Settled District, Pittsworth's population grew from a mere handful—sixteen—in 1881 to 231 in 1891. By 1896 it had reached 450. Unlike many other settlements the town was solvent and progressive from the beginning, escaping through adequate land resumptions, dairying and the new grain-growing techniques the tribulations of other centres. Built on rather open, level country with some silver ironbark and apple-tree vegetation, what Pittsworth lacked in physical attractiveness and character it made up for in Germanic respectability, fecundity and black bank balances.

> Today [1896] it consists of five hotels, Court House, Police Barracks, Post and Telegraph Office, four churches, two banks, some 28 stores and shops, several factories, and numerous private residences. The roll call at the State School . . .

[52] *Pugh*, 1895, p. 79 and *WE&T*, 31 July 1886, p. 2, c. 5.

[53] *BC*, 17 April 1901, p. 5, c. 1.

is now nearly 200 with three teachers employed . . . the building trade is very brisk and the three sawmills cannot keep pace with the demand [and] the rush for land continues unabated.[54]

All it lacked to complete the transformation from village to country town was a newspaper, doctor, flour-mill, hospital and a bunch of larrikins.

Along the Crow's Nest branch railway, opened on 6 December 1886, which stretched north-east from Toowoomba towards the Main Range, several thriving saw-milling villages were established during the 'sixties and 'seventies. At Highfields, three mills were at work by 1875, employing 76 men and producing over 57,000 feet of pine and hardwood timber every week.

Similarly, Crow's Nest, surveyed in 1876, expanded on the basis of the timber industry as did Killarney, twenty miles south-east of Warwick. As the timber was worked out the settlement either died like Highfields or expanded under the impetus of agricultural selection. Crow's Nest, by 1893, already had a population of 145, two churches, two stores, an hotel, school, blacksmith and the original sawmill as well as the usual government facilities. Killarney, with 387 people, was larger and more prosperous, boasting a School of Arts in addition to the usual publicans, sawmillers and tradesmen.[55]

Stanthorpe was the only large country town on the Downs that owed its growth to neither pastoralism nor intensive agriculture. Although an hotel and store, the 'Golden Fleece Inn', was established at Quart Pot Creek before Separation, the site remained nothing more than another rather desolate stopping place for the Northern Mail coaches travelling between New England, the Downs and Brisbane, and for drovers taking stock from the Maryland, Ballandean, Pikedale and Folkestone Stations to the southern markets.

The surrounding country, with its huge granite boulders, broken spurs, pink hills, small sequestered valleys timbered by dwarf gums, apple-tree and honeysuckle was watered by small streams flowing over flat granite beds. The little flats, broken spurs and ridges were neglected by the first agricultural selectors. The fruit-growing potentialities of the granite soils and the equable climate of crisp winters and hot summers were not recognized until the necessities of the 'eighties forced economic diversification.

In February 1872, however, Bartholomew Ross's hotel, a one-roomed bark erection with bar at one end, benches around the walls and spread straw and blankets on the earthen floors for nightly guests, experienced the greatest event in Quart Pot's history. Tin was discovered by C. S. McGlew and his partner D. Eisenstaedter in the nearby creek. This event followed finds in New England and Police Magistrate G. W. F. Addison's recollection that sandbags for windbreaks around the hotel had been filled with ore-bearing quartz. Indeed, the first specimen of crystal tin in

[54] Evans, *Garden of Queensland*, p. 55.

[55] *DDG*, 16 December 1876, p. 5, c. 4 and *WA*, 24 December 1887, p. 2, c. 6.

Queensland had been picked up by a wandering shepherd at Quart Pot in 1851.[56] Joseph Greer, a prospector on Nundubbermere run had also discovered stream tin in 1854 but this promising find had not been followed up, largely because the southern goldfields and the Gympie rush had diverted prospectors and miners from further investigating the area. Furthermore, the ore was not readily identifiable by the average prospector being found not in the usual metallic state but as an oxide of tin.[57]

By April 1872 a 'mad scramble' to the rich alluvial field had started. Two coaches a day, charging five shillings a trip, ran between Warwick and the new town of Stannum—Quart Pot was thought by thirsty miners to be the ideal name but ecclesiastics, officials and speculators all objected —and hundreds tramped in by foot. Applications for selections were lodged by special couriers riding hard to the Land Office at Warwick, thirty miles to the north. F. T. Gregory was appointed Land and Mineral Commissioner to clear up the muddle and chaos over mining claims and leases and on 22 April the first official mineral selection was taken up. A month later, on 26 May 1872 the Stanthorpe Town Reserve was officially proclaimed. By June 1872 there were 1,200-1,400 people on the field of some thirty square miles. A jumble of tents and humpies was already giving way, in spite of a timber shortage, to long lines of weatherboard and chamferboard houses. Four hotels and numerous grog shanties and stores were already doing a roaring trade with fossickers picking up and washing about fifty pounds of tin a day at sixpence a pound. McGlew, the discoverer, employed 25 men at his sluices on Quart Pot Creek and paid them two pounds per week and rations. He was extracting three tons a week by June.[58]

Eisenstaedter, his old partner, had, on his 640 acres, an even larger establishment which employed over one hundred men and was sending ten tons of ore every week to Sydney and London for smelting.

During September 1872 the first ore, 72 per cent pure tin, arrived in London, realizing £97.15s. net per ton. The early miners simply panned the stream tin out like gold in a mad scramble for the richest pockets. Such crude and destructive methods, combined with the charge of £3.13s. per ton for transporting ore by dray to Warwick, railway to Ipswich and steamer to Brisbane, encouraged the formation of mining and smelting companies floated with Sydney, Brisbane and Downs capital, and the employment of Chinese coolie labour at low wages.[59] Two undesirable features of Australian mining fields were thus introduced. Rampant speculation and the deliberate promotion of worthless ground became quite common. The Folkestone Company, floated by Toowoomba capitalists including James Taylor, was a case in point. The original

[56] *WE&T*, 13 May 1891, p. 2, c. 3.

[57] E. C. Saint-Smith, 'Geology and Mineral Resources of the Stanthorpe, Bullandean and Wallangorera Districts, 1913', *QSG Publication, No. 243*, Brisbane 1914, pp. 9-11.

[58] *BC*, 22 March 1872, p. 3, c. 1-4; *WE&T*, 25 May 1872, p. 2, c. 3 and 1 June 1872, p. 2.

[59] *Border Post*, 15 May 1874, pp. 2-3.

prospector, one Hannam, sold worthless ground to the promoters, they offered a misleading prospectus and the unfortunate shareholders lost their money.[60] Secondly, crude colonial racialism came swiftly to the Downs. Typically disorderly mass meetings of miners were held at Stanthorpe in December 1873 to condemn H. C. Ransome's rather precipitate introduction of Chinese wage-workers and to mildly persecute the unfortunate Orientals. Nevertheless, it is doubtful if there were ever more than 250 Chinese on the field at any one time and by 1878 they had almost all departed to the richer fields of the Palmer and the Herbert. A few remained as wage-workers and fossickers.

Meanwhile, the town expanded after the first sale of town allotments on 3 July 1872. The new slab, board and bark Theatre Royal with its melodramas, singing and itinerant dancing girls on their way to the northern goldfields was, by Christmas, doing good business but no school was built until late the following year. Nevertheless there were two churches, one Anglican, the other Roman Catholic, a clutch of government offices, three banks, three chemists, twelve large stores and twenty-two indispensable licensed grog shanties to slake the thirsts of the miners.[61]

Stanthorpe, by 1876, with 1,079 people in the town and a further 2,000 on the tin field was the liveliest and most colourful country town on the Downs. Furthermore, in 1883 the railway from Warwick arrived lowering freight costs and making commercial agriculture possible in the future. Five years later New England was also brought into communication by rail. But as physical conditions and urban amenities improved the yield of ore fell. The peak year 1873 produced 8,938 tons of tin ore worth £606,184. After then, both production and prices fell steadily, although the great decline in both did not commence until 1883 when only £40,233 worth of tin was extracted from a mere 817 tons of ore. Between 1872 and 1882 the field produced ore to the value of £2,315,659: but between 1883 and 1893 only £246,966 worth was extracted. During the latter year only 334 tons were mined yielding £10,284.[62] There was a brief revival of company sluice mining in the mid-'eighties and some silver mining further west at Silver Spur in the early 'nineties, but these failed to check the slide resulting from a combination of several factors; most of them common to all Queensland mineral fields. The alluvial tin was soon exhausted, capital preferred the richer and supposedly longer-lasting fields of North Queensland and the price of the metal slid slowly downwards after 1878. Severe droughts hindered sluicing for months on end in 1877-9 and 1886 but, on the whole, the chaotic nature of the early exploitation, the lack of reliable geological surveys and investigations and the haphazard application of capital ruined any possibilities the area might have had for a longer mining life.

60 *WE&T*, 29 June 1872, p. 2, c. 7 and *TC*, 1 February 1873, p. 3, c. 1.

61 *BC*, 11 November 1872, p. 3, c. 2-4 and *WE&T*, 7 September 1872, p. 2, c. 1.

62 Saint-Smith, 'Geology and Mineral Resources', p. 153.

But Stanthorpe's survival as a town in spite of its decline from 897 persons in 1886 to 735 in 1891, was ensured by three developments—the railway, the Grazing Farms Act of 1884 and the cultivation of the granite soils by retired miners. Peach, plum and apple orchards, combined with small market gardens, gradually spread over the flats and hills of the area, where the destructive operations of sluicing and the washed grey-green hillocks of abandoned tailings did not prohibit agriculture. The town itself consolidated around its legacies from a lustier past—the five substantial hotels, the government offices, the hospital, School of Arts, two halls, schools, and churches.

There was in 1893 even some small local industry—a brewery, tannery, sawmill and wattle-bark grinding mill. But Stanthorpe's great days were over. The colour was now in the blossom, not in the activities of men. No more were there the crowds in the streets, torchlight processions at night and rushes to new pockets or rich ore which made up the bustling life of an alluvial mining town. Market information had replaced mining news and stock exchange quotations, regularity of life and conduct had displaced informality and insouciance of the 'seventies. Life still remained in the town but now it gently pulsated rather than hummed and fluctuated. Stanthorpe had survived but its future now lay in the fields rather than the streams. Only a few old prospectors and the publicans lamented the change. The country-town storekeepers, clergymen and artisans were, in 1893, supreme. Their values, their controls, now dictated local life.

Two other types of villages remain to be considered: the pastoral hamlet and the railhead settlement. In 1891, Condamine, Inglewood, Jondaryan, Leyburn and Texas were examples of the former, Miles and Warra of the latter.

All these pastoral townships declined after 1875. Condamine had fewer people—106 in 1891—than it had twenty years earlier. Inglewood's population was stationary, and that of Leyburn and Jondaryan fell steadily.[63] The reasons are not hard to find. All were droving, drinking and administrative centres on old stock- and work-routes, bypassed by the railway, and unable to draw on any nearby agricultural settlement for compensation for the loss of their stockmen, carriers and publicans. Few were attractive enough or supported the minimum amenities that would prevent the more mobile of their inhabitants from cutting their losses and moving on, either to the towns of the east or to the pioneer settlements along the spreading fingers of the new western railways. None, for example, had permanent piped water supplies or reliable medical services. All lacked employment opportunities.

Leyburn, whose calm was broken by the brief Canal Creek gold-rush in 1871-2, was always 'a sleepy little town, clothed in dust' where the quiet monotonous life was broken only by the arrival and departure of Cobb and Co.'s twice-weekly coaches to Cambooya and Warwick, and the slow passage of teams and flocks through the town. Most men were

[63] *Australian Handbook*, p. 437.

either employed as carriers on the Toowoomba-Goondiwindi Road or else worked on nearby stations, rejoining their families at their Leyburn cottages on Saturday evening. A State School, an Anglican church, Police Station and Court House, two smithies, three stores, a sawmill and the inevitable three hotels made up the straggling, wooden town-centre along the Warwick road. Only the telegraph-poles, stretching into the distance were a permanent reminder of the world outside.[64]

While it had more hotels than stores in 1875, Condamine, like Leyburn, was 'a fair sample of an Australian bush township'. This hamlet, then of 166 souls and situated 77 miles north-west of Dalby, was, before the coming of the railway, the major stopping place for stockmen and carriers travelling between the Maranoa and the Northern Downs, needing water, food and a safe river ford.[65]

Most of the dwellings, however, were bark huts and the whole town, like most others in the bush, bore a temporary appearance, where life was 'neither remarkable for elegance or comfort' and where a 'good fire' was needed to improve the quality of the local scene.

The railheads were equally desolate. At Miles, no gardens, trees, flowers or shrubs relieved the fire-blackened gloom of the countryside and the knee-deep mud of the streets. For those not actually working on the railway, life was monotonous and, in case of pregnancy, diarrhoea or fever, dangerous and apt to be short. Many did not survive the eighty-mile journey to the hospital at Dalby, itself an institution with a high mortality-rate.[66] There were no churches for the 150 people in 1878 and no schools for the swarms of children camped in tents and huts along the track. For those who survived summer temperatures of 110 degrees in the shade, and the perils of illness, there were the fourteen public-houses and the three sly-grog shanties to supply liquid consolation. These followed the contractors so that when work moved on—as it did in 1882—the heart of the town stopped beating. But usually a general store, school and hotel remained to keep the new railway-station company and to service the usual cluster of poor grazing selectors around the new nuclei.

These then were the twenty towns and villages of the Darling Downs. Some, the mining and leftover pastoral villages, were declining; others had already attained their zenith; a few seemed to have reached a point where the agrarian multiples—the results of three decades of agrarian settlement, were coming into operation. But for the storekeepers of Clifton, Oakey, Crow's Nest, Miles and Pittsworth rosy hopes did not mean clinking tills. All over the white colonial world similar hamlets of a few hundred souls were, in 1893, really experiencing their Indian Summer. Most were too small and undifferentiated, too unsophisticated to both retain population and cater adequately for the expanding needs of the

64 *TC*, 9 March 1872, p. 2, c. 6.

65 *Town and Country Journal*, 10 July 1875, p. 68.

66 *Dalby Herald*, 17 August 1878, p. 2, c. 5 and *QPD*, Vols 22 and 23, (1877), pp. 16-20, 25-30.

prosperous agrarians and their sons who remained to farm in the new century. Henry Ford and World War I completed their relative ruin, the former by bringing the three larger towns within easy and cheap reach of almost every Downs family, the latter by cutting out the heart and hope of the country villages—an entire generation of young men. The garage and service-station may have replaced the blacksmith but banal statuary could not substitute for dead youth.

So, by 1893, the pattern was set. A distinctive regional capital, Toowoomba, had emerged, supported on both flanks by two sub-regional centres—pastoral Dalby and agricultural Warwick. Scattered along the railway tracks or at strategic posts like black currants in the rich plum cakes of the Downs were the villages. Some, Pittsworth, Oakey and Chinchilla were prospering. Others, like Stanthorpe, were stagnant. Most were sleepy, ostensibly tolerant, physically desirable places to live, and to rear children. All offered in some measure the crude framework of nineteenth-century western civilization. Except for market, show, church and race days, little human activity was observable in the dusty, bungalow and cottage-lined streets of these small towns. A buzz from the hotel bar and the general store, odd shouts from the school playground and the clip-clop of hooves at odd intervals alone indicated that the inhabitants were still alive. Only an imposing funeral or a contested election disturbed the general monotony. But while the tempo of village life may have been slow it suited the old and the very young. For the talented, the unusually skilled, the sensitive, as well as the young larrikin and the wage-worker, these advantages were not enough. Patriarchs had been replaced by petty babbitts and the values and satisfactions of progress association, church and municipal council, appeared to many to be neither as relevant as those of the successful farmers nor as rich, interesting and varied as those pursued in those marvellous creations of Victorian Australia, the cities of the eastern and southern seaboard.

Stephen Mehan's store, Drayton, 1856

By courtesy of the Royal Historical Society of Queensland

Mr George Clark's Talgai House, about 1880

By courtesy of the Oxley Memorial Library of Queensland

Washing sheep on Eton Vale, about 1870

By courtesy of the Royal Historical Society of Queensland

Stanthorpe in 1873 showing W. H. Groom's Hotel and Jacob Horwitz's store (*Queenslander*, 8 December 1932, p. 21)

By courtesy of the La Trobe Library, State Library of Victoria

F. H. Holberton's general store, Toowoomba, 1874 (*Town & Country Journal*, 19 December 1874)

Toowoomba at the turn of the century (*Queenslander*, 6 March 1920, p.18)

Prints by courtesy of the La Trobe Library, State Library of Victoria

The *Darling Downs Gazette* office, Toowoomba, about 1895 (*Queenslander*, 6 October 1900, p.7)

By courtesy of the La Trobe Library, State Library of Victoria

Harvesting a 300-acre wheatfield, Canning Downs, 1894

By courtesy of the Oxley Memorial Library of Queensland

Hayes' Steam Flour Mills, Warwick, about 1885 (*Centenary Souvenir 1840-1940*, p.105)

Prints by courtesy of the Oxley Memorial Library of Queensland

The famous Jondaryan Woolshed, 1894

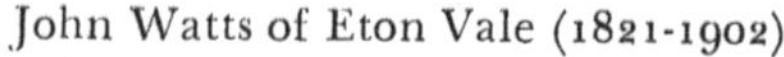

John Watts of Eton Vale (1821-1902)

Sir Joshua Peter Bell of Jimbour (1827-81)

William Henry Groom (1833-1901)

Prints by courtesy of
the Oxley Memorial Library of Queensland
except John Watts which is by courtesy of
the Royal Historical Society of Queensland

Sir Arthur Hodgson of Eton Vale
(1818-1902)

William Miles (1817-87)

James Morgan (1816-78)

Prints by courtesy of
the Oxley Memorial Library of Queensland

Contemporary cartoons of the Cambooya Election of 1888 (From the *Boomerang*, April and May 1888)

By courtesy of the
Oxley Memorial Library of Queensland

ROUGH ON CAMBOOYA.

"*I am more in touch with you than I could be with any other constituency for some time to come.*"—[PADDY PERKINS's Manifesto to the Electors of Cambooya.

THE POLITICAL·STY.

PART TWO

THE SELECTORS

The Darling Downs will not grow a cabbage.

John Watts of Eton Vale, c. 1860

The farming class are equally independent. Notwithstanding occasional dry seasons and consequent loss of crops, they fight their way through with eminent success, thanks to energy, a splendid climate, and rich soil. In fact, the farmers may be looked upon as the most thoroughly independent class in the country.

A. J. Boyd
Notes on Queensland for the Colonial Exhibition, 1886
London 1886, p. 20

The whole land question is enveloped in a fictitious halo—those called upon to speak or write on it, as a rule, not venturing to tell the whole truth for fear of giving offence—glossing over all that is unpleasant, and dwelling solely on its attractive points.

Hume Report, *QVP*, 1884, Vol. 2, p. 1089

CHAPTER 5

MYTHS AND REALITIES

AGRARIAN IDEALS AND PRACTICE ON THE DARLING DOWNS

Most contemporary observers of agricultural settlement on the Darling Downs during the nineteenth century noted that the high hopes and ideals which had inspired the great Lands Acts of 1863, 1868 and 1876 had not been realized. They testified with devastating accuracy to farming's slow and uncertain growth.[1]

Although socially affiliated with the hospitable squattocracy, the shrewd English novelist, Anthony Trollope, who visited the Downs in September 1871, fully agreed with the agrarian tenet that 'the encouragement of the genuine free-selector ought to be the first aim of colonial government.'[2] But Trollope considered that the Selection Acts had so far utterly failed to produce this thriving yeomanry:

> . . . the free selector can grow nothing on the Darling Downs for which there is a market. He finds it hard to get ready money. Wheat he cannot produce as it will fail twice for him every time it will thrive . . . transport costs are high . . .[3]

Commercial farming was a failure, he asserted, and advocated using the farm only for subsistence crops and depending upon seasonal work for a cash income. 'Terms for land', Trollope concluded, 'are not hard. Land is cheap because the struggle required to make it useful is severe.'[4]

Three years later, the perceptive 'Bohemian' noted that although some farmers on the 'pick of the Downs' were flourishing, the picture on the northern and western plains and scrubs was far from encouraging. Of the Irvingdale-Jimbour-Dalby district he concluded:

> . . . the feeling throughout . . . the district . . . appears universal, among rich and poor alike, that small areas will not pay hereabouts, and that at present agriculture cannot be successfully carried out, too many drawbacks existing independent of climatic conditions which do not themselves appear . . . very favourable.[5]

1 W. Epps, *Land Systems of Australasia*, London 1884, p. 178.

2 A. Trollope, *Australia and New Zealand*, London 1873, Vol. I, p. 39.

3 ibid., p. 180.

4 ibid., pp. 178-80.

5 *BC*, 30 May 1874, p. 5, c. 5.

A similar assessment was made by W. A. Tully, the Under-Secretary for Crown Lands, who saw that the very opportunities offered to poor men to select cheap homesteads had led to failures in some districts.

It is not providing the means of settling the people permanently on the land . . . instead of a large yeoman-class being established . . . the result is that the large estates are growing larger, and the very reverse of what was desired brought about.[6]

While Tully was 'aware that there are economic reasons for the general application of the land to pastoral pursuits, and that under certain conditions the land could not be applied to a better purpose' he maintained that many evils resulted from this form of settlement.[7]

Finally, the suppressed report on actual conditions on the Downs written by W. C. Hume, Resident Lands Commissioner, condemned the agitators of the country towns and forthrightly declared that although the outward appearance of agricultural settlement was prosperous the idyllic and automatic progress of selectors from near-poverty to comfort and affluence was generally illusory. Wheat could not be profitably grown in many districts, rust and drought scourged the better areas, many selectors were sinking into debt, and speculation and mobility, the antithesis of a yeomanry's characteristics, were rife. Hume gloomily remarked that until apparently hopeless disabilities were removed those selections outside the favoured Warwick-Allora-Toowoomba zone would eventually be absorbed by the great estates. This report, the most reliable document on the actual condition of settlement in existence, was deliberately withheld from publication by a Government which feared political consequences. Three years later, in 1884, it was released by the Griffith Government during the Land Bill Debates. Realistic arguments were again required to support completely novel and romantic legislation.[8]

These trenchant remarks were angrily refuted by urban politicians, the self-appointed spokesmen for the farmers and the publicists of agrarian ideals. Trollope's mind, the *Courier* shrilly and unfairly considered, 'had been warped by aristocratic or pro-Tory proclivities' and he had produced an account full of 'bias, errors and omissions'.[9] Toowoomba and Warwick newspapers passed strong and positively virulent strictures on Hume's report which had obliquely but bitterly attacked their proprietors. Groom's *Toowoomba Chronicle* confessed:

. . . that a more damaging report . . . and one more calculated to injure the character of the Darling Downs as an agricultural district was never written . . .

[6] *QVP*, Vol. 2, (1881), p. 142, 'Report of the Under-Secretary for Lands'.

[7] ibid., Vol. 3, (1877), p. 88.

[8] *QVP*, Vol. 2, (1884), pp. 1089-92. 'Report of the State of Settlement in the District of Darling Downs'. *QPD*, Vol. 43, (1884), pp. 253-420.

[9] *BC*, 27 May 1872, p. 2, c. 5-6. Overseas criticism, however valid and instructive, was never well received in the sensitive colonies.

it libelled a number of honest, industrious settlers in a way we think nothing can justify.[10]

Always willing to pronounce on land matters, the *Warwick Examiner* conceded truth by implication when it stated that:

We are not sufficiently versed in land matters to assert that its statements are untrue . . .[11]

These critics failed to examine dispassionately the charge that genuine settlement was flagging and basic aims had been ignored. Once again they fell back on the agrarian myth. As the farmers 'live nearer God, nearer heaven', argued the *Courier,* the escape from the 'sickly towns' offered by land settlement more than compensated for any lack of material success.[12] Such ideals were admirable for those who could afford them. But what the farmers wanted was bumper harvests and multiplying herds, high prices and cash in the bank. The agitations of the depression years revealed that they accepted the analyses of the critics. Romantic advocacy was no longer enough once cheap land had been made available.

Few farmers will ever admit to prosperity but an examination of the position of the Downs selectors reveals that most of the criticisms and complaints were valid and that it was difficult for homesteaders to survive, cultivate and prosper on their small holdings. For instance, of the 2,327 selections totalling 378,170 acres taken up in the Warwick and Toowoomba districts between 1877 and 1884, 339 portions of 38,788 acres were forfeited before the certificates of fulfilment of conditions had been obtained. This took place in the most favourable area for agriculture and casualties were much greater in less desirable localities. When subsequent transfers are taken into account and pastoralists' selections subtracted, the position is even more depressing.[13]

This conclusion is reinforced by a detailed study of the 353 small settlers who obtained the freehold in 1883. By 1903 only 181 farm families remained; the other 172 had previously failed, left or had sold out to their neighbours or new arrivals.[14] Even this with its nearly 50 per cent turnover, conceals the number forfeiting before freeholding and the differences between various areas.

On the Cumkillenbar Agricultural Reserve, settled under the 1866 Act by eleven intending agriculturalists, seven had walked off by 1874 and the remaining four had abandoned cultivation for pastoralism. By

10 *TC*, 12 August 1884, p. 2, c. 1.

11 *WE&T*, 16 August 1884, p. 2, c. 1-3.

12 *BC*, 23 March 1872, p. 6, c. 2.

13 *QVP*, Vol. 2, (1885), p. 1197. *Also*: *Queenslander*, 8 January 1876, p. 4.

14 *QVP*, Vol. 2, (1884), pp. 1003-40. 'Return of Deeds of Grant issued in 1883.' Evidence for the survival of farm-families has been drawn from: *Commonwealth of Australia*, Electoral Roll, Darling Downs Division, Brisbane 1903, 1905. It is possible that some families have remained undetected but they cannot affect the overall impression of mobility.

1884, only two were left.[15] These were 320-acre men; but on the East and West Prairie 640-1,280-acre resumptions, by Victorians with experience and capital, only six of the twenty-one 1877 lessees survived by 1903.[16]

A more illuminating example is a giant block of 80-acre selections taken up between 1876 and 1881:

WESTBROOK HOMESTEAD AREA[17]

SURVIVAL OF SELECTORS 1876-1903

Category	Number	Percentage
Original selectors	156	100
Forfeiting before obtaining freehold	27	17.5
Sold before 1903 after title obtained	72	46
Family farms still in possession of original selectors	52	36.5

Selectors on the Warwick Agricultural Reserve fared better. Only 35 of the original 108 who had selected during 1868-9 had disappeared by 1903.[18] This pattern reinforces the conclusion that farmers on good, well-watered land near markets, as these Swan and Freestone Creeks, Allora, Spring Creek, Clifton, Drayton and Toowoomba men were, had a far greater chance of success than post-1875 selectors. But even although they had partly succeeded in coming to terms with their environment, economic problems plagued them after the mid-'eighties.

This instability of settlement on the Downs, which goes far to destroy the legend of the sturdy pioneer fixing the character of the farm community, is reinforced by the selectors' failure to obey the injunction to cultivate. Less than six per cent of the total area of agricultural homesteads was tilled in 1878 and only 95,620 acres (less than three per cent) were cropped in the Settled District in 1892.[19] This was a poor result from the 2,808 cultivators then on the Downs. The result of the 1868 Land Act is even more striking as it excludes squatters and Conditional Purchase grazing selections.

Agricultural development in the Australian colonies, the United States and Canada was measured in terms of wheat production, wheat being

15 *BC*, 1 August 1874, p. 5, c. 2-3.

16 *QPD*, Vol. 30, (1879), pp. 1150-60, 1721-6 and *QVP*, Vol. 2, (1879), pp. 253-70. 'Report on the Petition of the East and West Prairie and St. Ruth Selectors.'

17 QGG, 'Selectors' Rent Lists', 1876-1886. *Surveyor-General's Office* Toowoomba Two-mile to the Inch Parish Map, Brisbane 1884. Commonwealth of Australia, Electoral Rolls, Darling Downs Division, Brisbane 1903, 1905. This 27,000 acre resumption is shown in Map 13.

18 *QGG*, 'Selectors' Rent Lists', 1870, pp. 312-14, 380-6 Commonwealth of Australia, Electoral Rolls, Darling Downs Division, Brisbane 1903, 1905. For a comparable area in the United States *see* J. C. Malin, 'The Turnover of Farm Population in Kansas', *Kansas Historical Quarterly*, Vol. IV, 1935, p. 339.

19 *QVP*, Vol. 2, (1878), p. 189 and *Queensland Statistical Register*, 1892.

AGRICULTURAL HOMESTEAD SELECTIONS, SETTLED DISTRICT, 1868-76[20]

Category	Land Agents' Districts		
	Toowoomba	Warwick	Dalby
Number of selections	464	273	1
Acres	101,022	60,786	157
Acres cultivated	4,801	2,419	15
Acres enclosed for stock	47,414	26,986	—
Cattle	5,323	4,413	5
Sheep	58,974	11,134	—

the only crop produced on the agricultural frontiers of the new nations for which a world market existed. The cultivation of wheat was central to the agrarian mystique. Producing the 'staff of life' was the only true farming and in some way superior to all other forms of landed endeavour.[21] Judged by this criterion, however, settlement on the Downs failed to fulfil all the hopes of its paper and platform protagonists and would-be producers. In 1892 only 433,941 bushels of wheat were reaped from a mere 31,222 acres and nine-tenths of Queensland's wheat and flour requirements had to be imported.[22] Queensland even imported large quantities of other grains, dairy products and fodder from the southern colonies as the Downs was unequal to the task of satisfying the home market.

The failure of agriculture to keep pace with the expansion of other sectors of Queensland's economy had significant repercussions in the political sphere and helped nurture a belief that the 'best elements' of the colony were being swamped by powerful rural and urban interests with entirely different ideals, aims and needs. Although the political power of the 'Old Guard' Downs pastoralists was smashed by 1875, the Queensland squatters continued their advance into vast new regions, where the agrarian selector could not follow. When tensions developed between the old 'Black Soil Men' of the Downs and the newer squatters of the north and west, the former had succeeded in conserving most of their original interests. The spectacular growth of gold and tin mining after 1866 diversified exports, attracted a flock of new immigrants and modified the political structure. Its effect on the struggling agricultural industry was fairly limited, except in a few favoured areas. Paradoxic-

20 The situation was worse on the 970 Conditional Purchases where only 3,804 acres out of 655,112 were tilled. But 26,240 cattle and 284,495 sheep were carried. *QVP*, Vol. 3, (1877), p. 95. 'Report of the Under-Secretary for Lands'.

21 A. Koch, and W. Peden, (eds), *The Life and Selected Writings of Thomas Jefferson*, New York 1944, p. 282. This attitude has traditional Classical roots.

22 *SR*, 1892.

ally, the only agricultural product exported in significant quantities was sugar—a crop grown not by sturdy yeomen but by planter-capitalists on large estates worked by black labour that was anathema to the small farmers of the south. The Darling Downs, whose aspirations and problems were once so central in the colony's affairs, seemed to the agriculturalists to be perpetually shrinking in importance by comparison with the rapid development of other parts of Queensland.

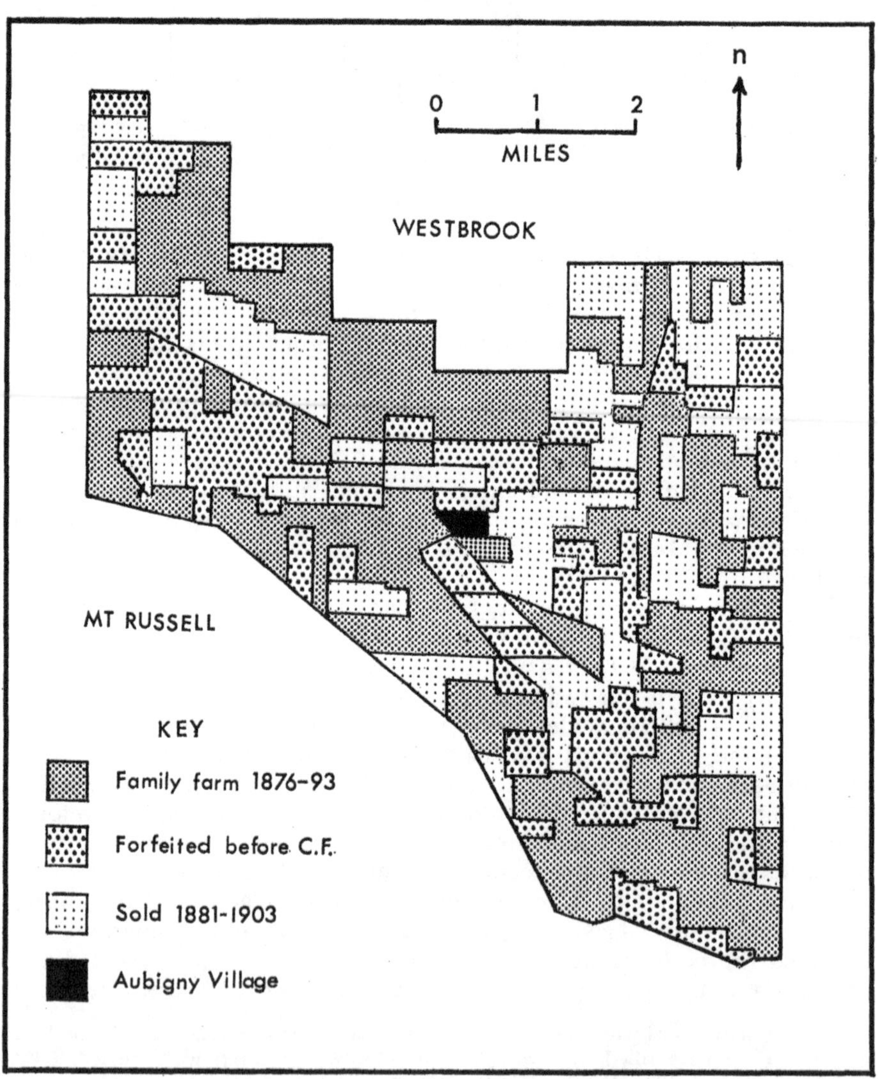

MAP 13 Westbrook homestead area: persistence of original small selectors of eighty acres, 1876-1903 (after *QGG*, 1876-89 and Queensland Electoral Roll, 1903)

Unlike the United States (where Jeffersonian concepts had triumphed with Jackson's Presidency) Queensland's dominant political values and ideas after Separation were formulated by a squatting oligarchy, entrenched on their vast stations and hostile to the concept of the yeoman farmer on his small selection. The squatters, wielding overwhelming political power, were a capitalistic-debtor class somewhat uneasily allied with the rising urban financial interests. The rural proletariat on the stations was powerless until the closing years of the century and was easily manipulated by the masters. The rapid rise of the larger towns, stimulated by assisted immigration, formulated needs and developed functions which seemed to clash with the desires of the country settlers. The expansion of Brisbane, the South Queensland metropolis, seemed to confirm the worst fears of the selectors. Such antagonisms are endemic in rural communities which consider that they are being exploited, crushed and mocked by the 'parasites' of the 'unhealthy cities'.

Jefferson's contention that 'the mobs of great cities add just so much to the support of pure government as sores do to the strength of the human body' was echoed on the Downs and strengthened in Australia by the unique concentration of population in several huge towns.[23] The Irish priest at Warwick, J. J. Horan, only articulated current rural thought when he declared that the moral health of the colony depended upon the rural yeoman and 'not the delicate and sometimes degenerate townsfolk'. Men of the soil, he continued, 'are more honest, less criminal and not as poverty stricken as those in the cities'. For the good of the country, asserted Horan, a large class of cultivators must be established on the Downs. Horan then went on to exhort his Catholic Celts to practise those supposedly Calvinistic virtues so necessary for survival in an age when economic relationships were assuming an ever-growing importance in the hearts and affairs of selectors.[24]

These crude Downs expressions of agrarian justification and ideology, matters of faith rather than fact, were expanded by Arthur Morgan when he maintained that the rural population was the only true productive force in Queensland:

> I do not mean the city people, whom some member well compared to drones; they are not really workers; they produce nothing; they are simply useful machines for paying taxes. It is the miner, the pastoralist, and the farmers who produce the wealth on which these people live and grow fat.[25]

That a yeomanry was automatically morally and physically 'healthier' than other sections and a strong stabilizing force against those urban elements who traditionally upset established notions of belief, institutions and property was widely believed.

23 Koch and Peden, *Thomas Jefferson*, p. 280.

24 *WA*, 30 August 1884, p. 2, c. 5-6. Horan had just taken up a large Allora selection which he intended to cultivate with tenant labour.

25 *QPD*, Vol. 55, (1888), p. 405.

. . . there are no measures more conservative, or more conducive to the maintenance of order in society, than those which facilitate the acquisition of property in land by those who cultivate it.[26]

Not only was the establishment of yeomanry a 'safety-valve' for accumulating urban distress but, as Archbishop Dunne stated, 'a man with a few acres of land is unlikely to become a socialist'.[27] Furthermore, the rural elements were 'the true supporters of their country, and the stock from which its best defenders must be drawn'.[28] These alone were the true Australians 'devoted to hearth and home' and not to the 'spurious nationalism of the town'.[29]

Obviously the agrarian spokesman did not really believe that their urban existence made them inferior beings. They were justified in assuming that closer settlement would ultimately bring a powerful reinforcement to the rights of property but they were unprepared for the practical consequences of the concepts they had so sedulously propounded once the so-called yeomen had established themselves and developed a spirit of class-consciousness. Then the old myths, solidly reinforced by economic interest, were used against their original promoters.

Humanity on the Downs was no different from anywhere else in the colonies. Larrikinism, larceny and libertarianism were not monopolized by the cities.[30] Civilizations are urban manifestations for it is not the 'children of the soil' who have developed the highest form of human endeavour. In fact, the nineteenth-century tendency was to replace these traditional rural values, for which the agrarians hoped they were providing the setting, with the more empirical and radical theories of the towns. Few new ideas ever germinated in the country and this one-way traffic was greatly accelerated by modern communications and technology.[31]

The advocates of yeoman farming in Queensland had no past golden age to draw inspiration from and were forced to borrow very heavily from the eighteenth-century English theorists, Continental idealists and North American experiences. In all cases the ideals of the articulates—the followers of Lang—were adopted as the guiding principles for the new agricultural interest in Queensland that was to spring into life once

26 *BC*, 9 January 1877, p. 2, c. 4-5.

27 *QPD*, Vol. 65, (1891), p. 1892; *BC*, 28 August 1878, p. 2, c. 5-6 and *QVP*, Vol. 4, (1892), pp. 59-204. 'Report of the Select Committee on Assisted Land Settlement'.

28 B. H. Hibbard, *A History of the Public Land Policies*, New York 1939, p. 143. This quotes Thomas Hart Benton, the great advocate of free land, whose influence on Australian land legislation, like those of other Americans, was not insignificant. *QPD*, Vol. 65, (1891), p. 1890.

29 *BC*, 15 April 1873, p. 3, c. 3; L. F. Heydon, *The Morris-Ranken Report*, Sydney 1883, p. 7; H. Mortymer Franklyn, *A Glance at Australia in 1880*, Melbourne 1881, pp. 120, 139.

30 The town and city, however, were magnets for individuals with anti-social tendencies. Isolated farms offered little scope for certain 'group activities'.

31 P. H. Johnstone, 'Old Ideals versus New Ideals in Farm Life', *United States Department of Agriculture Yearbook*, Part I, Washington 1940, p. 148.

the necessary legislation had been enacted.[32] Self-sufficiency, rural equality, the ennobling quality of country toil and the delightful freedom from the blatant commercialism of urban life were all contributions that were essential to the 'health' of the new colony. In fact, 'to transform pastoral territory into agricultural territory is an advance towards civilization'.[33] This doctrine, which implies that true 'progress' means the creation of a class intrinsically superior to all others—'the chosen people', as Jefferson described them—has also generally been accepted by historians of Australian land settlement. Most rather arbitrary estimates of the success or failure of colonial legislation have assumed that this goal was not only the most desirable but the only alternative to a permanent 'Bunyip aristocracy'. Conventional 'Whig interpreters' have accepted the ostensible aims of the agrarians without question. These assumptions, not necessarily wholly false, but sometimes founded on insufficient evidence, have hindered a more impartial and deeper examination of the actual problem involved and of other alternatives which might have been introduced with fewer 'evil results'.[34]

By the time that agricultural settlement was remotely possible in Queensland, farming could only be attractive if conducted on a commercial basis. Selectors had to earn a cash income in order to survive. Unfortunately for these guinea-pigs, many years elapsed before profitable agriculture was possible on the Downs. The homesteader was forced to make up the difference between subsistence and a cash income by taking part-time jobs and producing wool and meat that were always marketable. Thus the problems he faced when he tried to achieve a cash surplus moved closer to those experienced by the squatter whom he was supplanting in the supposed interests of the colony.

Some selectors, particularly the Germans, managed to survive and even thrive on a subsistence level, but most farmers were not prepared to accept such hardships for any length of time. They had not emigrated for this. All had been assured that the realization of the dreams of material betterment was merely a matter of 'energy, perseverance, and ordinary prudence' coupled with the exercise of other traditional rural virtues.[35] These, they soon discovered, were no longer enough in an expanding capitalistic economy. In any case, the self-sufficiency that some achieved was more often the result of poor communications and the absence of markets than of any inherent desire to permanently exist in such a condition.

What the propagators of the rural idyll failed to realize, or were not yet prepared to concede, was that mixed pastoral and agricultural farming on relatively large selections was the only way in which their yeoman protégés could flourish. A few pioneers on 40-acre and 80-acre

32 J. D. Lang, *Queensland, Australia,* London 1861, pp. 231-2, 278-9.

33 Speech by Hodgkinson, Minister for Mines: *QPD,* Vol. 65, (1891), p. 1886.

34 S. H. Roberts, *History of Australian Land Settlement,* Melbourne 1924, pp. 246-52 and C. J. King, *An Outline of Closer Settlement in New South Wales,* Sydney 1949.

35 Richard Daintree, *Queensland, Australia,* London n.d. [1873], pp. 42, 107 and Price Fletcher, (ed.), *Queensland, Its Resources and Institutions,* Brisbane 1886, p. 3.

'cabbage patches' survived and prospered but their success was attributable to favourable locational factors rather than to the possession of superior virtues. Most farmers were quick to abandon the practical implications of the agrarian ideals while tenaciously retaining for present comfort and future action the more invalid 'moral principles' which stemmed from them. The legislators, however, were extremely slow to make the modifications which the harsh experiences of the Downs agriculturalists had shown to be necessary.

The thesis that the urban middle-classes attempted to break the political and economic power of the squatters by the introduction of radical land legislation, while an over-simplification of the issues involved and neglectful of the very real belief in agrarian ideals of many of the protagonists, is supported by the fact that the practical concern of the former for the settlers dwindled once they had obtained their land. The selectors were left alone to cope with a harsh and unique physical and economic environment.[36]

Nevertheless Baker tends to exaggerate the clash between the squatters themselves and the final importance of the political alliance between them and the urban *bourgeoisie*. Conversely, he discounts the very real ideological conflict among the radical theorists who, however misguided in terms of contemporary economic realities, hoped to recreate equality of opportunity and by doing so provide rural Australia with a viable alternative to a squatting oligarchy. So far as Queensland and the Downs are concerned Baker's thesis underestimates the critical need for land revenue in the 'sixties and the catalytic role of the country town in formulating, expressing and representing rural needs and opinions.

Yet the doctrine that the yeoman farmer was the ideal man and the model citizen was not only a convenient shibboleth for the politician at the hustings or in the Legislative Assembly. This concept was implicit in the thoughts and attitudes of the small selectors themselves. It never, however, gained the acceptance and influence that the convict-based myths of the pastoral proletariat—the 'Australian legend'—achieved. Cockatoo farmers were figures of fun to townsfolk and derided by the pastoral workers and such radical journals as the *Bulletin* which were actively propagating a national religion on the basis of a relatively declining section. Even 'Dad' became prosperous and 'respectable' at last—the antithesis of the itinerant bushworker with his 'mateship', contempt for law and order and indifference, even hatred, towards property. The successful farmers were too close, socially and economically, to the great middle classes of the cities for their ideals to be seriously considered. Their rural ideology never 'became the most important basic component of the national *mystique*' as did that of the bushmen.[37] Yet both sets of attitudes had equal validity to those who

[36] D. W. A. Baker, 'The Origins of Robertson's Land Acts', *Historical Studies*, Vol. 8, No. 30, May 1958, p. 166 and A. A. Morrison, 'The Town Liberal and the Squatter', *JRQHS*, Vol. 4, No. 5, December 1962, p. 599.

[37] R. Ward, *The Australian Legend*, p. 5. *Also*, pp. 1-12, 221-40.

held them. Suitably romanticized, the bush *ethos* could appeal to most sections: to property, which could ignore its collectivism and theoretically subscribe to the image of the 'true Australian', and to the urban working classes which welded bush to asphalt in their own search for identity and economic security.[37a]

Yet the actual position of the selectors, with their individual and collective problems, triumphs and hardships, was for long hidden by the trumpetings of the urban agrarians and the bitter derision and conservatism of the threatened Downs pastoralists. Not until the turn of the century when selectors' sons such as Henry Lawson and Steele Rudd wrote of the would-be farmers with a sympathetic but wry, sardonic and often devastating realism, did the small men gain some of the recognition that their individual battles merited.[38] One critic has even claimed that 'Dad' that 'human old cocky . . . will be accepted as one of our Founding Fathers'. And why not? But this short period of brilliant portrayal was soon succeeded by the sentimental and unrevealing 'success stories' of their imitators. Possible interpreters turned their backs on the family farm. Rudd himself, son of a Welsh selector, was conscious that his Downs creations soon lost their earthly reality and richness. His tragedy was that, perceiving the stark, unattractive truth, he was unable to tell it. Caught by the seductive demands of urban success he exploited the farcical in his farmers. Yet he was always aware of the rich vein of deep human experiences that was available to him from his childhood at Emu Creek. 'I don't think comedy's my line', he once said. 'If I would let myself go I'd be gloomier than Lawson at his worst.' But he never really let himself go.[39] The golden age of the Australian selector has never been celebrated in poetry, prose and song as have the halcyon days of the outback pastoral workers. Soon it was too late for the selectors' own myths and real, equally valid experiences to be described and interpreted in a way that might have made a significant contribution to the national beliefs and illusions. The Australian farming middle-class never found its Tom Collins.

While the Downs farmers repudiated the 'Australian Legend's' egalitarianism once they had obtained their land, they did have some characteristics in common with the bushworkers. Many of them had emerged

[37a] The farmers certainly seem to have had the best of the bargain when they mentally exchanged mateship for respectability: secure in the belief that they had retained the valuable attributes of the Australian agricultural pioneer, they could afford to smile at their national image. This group of knockabout 'Dads' may have been laughable figures to urban sophisticates but their development of tremendous political strength, far beyond their real economic and numerical importance, has given satisfaction to the rural actors and not the urban audience.

[38] V. Palmer, 'Steele Rudd', *Overland*, No. 15, July 1959, pp. 21-2. No contemporary novelist of lasting stature emerged from the Downs or from any other part of farming Australia to sensitively interpret that unique 'combination of physical and spiritual experience' which the selectors underwent. Hamlin Garland, Willa Cather, W. A. White and O. E. Rölvaag perceptively and movingly examined the small settlers of the American Prairie States, but their counterparts were absent from the Australian scene.

[39] Palmer, 'Steele Rudd', p. 22.

from that group and attitudes could not be discarded with the swag. They shared its taciturnity, scepticism of intellectual and cultural pursuits, and talent for improvisation. These, however, were not unique manifestations of rural Australia. They were common to most Anglo-Saxon farming communities. The problems involved in mastering the environment, however, reinforced a sardonic, cynical, quasi-fatalistic attitude that was generally absent in New Zealand and North America, where the bulk of the selectors were not so sharply confronted by the perversities of nature. Hopes were usually deferred on marginal land.

The agrarian myth harmonized particularly well with the beliefs of the numerous free Irish immigrants to whom a small farm with its cultivation patch and tiny herd or flock was paradise indeed after the unbearable conditions in rural Ireland.[40] 'Our clear aim', maintained O'Sullivan, 'is a peasant proprietary in the Irish Tradition.'[41] Moreover, the agrarian ideal accorded with many of the social teachings of the Roman Catholic church to which most of the Irish selectors adhered.[42]

The frugal, hard-working and socially cohesive German element which provided more successful farmers in proportion to its numbers than any other national group, also regarded itself, in the early years at least, as a triumphant illustration of the validity of agrarian ideals. The Darling Downs with its cheap, rich land was an excellent nursery for those virtues which Isambert quoted as the finest features of the German peasantry from which most of the immigrants had been drawn:

> . . . all the members of the family . . . join in the glorious task of providing for their maintenance by their own free labour on their own free farms. No slave will or could work so hard . . . in order not to become dependent on others. And . . . these peasants, being inured by arduous labour to great endurance, in time of war generally render the best account in the defence of 'home, hearth, and beauty'.[43]

It is typical of rural communities that they tend to focus their grievances on particular groups which are held, rightly or wrongly, responsible for all their misfortunes and lack of economic success. The North American agrarians continually blamed the exploitation of eastern industrial capitalism and, later, the nefarious practices of the railroads

40 R. D. Edwards and T. D. Williams, (ed.), *The Great Famine—Studies in Irish History 1845-52*, New York 1957.

41 *QPD*, Vol. 23, (1877), p. 259.

42 The emergence of the National Catholic Rural Movement in the present century represents a return to the concept of the family farm as a bastion of faith and peasant virtues. Its practical achievements, however, have so far been limited and model Catholic group settlements have not multiplied to any great extent. T. A. Warren, 'Catholic Rural Policy in Australia', *unpublished B. A. thesis*, University of Queensland, pp. 38-42. Quoted by T. Truman, *Catholic Action and Politics*, Melbourne (rev. ed.) 1960, pp. 37-41, 131.

43 *QVP*, Vol. 2, (1886), p. 1110. Reprint of a letter from J. Isambert, German-born MLA for Rosewood, to S. W. Griffith opposing the leasehold principles of the 1884 Land Act, 6 May 1886. *QVP*, Vol. 4, (1892), 'Report of the Select Committee on Assisted Land Settlement'. Evidence of Heinrich L. E. Ruthning, pp. 119-21.

for the recurring economic depressions. In the Australian colonies the natural enemy was the squatter. It was perhaps inevitable that the powerful Downs squatters should be identified with past oppressors in the mother countries and regarded as 'malefactors of great wealth' impeding natural progress. By their personal petty persecutions and collective hostility towards the selectors many of the old 'grass dukes' aroused hatreds and opprobrium that poisoned squatter-selector relationships until the last of the Downs runholders had disappeared forever. This conflict was encouraged by the city and country-town 'liberals' who fished long and profitably in these muddy waters.

The Classical-cum-Jeffersonian idea that the 'small landholders are the most precious part of the State' was a concept which the squatters totally rejected.[44] They knew that they and not the agrarians were the true 'backbone of the country' and that the geography of Queensland would sustain this pre-eminence for generations to come.[45] On the other hand, the selectors were supplicants, handicapped by their inferior economic and numerical status and unable to demonstrate in a practical and conclusive fashion that their calling was uniquely important and essential to the well-being of the colony. In a sense, many struggling selectors were the victims of beliefs and suppositions that were not of their making and which were supplying a rickety theoretical basis for a hasty redistribution of limited landed resources. With too few regional modifications, all areas of nineteenth-century Anglo-Saxon agrarian settlement suffered from attempts to create a prosperous yeomanry by Act of Parliament. It was both tragic for the individual victims and unfortunate for the countries and colonies concerned that the process of adaptation was generally a long and painful one and that the solutions to national and local agrarian problems came too late to be of use to many disillusioned selectors. The Darling Downs' halting agricultural development convincingly confirmed the truth of the old New Zealand saying that 'the first selector breaks both heart and body, his successor is financially ruined, but the third farmer reaps handsome financial rewards and retires to the city to live on the proceeds from the sale of unearned increment'.

The basic argument of the agrarians was that of Locke: land is the common stock of society to which every man has a right and labour expended in cultivating the soil automatically confers title to it. Governments were created to protect property and the farms of the yeomen had a superior claim to all other forms of landed endeavour to be fostered and guarded by the State.[46]

44 Koch and Peden, *Thomas Jefferson*, p. 377.

45 'The New State of Augustus glorified the strong and stubborn peasants of Italy, laboriously winning from the cultivation of cereals a meagre substance for himself and a numerous virile offspring.' Yet, in spite of Virgil, the supreme poet and advocate for rural life, 'Italy was spared the realization of such perverse anachronisms'. R. Syme, *The Roman Revolution*, Oxford 1951, pp. 450-1.

46 M. Salvadori (ed.), *Locke and Liberty, Selections from the Work of John Locke*, London 1960, pp. 153-61 and R. I. Aaron, *John Locke*, Oxford 1937, pp. 279-83.

The Free Soil Democrats incorporated such thinking in their 1852 land policy:

> That all men have a natural right to a portion of the soil; and that, as the use of the soil is indispensable to life, the right of all men to the soil is as sacred as their right to life itself . . . the public lands . . . should be granted . . . free of cost, to landless settlers.[47]

Lilley's statement suggests that these concepts were also adopted by the Queensland radicals:

> . . . I hold that the State is not a merchant selling land, but a trustee holding it for equitable distribution among the people, so that it may be occupied and cultivated.[48]

This principle was reinforced by Queensland interpretations of the utilitarianism of John Stuart Mill which were implicit in all land legislation. The only justification for private property in land was the improvements made by the proprietor and of these, cultivation was by far the most valuable.[49] Swift's battered dictum that 'he who can grow two blades of grass where one was grown before, is a benefactor of mankind' was modified by the contention that 'the real value of land for the people is its capacity for settlement' and that the object was not to make one man rich but many men happy.[50] Rural happiness was the only true happiness which sinful mankind could achieve.

Mill's early opinions in favour of a peasant proprietary were widely quoted in Queensland and influenced 'advanced radicals' who were attempting to settle small farmers on the Downs.[51] The physical and economic structure, combined with Queensland's historical background, prevented any such transplanting of specialized European institutions. Furthermore, unlike conditions in North America where pastoralism, if it existed at all, was generally weak and short-lived in areas favourable for agriculture, the major problem confronting the infant colony was how to *transfer* interest in the land, not *establish* it. This invalidated much of the second strand of thought influencing Queensland policy—free homesteads on the American model. The United States Act of 1862 had a profound effect on Queensland policy. Groom, the foremost Downs agrarian, successfully inserted homestead clauses in the 1868 Act and often acknowledged his debt to America.[52]

Roberts has asserted that Queensland's unique pioneering in land policy placed her far ahead of other colonies. Although he was aware that the Acts had failed to stimulate agricultural settlement to the extent

47 Quoted by Hibbard, *Public Land Policies*, p. 357. H. S. Commager, *The Era of Reform, 1830-1860*, Princeton 1960, pp. 123-4. ('Vote Yourself a Farm'.)

48 *QPD*, Vol. 5, (1867), p. 427.

49 J. S. Mill, *Principles of Political Economy*, (new edition), London 1923; *QPD*, Vol. 5, (1867), pp. 427-9 and Vol. 23, (1877), p. 259.

50 *The Week*, 22 April 1876, p. 396 and *TC*, 30 November 1878, p. 3, c. 1-2.

51 Mill, *Political Economy*, 1848 ed., pp. 301-406.

52 *QPD*, Vol. 5, (1867), pp. 19, 423.

desired, he yet held that their theoretical basis was sound and admirable. The 1868 Act, he maintained:

. . . was twenty years in advance of the legislation of other Australian colonies, and embodied the provisions which they adopted piecemeal during the eighties . . . Queensland had become noted for the range of her experiments, many of them successful, all with good qualities. The State had gone far in land matters.[53]

Revolutionary features in Queensland legislation, however—the institution of easy terms for land and the restriction of free selection to specially proclaimed Agricultural Reserves and the resumed portions of pastoral leases—were prompted more by necessity than utilitarian convictions. Some legislators genuinely wanted a farming class to dethrone the Downs oligarchy. All Queensland radicals, whatever their motives, were forced to offer most generous terms in order to attract 'desirable' migrants to a new and distant colony with unique and unknown disabilities.[54] The most desirable class, men with adequate capital and experience, refused to invest money and labour in Downs farms. Squatting and storekeeping gave far better returns. And not only financial returns. Social and political rewards were greater for those who could choose to avoid the hard and dull routine of agricultural pioneering. Until the 'nineties, too, there was considerable social mobility in the colonies. On the Downs, there is some evidence to suggest that a tightening of opportunities for the sons of successful farmers stimulated the development of that rural radicalism which produced both the Farmers' Alliance and the shearing strikes. But this was later. Generally, only comparatively poor men took up selections.

In spite of paper precautions, the effect of ostensibly radical legislation was to place most Downs leaseholders in an unassailable position by enabling them to freehold large areas on virtually the same terms as the small selectors. Yet the devices used to evade the law fade into insignificance before the wholesale use of the pre-emptive right between 1858 and 1876. 305,309 acres of the finest land on the Downs were lost for small settlement in this way. Pre-emption not only curtailed the quantity of first-class land that was available for selection near markets and water, forcing many later selectors on to 'timbered slopes and waterless ridges', but it also enabled interested politicians to raise the cry of 'land hunger' when this was not really the basic problem facing those who were trying to establish commercial agriculture in the region.[55]

Excellent land was never short on the Downs during 1860-93 but few established or intending farmers had either the capital or the inclination to purchase private land at current rates when there was so much adjacent pastoral country available for selection. It was hoped and

53 Roberts, *Australian Land Settlement*, p. 252.

54 *QPD*, Vol. 5, (1867), p. 425.

55 *QVP*, Vol. 2, (1874), pp. 562-7. 'Return of Pre-emptive Purchases by Lessees of Runs.' *DDG*, 29 March 1869, p. 3, c. 1; *TC*, 8 January 1876, p. 2, c. 5-6 and *QPD*, Vol. 20, (1876), pp. 576-7. Groom castigated pre-emption as 'one of the most vicious systems ever introduced'. ibid., p. 576.

finally assumed by expanding grain-growers that the State would repurchase private land and resell it on more favourable terms once the so-called 'land famine' became too acute and political pressure was applied.

Their belief was justified. Between 1877 and 1882 a series of 'land exchanges' whereby the freehold squatters transferred 49,278 acres of agricultural land to the Crown for subsequent selection in return for 87,032 acres of pastoral country took place.[56] The largest exchange took place in June 1878. Edward Wienholt of Goomburra surrendered 20,611 acres at Allora in return for 41,222 acres on Jondaryan.[57] These exchanges, the result of direct storekeeper-selector pressure, were eventually successful although subsequent events showed that upset prices had been too high.[58]

Apart from the inevitable parochial jealousies aroused by these transactions—Dalby interests considered that the proposal 'is fraught with the most disastrous consequences to the present and future commercial welfare and prosperity of the town'—the suspicion remains that some exchanges were designed to aid supporters of the current Ministry.[59] The squatters did not lose by such transactions. Nevertheless, while it is significant that such deals took place so soon after settlement, they did provide a precedent for the fruitful State Repurchase Scheme inaugurated in 1894.

Repurchase was also a confession that yeomanry policies failed on the Downs.[60] During 1871 the repurchase of Westbrook was advocated and in 1881 and 1885 Kates unsuccessfully attempted to pass Parliamentary appropriations for land purchase. In 1891 a Government Bill was discharged after an inconclusive debate.[61]

Familiar arguments were advanced on the Downs in favour of such a scheme. It would increase the number of yeoman cultivators, provide them with first-class land on easier terms than they could privately obtain, satisfy squatters and their creditors by distributing lump cash or debenture payments, and act as a 'safety-valve' in times of depression and

[56] Appendix VI gives a list of the more important Exchanges. *QVP*, Vol. 2, (1878), p. 271 and Vol. 2, (1881), p. 149.

[57] *QVP*, Vol. 3, (1877), pp. 183-90 and *WA*, 29 November 1877, p. 2, c. 6.

[58] *WA*, 29 August 1878, p. 5, c. 1 and 21 March 1878, p. 2, c. 3.

[59] *QVP*, Vol. 2, (1879), pp. 249-50. 'Dalby Petition on the Irvingdale, Jondaryan, East Prairie and Allora Land Exchanges.' Earlier Exchanges were invalidated by legal opinion. These were even more favourable to the squatters who 'felt that they were doing the country a service'. *QVP*, Vol. 2, (1874), pp. 481-528. For critical comments on the political implications of these transactions *see*: *QPD*, Vol. 29, (1879), pp. 549-50, 624-5.

[60] And in the other colonies as well. All Australian colonies eventually followed the New Zealand and South Australian examples. W. P. Reeves, *State Experiments in Australia and New Zealand*, Vol. I, London 1902, pp. 271-98.

[61] Groom pioneered this innovation. *QPD*, Vol. 13, (1871-2), pp. 115-31; *WE&T*, 14 March 1874, p. 2, c. 1-2; *QPD*, Vol. 35, (1881), pp. 523-40 and Vol. 46, (1885), pp. 394-419; *TC*, 25 August 1885, p. 2, c. 1; *WA*, 8 August 1885, p. 2, c. 2 and *QPD*, Vol. 65, (1891), pp. 1383-7, 1802-1905.

bubbling unrest.[62] That most of the large freeholders were willing to sell to the State is confirmed by the rush to offer low-priced estates and the initial absence of compulsory purchase. By 1900, fifteen Downs properties aggregating 140,000 acres had been purchased from thirteen proprietors for £335,000–two-thirds cash. In only three cases was more than £2. 15s. 6d. per acre paid–452 agricultural leases were issued.[63] Previous attempts at private disposal, particularly by the Clifton syndicate, had partly failed through the resultant damage to the entire security, caused by such piecemeal disposal, the strict terms imposed and the prevailing depression.[64] State Repurchase solved the dilemma of redistribution to the satisfaction of the pastoralists, their creditors and the farmers.

Opponents for long delayed this necessary legislation. Most Liberals supported the concept in theory but not in practice; the innovation whereby the State invested in, rather than sold, Crown land was too great to be absorbed at once. They were joined by the outside squatters who maintained that this 'purely Darling Downs measure' was designed to relieve the freeholders of their financial obligations and to enhance the value of the remaining estates. As a result of the 'natural law of supply and demand' these properties would be automatically subdivided when land values rose and farmers really needed them.[65]

> . . . these artificial attempts (to restore prosperity) sapped the springs of self-reliance which is the only source of permanent progress.[66]

Nelson called the scheme an unwanted interference in private enterprise and an unwarrantable extension of governmental power. Millions of acres were still available and settlement had failed through adverse seasons and low prices rather than through the shortage of land. The 'credit of the colony' in London would be injured if loan funds were diverted to such a risky undertaking.[67]

These criticisms were reactionary and nonsensical. Repurchase was an outstanding success. Yet in some ways it marked a repudiation of past faith in the merits of the very small man. Settlers with experience and capital took up large, economic units suited to the physical characteristics of the area. The legislators had temporarily learned some lessons from past failures.

Apart from the competition for basic resources between squatters and agrarians, another fundamental conflict raged between the claims of the Treasury and the official colonial policy of encouraging agriculture. Treasurers naturally preferred assured squatting rents and huge land sales to a plethora of £5 rents from hundreds of poor selectors.[68] Rapid

62 ibid.
63 *QVP*, Vol. 2, (1917), p. 563.
64 *TC*, 29 January 1891, p. 2, c. 7-8.
65 *QPD*, Vol. 65, (1891), p. 1883.
66 *Pastoralists' Review*, Vol. 3, No. 9, 16 November 1893, p. 413.
67 *QPD*, Vol. 65, (1891), pp. 1883-4.
68 *BC*, 30 April 1879, p. 2, c. 3-4.

deferred payment alienations reduced the area of valuable land that could be sold for auction in times of financial crisis, and made nonsense of attempts to apply Wakefield's 'sufficient price' theory in Queensland. Lamb, Minister for Lands when the 1868 Bill was passed, was 'previously a disciple of Wakefield' and had known the prophet personally.[69] In any case the 'sacred principle' that land revenue should be used solely to promote immigration and reproductive public works was neglected in a colony obsessed with cheap British loans. That the Wakefield scheme was, in spite of the Benthamite and even mercantilist beliefs of its synthesist, a sociological rather than a scientific attempt to recreate in the colonies a fast vanishing and increasingly irrelevant eighteenth century squirearchy, is confirmed by an examination of its Queensland impact. Wakefield's main contribution was psychological rather than practical. He provided the colonial agrarian theorists with a seemingly logical framework supporting arguable proposals. These were useful oral weapons although the original oligarchic mystique with all its hated symbols and economic conservatism which Wakefield felt could only be preserved in the colonies, was anathema to the 'liberals'. Wakefield sought preservation, conservation and subservience: the colonials demanded opportunity. Both, however, looked to the soil rather than to the sheep. Furthermore, even if Wakefield intended to artificially 'manufacture wage workers' for British capitalists to exploit, the doctrine of the sufficient price made little allowance for varied geographical conditions.[70] On the Downs, one pound per acre in a lump sum was at once too dear for the intending agriculturalist and, as future events proved, too costly for the pastoralist. As a means of both assisting settlement and raising revenue it was, when incompletely applied, a total failure.[71]

Auction sales of homestead land were re-introduced in 1876 with the hope that 'those who give the highest price for land will also make the best use of it' and that a high rate of settlement could be combined with 'the maximum of revenue'.[72] This proposal which 'stank in the nostrils of the people of the Darling Downs' aroused intense opposition.[73] Those auctions actually held, however, failed to raise prices as selectors came to prior arrangements before the sale, bought off opposition and kept land values down to homestead rates.[74]

There is no question that intending settlers on the Downs were able to obtain land on terms which compared more than favourably with those in other colonies:

69 *QPD*, Vol. 5, (1867), p. 318 and *DDG*, 19 August 1876, p. 2, c. 3.

70 K. Marx, *Capital*, Vol. II, London 1930 ed., pp. 848-58; J. S. Marais, *The Colonization of New Zealand*, London 1927; M. Turnbull, 'The Colonization of New Zealand by the New Zealand Company, 1839-43', *unpublished thesis*, Oxford 1957.

71 *DDG*, 19 August 1876, p. 2, c. 3.

72 ibid.

73 *WA*, 24 August 1876, p. 2, c. 1.

74 *QVP*, Vol. 2, (1881), p. 142. 'Report of the Under-Secretary for Lands.' *BC*, 30 October 1880, p. 4, c. 5 and *QPD*, Vol. 20, (1877), p. 577.

CROWN LAND PRICES, 1860-84[75]

Land Act	Price
Acts of 1860 and 1863	£1 per acre upset price.
'Leasing' Act of 1866	Deferred payments: 2s. 6d. per acre over eight years.
Act of 1868	1. Auction lands Suburban: £1 per acre upset price Country: 15s. per acre upset. 2. Homesteads 3s. 9d. per acre: five annual payments of 9d. per acre for ag. land and 6d. per acre for pastoral. 3. Conditional purchases Agricultural land 15s. per acre 10 x 1s. 6d. annual payments. First-class pastoral 10s. per acre 10 x 1s. annual payments. Second-class pastoral 5s. per acre 10 x 6d. annual payments.
Land Act of 1876	1. Homesteads 2s. 6d. per acre. Five annual payments of 6d. per acre = £10 for 80 acres. 2. Conditional purchases To be fixed by Proclamation for each area at not less than 5s. per acre with 10 annual payments. All lands could be auctioned and upset prices raised.
Land Act of 1884	1. Agricultural farms Minus 160 acres: 2s. 6d. per acre after five years residence. Plus 160 acres: £1 per acre (later 10s. per acre). 2. Grazing farms Perpetual lease at reassessed rentals.

This provision of cheap land on easy terms reduced capital costs and enabled poor, landless men to take up small selections. As in New South Wales and Victoria, the great defects of the Acts have hampered impartial considerations of their solid achievements. The complete collapse of the Land Order system, however, indicated that newly-arrived immigrants without capital and experience were unwilling to take up land in the interior. This would mean economic suicide. Quite understandably, most accepted the cash offers of the brokers.[76]

75 This table is constructed from the original Acts in: *Queensland Statutes*, Brisbane 1860-84. Survey and deed fees were extra charges.

76 The Treasury lost £8 on every £20 order. *QPD*, Vol. 18, (1875), p. 141 and *QVP*, Vol. 2, (1867), pp. 958-60. 'Report from the Select Committee on Selections in Agricultural Reserves.'

II *The Selectors*

Few homesteaders took up land on the Downs with the express intention of capitalizing on the difference between the low rent (which eventually became the purchase price) and the market value of the land. Many conditional purchasers, however, could not resist attractive offers from pastoralists. A 320-acre selection costing £250 to freehold might fetch over £1,000 in cash and the temptation to sell was often irresistible. These 'traitors to their order' first appeared about 1872.[77] This coincided with the increasing release of Crown land which was then only fitted for grazing.

> . . . there is a method in this madness, . . . there is a greater desire to interpose between the resident squatter and the Treasury than to sit down and fertilize barren ridges with the never-ending sweat of unrewarded toil.[78]

The tendency to 'look upon the selection more as a chattel to be realized upon than as a farm to be used' was checked after 1883 when the margin between freehold and leasehold land narrowed following bad seasons and low prices.[79] Some squatters, aware that the value of their mortgaged security was falling, shuddered at the thought of acquiring more expensive land. Such speculation challenged the whole basis of agrarian thought. Selectors could never claim that their close communion with the soil had bestowed superior moral qualities upon them:

> Homestead and resident selectors have been the pets of administrators and of the public, not because they can lay claim to any personal merits of industry or morality, nor to any determined love of sacrificing themselves on the altars of their country, but because . . . there was a general agreement that in serving their own interests they must of necessity serve also the interests of the whole community . . . It has become patent that nothing but a very extraordinary love for the soil will prevent any man . . . from entering into a bargain to sell it.[80]

This characteristic New World tendency to speculate in land was encouraged by a freehold tenure and the rapid and cheap Torrens transfer system. Farmers as well as pastoralists and townsfolk were extraordinarily mobile and land was considered to be just another piece of exploitable property. Excepting the Germans, most Downs farmers would have scorned the European concept that the soil was a trust which they held on behalf of the nation and not a private plot to be mined, denuded and sold at will.

The Queensland Land Acts which established strict conditions for deferred payment selectors also pioneered a new trend in Australasian land legislation. Land classification, the staggered resumption of runs and the creation of homestead areas were all intended to avoid the evils

77 *BC*, 13 January 1876, p. 2, c. 3-4.

78 ibid.

79 *QVP*, Vol. 2, (1881), p. 156. 'Report of the Under-Secretary for Lands.' ibid., Vol. 2, (1879), p. 218.

80 *Queenslander*, 8 January 1876, p. 4. For an unconvincing defence of these selector-speculators on the Downs *see TC*, 13 January 1876. p. 2, c. 5-7.

CERTIFICATE CONDITIONS, 1860-84[81]

Act	Conditions
Crown Land Alienation Act 1860	'Must commence to occupy, improve and cultivate after six months.'
Agricultural Reserves Act 1863	Declaration after twelve months that he has resided for six months, erected residence, fenced, and cultivated one-sixth of total area.
Selectors' Relief Act 1865	Cultivation regulation reduced to one-tenth the area leased.
Crown Lands Act 1868	Homesteads Continuous personal residence and cultivation of one-tenth of area. Certificate after three years. Conditional Purchases Continual residence in person or by bailiff. Improvements to value of 10s. 6d. per acre for agricultural or first-class pastoral land and 5s. for second-class pastoral *or* 'fence in whole with a good and substantial fence' *or* if agricultural, cultivate one-tenth. Certificate after three years.
Land Act of 1876	Homesteads Compulsory personal residence for five years. Improvements to the value of 10s. per acre (80 acres = £40). Certificate after three years. Conditional Purchases Personal residence (on Darling Downs) 10s. per acre 'on any necessary improvements during lease'. Certificate after three years.
'Exchanged' Land Act 1879	Homesteads as above but improvements to value of 20s. per acre.
Land Act of 1884	Agricultural Farms Less than 160 acres: improvements to value of 10s. per acre. More than 160 acres: improvements to value of 15s. per acre, *or* equivalent in fencing. Certificate after five years. Grazing Farms To be fenced within three years. Certificate after three years.

81 *Statutes of Queensland*, Brisbane 1860-84.

of unrestricted free selection already apparent in New South Wales and Victoria.[82]

Before they could obtain their certificates, selectors had to fulfil certain cultivation, residence and improvement conditions. These varied from Act to Act but were gradually eased for the genuine selector.

These elaborate regulations were more exacting than in other pioneer regions. New South Wales simply required personal residence on conditional purchases for three years and improvements worth £1 per acre while South Australia gradually moved closer to Queensland's laws.[83] The United States Homestead Act made personal residence for five years the sole condition for a freehold title but land could also be 'communited' by cash payment after six months.[84]

The enforcement of such conditions not only required elaborate machinery but also the selectors' consent and compliance as well as complete impartiality by the supervisors. For many homesteaders, these conditions seemed a crushing burden, demanding capital investments beyond their reach and more than one man's labour. Some requirements, however, were absolutely essential for the establishment of a viable farm. The State had virtually given the land to the selector: surely it was the duty of the latter to reciprocate and make his practical contribution to the fulfilment of the yeomanry ideal.

But it was soon discovered to be both politically inexpedient and economically impossible for any Government to enforce the conditions so far as the agricultural selectors were concerned. Apart from the complete failure of the cultivation conditions in several areas, a fact recognized by their abandonment in 1876, relief measures were passed in 1865 and 1878 which relaxed other requirements.[85] The capitalists could always fulfil or evade conditions and those who most frequently failed to perform their obligations were the residents.

> Had the law been stringently enforced in agricultural reserves, they would now be almost exclusively waste land. It is only by putting the most liberal interpretation on the conditions . . . that occupants have been able to pull through . . . if the laws were stringently carried out, a great number of selectors would be ruined.[86]

82 *New South Wales Votes and Proceedings of the Legislative Assembly*, 1883, Vol. II, pp. 71-164. *Victorian Parliamentary Papers*, 1878, Vol. III, No. 65, 'Progress Report on the Settlement of the Country under the Existing Land System'. For a similar area to the Downs in the United States *see* P. W. Gates, *Fifty Million Acres: Conflicts over Kansas Land Policy, 1854-1890*, Ithaca 1954, pp. 99-103, 240-2.

83 Epps, *Land Systems*, pp. 116-35.

84 Hibbard, *Public Land Policies*, pp. 385-6. By 'communiting', vast freeholds on the Downs model were built up in the Western States.

85 *QPD*, First Series, Vol. II, pp. 37-43, 367-77 and Vol. 26, (1878), pp. 726-8, 966-7; *BC*, 20 February 1878, p. 2, c. 4 and 21 February 1878, p. 2, c. 5. For a discussion of this question see the debates on the abortive Selectors' Relief Bill of 1869. *QPD*, Vol. 9, (1869), pp. 599, 793, 856.

86 *QVP*, Vol. 2, (1867), p. 925. 'Evidence of A. C. Gregory, Commissioner for Crown Lands, before the Select Committee on Selections in Agricultural Reserves.'

In 1887, forty-seven indignant selectors on the Allora Exchange, threatened with forfeiture for non-compliance, were reassured by personal and abject apologies from the Lands Minister who waived the action.[87]

Apart from this governmental reluctance strictly to enforce the law, the Lands Department and their regional officers were, in spite of much ill-informed and politically motivated criticism, genuinely concerned to stretch the regulations in favour of the strugglers. That they did this on a more liberal scale for the squatters as well is beside the point. Hume asserted that:

> . . . it is no exaggeration to say that not a week passes without the department committing an illegal act—but, be it noted, not for the purpose of adding to the burden of the selector, but to relieve it.[88]

In all cases, 'no action is taken . . . unless the Crown Bailiff has reported actual abandonment'.[89] The selectors always got a second chance and the forfeiture rate was not a true indication of the number who failed to comply. Furthermore, in spite of the Land Courts and increasingly effective personal inspection by officials, it was difficult to refuse the prized certificate if the selector and the 'credible witnesses' were prepared to perjure themselves. The machinery was elaborate but often ineffectual in the face of prevailing political, administrative and moral attitudes.

The key to bona fide agricultural settlement was insistence on personal continuous residence.[90] These clauses were occasionally evaded and were the subject of much criticism.[91] Agitation for their removal usually came from speculative storekeepers and lawyers and from selectors who either needed more land or were forced to leave their selection to earn regular wages.[92] The older children were often sent off to camp on distant selections. Yet certificates 'were never refused except in cases of flagrant deception' and it seems that this regulation was effective in preventing wholesale speculation by smallholders, stopping the abuses so prevalent in Victoria and New South Wales and compelling genuine settlement.[93]

The expenditure of £40 on an eighty-acre homestead was not a harsh condition but small graziers under the Act of 1876 had validly complained that the compulsory investment of 10s. per acre 'was a useless

87 *WE&T*, 30 November 1887, p. 2, c. 4 and *WA*, 22 October 1887, p. 2, c. 5-7. Their votes were needed at the next election.

88 *QVP*, Vol. 2, (1884), p. 1089. 'Hume Report'.

89 ibid., p. 1090.

90 *QPD*, Vol. 14, (1872), p. 798. Speech of Thompson, then Lands Minister. *See* the insistence on a personal residence clause in the 1879 Land Bill by Groom, Kates and Horwitz. *QPD*, Vol. 30, (1879), pp. 916-27.

91 *QVP*, Vol. 3, (1888), p. 347. 'Report of the Downs Lands Commissioner.'

92 *WE&T*, 30 May 1874, p. 2, c. 1 and *BC*, 8 June 1874, p. 3, c. 5.

93 *QVP*, Vol. 2, (1884), p. 1090. 'Hume Report.' So far as the squatters were concerned, however, we have seen that the residence condition was the easiest of all to evade. Old men could always be procured for the movable huts in return for rations, grog and tobacco. *See* the evidence of G. Thorn who had used this method on Warra Warra. *QPD*, Vol. 5, (1867), p. 424.

hardship'.[94] On a 1,280-acre East Prairie or Dalby grazing farm the Act expected the selector to spend £640 over three years. This was £260 more than competent judges estimated was necessary.[95] In 1884 a suggestion made in 1881 by the Under-Secretary for Crown Lands that this condition should be abolished and that compulsory fencing was the best possible guarantee of genuine intention was adopted.[96]

Finally, the problem of fulfilling the conditions was not a major obstacle in the path of the genuine selector. Rigid conditions and elaborate machinery were necessary to halt the techniques developed and practised by the squatters to circumvent the early Acts. Once the damage was done the restrictions effectively stopped further pastoral encroachment. Conditions were still needed, however, to prevent similar frauds by the 'honest yeomen'. They could be, and were, relaxed as the exigencies of the situation demanded. The agrarians obviously could not allow small settlements to fail through the harsh imposition of the very laws passed to advance it.

The best size for a family farm was a more difficult problem. A 40-acre farm was an estate indeed to the impoverished Irish or German immigrant but was useless for profitable settlement unless adjoining a town and on good, well-watered land. Few Agricultural Reserves or Homestead Areas met these requirements.[97] Stock were needed to diversify income and insure against climatic vagaries. Once more the selectors were the victims of the yeomanry complex. Goldsmith's romanticism, transferred to land legislation, contained 'a most dangerous fallacy':

> Time was, ere England's griefs began,
> That every rood of land maintained its man.[98]

Agrarians such as Douglas and James Morgan believed that a 'peasantry on small holdings was the backbone of the country' and that 'eighty acres, in possession of an industrious man, . . . was quite as much as he could attend to'.[99] But commercial success usually meant mixed farming on relatively large selections. 'No man could carry on agriculture successfully without being in some degree a grazing farmer', stated one politician, while another asserted that 'eighty acres was an inducement to the settler's children to go bushranging. Such a man must always . . . be poor.'[100]

This major yet unpalatable problem occurred in other countries and

[94] *QVP*, Vol. 2, (1881), p. 142.

[95] ibid., Vol. 2, (1884), p. 1090. 'Hume Report'.

[96] *QVP*, Vol. 2, (1881), p. 142 and Epps, *Land Systems*, p. 97.

[97] *WA*, 10 February 1883, p. 3, c. 4. Views of P. Higgins, farmer and publican of Swan Creek. For other comments on the size of farms, *see The Australasian*, 11 December 1880, p. 760; *QPD*, Vol. 18, (1875), pp. 97-8; *WE&T*, 2 September 1876, p. 2, c. 2; *WA*, 18 February 1882, p. 2, c. 1-2 and 2 September 1884, p. 2, c. 5-7.

[98] *BC*, 17 February 1877, p. 5, c. 6.

[99] *QPD*, Vol. 26, (1878), p. 869 and Vol. 29, (1879), p. 642.

[100] *QPD*, Vol. 23, (1877), p. 256 and p. 330.

colonies. The New South Wales Morris-Ranken Report reached the same conclusions. There, a blanket 40-320 (later 640) acreage had applied ever since free selection began.[101] The first eighty-acre men in South Australia did well but acreage for agricultural credit selectors rose subsequently by 320 in 1868 to 1,000 in 1877.

> It was found that the concept of the small man was unreal. The small man was in fact too small a man.[102]

East of the 100 degree meridian in the United States the Homestead Act was resoundingly successful in promoting agricultural settlement. West of Iowa, conditions changed.

> . . . the idea of the farm small in acres within the semi-arid regions was tenacious but untenable . . . It was even vicious in its operation.[103]

The size of the holdings that could be taken up by intending Downs agriculturalists varied from Act to Act (*see* table p. 122).

These varying quantities, compared with the fixed areas in other colonies, seemed generous and admirably tailored to the requirements of the different localities within the Downs. But after 1870, good quality agricultural land that could be readily exploited under prevailing conditions was limited. Post-1876 resumptions in the great homestead belt were subdivided into eighty-acre portions. The entire Settled District was declared a Homestead Area in 1868.

Queensland attempted to overcome the difficulties imposed by blanket legislation by introducing a novel and promising system of land classification. Inaugurated in 1868, it was abolished in 1876.[104] This measure was unsuccessful owing to the lack of technical facilities for assessing the foreseeable potential of land, deliberate maladministrations by Lands Officers and the absence of all the apparatus of State which was needed to make such a system work when thousands upon thousands of acres had to be resumed, surveyed and selected.[105] Colonial beliefs in unlimited resources and social mobility, however, were very strong. Rigid allocation

101 *Votes and Proceedings of the New South Wales Legislative Assembly*, Vol. II, (1883), p. 110.

102 G. L. Buxton, 'South Australian Land Acts 1869-1885', *unpublished thesis*, University of Adelaide 1961, p. 99 and S. A. Kelly, *Rural Development in South Australia*, Adelaide 1962, p. 11.

103 Hibbard, *Public Land Policies*, pp. 385-8 and W. P. Webb, *The Great Plains*, Boston 1931, p. 511.

104 *BC*, 13 July 1874, p. 3, c. 4. Classification by an independent Land Board and selection after survey were reintroduced by the Act of 1884. By then, however, only 'the most wretched lands in the colony' were available for selection in the Settled District. *TC*, 7 April 1885, p. 2, c. 1-2; 6 June 1885, p. 2, c. 6 and 15 July 1884, p. 2, c. 1-3; *QPD*, Vol. 43, (1884), pp. 251-9.

105 A. C. Gregory also maintained that it was too costly and difficult to devise a proper system of classification. Yet he was responsible for administering the system and classifying much of the Downs. *QPD*, Vol. 6, (1867-8), pp. 876-84. Evidence of the Surveyor-General and Crown Lands Commissioner before the Bar of the Legislative Council. *WA*, 4 June 1874, p. 2, c. 1. This issue exposes classification abuses in the Warwick area.

SIZE OF HOLDINGS, 1860-93[106]

Act	Size of unit
Crown Lands Alienation Act 1860 Agricultural Reserves Act 1863	40-320 acres with leasing right of continuous land up to three times area of purchase. Usual size of genuine agricultural selections in Ag. Reserves 40 acres.
Crown Lands Act 1868	Homestead Leases Homestead Areas usually 160 acres (80 acres agricultural limit). Conditional Purchases Agricultural land: 40-640 acres. First-class pastoral: 80-2,560 acres. Second-class pastoral: 80-7,680 acres.
Homestead Areas Act 1872	Agricultural: total area 120 acres. Total area in Homestead Areas: 320 acres.
Crown Lands Amendment Act 1875	Maximum area for homestead selection extended to 640 acres.
Land Act of 1876	Homestead Areas only: 80 acres limit. Other homesteads 160 acres. Pastoral C.P. land 640-5,120 acres.
'Exchanged' Land Act 1879	Homesteads: 80-200 acres.
Land Act of 1884	Agricultural Farms Homesteads 160 acres. Others to 1,280 acres. Grazing Farms Limit of 20,000 acres.
Co-operative Communities and Land Settlement Act 1893	Limit of 160 acres per member.

and supervision were contrary to the spirit of an age in which pre-emption and free selection were but two sides of the same coin.

Such attempts that were made at classifying Goombungee selections, North Branch grazing farms and Westbrook homesteads were more praiseworthy but founded on considerable inter-regional variations of climate, soil and water resources. There was a complete lack of scientific data and the land was classified on the basis of appearance and type rather than potential.[107] No one knew what was a viable unit on the

[106] *Statutes of Queensland*, Brisbane 1860-93.

[107] *BC*, 19 May 1873, p. 2, c. 4 and 13 July 1874, p. 3, c. 4.

Downs in the nineteenth century. 'Farming was and is a way of life' and the complete answer to this question still awaits discovery.

> . . . It is not desirable to give the same weight to profitability measures as one would when considering other industries . . . It would be wrong to treat [economic] information as being the sole . . . factor in deciding whether or not to continue farming. Economics contributes towards decision-making; so do sociology, philosophy and psychology.[108]

The early agriculturalist could claim, and with some justification, that if he had accepted the red figures on an accountant's balance sheet, then the economy of the Downs would have remained a predominantly pastoral one. It is a measure of his success and a continuation of his tragedy that once the farmer had secured through political and technical action his economic base he often used his new security to condemn, by action and implication, the visions and faiths of other sections. The fragmented ideological beliefs which had sustained him in adverse times were later used to justify courses of action founded on selfish economic grounds. The pioneer needed his beliefs and myths even more than most other men. They were often all he could afford; they were necessary for personal survival. Success, however, often corrupted and fruitful myths became irrelevant delusions bolstering a new agrarian conservatism.

In 1876 power was given to Cabinet to alter acreages by regulation but such changes usually helped powerful friends rather than small selectors.[109] Struggling on 'stony soils and waterless ridges', far from markets, lacking capital and at the mercy of the seasons, the eighty-acre men, to take an extreme view, were often 'little better off than paupers or slaves'.[110] Dalby graziers maintained that their 640-acre selections were farcical and in 1874 demanded a minimum of 5,000 acres. Francis McKeon declaimed that:

> I have farmed for seven years in the Dalby district and it will take me seven years more to get out of the mess. A man must sell 100 head of stock per year to live properly. 640 acres were too small for mixed farming, the only means of survival.[111]

The grazing capacity of this district was then estimated at five acres per cow and one acre per sheep. Thus on a 320 improved selection only 65 cattle or 320 sheep could be carried. This would not support the selector and his family. The minimum acreage for a profitable small squattage was estimated at 1,280 acres in the Toowoomba area and 3,000-4,000 acres around Dalby.[112]

108 *Queensland Department of Agriculture and Stock*, 'An Economic Survey of the Wheat Growing Industry in Queensland', Brisbane 1959, p. 27.

109 W. H. Traill, *A Plain Explanation of the New Land Act of 1876*, Toowoomba 1877, pp. 5-8.

110 *BC*, 17 February 1877, p. 5, c. 6 and *The Week*, 21 April 1877, p. 529.

111 *Dalby Herald*, 2 May 1874, p. 2. Quoted by *BC*, 4 May 1874, p. 4, c. 5.

112 *BC*, 1 August 1874, p. 5, c. 3 and *DDG*, 15 November 1876, p. 2, c. 6-7. Even the *Argus* admitted that farms in the Allora district were too small and that more pasture was required. *WA*, 23 June 1883, p. 3, c. 1.

The more perceptive realized that acreages were invariably too small but it was difficult to increase them during the short formative years of agricultural settlement. Without direct political representation the farmers had to depend on the agrarians and the political opportunists to secure increases. The squatters, who had practical experience, were determined to oppose the enlargement of selections. J. F. McDougall of Rosalie Plains, a bitter opponent of grazing farmers, stated that:

> The small man would find to his cost that pastoral farming could only be carried out on a large scale. The more limited the area, the greater the effort of the agriculturalist to make it productive.[113]

Convinced that the yeoman would fail but fearing the small graziers, the Pure Merinos in the Legislative Council successfully blocked acreage increases. To conserve their personal interests, they even managed to reduce homestead areas in 1872 from 640 to 320 acres.[114] The urban radicals were often prepared to accept such ill-considered reductions in order to secure compromises on resumptions and thus satisfy popular clamour for land and the consciences of the idealists. The 'liberals' voted against the increase to 640 acres in return for further resumptions on the Downs and a restriction of the pre-emptive right.[115] The practical gave way to the political when farm sizes were arbitrarily fixed by compromise rather than by an examination of economic and technical factors.

Until land became scarce on the Downs after 1880, selectors were able to extend their holdings by utilizing the forfeited portions of their less fortunate neighbours and by surreptitiously invading the rough leaseholds of the adjacent squatters. Large town reserves and commonages were provided near urban and small farming areas. These were used for grazing selectors' surplus stock.[116] In 1890 thirty-three farmers grazed four hundred beasts on the Allora Reserve and the Warwick and Dalby Commonages were equally valuable.[117]

The failure of the practical application of the agrarian myth which

113 *QPD*, Vol. 14, (1872), p. 864.

114 ibid., pp. 865-904. *See* speeches by McDougall, Fitz and Taylor.

115 ibid., pp. 929-37 and *WE&T*, 24 August 1872, p. 2, c. 1.

116 *TC*, 17 April 1890, p. 2, c. 5.

Common	Date proclaimed	Acres
Warwick	31.7.68 and 2.10.68	12,800
Dalby	8.10.68	12,800
Allora	9.1.69	3,435
		TOTAL 29,035

(*Continued on facing page*)

117 *TC*, 17 April 1890, p. 2, c. 5. These Commonages, established by Macalister to catch votes, were sold for cash in 1889-91. *WE&T*, 21 August 1869, p. 2, c. 6 and 6 February 1889, p. 2, c. 2.

postulated that most of the Downs *had* to be settled by agricultural yeomen was not officially recognized until the 1884 Land Act paved the way for the establishment of a new group of small graziers with enough land to give them a fair living. Most of the pastoral leases on the Western Downs were resumed for this element.[118] Furthermore, a successful farmer in the Settled District invariably purchased more land. A Drayton freeholder built up his mixed farm from 20 to 91 acres between 1874 and 1909.[119] Another, farming on a much larger scale, expanded his mixed grain, dairying and breeding property from 760 to 3,000 acres between 1868 and 1900.[120]

Technology eventually made profitable farming on small selections possible. By then, however, farmers' expectations had risen with those of other sections of the community. The old standards were no longer sufficient and the farmers believed that they were entitled to a greater margin of profit. Farms on the Downs have tended to grow fewer and larger and there has been no return to the small homesteads. By 1959 the 'minimum size of a farm which will adequately cover interest on capital and the farmer's own labour' was estimated to be between 450 and 600 cultivated acres for a Downs grain property.[121] In spite of later radical attempts to defy the universal New World trend towards larger commercial holdings, increased capitalization, mechanization and diversification, the amalgamation of titles has continued on the Downs.

(*Footnote 116 continued from p. 124*)

Town reserve	Date proclaimed	Acres
Drayton-Toowoomba	13.8.63	58,240
Warwick	15.4.68	32,265
Dalby	10.3.65	52,200
Allora	24.10.68	10,350
Leyburn	3.10.65	20,160
		TOTAL 173,215

118 *QPD*, Vol. 43, (1884), pp. 251-65, 307-14, 314-84 and 390-468.

119 Mr J. Donges, *personal communication*, 20 June 1963.

120 *WE&T*, 18 August 1886, p. 5, c. 4 and *TC*, 7 October 1911, p. 5, c. 4.

121 *Q. Dept. of Agric. & Stock*, 'Economic Survey of Wheat-Growing Industry', p. 67.

CHAPTER 6

TEUTON AND SCOT

The selection years on the Downs were marked by the presence of a large national group whose origin, religion, language and social characteristics in some ways set them apart from other immigrants settling the scrubs and downlands. The Germans, with their love of land and careful farming methods, were living models of rural virtues. As such, they were universally praised by the agrarians. The decline of German immigration after 1879, their apparently rapid economic and political assimilation and the bitter consequences of two World Wars have, however, not only frustrated any repetition of past homage but also delayed an unprejudiced examination of their significant contribution to the agricultural development of the region. It is time for a balance to be struck between neglect, ignorance and disparagement of the German contribution and uncritical praise. Differences can, however, be exaggerated. Being mainly poor, assisted immigrants eager for land, the experiences of this group can also serve as examples for those of numerous others selecting on the Downs after 1860.

Apart from the unfortunate German missionaries and wandering adventurers, the first German migrants were shepherds, brought out under contract by Downs squatters between 1852 and 1855 to replace labour that had vanished to the goldfields.[1] These shepherds proved to be reliable, frugal and sober workers who invariably managed to save sufficient cash out of their wages of £20-30 per year (and rations) to enable them to take up land in the 'sixties. Their excellent reputation recommended them to Lang who was searching for Protestant yeomen 'with strict moral habits and strong religious faith' to counterbalance the threatened invasion of Roman Catholic paupers from Ireland and to form the flesh and blood for his agrarian campaign against the Pure Merinos.[2]

Lang's views were endorsed by Governor Bowen and the 1860 Select Committee on Immigration which hammered out a policy of assisted and land-order immigration. Thousands of Germans, recruited by agents,

[1] The first Germans in Queensland were the Moreton Bay missionaries who arrived in 1838. A. Lodewyckx, *Die Deutschen in Australien*, Stuttgart 1932, pp. 59-62, 146-9.

[2] M. E. Jackson, 'The Germans in Queensland in the Nineteenth Century', *unpublished thesis*, University of Queensland 1959, p. 4. Most Germans were recruited on the spot in 1853-4 by Edward Lord of Drayton who had been educated in Germany. *BC*, 30 July 1853.

emigrated to Queensland between 1861 and 1866 when the crash, drought, agricultural failures and Bismarck's wars stopped the flood.[3] Assisted migration was resumed on modified lines in 1860 although the flow was officially limited to 1,500 statute adults a year from Germany. By mid-1870s the stream was drying up although small numbers continued to arrive until the 'nineties. Confederation, the formation of an industrial Empire, anti-migration laws and obstacles and particularly harsh military service regulations discouraged emigration from Germany. Nevertheless, 17,360 German migrants arrived in Queensland between 1861 and 1879.[4]

The Darling Downs, with its existing pastoral German population, attracted many of the Government assisted migrants although most settled on the scrublands of Moreton. Logan, Albert, Caboolture, Rosewood, Laidley and Marburg all had a large German minority.[5] By 1864 there were 1,250 German-born on the Downs, comprising 10.4 per cent of the region's total population and 19 per cent of all Germans in Queensland. Twelve years later the 2,016 German-born represented only 7 per cent of the total Downs population but the area still harboured 20 per cent of all colonial Germans. After 1876, however, numbers relatively decreased. In 1891 there were 2,318 Germans on the Downs—15.5 per cent of all Queensland Teutons and 6 per cent of the area's population.[6]

The strong sense of national identity and resistance to complete assimilation, however, which many Germans successfully transmitted to their children, justifies the inclusion of native-born offspring in the minority group. Here the figures and estimates are approximate and tentative as there was a continuous drift from the Lutheran churches on the Downs. While religious affiliation alone serves as a numerical indication, census returns undoubtedly underestimate the true position. In 1891, a generation after the first wave of agricultural settlement, there were 4,286 professed Lutherans on the Downs—10 per cent of the total regional population and 18 per cent of all Lutherans in the colony.[7]

The English and Irish population was more numerous but the Germans were pre-eminently small farmers with a passionate love of grain and grape. It is this overwhelming concentration on a particular occupation

[3] *QVP*, Second Session, (1863), pp. 453-4, 459-61. 'Report from the Select Committee on the working of the Immigration Regulations.' M. A. Kleinschmidt, 'Migration and Settlement Schemes in Queensland', *unpublished thesis*, University of Queensland 1951.

[4] 1873, when 2,502 Germans arrived, was the peak-year for German migration to Queensland. Compared with other groups there was a very high proportion of married couples (45 per cent). 25 per cent of German migrants were children under 12 years and there was a fairly high ratio of female unmarried settlers. Yet in 1873, 101,900 Germans arrived at New York alone. *QVP*, Vol. 2, (1875), pp. 648-55, 734-5. W. D. Borrie, *Italians and Germans in Australia*, Melbourne 1954, p. 169.

[5] M. E. Jackson, 'Germans in Queensland', p. 27.

[6] *Censuses of Queensland*, 1864, 1876, 1891, 'Birthplaces'.

[7] ibid. It is probable that the 10 per cent figure is too low. Quite a few settlers were Catholics from the Southern Lander, others inter-married and changed their denomination, bringing up their children in the new faith. A figure of 15 per cent of the total Downs population in 1891 would not be too high an estimate.

and mode of life that gives this minority a significance and importance out of all proportion to its actual numbers among the selectors on the Downs.[8]

Moreover, the Germans first tended to congregate in a few localities. On Middle Ridge, around Drayton, Meringandan, Glencoe, Geham and Goombungee, more German than English was spoken. These small areas accounted for 54 per cent of all the Lutherans on the Downs in 1891.[9] Yet Germans were more scattered on the Downs than in South Australia, and West Moreton. German farmers were prominent at Warwick, Allora, Spring Creek, Emu Creek and Cambooya. These isolated settlers tended to have larger properties, intermarry more freely with their 'foreign' neighbours and become absorbed in predominant cultural patterns much more rapidly than Teutons further north.[10]

In the mid-'seventies when the Central Downs was resumed for small selection, foreign-born and native German settlers spread all over the Downs wherever there was a possibility of growing crops. For they were agriculturalists first and last and it was their ability and success in this field that gave them a particular value in an area where many settlers were trying to replace cattle with corn and sheep with wheat. The Germans, it was generally agreed, made better small settlers than the British. Their '. . . industry, frugality and care [stood] out in striking relief' and they 'lived in areas which other persons would have failed to live on'.[11] Certainly, the thriving German communities along the Crow's Nest Railway were a standing reproach to other national groups who had sold before seeing or quickly walked off.[12]

Contemporary opinion supported the assertions of the writer who maintained that:

> The Germans . . . have 'shaken down' in a remarkably short time into good, sturdy, plodding, self-reliant settlers, occupying our waste land and making them yield not only a subsistence but something more . . . by sheer industry and economy they have made the land keep them while they cleared and . . . cultivated. It is settling the country in the . . . best sense of the term.[13]

[8] Official figures do not correlate birthplace statistics with occupational data. This conclusion is based on secondary contemporary sources and Selectors' Lists in *QGG*, 1875-93.

[9] In 1876 there were 1,516 English/Welsh migrants in the Drayton-Toowoomba area, 1,493 Irish and 1,197 Germans. Even by 1891, when major German migration had long since ceased, there were more German-born than any other overseas settlers in the Highfields area, nearly as many as the English and Irish in Darling Downs North and half the number of English and 40 per cent of the Irish in Drayton-Toowoomba. *Censuses of Queensland*, 1876, 1886, 1891, 'Birthplaces'.

[10] This pattern was also characteristic of isolated Germans in the United States. S. Hawgood, *The Tragedy of German-America*, New York 1940, p. xiv.

[11] *QPD*, Vol. 30, (1879), pp. 1045 and 1041-5, 1122-8.

[12] For a description of the farms of the Meringandan Germans, *see BC*, 2 May 1877, p. 3, c. 2.

[13] *The Week*, 23 December 1876, p. 745. In general, however, the Germans were not innovators but slow, skilled and persistent adapters. 'His function was more often consolidation than it was innovation.' Hawgood, *Tragedy of German-America*, p. 33.

The belief that a higher proportion of Germans than other settlers retained their selections is confirmed by two sample surveys of post-1875 resumptions on the Central Downs:

DOWNS SELECTORS OBTAINING FREEHOLD, 1883-1903[14]

	All Selectors No.	Germans No.	Germans %	All others %
Title in 1883	353	53	15	85
Sold out by 1903	181	17	32	54·7
Remaining	172	36	68	45·3

THE FATE OF WESTBROOK SELECTORS, 1877-1903[15]

	All Selectors No.	Germans No.	Germans %	All others %
Total selectors	156	39	25	75
Forfeitures	27	4	10	15
Sold out by 1903	72	14	36	45
Remaining	57	21	54	40

This persistence was even greater in the traditional 20 and 40 acre plots of the eastern margin where the first German selectors gathered. The 'poetic intensity' with which these settlers regarded their land tended to weaken in subsequent generations but Schlunke's masterly description of a Riverina German describes the relationship well.

> But during the time Adolph had worked on the farm his obsession with it had developed into a passion. He felt a kinship with the land as he walked over it, as if his body and the earth were blood relations.[16]

Such small farming settlements where the Germans who supposedly preferred red scrub soils to black earths 'sold everything they could raise and lived on what they could sell' were the heart of the community. Nevertheless, it is true that the Germans, avid for land, only took up

14 *QVP*, Vol. 2, (1884), pp. 1005-27 and *Commonwealth of Australia*, Electoral Roll, Darling Downs Division, Brisbane 1903.

15 *QGG*, 1877-85. *Commonwealth of Australia*, Elect. Roll, DD Division.

16 E. O. Schlunke, *Rosenthal*, *Sydney Morning Herald*, 20 April 1939, p. 4, c. 5. This unpublished novel reveals Schlunke, with his feeling for country, character and culture, as one of Australia's few good, regional writers. While disagreeing with Semmler's view that 'a better novel depicting Australian pioneers has never been written', Schlunke was the only able and perceptive narrator and interpreter of the German farmers outside South Australia. *See also* C. Semmler, 'E. O. Schlunke: An Appreciation', *Meanjin*, Vol. 20, No. 4, 1961, pp. 407-18.

small acreages of scrub and bush because their limited capital and the shortage of first-class land dictated both area and locality. Many Germans, however, preferred to transfer from 'forest to forest'.[17] The life history of Christoph Donges furnishes a typical although rather unruffled example of an immigrant's economic and social assimilation and progress of such German '40-acre men' in particular and successful selectors in general.[18] Donges was born at Münchaussen, Hessen, on 3 August 1842, the son, as most Germans were, of an independent peasant.[19] At the age of nineteen he emigrated with a batch of his fellow townspeople in order to improve his economic circumstances. Like most Germans and Scots he had had an excellent primary schooling followed by agricultural experience on the family property. A nominated immigrant, he contracted to serve McLean and Beit at Westbrook for two years after his arrival on the Downs in 1862. After his initial contract expired he became a shepherd and later a boundary-rider for Kent and Wienholt at Jondaryan. There he stayed until 1876, enjoying excellent relations with his employers.[20] Donges married a German-born Highfields selector's daughter in 1867, and the union produced the customary large family of ten sons and four daughters, twelve of whom survived beyond infancy.[21]

By 1874, when he purchased 20 acres at Drayton, he had accumulated £270 in cash, household furniture, milch goats, and seven horses worth over £20 each which he had bred and grazed on the station. After leaving Jondaryan in 1876 he carefully improved his farmlet and eventually extended it to 91 acres. With an excellent team and implements he earned a supplementary cash income by contract ploughing. His wife's eggs, butter, fruit and vegetables were bartered at Toowoomba and Donges, an excellent farmer convinced of the value of thorough tillage and fodder conservation, grew cereals, kept a few pigs and milch cows and bred two or three young horses every year. This diversity was characteristic of most German farmers.

Although a staunch Lutheran and elder of the Church, Donges soon acquired an excellent knowledge of English, educated his family in this language and enjoyed cordial relations with the dominant British

17 Graham in *QVP*, Vol. 2, (1879), p. 270 and Hawgood, *Tragedy of German-America*, p. 27.

18 Mr Jacob Donges, *personal communication*, 20 September 1963. Donges' experiences were paralleled on a larger scale by those of Henry Saal of Spring Creek. *BC*, 22 September 1913, p. 9, c. 3.

19 Most Downs Germans came from Prussia, Pomerania, Hesse, Baden, Schleswig-Holstein, Württemberg and Silesia. E. V. H. Gutekunst, 'German Settlement of the Darling Downs', *Darling Downs Centenary*, p. 47.

20 Others, such as Maas Hinz and Philip Imhoff, worked as navvies on the Downs railways. *TC*, 7 October 1911, p. 5, c. 4. Mrs P. Imhoff, *personal communication*, 28 October 1963.

21 No statistics exist to support the contention that the Germans tended to have larger families than even the Irish. Still, Gustav Jentz of Pittsworth with his 18 children was not an unusual example. *Queenslander*, 20 January 1929, p. 17.

majority. A year after his death in 1914, a son unsuccessfully contested a Parliamentary constituency as a Labour candidate.[22]

Not all Germans followed Donges' path to prosperity and place on the Downs. The community had its murderers, ne'er-do-wells and failures as well as its stolid, 'God-fearing', and docile members. On the whole, however, the group became unshakeably 'petty *bourgeois*' in its Queensland search for property, security, acceptance and 'respectability'.

Most Germans, emigrated from depressed farming areas, came to the Downs in family units determined to preserve these standards and attitudes which they felt were threatened in the new Germany:

Work was the best preventative for immorality and shiftlessness, and work was just not available.[23]

These objectives were very similar to those of the South Australian Silesians. But they, on the contrary, had emigrated primarily because of religious conflict and persecution, established strong group settlements and retained their cultural identity through the church's active opposition to most forms of assimilation.

From the very start these early immigrants kept to themselves and pursued their own way of life comparatively unaffected by the remainder of the colony. This way of life was, naturally, an almost exact replica of their life in Germany. German language, customs, methods of work, architecture, etc., prevailed wherever they settled; to the understanding eye it might have seemed as though a little piece of Silesia had suddenly taken wings and flown complete and undisturbed to a new land many thousands of miles away.[24]

Miniature rural Germanies were rare on the Downs and did not persist. Here forces of resistance were much weaker and the evidence suggests that partial social assimilation was more rapid than in South Australia. The family farm replaced the peasant village, improved communications broke down isolationism, there was a much greater participation in political life and German schools were never successful.[25] Most important of all, the Lutheran Church 'the most powerful institu-

22 The Downs Germans' involvement in and contribution to Queensland political life appears to have been relatively greater than that of their fellow-nationals in South Australia. I. A. Harmstorf, 'Germans in the South Australian Parliament', *unpublished thesis*, University of Adelaide 1961, (microfilm copy, ANU library). Donges' preference for partly-improved land close to a market was also characteristic of the Germans in the United States. Hawgood, *Tragedy of German-America*, p. 33.

23 M. E. Jackson, 'Germans in Queensland', p. 22.

24 C. A. Price, *The German Settlers in South Australia*, Melbourne 1945, p. 14.

25 The only important and relatively long-lived German day-school on the Downs, St Paul's of Toowoomba, closed in 1895. The final step towards complete assimilation, intermarriage, was at first resisted by the Lutheran Church. Nevertheless, two Downs Parliamentary representatives, William Lovejoy and Francis Grayson, both had German wives, and many single Teutons married British or Australian women. For another example of assimilation, *see* the case of George J. H. Wieck of Goombungee who 'managed community affairs behind the scenes', acted as liaison officer between Briton and Teuton, helped new Germans to become established, and was a key figure in Aubigny local and regional politics. Col. G. Wieck, *personal communication*, 27 September 1963.

tion in the persistence of German culture in Australia' was weaker, more fragmented and often incapable of enforcing effective group conformity to religious and social ideals.[26]

Nevertheless, the church was the pivot of most German settlers' existence, and the only tangible link with the customs of the 'Vaterland'.

No understanding of the early group *ethos* can be complete without a consideration of this puritanical, fundamentalist and all-embracing religious organization:

> Members believed in verbal inspiration and Luther's interpretation of the Bible . . . the Church claimed no secular power but it influenced all activities. It reserved the right to discipline its members; disputes among them were settled by committees appointed by the Church. It was a gross breach for a member to take another to law. A member who committed a gross or flagrant sin was admonished three times . . . If he refused to repent he was called before the congregation; if he persisted in error he was expelled from the Church. This was regarded as complete and utter disgrace as it carried not only social ostracism but eternal damnation. However, the door was always left open for a genuine repentant.[27]

Sunday church was the only social gathering for many isolated settlers and special burial, baptismal, wedding, folk-singing and thanksgiving customs were perpetuated within its walls. The German-born pastors, the real leaders and prophets of this community of Israelites in the wilderness, attempted to exercise the same degree of spiritual and temporal control over their flocks as they did in Germany. This aroused great resentment among the Australian-born who felt that such anachronisms as the penitential seat were humiliating and unnecessary in an open society.[28]

The most important problem was that of the retention of the German tongue. 'Many staunch Lutherans believed that the loss of the German language meant the total loss of the Lutheran faith.'[29] Not until after World War I were services held in English. This blind adherence to the German language strengthened the 'Deutschtum' of the older generation but lost the church many native-born settlers.

> If a dual Volkstum [national way of life] is placed before the young German-Australian, and two languages are impressed upon him [one inherited from his forbears and the other given him by the land of his birth] . . . then for a few generations he will think it a divine ordinance to retain both tongues and both ways of life. But all the time the voice saying, 'It is your sacred duty to hold fast your German heritage' will become weaker and weaker. Youth, without experience of the spiritual and cultural riches of the German language, says simply, 'We are living in an English country.'[30]

[26] W. D. Borrie, *Italians and Germans in Australia*, p. 199.

[27] E. O. Schlunke, *Rosenthal*, 19 April 1939.

[28] F. O. Theile, *One Hundred Years of the Lutheran Church in Queensland*, Brisbane 1939, pp. 78-83.

[29] ibid., p. 89 and A. Brauer, *Under the Southern Cross. History of the Evangelical Lutheran Church of Australia*, Adelaide 1956, pp. 164-5.

[30] T. Hebart, *The United Evangelical Lutheran Church in Australia*, Adelaide 1938, (English edition), p. 103.

Accentuating the drift was the scattered nature of Downs settlement, the difficulty in obtaining German pastors, the total failure of German education and the different dialects used by church and adherents.[31]

Borrie has declared that the splits which rent the Lutheran Church all over Australia 'encouraged faith and adherence'.[32] Such a conclusion is difficult to accept when the Germans on the Downs are considered. Doctrinal disputes where 'personal antipathy and personal misunderstanding, much narrowmindedness and imputation of motives was intermingled with the fight for principles' did much damage on the Downs where the church was relatively weak and isolated potential congregations were 'neglected and lost'. The Warwick Germans, numbering 306 in 1864, never obtained a pastor and were virtually lost to the Lutheran faith.[33] When it was realized that although social assimilation was inevitable the church could still survive and even flourish with the English language it was too late to recover lost ground. In 1893, ten Lutheran congregations, served by five pastors, were in existence on the Downs. With the exception of Westbrook, all were in the Toowoomba-Highfields-Goombungee area. Most Downs Germans could not cope with the conflicting problems of pioneering in a new environment and, at the same time, preventing absorption and adaptation to prevailing British and colonial cultural patterns. The German-born and their pastors undermined as long as they could the power of the environment to modify human character. They backed heredity and the Bible. But their neighbours were at once more prosaic and utopian. Concerned with material improvement on this earth they were convinced that a New World in human terms was indeed possible on the Downs. However, 1915 cruelly demonstrated that one age of innocence was over.[34]

The Queensland church's inability to retain its dominating influence and numerical strength meant that the survival of the 'Volk' consciousness which marked the South Australian community was less in evidence in the northern colony. There was jubilation in 1871, some tendency towards Pan-Germanism, and apprehension after 1899 for the future relationship of the two Empires but in general, nationalistic forces appear to have been quite weak on the Downs. The Germans' initial willingness 'to hire themselves for whatever they can get' was an early source of friction but, in general, they were not competitors on the labour market. British-German relationships were considered to be 'excellent on the Downs during the nineteenth century' but cordial, surface attitudes did conceal some economic and political animosity. The Germans' farming successes and their 'liberal' block-voting were sometimes resented. Inflamed by World War I, latent antagonisms emerged much later on the Downs.[35]

31 F. O. Theile, *One Hundred Years*, pp. 89-90.

32 Borrie, *Italians and Germans in Australia*, p. 198 and A. Brauer, *Under the Southern Cross*, p. 337.

33 F. O. Theile, *One Hundred Years*, p. 21.

34 ibid.

35 E. Thorne, *An Eight Years' Resident*, London 1876, p. 123 and E. V. H. Gutekunst, 'German Settlement', p. 49.

What was present was an undercurrent of isolationism, temporarily exposed by Federation and the conscription referenda, which, if the Downs Germans had been more numerous and less economically integrated, might have produced a small scale Queensland 'Middle West'. Certainly the 'Bible in State Schools' referendum of 1910 demonstrated the Teuton's strong concern with religious fundamentalism and paternal social ethics.[36]

On the whole, however, the German farmers were the agrarians' ideal settlers. Determined to regain lost status and improve existing standards of agricultural life, offering little competition in the labour market, white, Protestant, apparently 'liberal' and present in 'manageable numbers', their initial failure to immediately conform to all dominant social *mores* was temporarily overlooked by the British minority. Two World Wars brutally interrupted an apparently untroubled slide into complete assimilation. Seventy years later, however, only the surnames, an anglicized religion and a few insignificant customs and attitudes distinguish those of Teuton descent from those whose grandparents migrated from the British Isles.

The Scots farmers shared some of the valuable and desirable agrarian attributes of the Germans. Although scattered throughout the Settled District, in smaller numbers and with less overt religious participation and supervision, they also were dogged, reasonably well-educated, thrifty and diligent farmers with a keen regard for site and soil. More inclined to experiment, innovate and improve their stock than the majority of Germans and providing more than their share of emerging rural leaders, the Scots tended to farm larger areas than other national groups and to graduate more quickly to 'boss-cocky' and even grazier status.[37]

The almost transcendental attachment to the land as a 'sacred trust' and the social and economic conservatism of pre-industrial peasant Germany which the Lutheran church attempted to preserve on the Downs were absent in the Scots. They intended to be progressive capitalists rather than stagnant agrarians. True, they cherished their land and practised without question the traditional rural virtues. After all, their

[36] In the Aubigny, Toowoomba and Cambooya electorates where the German element was strongest, the voting figures for the Federation referendum demonstrate the effect of the German vote:

Constituency	For Federation	Against Federation	Majority
Aubigny	169	974	805
Toowoomba	982	1,129	147
Cambooya	278	938	660

QVP, Vol. 1, (1899), p. 753.

[37] Six Emu Creek farmers—Smith, Mackintosh, McPhee, McIntyre, McPherson and McPhail—illustrate these contentions. In 1874 these selectors held 3,443 acres between them, averaging 574 acres. Of this area, they cropped an aggregate of 315 acres. All had cows, pigs and bullocks and these Scots grazed nearly 5,000 sheep between them. Renowned for their Lothian-type farming practices, the Emu Creek men made extensive use of machinery. *BC*, 16 May 1874, p. 5, c. 5-6.

fiery sponsor, John Dunmore Lang, was an agrarian without peer in the colonies. Yet these sons of Lowland farmers and hinds regarded the land in a different light—as a source of profit and advancement—much earlier than those of Teuton blood.

> . . . they believed in land—these Scotch pioneers, and in sheep, and in wheat, and in horses, and cows—in all things, in fact pertaining to the soil—and the soul.[38]

In short, they believed in the land rather than loved it.

The Scots' concept of agriculture as a business, which so well fitted them for soil-breaking in the colonies, was an attitude they brought with them from Scotland itself. Between 1770 and 1830 the Lowlands in particular experienced an agricultural revolution. Even by 1815 'production was essentially for profit [and] . . . business motives were increasingly dominant and powerful within the sphere of production itself'.[39] But new methods and new ideas meant status, profits and privilege for a few and economic and social depression for the great majority. All of Scotland was held by less than 8,000 proprietors and the rich mixed farmers tended to grow wealthier and fewer. Advancement in agriculture became all but impossible and those who wanted land of their own were forced to emigrate to secure it.[40]

Yet Scots selectors never became as significant as those of their countrymen who became squatters or merchants. Land and profits on a grand scale were the aims of most Celts.[41] By the time that the Downs was opened for selection, however, opportunities in the pastoral and even mercantile fields for men of energy and ambition rather than capital were fast diminishing. Moreover, those Scots who settled on the Downs after 1865 tended to have limited cash resources (although more than most Germans and Irish) and few influential connections. The Leslie epoch was very definitely over.

In 1891 there were only 1,295 Scots-born settlers on the Downs. They represented only 5.78 per cent of the total population of the region. There were then only half as many Scots as Germans and only one-quarter as many Scots as Irish. Nearly 18 per cent of all Scots resided on the Central Downs and a further 31 per cent lived in the Toowoomba district.[42] Some localities such as Caledonian Valley near Greenmount, Allora, Swan Creek and Yangan had relatively strong Scots farming communities but these minor concentrations were the result of coincidence, patriarchal 'lairdship' and family settlement rather than any conscious attempt at group settlement.

38 Steele Rudd, *Duncan McClure*, Sydney 1909, pp. 1-2.

39 L. J. Saunders, *Scottish Democracy, 1815-1840*, Edinburgh 1950, p. 8.

40 ibid., p. 55.

41 'They were men who had been accustomed to have property and were determined to have it again.' H. I. Cowan, *British Emigration to British North America, 1783-1837*, Toronto 1928, p. 122. Quoted by M. Kiddle, 'Scottish Lowland Farmers, c. 1830-50', *unpublished seminar paper*, ANU, 13 May 1954, p. 17.

42 *Census of Queensland*, 1891, 'Birthplaces'.

Such co-operative ideas were anathema to the Presbyterian Scots.[43] Although most Scots selectors were firmly attached to the Kirk many of its assumptions and social controls were never accepted by its colonial adherents. In any case, its secular powers were rapidly waning in Scotland itself. Nevertheless, like the German Lutherans, the Scots Presbyterians whose basic Calvinism equated material success with individual virtue, had the benefit of religious teaching whose precepts were well adapted to successful selection.[44] Between the brass bands, Sunday wine-gardens and gay festivals of the Toowoomba Germans, however, and the strict Sabbatarianism of the Allora Scots a wide gulf was fixed which took several generations to bridge.

While Weber's thesis stressing the Calvinist contribution to the development of modern capitalism is open to serious objection in its European and New England setting, any attempt to apply it to the agrarian regions of the Australasian colonies seems a rather sterile academic exercise. That the Scots considered that thrift, frugality and hard work led to inevitable rural success can be accepted. But these beliefs were also held by many successful Irish Roman Catholic boss-cockies. What is indisputable is the triumph of urban capitalistic techniques and controls in New World agriculture. Religious beliefs, as such, however, played only a minor part in this economic development.[45]

[43] Presbyterian churches at Allora (1873), Greenmount-Emu Creek (1886), Killarney (1887), Emu Vale-Swan Creek (1886) and Clifton (1890) give some indication of the distribution of Scots rural population.

[44] But the thesis propounded by Professor Manning Clark regarding the importance of the distinctive Catholic Protestant and Enlightenment contributions to the shaping of the mental environment of the colonists is another matter. Even if not wholly acceptable, his ideological approach is certainly a more stimulating way of commencing a deeper analysis of Downs attitudes. This awaits future research.

[45] M. Weber, *The Protestant Ethic and the Spirit of Capitalism*, London 1930; H. H. Gerth and C. W. Mills, *From Max Weber: Essays in Sociology*, London 1947; 'The Protestant Sects and the Spirit of Capitalism', pp. 302-22; 'Capitalism and Rural Society in Germany', pp. 363-85 and C. M. H. Clark, *A History of Australia*, Vol. I, Melbourne 1962, pp. 21-41.

CHAPTER 7

BLACK SOIL AND SUMMER RAIN

PROBLEMS AND STRUGGLES OF THE PIONEER SELECTORS ON THE DARLING DOWNS

The Pure Merinos have for long obscured the role of the small farmers in Downs history. Temporarily concealed by the clash of squatter, lawyer and storekeeper, a growing but mute third force—the farmers of southern Queensland—increased in numbers and economic importance. As the only region in the colony capable of sustaining a large group of small commercial graingrowers, the Darling Downs acquired a special significance in the struggle for land and survival.

Statistics indicate the considerable progress made by the small settlers between 1860 and 1893, and dispel both the fervent claims of their flatterers and the gloomy conclusions of their detractors.

The speed and thoroughness of selector penetration, as elsewhere in Australia, has been under-estimated. Gold stole and retained the glamour. While incoming pioneers faced years of adjustment to novel conditions, those who failed or recoiled from the task were always replaced by optimistic new arrivals. Disappointments, while expected, were frequently overwhelming. Many fell victim to the environment and economic fluctuations. Others were unable to adapt themselves to the monotony, drudgery and loneliness of farm life and retreated in defeat to the towns. The small personal victories of the remainder, however, and the mounting population, production and overall development of the Downs were just sufficient to confirm the belief of the majority that 'progress' was a reality, and that the land did offer a means of escape from servitude abroad and wage-slavery in Australia. That a man and his family could acquire land of their own and what passed for independence and respectability in an evolving community was firmly believed. On the Downs there was always sufficient evidence to prove, in the selectors' eyes at least, that these aspirations were valid and realizable.[1]

Agricultural settlement on the Downs was at first a subsidiary offshoot of the small town (Warwick, Drayton-Toowoomba and Dalby) which had

[1] For an examination of these factors in another setting, *see* W. A. Mackintosh, *Economic Problems of the Prairie Provinces*, Canadian Frontiers of Settlement Series, Vol. 4, Toronto 1935, p. 11.

arisen in the late 'fifties to serve the immediate needs of the pastoral industry. Years before each of these towns acquired their limited, sometimes ill-chosen, agricultural reserves a few farmers had commenced supplying them with foodstuffs and fodder. Even some 'dangerously advanced' squatters such as Frederick Bracker of Warroo had proved, as early as 1842, that agriculture was possible, but these rash and successful experiments were abandoned when the implications of their success were comprehended.[2]

Only after Separation, when legislative action, assisted migration and a small but important group of station hands with experience and capital, provided a nucleus of likely farmers did agriculture really expand. Between 1861 and 1864, the area cultivated on the Downs increased from 1,175 to 4,032 acres—a gain of 343 per cent in less than four years. In 1864, 153 farmers and their 431 employees represented 11 per cent of the total male workforce on the Downs.[3] Twelve years later, in 1876, 24,148 acres, a staggering increase of 591 per cent, were being tilled by 1,748 farmers and 628 labourers who together comprised over 20 per cent of the working male population on the Downs and were easily the most numerous by occupation.[4] By 1891, 74,522 acres were under crop—a 308 per cent rise over 1876. The number of agriculturalists failed to keep pace with the dramatic increase in cultivation. Although 6,329 farmers and labourers worked on the Downs they were now only 15 per cent of those gainfully employed although still the largest single occupational group.[5] Such a relative decline was to be expected once the first great era of settlement had ended and consolidation and rapid increases in per capita production had commenced.[6]

The first selectors were clustered together at Drayton, Toowoomba, Allora and the Condamine's Warwick tributaries. This latter area, with its 3,605 acres under cultivation in 1864 (30 per cent of all land tilled in Queensland, 60 per cent of cultivation on the Downs) and more than half the regional farm population, was already renowned for its cereal production and potential. Its 'golden valleys of waving grain' were the prototypes for future development all over the Settled District.[7]

By 1876, however, the position had altered. The consolidation and extension of the agricultural reserves had intensified the small farming population around the two original nuclei and the Land Act of 1868

[2] Two years after their arrival, the Leslies grew wheat at Canning Downs (1843). Their example was followed by John Campbell of Westbrook (c. 1845) and Arthur Hodgson of Eton Vale (1846), both of whom grew 'splendid crops'. *DDG*, 12 October 1878, p. 5, c. 5 and *BC*, 20 November 1903, Harvest Supplement. 'Reminiscences of Harry Bracker', *Darling Downs Centenary Souvenir*, p. 61.

[3] *Census of Queensland*, 1861 and 1864. *SR*, 1861-4.

[4] ibid., 1876.

[5] ibid., 1891.

[6] In 1891, 219 sugar-growers employed 8,799 labourers. On the Downs, less than one-fifth of the employed male farm population worked for wages. ibid., pp. 1090-1.

[7] For a description of this area, *see BC*, 14 October 1876, p. 6, c. 4 and 20 October 1880, p. 5, c. 3-5.

had scattered selectors all over the eastern part of the Settled District not already freeholded by the squatters. Under this Act, 2,319 selectors took up 1,242,269 acres in nine years. Of these, 931 were homesteaders securing 234,189 acres and 1,229 were conditional purchasers selecting 876,091 acres.[8] Agriculture for the first time penetrated beyond the 'suburbs' of the towns to the Highfields ridges, the resumed halves of the great runs of the Central Downs and the Dalby creeks.

Most selectors concentrated in a belt about sixteen miles wide which extended for sixty-five miles between Geham in the north and Killarney in the south. This 'selector zone' included the farming areas of Meringandan, Emu Creek, Spring Creek, Greenmount, Clifton, Back Plains and Freestone Creek, Yangan, Lord John Swamp and Swan Creek where agriculture was the rule on most selections.[9] Over half the farmers (839), however, were still congregated around Drayton-Toowoomba while a further 214 resided in the Warwick district. A mere 98 agriculturalists had selected on the huge expanses of the Northern and Western Downs by 1876.[10]

The second great stimulus to small settlement, the Land Act of 1876, resulted in a further 3,440 selections totalling 849,728 acres being taken up on the Downs. Homestead selectors numbering 2,021 accounted for 214,019 acres and the remainder were conditional purchases.[11] Between 1876 and 1881 homestead selection was at its peak on the Downs and the last resumptions in the Settled District then thought suitable for small farmers were taken up. These included the western portions of the East Prairie, St Ruth, Westbrook, Beauaraba, Felton, Eton Vale, North Branch and Toolburra Runs where the bulk of the new selections were made. Grazing farmers on larger units also began to spread along the banks of the Condamine River from Dalby in the north to Leyburn and Milmerran in the south-west.

A marked decline in the rate of small agricultural selection took place after 1883. Although between 1885 and 1893, 2,160 selections totalling 932,981 acres were made under the 1884 Act, most of these were comparatively large agricultural and grazing farms to the north, south and west of the Settled District where pastoral leaseholds were being subdivided for the first time. Around the townships of Stanthorpe, Inglewood, Miles and Condamine, the grazing selector became prominent.[12] Nevertheless, there was no marked extension of the small farming belt

[8] These and subsequent Land Act statistics are drawn from *QVP*, 1868-93, 'Reports of the Under-Secretary for Crown Lands' and *SR*, 1868-93.

[9] *See* Map 14 indicating areas of selector-settlement.

[10] *Census of Queensland*, 1876.

[11] Some selectors were farmers taking advantage of the Act to increase their holdings, while others were family-members intending to amalgamate the individual selections once they had obtained their certificate. At most, about half the homestead selectors would join the ranks of the permanent farmers.

[12] 131 selectors took up agricultural farms (20,966 acres) and 27 grazing farms (95,099 acres) under the 1884 Act in the Stanthorpe Land Agent's District alone between 1885 and 1893. *SR*, 1893.

beyond the eastern half of the Settled District although mixed farming on larger areas was growing in popularity all over the Downs.

By 1891 the distribution of the farming population on the Downs was well defined and relatively stable. While the large freehold pastoral estates still appeared as gaping voids in an area otherwise covered by hundreds of small homesteads, agriculture associated with grazing was now the dominant activity in the several districts of the old 'selector zone'. The actual pattern, however, had changed little since 1876. Nearly 20 per cent of all farmers were located around Drayton-Toowoomba and a further 12 per cent were in the Highfields district. Most of the remainder were spread along the Toowoomba-Warwick railway and its branches to Pittsworth and Killarney.[13] The actual number of farmers in each district and the acreages they cultivated in 1893, give a more accurate indication of the spread of the small settlement.[14]

Number of Farm Proprietors and Area of Cultivation per Holding, 1893

Petty Sessions Districts	5 acres		5-20 acres		20-25 acres		50 acres		Totals	
	Prop.	AC.	Prop.	AC.	Prop.	AC.	Prop.	AC.	Prop.	AC.
Crow's Nest	30	79	43	413	4	99	—	—	77	591
Highfields	27	77	253	3,078	128	3,624	16	1,106	424	7,885
Toowoomba	282	649	439	4,928	280	8,690	76	8,570	1,077	22,837
Allora	5	10	32	375	109	3,643	157	15,796	303	19,824
Killarney	8	27	28	363	43	1,209	20	1,985	99	3,584
Warwick	61	142	115	1,384	123	3,966	101	9,757	400	15,249
Condamine	1	2	1	6	—	—	—	—	2	8
Dalby	51	116	66	661	11	288	1	150	129	1,215
Inglewood	25	59	18	162	5	168	—	—	48	389
Stanthorpe	64	122	31	319	11	311	1	58	107	810
Darling Downs	571	1,315	1,034	11,764	715	22,920	372	37,422	2,692	73,421
Queensland	2,711	6,342	4,616	50,901	2,724	80,343	890	114,489	10,941	252,075

This table discloses that the Warwick-Allora-Killarney district with its 802 farmers cultivating 38,057 acres (50 per cent of the acreage cropped on the Downs and 15 per cent of the Queensland total) was not

13 *Census of Queensland*, 1891.

14 Toowoomba in 1893 had more cultivating proprietors than any other district in Queensland. Warwick was in fourth place and Allora in twelfth position. So far as acreages were concerned Toowoomba again led, Warwick was third and Allora fifth. The average acreage cultivated for all groups was 23 acres for Queensland and 27 acres for the Downs. Warwick farms, however, averaged 38 acres of cultivation per unit—the highest figure in the colony. *QVP*, Vol. 3, (1893), 'Returns of Agriculture and Livestock for 1893', pp. 1519-20.

only the premier agricultural portion of the colony but also had the largest farms. Farms were smaller and more diversified within a twenty-mile radius of Toowoomba where 58 per cent of all agriculturalists on the Downs cropped 3,412 acres. Many Toowoomba agriculturalists were not so much farmers as horticulturalists and market-gardeners. They

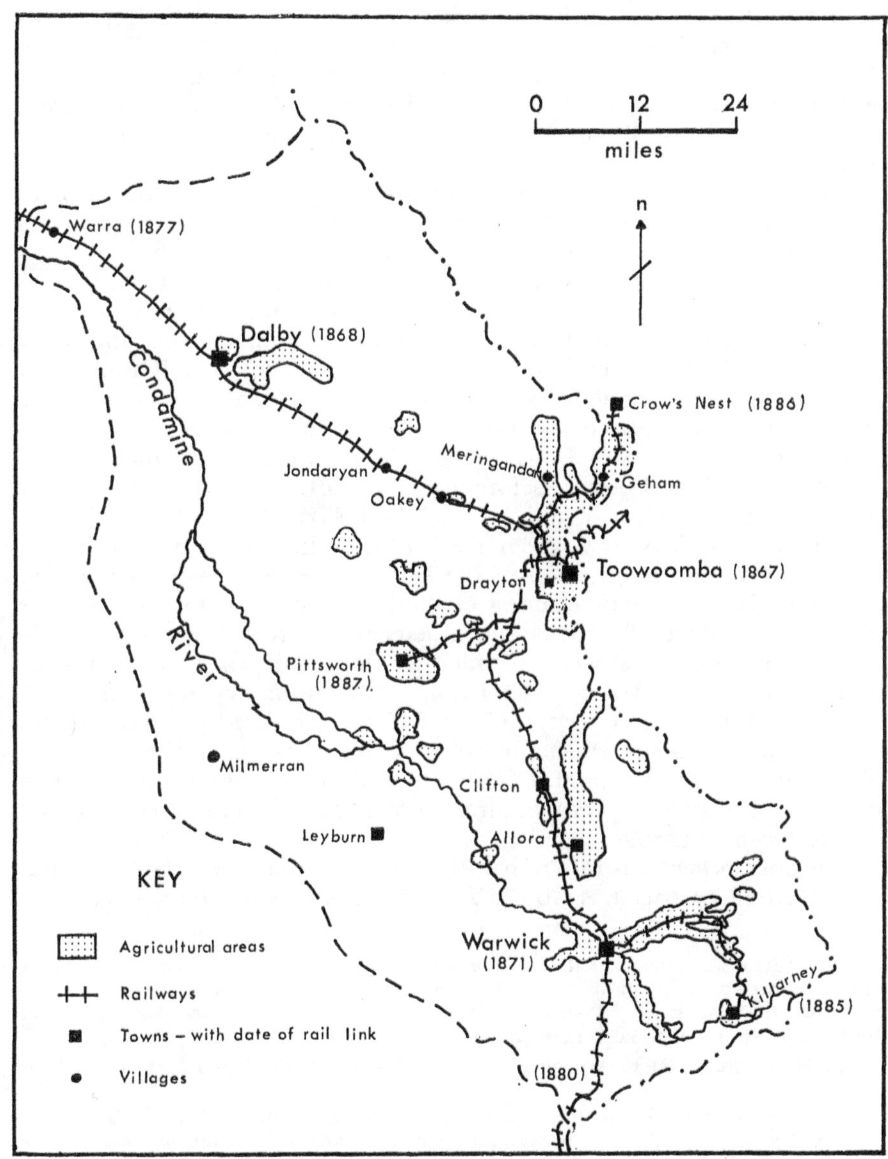

MAP 14 Settled District agricultural areas, 1860-93 (after Parish maps and *QGG*, 'Rent Lists')

supplied the growing urban market with a tremendous variety of produce and their diversified skills were always welcome. Such specialization was characteristic of the environs of most country towns in the great crescent of the continent. The considerable significance and sometimes the very existence of these small holdings has been observed by the drama of selection taking place over much larger, but less profitable, areas.[15] Apart from these areas, and isolated pockets in the more favoured portions on the Central Downs not in the possession of the pastoralists, there were few other patches of cultivation in the Settled District. All in all, only 0.7 per cent of this district was tilled in 1893 and an infinitesimal part of the gigantic Pastoral District to the west had been ploughed for profit.

The physical environment was overwhelmingly important in the lives of these settlers. Settlement on the Downs derived immeasurable benefits from the early delineation of the Settled District to which it was restricted. Although much of this district could not be cultivated with the techniques available in the three decades following Separation, its western boundary did roughly correspond with existing climatic, soil and vegetation controls. While events have proved the fallacy of environmental determination, first crudely expressed by the diehard squatters and later refined and systematized by Griffith Taylor and others, the unique physical characteristics of Downs geography enforced a long and arduous period of trial and error before even a portion of the agricultural potential of the region could be exploited.[16] While the 'utilisation of land in any country at a given moment is a highly complex effect of many causes', the peculiarities of the Downs climate in particular called for the evolution of new farming methods and material to combat these grave disadvantages.[17] During the nineteenth century it is indisputable that 'seasons and soils' were of much greater significance to the Downs selector than S. M. Bruce's later trilogy of 'men, money and markets'.[18] This is not to suggest that the latter three requirements were unimportant factors on the Downs between 1860 and 1893. As the process of adaptation accelerated and techniques and tools were evolved which gave some insurance against natural hazards, finance and prices assumed a more prominent role.

The only other Australian parallel to the rather fortuitous creation of the Settled District was Goyder's Line in South Australia which, when

15 ibid.

16 *See* Taylor's statement that '. . . the distribution of human settlement is almost entirely determined by natural controls', in Griffith Taylor, 'The Pioneer Belts of Australia', I. Bowman (ed.), *Pioneer Settlement*, American Geographical Society Special Publication No. 14, New York 1932, pp. 360-91.

17 S. M. Wadham, R. K. Wilson and J. Wood, *Land Utilization in Australia*, Melbourne 1950, p. 1.

18 ibid., p. 367. For illuminating discussions on this problem, *see* W. A. Mackintosh, *Economic Problems*, pp. 1-11; R. W. Murchie, *Agricultural Progress on the Prairie Frontier*, Canadian Frontiers of Settlement Series, Vol. 5, Toronto 1936, pp. 1-72; J. C. Malin, 'The Adaptation of the Agricultural System to a Sub-humid Environment', *Agricultural History*, Vol. 10, No. 3, July 1936, pp. 117-18, 140.

officially adopted in 1872, marked the northern limit of profitable commercial agriculture on small holdings. After the spectacular success of agricultural pioneering south of the line, however, the more arid land to the north was thrown open with calamitous results.[19] This pattern was repeated in parts of New South Wales, the Victorian Wimmera and the American states of Kansas and Nebraska.[20] On the Darling Downs, however, the task of introducing commercial grain growing to the region was sufficiently intricate and unrewarding to inhibit any genuine demand for agricultural selections further west.

The selector on the Downs pioneered with certain advantages not always enjoyed elsewhere. Contrary to the conclusions of some writers, the Downs was not a frontier community, even if that much used and abused term can be applied to the peculiar Australian conditions.[21] The selector was not a pioneer in the American sense. It is true that the selectors were laboriously attempting to alter the pastoral foundation of the Downs economy but actual settlement, however sparse, had preceded them. The towns, however small, and much of the apparatus of Western civilization had already been established. The farmers were 'mopping-up' in an area which Europeans had already occupied and started to exploit. The aborigines had been decimated and while squatter-selector relationships were often strained and unpleasant there was certainly no range-war or armed violence.

The agriculturalists had one great advantage. The soils that they were expected to cultivate were among the finest in the world. The heart of the Settled District was overlain by an immensely deep black soil, similar to the Russian chernozems, capable of being cropped for many decades without expensive fertilizers. Formed under a grassland régime subjected to summer rainfall and winter drought and derived from volcanic or calcareous rocks, these soils were well supplied with vital plant nutrients. With their high clay content, these soils retained moisture for winter growth, and although sticky after heavy rain, were self-mulching, friable and easily ploughed.[22] The fertility of the black

19 *BC*, 17 December 1879, p. 6, c. 5-6; *South Australia Parliamentary Papers*, Vol. II, No. 28, (1888), 'Report of the Committee on the Land Laws of South Australia', pp. v-viii, xxiv, xvi-xiiv; G. L. Buxton, *SA Land Acts*, pp. 48-79; D. W. Meinig, *On the Margins of the Good Earth*, Chicago 1962.

20 *Victoria Parliamentary Papers*, Session 1878, Assembly, Vol. 3, No. 65, 'Progress Report by the Royal Commission on the Agricultural Progress of the Colony', pp. 669-72. The belief that 'rain follows the plough' was firmly held on the American prairies. J. C. Olson, *A History of Nebraska*, Lincoln 1955, pp. 168-77.

21 For a discussion of this point, *see* Norman Harper, 'The Rural Urban Frontiers', *Historical Studies, Australia and New Zealand*, Vol. 10, No. 40, May 1963, p. 401-21.

22 This section is based on A. R. Callaghan and A. J. Millington, *The Wheat Industry in Australia*, Sydney 1956, pp. 62-4; J. Hart, 'Agriculture on the Darling Downs', *QAJ*, Vol. 69, Part 1, July 1949, and Part 2, August 1949, pp. 1-9, 63-74; F. A. L. Jardine, 'Horticultural Districts of Queensland. 1. The Granite Belt', ibid., pp. 78-83; N. S. Noble (ed.), *The Australian Environment*, (second edition), Melbourne 1950, pp. 37-8; J. A. Prescott, 'The Soils of Australia in Relation to Vegetation and Climate', *CSIRO Bulletin No. 52*, Melbourne 1931. (The pioneer study adopting the

(Continued on next page)

earths giving extremely high yields of grain helped offset climatic disadvantages. But it was the justifiable grievance of intending selectors that these desirable soils were the ones most monopolized by pastoralists.

On the eastern fringe of the Downs, was a less extensive but fertile belt of red, loamy soil also of volcanic origin and with excellent water-retaining capacities. Slightly inferior to the black earths, this soil was also highly suitable for cropping. Scattered in patches throughout the region was a moderately fertile red-brown sandy soil which, with its lesser moisture holding qualities needed more management and produced smaller yields.[23] To the north-west of Dalby lay a heavier and less-fertile variant of the black earths proper. Less friable than the soils further south, it responded well to cultivation although little exploited during the period. South-west of Warwick, the granite soils of the Stanthorpe area were beginning to attract smallholders by the turn of the century.[24] These soils were not suitable for cropping although it was beginning to be realized that the area was a potential apple and stone-fruit growing district.

Except on black earths of Central Downs, trees cost the homesteaders much arduous labour. On the eastern slopes and foothills continuous stands of bluegum, stringybark and ironbark had to be cleared before the selectors of Middle Ridge, Crow's Nest and Highfields could sow their crops. The ironbark and cypress pine forests of the western margin of the Settled District, however, as well as the brigalow-belah associations of the Western Downs and the open poplar box country around Dalby were not invaded by axe, saw and fire during this period and were merely thinned by ringbarking.[25] But the main obstacle to the successful cultivation was the capricious summer rainfall of the area. In comparison with the Western Downs and the southern portions of the Australian wheat crescent, the Settled District received copious precipitation which averaged twenty-six inches per annum. There was a concentration in the three summer months of January-March when the area received over one-third of its total precipitation. The five months between May and September were virtually dry. Most rain fell during periods of high temperature with considerable potential evaporation and transpiration rates. Even in winter, falls of less than fifty points were

Russian (Dokuchaiev and Glinkas) system of soil classification based on the characteristics of the soil itself and their relationship to climate and vegetation): *Queensland Bureau of Investigation*, 'Eighth Annual Report, 1951', Brisbane 1952. (This report includes the only detailed soil map of the Settled District and a brief survey of the wheat-growing potentialities of the region.)

23 This loam covered the 'scrubby ridges' in the Oakey-Westbrook-Pittsworth districts which were settled by the eighty-acre men in the late 'seventies. J. Hart, 'Agriculture on the Darling Downs', *QAJ*, Vol. 69, Part 1, July 1949, and Part 2, August 1949, p. 7.

24 ibid., and F. A. L. Jardine, 'Horticultural Districts'.

25 ibid. For a first-hand account of clearing a heavily-timbered Toowoomba farm, *see* J. Donges, 'Early Agriculture in the Toowoomba Area', Address to the Toowoomba and District Historical Society, *TC*, 20 February 1960, p. 6, c. 6-9.

useless unless followed by further showers. The growing season, however, in contrast to areas further south, was twelve months long and the chances of receiving sufficient rain for optimum plant development—the maximum growth factor—were reasonably good. Although the moisture stored in the soil was the factor which made early agriculture possible on the Darling Downs, the heavy falls needed to provide this reservoir were unreliable. Summer rains were characterized by brief, intensive thunderstorms accompanied by violent thunder and lightning. These usually commenced in mid-October and the series ceased in early January. Such torrential downpours were local in character and tended to follow well-defined paths across the Downs from west to east so that falls were irregular in intensity and distribution.[26]

Long droughts, often temporarily broken by intermittent and ineffective showers, caused disastrous crop losses in 1864-5, 1871, 1877-8, 1885-6 and 1888-9.[27] The Downs squatters, however sorely stricken at times, never faced such complete disaster as the loss of their entire investment. Droughts were feared most of all, destroying a cash income from crops and requiring the hand-feeding and watering of stock.

Serious floods, drowning men and stock and sweeping away crops and fences, occurred during the summer of 1862, 1863, 1873, 1887, 1890 and 1895.[28] On 21 January 1887 the Condamine River rose thirty-five feet at Warwick, drowned thousands of sheep and destroyed the 'splendid crops' of unlucky selectors at Swan Creek, Killarney and Freestone Creek.[29] In March 1890, further floods took a heavy toll in the Warwick-Allora district and the disastrous deluges which devastated Brisbane in the first week of February 1893 were repeated all over the Downs a week later. The damage was at its worst at Highfields where 'most crops were destroyed' and there was 'complete devastation in the district'.[30]

Bush fires, although a menace to the isolated selector, never threatened the Downs although prolonged summer heat waves wilted standing crops and lowered maize yields. Hail was always a hazard and late frosts and biting westerly winds, particularly on the Central Downs, retarded crop growth.

The Settled District was comparatively well-watered by river and creek.

[26] W. T. Brooks, 'The Climate of the Queensland Wheat Belt', *Economic News*, Vol. 19, No. 1, 1950, pp. 1-2; A. R. Callaghan and A. J. Millington, *Wheat Industry*, pp. 42-5; R. H. Greenwood, 'The Rural Pattern of South-Eastern Queensland', reprinted from *The Australian Geographer*, November 1956; L. G. Miles, 'The Relationship of Crops to Dry Farming Practices in Queensland', *QAJ*, Vol. 73, August 1951, pp. 109-15; P. J. Skerman, 'Average Expectancy of Worthwhile Rain on the Darling Downs', *The Queensland Graingrower*, Vol. II, No. 7, 5 October 1960, p. 9.

[27] J. C. Foley, 'Droughts in Australia', Bulletin No. 43, *Commonwealth of Australia, Department of Meteorology*, Melbourne 1957.

[28] *Warwick Mail*, 18 February 1862. Quoted by *BC*, 25 February 1862, p. 3, c. 3. ibid., 24 June 1873, p. 4, c. 1.

[29] *WE&T*, 26 January 1887, p. 2, c. 1-7. During January 1887 the Toowoomba district received eight inches of rain in one week. *TC*, 25 January 1887, p. 3, c. 1-7.

[30] *WA*, 15 March 1890, p. 2, c. 1 and 29 March 1890, p. 2, c. 5; *TC*, 21 February 1893, p. 3, c. 1-5; *WA*, 14 February 1893, pp. 2-3; 21 February 1893, p. 2, c. 3 and 13 June 1893, p. 2, c. 5.

The sluggish Condamine River, flowing from south to north along the western margin of the area drained several creeks flowing from the eastern slopes of the Main Range. Except in times of prolonged drought these streams—Freestone, Swan, Glengallan, Hodgson, Oakey and Myall Creeks—provided permanent water but their small tributaries were usually dry in winter months and were often little better than stagnant ditches in summer. Some areas of small settlement were completely without surface water and most of the creek frontages had long been pre-empted by the pastoral 'cormorants'. The 27,000 acre Westbrook Homestead Area was totally waterless. Sub-artesian supplies, however, were to be found at reasonable depths all over the Downs although in some areas such as East Prairie the selectors were compelled to dig expensive wells over 200 feet deep in order to obtain water for stock and domestic purposes.[31] The introduction of the geared windmill after 1876 solved the problem of providing water all the year round for stock on small selections but the drought losses which continued to plague the small selectors after towers and tanks dotted the landscape were not so much due to 'thoughtlessness' and 'careless improvidence' as the critics claimed but to the selectors' inability to pay for the construction of these invaluable devices.[32] Irrigation was but the dream of a few prophets and is, even now, still in its infancy.[33]

The native fauna of the Downs (wallabies, flying foxes and kangaroos) nightly sallied forth from the thick scrubs and waste land to eat crops unprotected by tall sapling fences. At their worst around Toowoomba in the 'seventies and Warwick in the late 'eighties they were finally annihilated by a campaign of ruthless extermination waged by settlers who saw the animals as competitors for grass and grain.[34] Ideas of preservation and the maintenance of ecological balance were anathema to the pioneer.

Apart from minor local variations, selectors all faced the same processes and problems in establishing the family farm. Michael Brewer at Mount Sturt, John Truss at Middle Ridge, Maas Hinz at Bark Plains, James Bourke at Clifton, John Collins at North Branch and John Mathieson at Goombungee were confronted with the same never-ending rituals which were necessary if they were to convert their environment from pasture to paddock.

31 Contractors charged one pound per foot for digging wells in 1878. *QVP*, Vol. II, (1879), 'Report of the Select Committee on Relief for the East Prairie Selectors', pp. 257-8.

32 *QPD*, Vol. 24, (1877), pp. 1295-8. The first American-type windmill was erected at a cost of £117 in 1876 by the Railways Department at Gowrie Junction. *DDG*, 2 August 1876, p. 5, c. 4.

33 Francis Kates was the leading advocate of irrigation on the Downs but his efforts were fruitless. *QPD*, Vol. 49, (1886), pp. 814-23 and Vol. 52, (1887), pp 75-7.

34 *QAJ*, Vol. 3, Part 3, August 1898, pp. 116-19. There were 'scenes of sickening slaughter' as thousands of marsupials were clubbed to death in special palisade traps. *WE&T*, 18 September 1875, p. 2, c. 5. Nearly 60,000 marsupials were killed in five months in the Warwick district alone in 1878. *WA*, 4 July 1878, p. 2, c. 6. Bounties gave selectors a good cash income for a few years.

Let us follow a Downs selector of the late 'sixties during his first critical months of pioneering. Once he decided to take up land on the Downs he usually went to the nearest Land Office and inquired exactly which areas were open for free selection.[35] Some intending farmers had liquid capital and preferred to purchase partially improved selections which were offered by many original selectors once they had obtained their certificates. A small group of agricultural pioneers on the Downs acted in a similar way to their American contemporaries by fencing, clearing and ploughing new land and then selling out after a season or two and moving on to the next property.[36] Established farms were readily available for private sale after 1875. Initially prices were fairly high and there was often much work to be done before they became profitable.[37] After 1879 land values followed actual farm returns down to very low levels and by 1884 it was possible to purchase a 600-acre semi-improved Warwick mixed farm for £2 per acre.[38] Rough grazing properties could be bought for considerably less.[39]

Private purchase, however, even when terms were available, was beyond the means of most and dangerously depleted the capital of others. The majority of newcomers selected or purchased cheap Crown land after they had inspected it in company with the local agent or a knowledgeable farmer. Hasty selection often meant rapid ruin. It was no accident that pastoral employees who selected on the stations on which they had worked generally picked choice situations and eventually prospered.

After selection, the lessee would bring his family and possessions to the property by dray, buggy, sled, horseback and even wheelbarrow. A few of the earliest settlers walked across country to their new home. Men usually camped for a few months and constructed accommodation before their families joined them. A long period of isolation ensued. Even when neighbours arrived they were often miles away and the local school, store, hotel and church much further.

To most, the initial satisfaction of their genuine land hunger at first more than compensated for the initial isolation and hardships. All of Rudd's later sentimentalism cannot conceal the genuine, deep joy the new selector felt for his own portion.

35 *Queensland Lands Department*, 'Selectors' Guide', Brisbane 1883.

36 John Glasheen selected three farms at Sandy Creek, Allora and Clifton between 1871 and 1889. Each was larger and more profitable than the one preceding. *Queenslander*, 14 August 1930, p. 19.

37 Christoph Donges purchased 20 acres at Drayton in 1874 for £200 cash. There were no stock and implements although six acres had been cleared, the whole fenced and a humpy erected. This was an exceptional case although favourably-situated Drayton farms always fetched good prices. Donges, *personal communication*, 20 June 1963.

38 *WA*, 8 January 1884, p. 3, c. 4. 95 acres at Glencoe, complete with fences, water, cottage and barn, sold for £8.2.0 per acre in 1890 although the £2.7.0 per acre paid by W. Ryan for Billy Dwyer's 80-acre Westbrook homestead was a more usual price. *TC*, 24 July 1890, p. 3, c. 2.

39 'Overton' at Geham of 2,059 acres was sold for only £1.4.0 per acre in 1890. ibid.

> You'll ride all over it filled with the proud spirit of ownership. Every inch of it and everything on it will be yours—the growing timber; the logs and firewood lying about; hundreds of fencing-posts that some poor cove's split and had to abandon; the old sheepyard and shepherd's hut that were erected by someone who went insolvent; even the wild flowers and darn stones'll be yours! How you'll admire it all![40]

The equipment brought by the selector varied in quantity, cost and quality, but a minimum number of essential items was required for successful farming. The Germans and some Irish occasionally managed with nothing but the simplest hand tools—American axes, grubbers, picks, cross-cut saws, carpenters' and fencing tools and shovels.[41] Most, however, had a single-furrow iron mouldboard plough, a set of wooden harrows, harness and saddles. Household supplies were also necessary. These usually consisted of a 200-pound bag of flour, tea, sugar, salt beef, pickles, jam and tobacco as well as cutlery, soap and blankets.[42] A few sticks of jealously guarded furniture were sometimes a woman's only reminder of the comforts she had left behind and a symbol of femininity in what was essentially a brutal, primitive male world.

Horses were costly but essential, though it was not unknown for poor selectors to put their first crop in by hand. A good plough and saddle horse might cost anything from eight to twenty pounds or more and its loss represented a major catastrophe. Horses were almost as valuable as people—some even considered that they were worth more. Selectors usually arrived with one or two cows, a score or so of sheep and sometimes goats. All had poultry, dogs and a cat, while a sow in pig was considered a necessity. For a few years, farmers had to depend upon natural increase until better stock could be purchased and the old, inferior animals culled.

Provision of shelter was the new selector's first task. The poorest raised a crude humpy constructed on a framework of sapling timber walled and roofed with large sheets of bark delicately removed from living trees.[43] Corrugated iron huts which appeared on the timberless areas after 1880 were universally detested as habitations. After some successful seasons he might erect a slab cottage with frame and rafters of trimmed gum and ironbark saplings and walls of split eight-foot slabs. Shingles covered the roof and floors were of adzed slabs or pounded earth strewn with skins. By the 'seventies, some cottages were appearing on raised piles although this practice was not general on the Downs until much later. Cottages were usually of two to three rooms with a chimney at one end serving an open fire or colonial oven though sometimes cooking was done outside.[44]

40 Steele Rudd, *The Green Grey Homestead*, Sydney 1934, p. 11.

41 E. Thorne, *An Eight Years' Resident*, London 1876, pp. 216-19; 'Selectors' Guide'; Price Fletcher (ed.), *Queensland*, pp. 1-30; J. Donges, 'Early Agriculture'.

42 ibid.

43 ibid., *Queensland Lands Department*, 'The Illustrated Guide for the Use of Farmers, Fruit-growers, Vignerons and Others', Brisbane 1888.

44 ibid.

The final stage for the successful selector was the construction of a permanent four- to six-roomed house.[45] Most Downs farm houses were unpretentious iron-roofed weatherboard buildings with long, shady verandahs at front or side, and with brick or stone chimneys. Their honest functionalism was often superior to the more 'advanced' architecture favoured by the urban middle classes. At the rear of the house was usually a large vegetable garden, an orchard, piggeries, barns, stockyards and fowlhouses.

Progress from humpy to homestead, however, while common, was not a fixed rule. Farmers with capital built cottages or large houses soon after arrival.[46] Others deliberately refrained from what they considered to be an unremunerative investment and applied their profits to other purposes. The standard of rural accommodation varied considerably. A fine house was not necessarily an accurate indication of the financial status of the occupant and many a comparatively wealthy Downs farmer lived and died in a small cottage. In the older-established Warwick Reserve were houses, which, with their 'air of comfort . . . [and] verandahs whose posts are festooned with trailing shrubs and vines' gave an appearance of permanent and 'comfortable' settlement.[47] A few Warwick farmers used the excellent local stone to good effect. Further west, and on the eastern ridges and in the Goombungee scrubs, conditions were harsher and farms much newer. Here, humpies and huts, interspersed with small cottages, were more common. The unfortunate farm labourers, perhaps the most silent, downtrodden and ill-paid group on the Downs, lived in even more primitive conditions. Sometimes they were lucky and secured the original hut and cottage when the farmers moved to a grander dwelling. Downs homesteads nevertheless were more substantial and comfortable than in most other parts of Queensland.

Next the selection had to be fenced laboriously and perhaps cleared. Boundary fences were constructed from hardwood posts and two or three rails morticed into the huge ten-by-four posts. 'Chock and log' fences were two-thirds cheaper and could be built quickly with unskilled labour. Near the house, a stockyard with five rails six feet high was built with a milking bail in one corner. Rail fences were valued at about £20-30 per mile during the 'seventies and the more easily erected six and seven wire fences which later appeared cost a similar

[45] A typical Drayton house cost £80 in 1876, with an additional £20 for the popular detached kitchen. While some new homesteads cost £200 or over, a modest dwelling could still be built for about £120 as late as 1890. J. Donges, 'Early Agriculture'. See list of improvements on the Clifton Estate farms which were privately purchased in 1889, *QVP*, Vol. 4, (1896), pp. 649-53.

[46] H. C. Frederic of East Prairie rather foolishly spent £450 of his capital on a seven-roomed house soon after his arrival from Victoria in 1878. He survived, but repented of his folly during the drought and depression of 1878-81, *QVP*, Vol. 2, (1879), p. 258.

[47] A. J. Boyd, *Queensland*, London 1882, p. 23; *The Week*, 9 December 1876, p. 674 and *BC*, 2 October 1876, p. 3, c. 6.

amount.[48] Very few selectors could afford to employ contractors. Trees and scrub were chopped, grubbed and burnt. On the timbered slopes of the Eastern Downs, small fires marked the site of each homestead as the blackened, sweaty selectors chopped, dragged and fired. After several months, three or four acres of cleared scrub would be ready for the first crop of maize.

Although selectors provided their own labour to reduce costs, this versatility, combined with cheap land, was never sufficient to enable the farmer to do without a moderate cash income. Financial outlay was still considerable, and capital investment had to be carefully allocated. Too little, and the selector would be reduced to the status of a peon. Too prodigal an application of capital and the farmer might more easily fall victim to drought, rust or storekeeper. Years of progress and toil could be destroyed in a week. The most difficult of all misfortunes to accept was a steady fall in the standard of living resulting from waning prices.

The minimum capital outlay naturally varied, connected as it was, with capital resources (either liquid or in the form of stock, tools, etc.) and living standards. All estimates of costs and investments must be regarded as suspect but the following table indicates some of the minimum requirements to commence farming on an 160-acre completely unimproved Downs agricultural selection.

The old yeoman ideal of the family farm was the basis of Darling Downs agricultural selection. Most farmers could never have managed without the arduous and unpaid services of their families. Indeed, it may be claimed that an essential ingredient in successful farming was to have as large a family as possible. To be fruitful was farsighted. Three Crow's Nest pioneers who took up selections when the area was thrown open in 1875-6, J. T. Littleton, Matthew Gleeson and Thomas Williams, had twenty-seven children between them. Another three, Charles Byrnes, Joseph Gould and Pat Skelly, had a further forty-nine offspring. This pattern was repeated all over the Downs. The German settlements in particular swarmed with children.[49] Although the family group with its close, interdependent relationships had many desirable characteristics—the creation of a strong sense of family loyalty and duty and the feeling that all had a share in the making of the property, and, by implication, the colony—the precarious nature of commercial farming meant that the farmer was not only risking his own capital and labour but those of his entire family as well.

This system had a profound psychological effect on many family

48 E. Thorne, *Eight Years' Resident*, pp. 218-29. In 1874 the following fencing costs were current on the Downs:

Paling fence, per mile	£100
One-wire fence, per mile	£25
Top-rail and 2 wires, per mile	£65

QVP, Vol. 2, (1874), p. 502.

49 Robin Smith, *Crow's Nest History*, 1958, pp. 40, 125.

MINIMUM CASH OUTLAY FOR A DOWNS SELECTOR, 1892[50]

	£	s.
Rent (160 acres at 2s. 6d. per acre)	20	0
Deed fees	1	10
Rates	8	0
Fencing (two miles at £30 per mile including labour)	60	0
Dray and harness (£4.10s. for harness)	14	10
Plough and harness (£5 each)	10	0
Harrows	3	10
Tools	4	0
House materials	20	0
Rations and clothes (family of three)	50	0
Two horses at £8 each	16	0
Two cows at £4 each	8	0
Sow	1	10
Fowls		10
Seed	4	0
TOTAL	£221	10

heads who, although they soon realized that they had adopted the wrong vocation, were forced to continue with a way of life of which they had wearied and whose underlying assumptions and beliefs they had unconsciously discarded. A sense of frustration often permeated the whole atmosphere. Schools emptied at harvesting time, and children were forced into heavy farm duties at an early age without any choice. Compulsory school attendance was not introduced in Queensland until 1900. Adolescents worked without wages. Racking tensions between patriarch and his sons were not uncommon and remorseless routine often made drudges of the women who bore the brunt of pioneering.[51] Yet the necessity for free family labour sustained a terrific drive and determination to conquer the 'bush' and reinforced the old agrarian myths and arguments as the selector conjured a vision of himself and his family standing almost alone against the evil and impersonal tides of world mercantilism.

[50] This guide, compiled from composite sources, does not include the actual expenses incurred during the first year's farming which invariably resulted in a theoretical loss. Furthermore, the all-important element of family labour is excluded.

[51] *QVP*, 1875-93. 'Department of Education, Inspector's Reports'. These refer to the chronic absenteeism among primary school-children on the Downs and the reluctance of some parents to send their child labour to school at all. For first-hand evidence, *see:* Colonel G. F. Wieck, *personal communication*, 27 September 1963: 'I grew up conscious of a man able in one field trying to rear a large family (nine children) in a field for which he was neither trained nor suited. I left school at the age of ten years and after seven years of very hard work and sacrifice became restless and unhappy . . .'

Mixed farming on moderately sized selections was the key to success. Yet it was the cash crop which provided most of the income in good years and which was really the sole economic justification for small settlement. The successful cultivation of grain and fodder crops, as the East Prairie selectors soon found out, not only meant the difference between an 'adequate' income and plain subsistence but also made possible an increase in carrying capacity and the ability to graze the more profitable fat stock.[52]

A variety of crops was grown by the selectors, the most important being maize, lucerne and wheat, which accounted for nearly 90 per cent of the total area tilled. Maize, the universal mainstay, was easily grown, capable of giving high yields and required little attention. Food for humans and animals alike, it was especially popular with the poor incoming selectors for it was rarely a total failure. There was a distinct correlation between the expansion of small settlement and the growth of a maize harvest. Established farmers concentrated on the more profitable but hazardous cultivation of wheat which required greater preparation and investment in machinery. Introduced by Bracker of Rosenthal in 1842 and the Leslies in 1843, by 1861 maize accounted for 35 per cent of all land under cultivation. In 1870 the proportion was 40 per cent and by 1875 it had risen to its peak of 43 per cent. After then, however, the proportion devoted to maize fell as wheat and lucerne growing expanded. By 1885, only 25 per cent of such land was under maize although the figure temporarily rose to 35 per cent in 1893. In the latter year, the Downs crop of 556,264 bushels represented about 30 per cent of the total Queensland production. This figure had remained fairly constant since 1865.[53]

Maize cultivation was concentrated in a few, relatively small, districts on the Eastern Downs where the slopes of the Main Range and the red-soil scrubs were especially favourable.

Yields per acre fluctuated between 20 and 30 bushels but on new scrub land some farmers managed to secure up to 100 bushels to the acre.[54] Production was hindered by the unreliable rainfall, the hot, dry, westerly winds which swept over the Downs just when the plant was flowering and the backwardness of the pig industry which inhibited development of a profitable American 'corn-belt' style of farming.[55]

Crops were planted between mid-September and mid-December and harvested in May, though sometimes a second crop was secured in winter for grazing and fodder. After a light ploughing, seed would be sown broadcast and the field gently harrowed. Rough and ready methods gradually gave way to more thorough and less costly techniques.[56] The cobs were pulled, heaped and carted to a shed where they were either shelled by a hand machine filling twenty bags a day or

[52] *QVP*, Vol. 2, (1879), pp. 259-72.

[53] *SR*, 1861-93, 'Crop Statistics'.

[54] E. Thorne, *Eight Years' Resident*, p. 199. Lucerne hay was also a most profitable commercial crop although the 1870 price of £6.7.0 per ton was almost halved by 1893.

[55] ibid. [56] ibid.

threshed by a steam-driven device capable of processing and bagging 100 bushels an hour or 1,200 per day. This machine reduced costs from 6d. to 8d. per bushel to as low as 1½d. The stalks, with typical colonial wastefulness, would be mowed, hoed and burnt.[57]

Lucerne was the most valuable of all other crops except wheat. English pasture grasses refused to thrive in the Downs climate, but lucerne, especially suited to the rich soils, was the ideal crop for artificial pasture and hay production. After the first season, lucerne would yield up to seven tons per acre for over ten years before renewal was necessary.[58] Unfortunately, few new selectors could afford to cultivate this crop at first as seed and preparation were expensive, and there was no immediate cash return. Lucerne was a rich man's crop. First grown by Frederick Bracker in 1851 and by Patrick Leslie of Goomburra a year later the crop was introduced commercially by Charles and William Gillam of 'Ardendeuchar' in 1863. Lucerne gradually spread from the Allora-Warwick district northwards until it was grown all over the Settled District.[59] In 1870, 1,572 acres were sown in artificial grasses but by 1875 there were 3,981 acres. Ten years later, 17,478 acres were under new pasture, although by 1893 the area had fallen to 8,470 acres—60 per cent of all lucerne grown in Queensland. The Allora (2,167 acres), Warwick (1,980 acres) and Toowoomba (3,594 acres) districts accounted for 5,138 tons of the 6,298 tons of lucerne hay harvested on the Downs in 1893. This figure represented but 33 per cent of the Queensland total as more farmers preferred to graze stock on the large green paddocks rather than cut them for marketable hay.[60] The only other crops of any real significance were oats, barley and potatoes. Of these, potatoes were the most important and rewarding. This hand-cultivated crop, supplied, in conjunction with flour, mutton, pumpkins and tea, the staple diet of the small selector. Planted in late September, a good crop would yield two tons to the acre, selling for £6 to £7 in the 'seventies and £3 to £5 in the late 'eighties and early 'nineties.[61] In 1861 only 149 acres on the Downs were planted but by 1865 the area had reached 529 acres (40 per cent of the Queensland total). Two-thirds of the crop was grown near Toowoomba. After 1870 the area devoted to potatoes did not greatly increase as selectors' needs were soon satisfied, local markets were quickly saturated and the metropolis was inaccessible. Only 669 acres were planted in 1875 and 823 in 1885. By 1893, the industry had revived, the Downs then producing 3,826 tons from 1,504 acres—only 13 per cent of the Queensland output. Over 48 per cent of the crop was grown in the Highfields district where German farmers industriously cultivated very small plots. The remainder was produced near Toowoomba (20 per cent) and Warwick (16 per cent).[62]

57 ibid., p. 200. 58 ibid.

59 T. Hall, *The Early History of Warwick District and Pioneers of the Darling Downs*, Warwick n.d. [c. 1926]. *Early History*, p. 92.

60 *SR*, 1861-93, 'Crop Statistics'.

61 ibid. 62 ibid.

Oats and barley, cultivated in the same way as wheat and maize, were even more sensitive to climatic conditions. Both were grown for hay, stacked for future use or baled for sale. 7,062 tons of hay was made from these grains in 1885 and 4,084 tons in 1893.[63] Many farmers, however, did not care, or could not afford, to conserve fodder for supplementary feeding and emergencies with drastic consequences which might easily have been averted. Farming practices on the Downs lagged well behind those of other colonies. Only small areas were under oats and barley:

OATS AND BARLEY DOWNS, 1870-93[64]

	1870	1875	1885	1893
Oats Downs	773	1,355	2,594	2,755
Queensland	2,386	4,119	8,039	12,653
Barley Downs	555	794	775	768
Queensland	760	1,292	1,593	1,381

(Figures in acres)

Other commercial crops (e.g. rye, sorghum and millet) were tried between 1860 and 1893 but none attained any prominence. Cotton was successfully grown at Warwick and Toowoomba but the collapse of the market after the end of the American Civil War destroyed any further prospects of expansion.[65] There was a remarkable development in the cultivation of tobacco in the Texas and Killarney areas after 1885, and a large and thriving wine-making industry established by the Germans of Middle Ridge in the early 'seventies expanded until killed at the end of the century. Reciprocity with South Australia, the imposition of heavier excise duties and licence fees, the fruit fly and the climate (which prohibited the production of first-class vintages) were responsible for the eventual collapse of the wine industry. Nevertheless, in 1893, 245 makers on the Downs produced 38,017 gallons of light white and red table wines from 340 acres of vines. Three-quarters of the output came from the Toowoomba ridges.[66] Small

[63] ibid. [64] ibid.

[65] T. Hall, *Early History*, p. 93, 'Splendid cotton was grown at Warwick at the Old Hermitage Farm by Armistead and Parr.' The industry was protected by a bonus of £3 per ton which was removed in 1868.

[66] W. MacPhillips was the first selector on the MacIntyre River to grow tobacco, in 1881. By 1883 he was cropping 14 acres and the settlers were already talking about 'the Virginia of Australia'. *WA*, 3 May 1884, p. 2, c. 3. 'Several tons' of leaf came from the Killarney area in 1889-90. *WE&T*, 21 June 1890, p. 2, c. 2. In 1893, 475 acres of tobacco on the Southern Downs (Killarney, 214 acres and Stanthorpe-Maryland, 140 acres) yielded nearly 229 tons of leaf. *SR*, 1861-93, 'Crop Statistics'.

orchards and Chinese market-gardens flourished in the Warwick and Toowoomba suburbs.

'When wheat shall be grown on the Darling Downs' was for long an expression among Australians of extreme improbability. As soon as the first selectors appeared, however, wheat became the most important single crop. Grain growing was developed in spite of grave climatic disadvantages and falling prices. There were tremendous fluctuations in production, yet farmers never stopped trying to expand wheat acreages and production. Even such a successful farmer as Donald Mackintosh could state in 1899 that '. . . for the last thirty-six years I have not got more than one good crop every three years . . . the highest crop I ever had was forty-two bushels to the acre, but the general average in a good season is from twenty-four to twenty-six bushels . . .'[67] Under optimum conditions wheat could be an extraordinarily profitable crop. One bumper harvest and success would be assured. It was not unusual for farmers to clear as much as £1,000 from a season's crop and an annual return of £500 to £800 was common in the Warwick district.[68] Such incomes enabled farmers to withstand a run of bad seasons and low prices but if these came during the first season or two on the selection this violent oscillation had a catastrophic effect.

Overall yields were, nevertheless, higher on the Downs than in all other colonies except failing Tasmania. They varied greatly, however, from area to area within the region. Some Warwick-Allora farmers consistently obtained forty bushels per acre from a few selected fields, but twenty-five bushels to the acre were more common and seventeen to twenty-two the usual return in the district.

AVERAGE WHEAT YIELD PER ACRE, 1860-94[69]

Years	Downs (bushels)	Australian Colonies (bushels)
1860–9	15.8	12.9
1870–9	18.0	10.9
1880–9	15.0	8.0
1890–4	18.0	8.5

67 *QPD*, Vol. 81, (1899), p. 377.

68 *WE&T*, 7 April 1882, p. 2, c. 6.

69 E. Dunsdorfs, *The Australian Wheat-Growing Industry, 1788-1948*, Melbourne 1956, p. 534. Between 1884 and 1894 South Australia and Victoria, the two major producers, obtained overall yields of only 6.8 and 9.9 bushels to the acre, respectively. The United States figure was 12 bushels, the New Zealand 23.7, the British 28, and the French 18. Queensland, with an average of 14.9 bushels, was in a high position. *QVP*, Vol. 4, (1897), 'Report of the Registrar-General on the Returns of Agriculture and Livestock', p. 957. 30 Allora farmers, with an aggregate wheat crop of 300 acres, produced 11,562 bushels in 1872-3—an average yield of 38.32 bushels per acre. *WE&T*, 7 March 1874, p. 2, c. 6.

But in spite of the considerable, although unco-ordinated and unscientific, attention devoted to wheat growing the Downs output was for long an insignificant fraction of the total Australian production. The problems of the Downs graingrower were considered to be of purely regional interest. Yet these drawbacks were shared by other parts of the fertile crescent, particularly the New England area. Acreages devoted to wheat on the Downs expanded as follows:

INCREASE IN WHEAT CULTIVATION, 1861-93[70]

Year	Acres	Year	Acres
1861	375	1881	15,038
1866	2,510	1886	14,663
1871	3,061	1890	11,582
1876	5,854	1893	28,766

ACRES SOWN WITH WHEAT

Police District	Years			
	1861	1871	1881	1891
Allora	—	—	—	6,563
Warwick	356	2,318	10,332	6,964
Toowoomba	19	743	4,635	4,797
Highfields	—	—	—	720
Other districts	—	—	68	262
TOTAL DOWNS	375	3,061	15,035	19,306

The percentage of land sown with wheat was thus fairly constant although in the early 'nineties maize was overtaken as the leading crop

70 Acreages devoted to wheat on the Downs expanded as follows:

Year	Acres	% Cultivated land	Year	Acres	% Cultivated land
1861	375	25	1881	15,038	39
1866	2,510	27	1886	14,663	23
1871	3,061	23	1890	11,582	18
1876	5,854	24	1893	28,766	37

SR, 1861-93, 'Crop Statistics'.

on the Downs. The last decade of the nineteenth century marked the end of thirty years of experiment and the beginning of the spectacular expansion on the Downs.

Warwick-Allora, where wheat growing first began on a commercial scale, remained the heart of the industry although during the 'seventies there was some expansion on the Central Downs and around Toowoomba.

While most wheat in the Toowoomba-Highfields area was grown on numerous small plots, the graingrowers of Warwick-Allora were concentrated in several contiguous districts and harvested much larger acreages. Each farm had a greater proportion of its area planted with

ANALYSIS OF FARMS IN THE WARWICK-ALLORA WHEAT BELT, 1882[71]

Locality	Selectors	Total Acreage in Wheat	Range of Wheat Acres	Average Per Farm
Lord John Swamp	17	416	8–45	24
Emu Vale	17	606	3–100	38
Darkey Flat	14	248	6–65	18
Killarney—Farm Creek	12	284	3–70	24
Sandy Creek	7	110	7–35	16
Lower Swan Creek	46	2,030	8–130	44
Upper Swan Creek	22	694	8–80	31
Warwick Municipality	7	177	10–40	25
Freestone Creek	48	2,451	9–240	51
Glengallan Creek—North	15	319	6–38	21
Glengallan Creek—South	52	1,719	4–96	33
Goomburra Homestead	13	350	8–85	27
TOTAL DISTRICT	270	9,404	3–240	29

wheat than in other districts. In 1880 some farmers at Freestone Creek were sowing up to 50 per cent of their holdings with the cereal.[72]

These farms then accounted for 69 per cent of the total Downs wheat acreage.

Though acreages slowly increased actual yields fluctuated wildly. Rust, smut and drought caused tremendous losses between 1869 and 1893.

The following table indicates that the menace did not attain serious proportions until 1878 when many wheat farmers were fairly financially

[71] 63 farmers, holding 21,551 acres at Freestone Creek, then had 4,731 acres under wheat, an average of 75 acres per farm. *WE&T*, 26 June 1880, p. 2, c. 3.

[72] *WA*, 26 August 1882, p. 3, c. 1 and 12 September 1882, p. 3, c. 1.

THE DOWNS WHEAT HARVEST AND THE RAVAGES OF RUST, 1870-93[73]

Year	Harvest (bush.)	Areas Affected by Rust %	Year	Harvest (bush.)	Areas Affected by Rust %
1870	39,787	30	1882	144,531	49
1871	55,439	9	1883	42,154	9
1872	78,734	9	1884	194,790	10
1873	81,161	6	1885	51,598	7
1874	71,723	6	1886	17,921	54
1875	96,381	4	1887	170,978	14
1876	99,409	19	1888	7,465	91
1877	91,764	13	1889	128,204	75
1878	129,293	50	1890	195,351	11
1879	26,620	28	1891	380,282	9
1880	219,062	14	1892	435,953	5
1881	37,186	40	1893	391,506	12

secure.[74] When one rust-ridden season followed another, as in 1881-2 and 1888-9, the consequences were severe. Nearly the whole crop was wiped out in 1888 when farmers harvested with matches rather than mowers.[75]

The climate provided optimum conditions for stem rust (*Puccinia graminis*) to invade the soft, late-maturing wheats. The popular imported White Llammas, Purple Straw and Steinwedel varieties were prolific, easily harvested and favoured by millers. They were also ideal hosts for the fungus.[76] Old World practices and traditions, combined with unreasoning prejudice and reliance upon incantation and haphazard experimentation rather than scientific research, delayed improvement. Remedies were at first sought instead of resistant varieties. Seed was pickled by bluestone, treated with other chemicals and hidden away, to protect it from 'malign influences' in the air and spontaneous generation. Some farmers advocated liming and drainage as it was also

[73] A sharp, early drought could add to the severity of the attack. In 1880, it was stated that 'wheat operations in the Warwick area are as near total failure as they could be'. *WA*, 28 September 1880, p. 2, c. 1. In 1881, three-fifths of the area sown was unproductive through drought, and one-third of both the 1885 and 1886 crops similarly failed. *SR*, 1870-93, 'Wheat Returns'.

[74] *SR*, 1870-93, 'Wheat Returns'. A rust attack did not always result in total loss. If harvested in time, some of the crop was usually saved, although yields were much lower in the stricken areas. Under prevailing conditions and with the high yields of the region, an infestation rate of less than 20 per cent was not regarded as particularly serious although the fungus might destroy one farmer's crop and leave his neighbour's unscathed.

[75] *WA*, 20 December 1881, p. 2, c. 1-2. 1888 'was the most disastrous season in the history of Warwick. . . . Last year was a terrible one of woe and completely ruined many a farmer who had sunk his little all on his first season's crops.' *WE&T*, 7 August 1889, p. 4.

[76] *WA*, 23 October 1880, p. 2, c. 1 and 20 December 1881, p. 2, c. 1.

thought that the rich black soil harboured the disease.[77] One enthusiast strung copper wire throughout his fields to divert the 'magnetic electricity' which, attracted by the iron in the soil, descended from the clouds and stimulated the fungus.[78]

After the 1879 disaster, however, farmers realized the value of experimentation with new varieties. While the £500 reward offered by the government for a rust 'cure' remained unclaimed, millers and advanced farmers began importing early maturing varieties such as Talavera, White Tuscan and Defiance.[79] Sown earlier, they proved partially rust-resistant, particularly Allora Spring, the '90-day wheat' from California obtained from William Farrer whose cross-breeding was beginning to attract attention.[80]

By 1890, breeding for resistance rather than prevention was accepted as the logical procedure, though public research was still negligible. The Queensland Government, notoriously averse to expenditure on 'impractical, coddling research' for a minor section, did little to help. What initiative there was, and the Downs seems to have stimulated inquiry and experiment when more productive regions did not, came from the advanced farmers and the hardheaded millers. Adversity bred investigation.[81] It is astonishing that the field plots, scattered over the Downs in the late 'eighties and early 'nineties and attended by enthusiastic amateurs, produced such remarkable wheats as Canning Downs Rust-Resistant, Miracle and Balatourka. All of these were used by Farrer in his own trials. The Darling Downs with its extreme conditions was the ideal proving ground for new wheats. During this period of experimentation the region played a part out of all proportion to its importance in Australian wheat production. There was a considerable two-way traffic between the Lambrigg genius and the Downs millers and farmers whose future he was to assure.[82]

Farrer, with his theoretical foundation, systematic experiments and practical objectives eventually revolutionized the Downs industry. Selective cross-breeding so mitigated the effects of rust, smut and drought

[77] J. T. Wilson stated in 1879 that deep drainage 'was a better preventative than new varieties'. *BC*, 13 August 1879, p. 5, c. 2. For similar remarks by South Australian farmers, see a discussion in the *South Australian Register*, 12 January 1881, Supplement, p. 2 and 19 January 1881, p. 6, c. 7.

[78] *BC*, 30 December 1871, p. 7, c. 4. Many farmers dressed the seed with salt or lime or pickled it in bluestone. Some picked seed on 'feeling' or 'the look of the grain'. ibid., 20 October 1880, p. 5, c. 3.

[79] N. A. Cobb, 'A Contribution to an Economic Knowledge of Australian Rusts', *Agricultural Gazette of New South Wales*, Vol. 3, (1893), pp. 443-60. 'Defiance', imported from N.S.W. by A. Wilson and distributed to his neighbours, was 'a great success' at Warwick. *WA*, 6 November 1883, p. 2, c. 2.

[80] ibid., 'Allora Spring Wheat', *Agricultural Gazette of New South Wales*, Vol. 9, (1898), pp. 608-9.

[81] Opposing the offer of a reward for a rust-cure, the squatting members derided scientific experiments as a waste of money. *QPD*, Vol. 29, (1879), pp. 593-6.

[82] *WE&T*, 2 November 1892, p. 3, c. 5 '. . . The soft wheat varieties are going right out of favour'.

that planting expanded throughout the Settled District. Yet Farrer, although his work first became prominent at the five Rust in Wheat Conferences held between 1891 and 1896, was unknown to most on the Downs in 1893.[83] Few read technical or Parliamentary papers. Even official circles afforded him little recognition.

Scientific methods solved the problem of rust but the equally pressing difficulty of falling prices, associated with the necessity for increased capital investment on Downs farms was a much more intricate and difficult proposition. Downs farmers in their first decade relied on a regional economy rather than a colonial one, but farm prices soon began to fluctuate in closer accord with metropolitan and world movements.[84]

Although there were periods of relatively high prices, 1866-95 was a period of falling returns. Wheat was 10s. per bushel on the Downs in 1861, 5s. in 1866 and 2s. 9d. in 1893.[85] The prices for other commodities fell in proportion. Maize was 4s. 6d. a bushel at Warwick in 1878 and 1s. 2d. in 1892.[86] Short slumps occurred in 1866, 1879-80 and 1882-3 with a long depression commencing in 1888. The 'selection years' of the late 'sixties and mid-'seventies, however, were characterized by moderately good prices. The following table indicates the extent of the price slide on the Downs between 1878 and 1892, as well as the short slump of 1879-80. These figures hide the farmers' actual net returns. Month-by-month and even day-by-day fluctuations had a far greater impact on the individual selector than the more imperceptive yearly declines. 'Average retail prices' meant little to those forced to sell in a glut or others lucky enough to survive a drought with surplus produce. The pattern of maize prices at Ipswich and Toowoomba illustrates this contention.

The farmer had two powerful, indispensable and decisive allies—family labour and an increasingly efficient technology. These overcame,

83 W. Deacon, 'Wheat Cultivation on the Darling Downs', *QAJ*, Vol. 1, No. 2, (1897), pp. 149-51. In 1887 the new Department of Agriculture placed the distribution of seed and field-trials on a systematic basis. For the Report of the last Rust in Wheat Conference (Melbourne, 1896) which completely accepted Farrer's results and recommendations, *see Agricultural Gazette of New South Wales*, Vol. 7, Part 7, July 1896, pp. 438-43. Farrer's masterly paper on the whole problem and his experiments is printed in the above journal: ibid., Vol. 9, Part 1, (1898), pp. 132-243. *See also* A. Russell, *William James Farrer*, Melbourne 1949.

84 The wholesale prices given by Coghlan and the index for 1861-1938/9 constructed by Butlin can only be used as rough guides when dealing with actual regional fluctuations. These figures, and those published in the Statistical Registers on which they are based, give little indication of the real return to the Downs farmers at any given time. Drought, rust and glut could and did make nonsense of metropolitan quotations. T. A. Coghlan, *Labour and Industry in Australia*, Vol. 3, London 1918, pp. 1608, 1614-26. N. G. Butlin, *Australian Domestic Product, Investment and Foreign Borrowing*, Vol. 1, Cambridge 1962, pp. 454-5.

85 Wheat prices were fairly close to Adelaide and, after the colonies had achieved a surplus in 1879, world quotations. Transport costs, local shortages and millers' rings, however, did cause significant Downs variations.

86 These prices and those in the following table are taken from the following newspapers: *WA*, 18 July 1878, p. 2, c. 1; 17 July 1879, p. 2, c. 1; 1 October 1889, p. 2, c. 1 and *TC*, 27 August 1892, p. 3, c. 1.

WARWICK-TOOWOOMBA MARKETS—PRODUCE PRICES, 1878-92[87]

Commodity	1878 (July)	1879 (July)	1889 (October)	1892 (August)
Wheat (bushels)	5/6	4/6	4/–	3/9-4/–
Maize (bushels)	4/6-5/–	2/–-2/3	4/1	2/–-2/9
Potatoes (ton)	£8-£9	£3	£4	£2.15.0-£3.10.0
Chaff	£8.10.0	£4	£2.5.0	£1.15.0-£2.0.0
Lucerne hay (ton)	£9	£3.10.0	£1.10.0-£2.0.0	£1.10.0-£2.0.0
Butter (lb)	1/9-2/–	10d.-1/–	8d.-1/3	9d.-11d.
Cheese (lb)	10d.-1/3	n.a.	6¾d.-7¾d.	8d.
Eggs (dozen)	1/9-2/–	1/–-1/3	n.a.	6d.

or enabled the farmer to disregard labour charges, the largest single item in the cost structure. Reaping and threshing rapidly and efficiently farmers were able to reduce the ever-present risk of crop damage. Farm machinery and improved techniques not only eliminated much harsh toil, increased yields and dramatically lowered costs but enabled complete new farm activities—dairy farming and fat-stock production—to become established. These diversified Downs farming at a critical time. Ridley, Farrer, refrigeration and Separation saved the small selectors. Paradoxically the development of machinery and ocean steamers helped farmers in the southern colonies far more than the Downs producers. Victoria and South Australia were able to produce huge quantities of cheap grain on comparatively poor soils while the Queensland industry was still in the nursery stage.

The old primitive implements were soon replaced by modified local models and imported machinery. By 1891 a successful Warwick grain-grower might invest nearly £200 in farm implements. The introduction of Australian and American harvesting equipment was the most revolutionary technological development on the Downs after railways. The Downs farmer entered the machinery age twenty years behind his South Australian counterpart. By 1870, mowers had replaced scythes on many farms and the Adelaide wheat stripper and the reaper were making

87 WHEAT PRODUCTION IN FOUR COLONIES (bushels)

Season	Queensland	New South Wales	Victoria	South Australia
1880–1	223,243	3,717,355	9,727,369	8,606,510
1890–1	207,990	3,649,216	12,751,295	9,399,389

Commonwealth of Australia Yearbook, 1910, p. 367.

their first appearance.[88] Combined reapers and binders were demonstrated at Warwick in 1877 and mobile machines in 1875.[89] H. V. McKay's famous combine harvesters were at work in the Warwick-Allora area by the mid-'nineties. After 1888 the pace of mechanization accelerated as grain acreages rose and farmers found that they could not compete without the latest implements.[90]

Considerable savings were made in labour, time and money. Reaping carried out by men with scythes and sickles cutting a quarter-acre per day, cost from 25s. to 40s. per acre in 1865. A reaper and binder, operated by two to three men and cutting 12-15 acres per day, cut this to £1 per acre by 1875. By 1895, 25 acres were being cut by one man for less than 10s. per acre. Hand threshing with flails cost from 1s. 3d. to 1s. 8d. per bushel in 1865 when 20 bushels was a fair day's work. Stationary steam threshers reduced the cost to 6d. per bushel by 1870. Mobile plants, processing 500-800 bushels per day, lowered the price to 10d.-1s. 4d. per bag of 40 bushels (plus labour) during the following decade.[91]

The graingrowers' production costs varied enormously according to individual and regional circumstances. A questionnaire, posed in 1895 by the Queensland Department of Agriculture to 213 wheat farmers, revealed surprising discrepancies and 'great and unaccountable differences in the cost of production'.[92] 137 farmers considered that the crop was profitable, 47 stated that it was ruinous (although 30 of these showed a good profit when prices were at their lowest point ever) and 29 were indecisive. There were marked differences between large and small growers. Larger farmers tended to have lower working costs although their capital investment was higher. Hidden costs such as establishment, interest, rates and maintenance are impossible to assess precisely. In 1893 a Warwick farmer published more detailed figures which, taken in conjunction with the previous survey, give a reasonably accurate estimate. If the 100 acres produced an average yield of 35 bags (1,400 bushels) the farmer would gross £245 and make a net profit of £34. 10s. If the price

88 B. M. Sims, *Allora's Past*, p. 40. R. Williams first made farm implements at Toowoomba in 1864. Prices fell immediately—two-horse ploughs sold for £6.10.0, iron harrows for £5 and hoes for £3.6.0 each. *DDG*, 25 July 1865, p. 3, c. 6.

89 In 1871 there were 3 mowers, 4 reapers, 8 strippers and 16 threshers on the Downs. By 1875 the respective figures were 85, 85, 9 and 28. *SR*, 1871 and 1875.

90 In 1891, a successful Warwick graingrower estimated that a total investment of at least £188 was needed for farm machinery. *WE&T*, 1 November 1893, p. 2, c. 6.

91 B. M. Sims, *Allora's Past*, p. 40; Rev. J. D. Lang, *'Queensland'*, pp. 181-4; *WE&T*, 18 December 1875, p. 2, c. 2 and *WA*, 5 December 1878, p. 3, c. 6.

92 T. Weedon, *Queensland*, Brisbane 1897, pp. 281-4. For six large growers the total cost per acre ranged between £1 and £3.8.0, with an average cost of £2.0.8. The average cost per acre for ten small growers was £2.10.4½. In 1897-8 the estimated cost per acre for 'an average Downs farm' (and there was really no such thing) was £2.5.11. *QAJ*, Vol. 3, Part 3, August 1898, pp. 90-3. South Australian farmers, working larger acreages with modern machinery, had much lower costs but low yields per acre returned them only half the profits secured by Downs farmers from similar areas. *QAJ*, Vol. 4, Part 4, April 1899, p. 258.

Costs of Production—100-Acre Warwick Wheat Farm, 1893[93]

	£	s.
Plough, harrow and sow 100 acres	100	0
Seed 100 bushels at 3/6 per bushel	17	10
Reaping and binding at 37/6 per acre	37	10
Stocking, carting and stacking	20	0
Threshing 350 bags at 1/– per bag	17	10
Threshers' wages and food	18	0
TOTAL	£210	10

of wheat rose above 3s. 6d., profits would also rise but a fall would lower margins. A decline of 6d. per bushel might produce a net loss.[94] Fortunately, yields were usually higher than this in the areas whose farm economies were based on wheat—a 20-bushel crop and the Warwick-Allora grower could withstand a considerable price fall. Careful farmers on good soils and with favourable climatic conditions suffered less.

Few Downs farmers ever earned a reasonable dividend on their capital investment once prices fell. Those who could afford to increase the gross area under cultivation, invest heavily in machinery and strike a balance between crop and livestock suffered little. All were prepared to accept in lieu of interest 'the inherent satisfaction in owning land which also provides [them] with a home'.[95] They had no other alternative. But psychological factors modified the consequences of economic changes. Rural ideals were not always purely emotive and ineffective. The penetrating statement of the Wheat Industries Commission was as true in 1893 as it was when it first appeared in 1936:

> . . . agriculture is rather more a way of life than a method of making profits, and that, generally speaking, the interest which can be earned upon the money invested in agricultural pursuits on the basis of land values and costs of providing fixed assets on a farm, is considerably lower than the rate of interest expected from investments either in gilt-edged securities such as government bonds or in industrial enterprises.

93 *WE&T*, 1 November 1893, p. 2, c. 6.

94 ibid.

95 *Commonwealth Parliamentary Papers*, 1934-7, Vol. 4, 'Report of the Royal Commission on the Wheat, Flour and Bread Industries', pp. 126, 680.

CHAPTER 8

STOREKEEPER AND BANKS

FINANCIAL PROBLEMS OF THE DOWNS SELECTORS

The original capital of the selector was usually quickly dispersed in land purchase or rent, compulsory improvements and initial living expenses. Although the deferred payments system reduced the capital outlay—a 160-acre agricultural selection taken up under the Act of 1868 only required an annual cash payment of £12—this assistance only gave the prospective farmer his land and did little to help him make a commercial success of his selection. Other inescapable establishment charges meant that few selectors could afford to work their holdings without some kind of part-time or off-season job. Warwick farmers 'who had the greatest difficulty in living' in 1867 only survived by such station work. An annual shearing cheque of some £20-30 was often the margin between failure and success. Many selectors had had previous station experience on the Downs and were in keen demand by adjacent squatters who regarded them as reliable and skilled contractors. This labour did much of the shearing, washing, fencing and craftsman's work on the freehold estates. In some instances their selections formed a miniature closely-settled zone on the station boundaries which operated to the advantage of both squatter and the selector.[1] Some selectors laboured on neighbourhood roads and returned to their farms for food and shelter at nightfall while others secured employment on railway works or in the sawmills of the Range. Several kept hotels or small stores and a few built up lucrative harvesting businesses. Such selectors were the threshing contractors Robert Cooke of Allora and W. D. Lamb of Yangan and Christoph Donges, a Drayton ploughman.[2] Windfalls, such as the discovery of tin at Stanthorpe in 1872, occasionally enabled selectors to accumulate a capital reserve in a short space of time but such opportunities were limited on the Downs.

Downs farmers, although the country-town myth-makers and Brisbane legislators refused to recognize it, were really small businessmen in an

[1] *QVP*, Vol. 2, (1867), 'Minutes of Evidence Taken Before the Select Committee on Agricultural Reserves', pp. 964-5.

[2] *WE&T*, 18 December 1875, p. 2, c. 2; Morrison, 'The Town Liberal', *JRQHS*, Vol. 3, Supplement; J. Donges, *personal communication*, 20 June 1963.

age of rapidly expanding capitalistic enterprise. Like any other commercial class the pioneers needed credit if they were to survive. Some of the most successful were thrifty and had an aversion to the use of outside capital, only purchasing new implements and more land when they had the cash to pay for them. Thus Donald Mackintosh of Greenmount was opposed to borrowing to finance further improvements.[3] This was particularly true of the German and Scots elements. Between 1860 and 1893 the increasing use of capital in farming became essential to the reduction of costs of production demanded by the continual fall in prices. It became increasingly impossible for the aspiring Downs farmer to triumph: external capital was required if the selector was to graduate from the ranks of the 80-acre homesteaders to those of the 'boss-cocky' group farming over 500 acres. A 640-acre conditional purchase under the 1868 Act required an annual cash payment of some £48 as well as an expenditure of £320 on improvements over the period of the lease.[4]

But it had always been usual for agricultural credit to be harder and dearer to obtain than advances for other forms of commercial endeavour. The farm business was small, it was controlled by numerous independent operators with all the idiosyncrasies of individuals, and it was spread over a wide area. Though farming was much less specialized than either commerce or manufacturing, each type prescribed a different type of credit. The Drayton dairy farmer needed less long-term credit than the Freestone Creek graingrower with his less regular returns, high labour costs, greater capital investment and seasonal fluctuations. The East Prairie small grazier had a large initial investment in stock and his capital needs were similar, though smaller, than those of his squatter neighbours.[5]

Moreover, each farm demanded several types of credit which were classified according to the length of the loan and depended on the use the farmer intended to make of his borrowed capital. Thus long-term credit (over three years) was necessary for land purchase and standing improvements; intermediate credit (six months to three years) financed stock, machinery and crops when the time lag between investment and sale or produce was especially great; short-term credit (a few months) purchased household needs and paid labour.

Belshaw has formulated three requisites for an adequate system of rural credit. Firstly, the cost of credit to agriculture should be virtually the same as that for other enterprises, allowing for differences in risk, convenience to the lender and special expenses. This presupposes the creation of specialized credit agencies or the adaptation of existing institutions. Secondly, the convenience of the farmer should be safeguarded

[3] *QPD*, Vol. 86, (1900), p. 2403.

[4] *QGG*, 22 February 1868, No. 27, Supplement, pp. 172-201.

[5] *See* the grievances of the East Prairie selectors: *QPD*, Vol. 26, (1878), pp. 865-73 and *QVP*, Vol. 2, (1879), pp. 253-70. 'Report of the Committee on the Petition of the East Prairie Selectors'. Some of the problems of the Highfields farmers are discussed in: *BC*, 2 May 1877, p. 3, c. 2. For the Felton and Westbrook homesteaders, *see*: *TC*, 8 January 1876, p. 2, c. 5-6.

by ensuring that loans are for a long enough period to cover the productive processes for which they are needed. Thirdly, the equity of the farmer must be safeguarded in the event of liquidation.[6]

Few of these conditions were met by individuals and institutions which provided credit for Downs farmers between 1860 and 1893 when glaring defects and haphazard and reluctant allocation of agricultural finance were evident. However, Downs agriculture was subject to unpredictable risks which made both lending and borrowing extremely hazardous unless the security was more than adequate.[7]

The key to all credit is the security the borrower can provide. The incoming selector was at a serious disadvantage. Few could provide sufficient chattel or collateral security, and personal notes or promises to pay were not very tangible assets although they were all many homesteaders could offer. Crop liens were virtually worthless in this period of agricultural adaptation and the selectors' stock was too scanty and poor to be a worthwhile security. Few would disagree with the axiom that:

> The most important real security a lender can have is an honest and industrious farmer who is a good farm manager and who has an efficient and profitable farm business.[8]

Distinctions were difficult to make among the host of new selectors, and few pioneers on the Darling Downs had an 'efficient and profitable farm business' within the first three years of settlement. The first sign of rural prosperity was usually the acquisition of more land after the selection had been freeholded. 'Prosperous and free from debt' Allora farmers such as John Glasheen and James Bourke were demanding—and obtaining—more land by 1874; six years after initial selection. But these were the exception.[9]

The only negotiable security most small selectors had was their land. But this was of dubious value in the years before a certificate of fulfilment of conditions was granted. It was during these very years that the selector most needed cheap, ready, reliable credit. But the politicians and their advisers in the Lands Office were at pains to prohibit the mortgaging of selectors' leases. The Crown Lands Act of 1860 and the Agricultural Reserves Act of 1863, as well as the three key Darling Downs Settlement Acts of 1868, 1876 and 1884, specifically forbade borrowing by mortgage or any other charge on the security of the Crown lease. During the currency of the original lease the land could neither be transferred nor taken for execution of a debt unless the selector be-

[6] H. Belshaw, *The Provision of Credit with Special Reference to Agriculture*, Cambridge 1931.

[7] As the necessary statistics do not exist, it is impossible to estimate the precise extent of selector indebtedness on the Darling Downs. The historian can but sigh for source material such as that available to the student of rural finance in contemporary India—e.g., M. Darling, *The Punjab Peasant in Prosperity and Debt*, Bombay 1925.

[8] I. W. Duggan and R. U. Battles, *Financing the Farm Business*, New York 1950, p. 81. *See also*: W. G. Murray, *Agricultural Finance*, Third Edition, Ames, Iowa 1953.

[9] *BC*, 28 April 1874, p. 3, c. 4-5. 'Agricultural Settlement on the Darling Downs'.

came hopelessly insolvent. Under the Act of 1884 deeds of grant in fee simple were refused to all mortgaged lands.[10] These interdictions were intended to prevent speculation and dummying. It was also hoped that they would safeguard selectors from falling into the hands of unscrupulous men eager to acquire their land by default or loss. But these regulations actually impaired the distribution of credit, a fact which was recognized by the Act of 1884 when lending on the security of a Conditional Purchase or agricultural and grazing farm leases was made easier.[11]

Nevertheless, homestead selectors under the Acts of 1868 and 1876 had to wait five years before they could obtain their certificates. Conditional purchasers had to wait three years and lenders were not always willing to advance solely on the strength of such certificates.[12] Freehold securities were a different matter. Mortgaging of such property was conducted under the provisions of the Queensland Real Property Act of 1861 (25 Vict. No. 14) which simplified legal processes and assisted transfers. Under this Act, when land was charged or made security for a mortgage, a bill could either be executed and registered or the land could be charged merely by depositing the documents of title with the mortgagee. The latter was common practice on the Downs but from the lender's point of view it was rather a precarious undertaking. All such bills were not transfers but were only security for the sum borrowed although on default the mortgagee was entitled to sell the land.[13] This Act was replaced by the consolidated Real Property Act of 1877 (41 Vict. No. 18) which created equitable mortgages that had to be registered. These Acts, which established the Torrens system of land transfer in Queensland, helped selectors by making cheap transactions possible, and by providing them with a good, easily recognizable security for loans.[14]

[10] The judgment of the Supreme Court of Queensland in the case Miskin and Another *v.* Attorney-General (22 December 1871) did, however, give lenders some security. The judgment declared that an insolvent selector must surrender his conditional purchase to his assignees. They could then dispose of the estate as they wished. *BC*, 25 December 1871, p. 3, c. 5. *Acts and Regulations Relating to the Waste Lands in the Colony of Queensland*, Government Authority, Brisbane 1861, pp. 15-16. *QGG*, 22 February 1868, No. 27, Supplement, Crown Lands Act of 1868, pp. 172-201. *QPD*, Vol. 20, (1876), pp. 564-5. Debates on the mortgaging clauses (28, 32, 34-35, 49) of the Crown Lands Act of 1876. Homesteads were specifically excluded from passing to creditors or being mortgaged or transferred during the first five years. *Consolidated Statutes of Queensland*, Vol. 1, Brisbane 1889, pp. 1154-7. Crown Lands Act of 1884, Clauses 66-8, 74.

[11] ibid.

[12] ibid. *Also: Australian Joint Stock Bank*, Confidential Instructions to Officers, Sydney 1886, pp. 20-6. Unpublished. BNSW Archives, Sydney. For the practice in New South Wales, *see: Votes and Proceedings of the New South Wales Legislative Assembly*, Vol. II, (1883), pp. 161-4. Morris-Ranken Report.

[13] *QPD*, Vol. 22, (1877), pp. 251-4.

[14] ibid. *Consolidated Statutes of Queensland*, p. 2200. G. A. Eagar, 'Bankers' Securities', *Journal of the Institute of Bankers of New South Wales*, Vol. 3, Part 6, 25 June 1894, pp. 236-50, 277. The Torrens system also encouraged land speculation—freehold fetters! *BC*, 7 August 1876, p. 2, c. 4-5.

Even a part-time cash income and plentiful family labour, however, were insufficient to provide the farmer with enough cash to bridge the gap between ploughing and harvesting and to carry him over the frequent bad seasons. As in the other Australasian colonies 'reliance on borrowed money was the bane of the selector' but it was unavoidable.[15] For this essential short-term credit most farmers were forced to rely on the local storekeeper, town miller or commission agent. Unfortunately for the selectors, these people provided the most costly, unreliable and exacting credit facilities of all. Yet, as one Victorian farmer pointed out, many ensnared selectors considered that they had no alternative but to accept the system as one of the facts of life. This had important social and political repercussions. Trapped in an apparently never-ending cycle of debt and drought, some selectors never escaped from their financial commitments. Moreover, boss-cockies who had themselves survived what many considered to be part of the Darwinian struggle for survival on the land were reluctant to help the later selectors escape these financial toils. Some selectors, it was claimed:

> . . . became so degraded morally and intellectually that they were incapable of the rational and manly discontent of freemen.[16]

The slow provision of farm credit by the state in Queensland was partly the result of this process and these attitudes.

Storekeeper credit usually took the form of a simple advance of goods, the price of which would be deducted from the farmer's cheque when the crops or livestock were sold. Occasionally this advance was secured by a written agreement giving storekeepers first call upon the certificates of fulfilment. Upon the grant of a freehold, the notes would be retired and the new deeds deposited. Not only did these arrangements compel the farmer to pay whatever prices the storekeeper demanded, but they gave him no choice in the marketing of his produce and he was forced to take whatever returns the latter had managed to secure. Steele Rudd's realistic and masterly description of Dad's first harvest graphically illustrates the operation and consequences of storekeeper credit:

> Fifteen bags we got off the four acres, and the storekeeper undertook to sell it . . . Dad expected a big cheque.
>
> Every day for nearly three weeks he trudged over to the store [five miles] . . . Each time the storekeeper would shake his head and say, 'no word yet.'
>
> Dad couldn't understand. At last word did come. The storekeeper was busy serving a customer when we went in, so he told Dad to 'hold on a bit'.
>
> Dad felt very pleased—so did I.
>
> The customer left. The storekeeper looked at Dad and twirled a piece of string round his first finger, then said, 'Twelve pounds your corn cleared, Mr. Rudd, but, of course,'—going to a desk—'there's that account of yours which I

[15] ibid., 29 February 1876, p. 2, c. 5-6. This was also the case in most areas of the world where commercial agriculture was being established. G. R. Anderson, 'From Cattle to Wheat. The Impact of Banking in Early Wichita', *Journal of Agricultural History*, Vol. 33, No. 1, January 1959, pp. 3-15.

[16] A. Moffat, 'Speech at the Bundaberg Agricultural Conference', *QAJ*, Vol. 9, Part 1, 1 July 1901, p. 28.

have credited with the amount of the cheque. That brings it down to just three pounds, as you will see by the account.'

Dad was speechless, and looked sick.

He went home and sat on a block and stared into the fire with his chin resting in his hands, till Mother laid her hand upon his shoulder and asked him kindly what was the matter. Then he drew the storekeeper's bill from his pocket, and handed it to her, and she too sat down and gazed into the fire.

That was our first harvest.[17]

Several Downs storekeepers tried deliberately to tie the farmers to them while the flourmillers frequently acted in collusion to fix prices and even compelled the farmer to remain shackled to the obnoxious truck system. Farmers deeply in debt found it almost impossible to transfer their accounts and could only escape by good crops and rising prices. Isolated storekeepers had a virtual monopoly of the homestead areas they served. Near Toowoomba and Warwick, however, business competition was keen and the storekeepers were eager to attract farm custom. It was near these towns, though, that the most prosperous farms were situated.[18]

The poorest selectors were reduced to the simple barter system and the storekeepers usually got the best of these transactions. It was customary for these homesteaders to receive what amounted to 10 per cent less for their produce and to be charged 10 per cent more for the store goods. As far as the merchant was concerned it was always a buyer's market. Selectors without sovereigns had no bargaining power. Interest rates were invariably exorbitant; it was common to pay at least 15 per cent for 12 months' accommodation and 30 per cent for loans maturing in 6 months. Warwick 'money-grubbers' charged 33 per cent interest on short-term loans in 1870 and Highfield storekeepers imposed rates ranging from 20 to 30 per cent in 1879. Even 'established' selectors were being charged 12 per cent interest, plus 10 per cent commission, on all overdue accounts by the Downs storekeepers in 1868.[19] Stiff booking fees were often demanded—there was sometimes a difference of between 5 per cent and 60 per cent between cash prices and charged goods—and the pitiless accumulation of compound interest often pushed debts to fantastic levels.[20]

17 Steele Rudd, *On Our Selection*, Sydney 1961, (New Edition), p. 6.

18 J. J. Kingsford in 1862 attempted to regain his lost monopoly of Warwick farmers' business by raising wheat prices to 8/- per bushel and thereby forcing the new flourmill out of business. He failed, but the mill, itself a monopoly, continued the old truck system. *DDG*, 13 February 1862, p. 3, c. 6.

W. T. Lovejoy declared in 1890 that his Meringandan hotel and store 'commands all the trade of the area', while James Mowen, 'The laird of Clifton', was in a similar strategic position. *TC*, 7 October 1890, p. 2, c. 3 and *WE&T*, 31 July 1886, p. 2, c. 5.

19 *WA*, 22 April 1868, p. 2, c. 1-2; *WE&T*, 12 November 1870, p. 2, c. 7 and *QPD*, Vol. 29, (1879), p. 691.

20 A. Moffat, 'Speech at Bundaberg Conference', p. 24. Even E. L. Thornton (MLA for Warwick and later Eastern Downs), (1868-73), a gentleman-farmer with 836 acres, was forced to pay 12 per cent interest to Horwitz in 1881. He was later declared insolvent. *WA*, 7 July 1883, p. 3, c. 3.

A few country storekeepers exploited the farmers whenever they could and their granting of credit was often an arbitrary transaction based on personal whim rather than a purely business proceeding:

> It is just as well to frighten them [the selectors] . . . the rate of interest . . . was just according to the temper I was in when they came to see me.[21]

But other merchants were conscious of their responsibilities to an agricultural interest that many felt would ultimately dominate the Downs economy. Cribb and Foote of Ipswich, and F. H. Kates of Allora all earned a reputation for fairness and unwillingness to press farmer debtors in hard times. Yet a rival storekeeper, H. Benjamin, alleged in 1883 that 'Jacob Horwitz of Warwick possesses a number of selectors' and farmers' deeds in his safe . . . which enables him to exert political control . . .' This, although splenetic, was true.[22] But the principals of all these firms were actively engaged in Queensland politics and relied on their clients' assistance for electoral victory. Kates claimed that his several political triumphs between 1878 and 1903 would not have been possible if his money-lending, storekeeping and milling practices had oppressed selectors.[23] No doubt there is some truth in this contention but it can be argued that the existence of book debts gave these aspiring politicians the whip-hand over their constituents.[24] Once again the majority of farmers were unwilling to associate what they regarded as the indirect economic oppression of the entire capitalist system with the exactions of their local storekeepers.

Yet the storekeepers had some grounds for defence. It must again be emphasized that only those with no real security borrowed from storekeepers. Unregistered personal acceptances were almost worthless in point of law and the selections themselves were usually forfeited to the Crown after their unsuccessful lessees had walked off and left their creditors lamenting. Even when the selections did fall into storekeepers' hands this usually coincided with a period of low land values. Such selections were not readily saleable in times of agricultural distress and few storekeepers could afford to have capital locked up in partially improved land. Moreover, the incoming selector would demand as much credit as his unfortunate predecessor. The storekeepers themselves had to pay heavily for credit from the Brisbane and Sydney merchant houses who in turn borrowed from the banks. A major failure in Brisbane would create a chain reaction which would soon affect the Downs. Overextended storekeepers found it impossible to call in all loans and debts at a moment's notice. They could not refuse the farmers' call for assistance at particular times of the year and their economic position was

21 Evidence of R. W. Bennett, a hard-headed, unsympathetic storekeeper and commission agent, of Horsham, Victoria: *Victorian Parliamentary Papers*, 1879-80, Vol. 3, No. 72, pp. 17-19. 'Minutes of Evidence Given Before the Crown Lands Commission of Inquiry'.

22 *WA*, 29 September 1903, p. 3, c. 2.

23 *WE&T*, 29 September 1883, p. 3, c. 1.

24 For Kates' defence, *see: QPD*, Vol. 49, (1886), p. 755.

often only a little above that of their struggling customers. There was a particularly high failure rate among the 'gombeen men' on the Darling Downs which reflected the problems and difficulties of their clientele.[25]

A few fortunate selectors had other and more reliable sources of cheap credit. After 1880, second-generation farmers began to take up new selections with finance provided by their fathers or other relatives.[26] Others had personal friends in country towns and some lawyers were often willing to oblige. Local commission agents such as T. G. Robinson of Toowoomba and William Deacon of Allora also advanced on good security and a small number of squatters were prepared to finance prospective tenant farmers.[27] But such arrangements reached only a few farmers and the terms were often unsatisfactory from the selectors' point of view.

Satisfactory long-term credit from the banks was even harder to obtain although the 'respectable' established farmers could generally secure bank advances for more land, stock or improvements. In 1888 one large Warwick farmer had, to the chagrin of the Bank of New South Wales' head office, an overdraft of nearly £818 without the security of registered mortgages.[28] The introduction of expensive, but essential labour- and cost-saving machinery during the 1870s forced most farmers to resort to the lending concerns. Apart from the banks, only the stock and station agencies, which flourished during the 1880s, lent freely on landed securities. But these mortgage investment and trading companies catered only for the pastoralist and the small farmer was unable to tap the stream of British deposits flowing into these institutions.[29]

The banks themselves would not advance on most agricultural securities until the 'seventies and this class of business was always regarded as inferior to other banking transactions although this conservatism slowly changed over the years. But, as a leading Victorian capitalist asserted:

> The property of the selector and farmer is, as a class, of an inferior character as a security, and it is obvious that lenders must take this fact into account, and those who do not will eventually lose on the transactions.

25 Clark was alleged to have 'put the screw on his 50-60 mortgagors' during the 1868 Warwick election. Nevertheless, he lost the fight. *WA*, 23 September 1868, p. 1, c. 1-4.

26 E.g., W. D. Wilson, a prosperous Warwick storekeeper and Mayor of the town in 1885, was declared bankrupt in April 1890 with liabilities which exceeded £8,000. Like others, he attributed his misfortune to the agricultural depression and crop-failure. *WA*, 14 July 1891, p. 2, c. 7.

27 The Clifton Estate, part of which was subdivided between 1889 and 1891, was almost entirely taken up by prosperous Central Downs farmers and their sons. *WA*, 16 February 1889, p. 2, c. 1 and 5; *TC*, 29 January 1891, p. 2, c. 7-8 and *QVP*, Vol. 4, (1896), pp. 649-56.

28 Robinson advanced on the security of produce and stock. *TC*, 29 March 1883, p. 2, c. 5. *See* chapter on the 'Middlemen'.

29 General Manager to Inspector, 21 October 1888, S/1/72 *BNSW Letters to the Queensland Inspector*, 1886-91, p. 519. mss BNSW Archives, Sydney.

Yet the standard practices of English banking had already been violated by pastoral lending which events proved to be extremely dangerous. In many cases, loans to farmers were certainly no more hazardous but the old pro-squatter prejudices took years to disappear.[30]

The period 1868-88, when the bulk of the selections were taken up on the Darling Downs, was also the age of bank flotations, managerial individualism and competition in Queensland. In 1872 only five banks operated in the colony but by 1888 ten were seeking advance business. In 1880, the five banks on the Downs had a mere eleven branches confined almost entirely to Toowoomba, Warwick and Dalby, but eleven years later six banks operated twenty-three branches spread throughout the farming areas. Some of these depended almost entirely on 'sound agricultural lending'.[31] Evidence exists, to support the theory that the aggressive native banks with their close political ties, strong beliefs in the future potential of the country and willingness to take speculative risks on a large scale, forced the older banks into competition for the limited advance and deposit business.[32] Rural customers benefited by such competition although most of the advantages were secured by speculators, merchants and pastoralists.

The Queensland National Bank, that 'institution of adventurers, speculators and optimists', had seven branches on the Downs by 1890. In the late 'eighties this bank opened agricultural branches at Allora, Clifton, Pittsworth and Killarney on the Downs.[33] Two years previously, F. H. Hart, the chairman of directors, had stated:

> We have every reason to be satisfied with the progress made at the offices established in agricultural districts . . . the public generally in these districts having shown their appreciation of our efforts to afford them legitimate banking facilities.[34]

This bank, with its corrupt general manager, rash lending policy, pastoral speculations and virtually autonomous branch managers, had lost over £3.5 million by 1896. But of this sum, only £243,542 (6.96 per cent) consisted of losses on agricultural advances. As most of the latter

30 An examination of the papers of a representative Australian concern of this nature failed to reveal any interest or activity in the sphere of agricultural finance: *Goldsbrough, Mort and Co. Ltd*, Collection, ANU Archives. This state of affairs was reversed in the United States where similar land-mortgage and mercantile companies lent directly to the grain growers of the prairie states. The pioneer pastoral industry had of course been extinguished or had never put down a hoof in this area. A. G. Bogue, 'The Land Mortgage Company in the Early Plains States', *Journal of Agricultural History*, Vol. 25, No. 1, January 1951, pp. 20-33.

31 G. S. Griffiths, 'The Farmer: His Wants, His Security and His Loan-Supplies, From a Financial Agent's Point of View', *AIBR*, Vol. 12, No. 4, 16 April 1888, p. 206.

32 *Pugh*, Brisbane 1880 and 1891, *AIBR*, Vol. 15, No. 12, 20 December 1891, pp. i-xiiv.

33 General Manager to Inspector, 25 June 1887, GM/1/230 *BNSW General Manager's Letter-book*, 1884-94, p. 390. mss BNSW Archives, Sydney; ibid., 1 February 1888, p. 445 and S. J. Butlin, *Australia and New Zealand Bank*, Sydney 1961, pp. 220-1, 231.

34 G. Blainey, *Gold and Paper, A History of the National Bank of Australasia Limited*, Melbourne 1958, p. 190.

were loans to the ailing sugar industry the Downs farmers' share of this welter of lending was infinitesimal.[35]

On the other hand, the Royal Bank of Queensland, founded in 1885, was more wary of pastoral investment and concentrated on mercantile, mining and agricultural business. This bank with its 'smooth and cautious lending policy' was closely associated with the economic development of the Darling Downs. Two of its directors, Miles and Kates, were both protagonists of the agricultural interest on the Downs and the bank generally adopted a relatively liberal advance policy towards the more prosperous farmers.[36]

The conservative and canny Bank of New South Wales, orientated towards the squatters and merchants, operated with tight head office control over their regional managers. This bank was generally reluctant to lend to agricultural selectors on the Downs until the mid-1880s when their original pastoral bias was modified. By the last decade of the century it was evident that the bank in both New South Wales and Queensland was keen to lend on small farming securities.[37]

Likewise, the Australian Joint Stock Bank with its traditional associations with the Darling Downs pastoral industry and its rigid head office control over both the Brisbane inspector and the managers in the field, was not prepared to take mortgages over livestock and small farm property until the mid-1870s. In 1893, however, Friend, the chairman of the reconstructed bank, noted that:

> It has long been the policy of the bank to open branches in rising country towns and much valuable business has been secured that way . . .[38]

In that year loans to small farmers accounted for approximately 13 per cent (£1.24 million) of the total advances.

Bank policy was as diverse as the various types of security a farmer could offer. Practices varied from year to year, from head office to head office, and from manager to manager. Head offices would sometimes ignore country managers' practices of lending on certificates without registration until the all-important ratio of deposits to advances fell. Then there would be fiery letters from the general manager and threats of dismissal would follow a few weeks later.[39] These erratic decisions meant that the Downs farmers could not *rely* on credit which was often arbitrarily restricted when the farmer needed it most. Fluctuations

35 In the late 'eighties, this bank opened agricultural branches at Allora, Clifton, Pittsworth and Killarney on the Downs. *AIBR*, Vol. 12, No. 8, 16 August 1888, p. 518.

36 ibid., Vol. 21, No. 12, 18 December 1897, pp. 799-800.

37 G. Blainey, *Gold and Paper*, p. 202. William Miles, to whose 'tact and widespread influence' the high position of the Royal Bank was attributed, represented the predominantly agricultural constituency of Darling Downs (1878-87). A 'liberal squatter', he sympathized with the farmers so far as their interests did not clash with those of his own group. *WE&T*, 24 August 1887, p. 2, c. 4-5.

38 General Manager to Queensland Inspector, 13 April 1890, S/1/172, *Secretary's Letter-book*, 1886-91, p. 831. mss BNSW Archives, Sydney.

39 *AIBR*, Vol. 17, No. 10, 19 October 1893, p. 956 and Vol. 21, No. 6, 19 June 1897, pp. 373-4. Annual reports of AJS Bank.

on the London money and staple exchange markets would not only eventually affect prices for rural produce but would usually curtail advances that were necessary to cushion the effects of such depressions.

Occasionally, the banks were willing to lend on the personal guarantee of the selectors' friends or business associates:

It has long been the practice of the banks in agricultural districts to assist the selectors, while licensees, by discounting for them an acceptance of their neighbour's, with an understanding that these will be renewed when they get their leases, when they will retire the accommodation bills by taking up money on their own security.[40]

These advances seldom exceeded £100 but there was little real security for the lenders and the practice was generally frowned upon by head office. All banks would not, and legally could not, lend on leases alone until the certificates of fulfilment of conditions were obtained. The few months which followed the issue of such certificates showed whether the Downs lessee was a dummier, speculator or genuine farmer. The Bank of New South Wales, however, was reluctant to lend on any Conditional Purchases as there was no security beyond mere deposit of deeds and the bank could not force the sale of such land to liquidate the debt.[41]

This differed from the usual practice of the banks in Victoria where they were prepared to lend on seven-year leases, made under the Grants Act of 1869, once the three-year probationary period was over. Advances in Victoria were even made before certification:

The transfer of a Conditional Purchase vitiates the right to purchase the Conditional Lease if made before five years have expired, but a legal mortgage over a Conditional Purchase and Conditional Lease *without* a transfer is valid security to the Bank, the mortgage being duly registered. The transfers might be held but must not be put through.[42]

By the mid-1880s the Australian Joint Stock Bank was advancing to conditional purchasers whose leases were supposed to be transferred to the bank although this was often disregarded by local managers.[43] Later in

40 General Manager's Circulars to NSW Branches, 269 of 3 April 1891, 271 of 2 May 1891 and 303 of 3 December 1892, *AJS Bank Letter Book*, pp. 139-64, mss BNSW Archives, Sydney. AJS Bank, Confidential Instructions to Managers, Sydney 1886, pp. 18-26. Unpublished. Bank of NSW Archives, Sydney.

41 *AIBR*, Vol. 4, No. 10, 8 October 1880, p. 334. *See* the consternation created in banking tabernacles by the Victorian Supreme Court judgment in Commercial Banks *v.* Carson. This case decided that guarantors were not personally liable for acceptance on leasehold property.

42 As early as 1868, however, the Bank of N.S.W. was lending on Downs leaseholds so long as the security was adequate. This practice was discouraged and censured by Head Office. *See*: Bank of N.S.W. *v.* W. T. Perkins, Supreme Court, Brisbane, 22 March 1880. Perkins, of Highfields, had been given a mortgage at 12 per cent interest over one freehold and two leasehold selections. There was, however, a store and hotel on the property which presumably constituted sufficient security. This mortgage was due on demand. *BC*, 23 March 1880, p. 3, c. 3.

43 Secretary to Victorian Inspector, 7 February 1887, S/1/158, *BNSW Secretary's Letter-book*, 342, BNSW Archives, Sydney. AJS Bank, Circulars, p. 20.

the period unregistered mortgages were taken but the mortgagor had to sign a blank form of agreement.[44]

By 1890, the Bank of New South Wales was lending freely to conditional purchasers on the Western Downs who had obtained their certificates for their large grazing selections. This is confirmed by the following extract from a letter, dated 8 May 1890, from head office to the Brisbane Inspector:

If the Conditional Purchasers . . . are such as hold certificates of conformity . . . to enable them freely to transfer their holdings, then we have to inform you that the advance business in this Colony at our Country Branches is largely built on such securities, which are as valid in themselves and as realizable as Freeholds. There can be no reason therefore why our Goondiwindi Branch should not make similar advances and the fact that they have been discouraged from doing so, in some measure accounts for the poverty of business at a Branch of which, from its situation, we expected better things, and also explains how it is that the Commercial Bank should have thought opening there, our restrictiveness, of which the Head Office was ignorant having clearly given them the opportunity.[45]

Homestead leases under the parallel Queensland and New South Wales Acts of 1884 and their amendments were also regarded as worthwhile securities by the Australian Joint Stock Bank:

. . . in cases where we can pick our men, and we are quite sure of not only their present bona fides, but also of their future compliance with the very stringent law bearing on Homestead Leases.[46]

But these leases could not be freeholded, they were often forfeited for non-compliance with the conditions and they were taken up in areas on the Downs that were subject to droughts and all the hazards of pastoral enterprise.

Because farm securities were always considered to be second-rate investments the banks forced most farmers to pay more than the current rates for advances and were reluctant to lend over long periods. The banks preferred to grant a fluctuating overdraft that, while due on demand was really a long-term loan, or to issue renewable three or six months' bills. Such short-term loans or 'cash credits' carried interest charges that were 20 per cent or more above the ruling rates.[47] Expensive servicing charges were also imposed. By the end of the century, however, it was possible for debt-free Downs freeholders to obtain advances with interest charges considerably below the ruling rates. This group was very small and did not need much external financial assistance. For those who needed credit most—the small pioneer agricultural selectors—the banks could offer little comfort.

44 AJS Bank, Confidential Instructions, p. 20.

45 ibid.

46 Assistant Secretary to Acting Inspector, Brisbane, 8 May 1890, S/1/172, *Secretary's Letter-book*, p. 848, BNSW Archives, Sydney. Queensland Inspector to Manager, Goondiwindi, 24 November 1893, 84/17, BNSW *Circular Book*, 1873-93, mss BNSW Archives, Sydney.

47 General Manager to Branches, 8 January 1891, 263, AJS Bank, Circulars, p. 139.

Queensland bankers were convinced that it was cheaper, more profitable, safer and more dependable to advance large sums to a relatively small number of individuals or companies operating 'sound' export industries or dealing with urban lands which did not depend for their productivity on the vagaries of the weather and the fertility of their soils. The long depression of the late 'eighties which culminated in the financial disasters of 1893 modified if they did not destroy many of these rather ill-founded 'principles' of colonial banking. Rural land values on the Darling Downs generally remained fairly static after 1885 and did not greatly appreciate until near the turn of the century. But at least those who lent on farm securities in the region were not faced with the catastrophic fall in values which marked the speculative urban subdivisions in Brisbane and Melbourne.

The close social, psychological and political ties between the bank manager and squatters had a considerable but unmeasurable influence on the extension of credit to Downs selectors. Allied with the pastoralists during the squatter-selector struggles on the Downs during the first two decades following Separation, the managers and their metropolitan superiors were sometimes unwilling to disturb the traditional pattern and seek new business from the expanding small farmer interest.[48] As such business depended on close rural contacts and managerial ability in assessing risks and agricultural securities, the banks tended to ignore potential customers when local managers were incapable of exercising that '. . . wisdom . . . in judging the character of borrowers' that was so essential to sound lending.[49] On the other hand, there were a few

[48] Ruling interest-rates for N.S.W., as fixed by agreement between the banks, were as follows during 1873-4: 65 days 5%; 95 days 6%; 125 days 7%; 155 days 8%; over 155 days 9%. Cash credits 8%; overdrafts 9%. Queensland rates were often 1% higher. BNSW *Board Minutes*, 1850-77, BNSW Archives, Sydney.

The average rate of interest on Queensland mortgages registered under the Act of 1861 was as follows:

Year	Rate %	Year	Rate %	Year	Rate %	Year	Rate %
1874	8.8	1879	11.0	1884	9.3	1889	8.7
1875	9.1	1880	10.2	1885	8.2	1890	8.2
1876	10.0	1881	8.1	1886	8.7	1891	8.24
1877	10.0	1882	8.4	1887	8.2	1892	8.16
1878	10.2	1883	9.4	1888	7.6	1893	8.02

These rates of course applied to securities which lenders considered to be first-class. Few Downs farms would fall into this category. T. Weedon, *Queensland, Past and Present*, Brisbane 1898, (Official Yearbook).

[49] For instance, William Thompson, the first manager of the Bank of New South Wales at Warwick, was an unsuccessful Western Downs squatter who had originally been a London and Sydney merchant. While managing at Warwick, Thompson was personally involved in dummying on Canning Downs. His daughter married W. B. Slade, a partner in Glengallan Estate. *WE&T*, 7 November 1888, p. 2, c. 5; *QVP*, Vol. 2, (1867), pp. 975-6.

score successful farmers on the Downs whose 'industry and faith . . . had an excellent reputation in bank parlours'.[50]

But this aloofness, suspicion and distrust between those who donned silk top-hats and those who favoured the cabbage-tree style, was not a monopoly of the bankers. Some Downs farmers regarded the banks in much the same way as the American Grangers viewed the railroad monopolies and the Canadian graingrowers the elevator companies.[51] Not only did these pillars of the ruling metropolitan establishment fail to help the selector, who succeeded almost entirely by the practice of the traditional rural virtues, but they were only prepared to help when their interest seemed impregnable. When a selector needed immediate financial assistance to avert disaster or when he was faced with total failure, the banks more often than not appeared as soulless and merciless blood-suckers.[52]

With their high façades, opaque windows and forbidding doors and grilles, the rural versions of 'Drury's temple' in Warwick and Toowoomba were surrounded by a mystique that many selectors refused to penetrate. 'Most of the selectors were shy of the banks in those days' recalled the son of a German immigrant and this tendency was reinforced by the prevailing ignorance and want of 'book-learning' and the inability or refusal of many to practise even the most simple techniques of farm accountancy.[53] When the banks on the Downs closed their doors during the smash of 1893, some farmers at least echoed the sentiments of 'Banjo' Paterson in his verses titled 'Reconstruction' which were approvingly reprinted by the *Warwick Argus*:

So the bank has burst its boiler! And in six or seven years
It will pay me all my money back—of course!
But the horse will perish waiting while the grass is germinating,
And I reckon I'll be something like the horse.

There's the ploughing to be finished and the ploughmen want their pay,
And I'd like to wire a fence and sink a tank;
But I own I'm fairly beat how I'm going to make ends meet
With my money in a reconstructed bank.

I can draw out half my money, so they tell me, from the Crown;
But—its just enough to drive a fellow daft—
My landlord's quite distressed, by this very bank he's pressed,
And he'd sell me up, to pay his overdraft.

There's my nearest neighbour, Johnson, owed this self-same bank a debt
Every feather off his poor old back they pluck'd,
For they set to work to shove him, and they sold his house above him
Lord! They never gave *him* time to reconstruct.[54]

[50] S. J. Butlin, *ANZ Bank*, p. 252.

[51] *AIBR*, Vol. 1, No. 7, 7 July 1877, p. 283. Editorial on the banks and selectors.

[52] P. F. Sharp, *The Agrarian Revolt in Western Canada*, Minneapolis 1948.

[53] *QPD*, Vol. 55, (1888), p. 405.

[54] *The Bulletin*, 17 June 1893, p. 5, c. 3. Quoted by the *WA*, 20 June 1893, p. 3, c. 2. Five verses are omitted from this quotation.

Although the shearing strikes of 1891 and 1894 proved that, in the final analysis, most Downs farmers were on the side of property, the theme of cynical comparison in the preceding verses with their near-approval of the fate of the banks corresponded with current rural thinking that all forms of the capitalist system were not sacrosanct. Beset by falling prices, dear credit and other disabilities, the selectors were inclined to seek new solutions for old problems and to allow the usually submerged streak of rural radicalism to come to the surface again for a short while.

By the early 'nineties many Downs farmers were convinced that the problem of rural credit could only be solved by the intervention of the State with its superior financial resources and borrowing power. The old order had been tried and found wanting and the need to create new channels for the distribution of rural credit was a significant aspect of the remarkable political upsurge which took place among Downs farmers between 1890 and 1893. This movement, which found expression in the Farmers' Alliances, was not peculiar to Queensland but was common to all the Australasian colonies and had its counterparts in the Alliance and Populist movements in the United States.[55] But whereas the American graingrowers, with their 'Greenback' traditions, declaimed against eastern monopolies and advocated such financial nostrums as the free coinage of silver and the creation of a sub-treasury to stabilize farm prices and provide finance, the Australian agriculturalists regarded direct or guaranteed State advances to settlers as but a further and legitimate extension of the powers of Government. Rural ideology aside, what Siegfried had noted as 'this perfect mania for appealing to the State' for all manner of assistance had long been a key feature of Downs politics.[56]

State advances to Queensland farmers were first mooted in Parliament by John Walsh during the 1879 debates on the Allora Exchange Lands and the financial needs of the incoming selectors.[57] This rather premature discussion coincided with the Report of the Victorian Crown Lands Commission which recommended the creation of State Mortgage Banks and the agitation of the new Victorian Farmers' Union for similar institutions.[58] This interest died away with the return of rural prosperity and it was not until ten years later that similar proposals were revived in all southern colonies.

The great depression renewed interest in agricultural banking. New political organizations operating outside the traditional order gave expression to radical remedies for the ailing sectors of the Queensland

55 J. Donges, *personal communication*, 20 June 1963.

56 *See*: J. D. Hicks, *The Populist Revolt: A History of the Farmers' Alliance and the People's Party*, Minneapolis 1931 and F. A. Shannon, *American Farmers' Movements*, Princeton 1957.

57 A. Siegfried, *Democracy in New Zealand*, London 1913, p. 16. *See also*: W. P. Reeves, *State Experiments in Australia and New Zealand*, Vol. 1, London 1902, pp. 333-57.

58 *QPD*, Vol. 29, (1879), pp. 651, 688-91.

economy. Both the Labour Party and the Darling Downs Farmers' Alliance, with which it had a tacit understanding, incorporated planks in their 1893 election platforms which pledged the inauguration of a State Land Bank.[59] Although the theorists had canvassed support for their ideas before the 1892 Select Committee on Assisted Land Settlement and while there had been some rather academic discussion on the Downs, the 1893 proposals were the first-fruits of a widespread and genuine radical movement among the Downs farmers themselves.[60]

For once, the country-town representatives of the farmers did not play a leading role in the formulation and expression of political issues. The old generation of Darling Downs politicians were hopelessly split on trivialities and showed some reluctance to lead the fight against Queensland's financial establishment. It was the new men who had risen from the ranks of the selectors who were unequivocally in favour of cheaper credit.[61]

Considerable support for the movement came from the large German element who were well aware of the successful operation of farmers' banks in the Fatherland which, though attuned to the stable social structure and co-operative traditions of small-scale agriculture were not readily adaptable to Queensland conditions.[62] The more mobile Downs agrarian population with its individualism, direct political powers and susceptibility to commodity price fluctuations demanded a specifically colonial solution.

With the institution of State subsidies to the sugar, meat-freezing and dairying industries in 1893 and the Alliance victories at the elections later in the year it appeared likely that some system of State advances to farmers would follow. Yet not until 1901 was an Agricultural Bank established by Parliamentary action. Queensland thus had the dubious distinction of being the last Australasian colony to introduce such legislation. Moves in 1894 for a Select Committee to examine the subject and a Bill introduced by J. M. Cross in 1897 and again in 1898 were all defeated by substantial majorities.[63] Even although the banking scandals of 1893 and 1896 had challenged the hitherto sacred creed of *laissez-*

59 *Victoria Parliamentary Papers*, Session 1878, Vol. 3, pp. 669-75. *Australasian*, 20 December 1879, p. 794 and 7 February 1880, p. 183. These proposals for state mortgage banks for farm borrowers were derided by the Brisbane mercantile class. *BC*, 16 March 1878, p. 4, c. 6-7.

60 For the 1893 Queensland Labour Party platform, *see: WE&T*, 21 January 1893, p. 3, c. 6. For the platform of the Aubigny Farmers' Alliance, *see:* ibid., 18 March 1893, p. 3, c. 1-2.

61 *QVP*, Vol. 4, (1892), 'Report of the Select Committee on Assisted Land Settlement', pp. 65-7.

62 Thus Henry Daniels, a Back Plains farmer, could confidently assert to the Cambooya electors in 1893 that 'he was of the farmers and for the farmers'. *TC*, 8 April 1893, p. 2, c. 5.

63 The Landschaften Co-operatives of Prussia (1769), the Schulze-Delitsch Popular Banks (1852) and the Raifeissen Agricultural Banks (1869) were all based on a system of mutual guarantees by the peasants themselves and were partly concerned with furthering certain social objectives. H. Belshaw, *Provision of Credit*, pp. 128-33, 217-34.

faire finance, the Downs farmers were still too weak politically and economically to influence the safe and stodgy policies of the 'Continuous Ministry' which had been formed from the property-conscious remnants of the old major parties. It feared that concessions to the rising farming interest would create an undesirable precedent of Government interference with the money market which was regulated by supply and demand and interest rates which were fixed solely on the value of the offered securities:

> . . . the project requires the Government to undertake duties foreign to its nature, and for the execution of which it is disqualified. The lending of money is a trade, and trading is not a function of the State.[64]

Not only would such an enterprise hamper Queensland's attempt to restore the confidence of the London investor in her possibilities, the critics claimed, but it would inevitably lose money and encourage speculation by selectors and hasty and uneconomic rural settlement.

Having legislated for so long in the interests of certain groups, the politicians were reluctant to acknowledge the appearance of a new interest with its own demands. They clung to the old agrarian shibboleths which had served in the past and ridiculed the pleas for a 'potato bank' which would sap the sturdy individualism of the Downs farmers. G. Glenross Smith, a Toowoomba mixed farmer, who ironically enough, was soon to be forced into bankruptcy by the institutions he defended so enthusiastically, expressed the old individualistic view that State banks were a Utopian 'dream of the sweet bye-and-bye'.[65] Besides, political leaders feared that 'a mass of discontented peasantry' in debt to the State would form a political force that could enforce financial concessions in bad times and 'endanger the independence of Parliament and injure the credit of the colony'. It was felt by conservatives that even 'the slightest discussion of a bank' or alternative methods of finance amounted almost to sacrilege and was a dangerous interference with 'interests outside the jurisdiction of Parliament'. Yet the legislation which saved the Queensland National Bank in 1893, and again in 1896, was in itself a form of State intervention and even an acceptance of the need for some form of control over at least part of the banking system of the colony. The two crises of the Queensland National Bank, with its close ties with the ruling Coalition, hindered the inauguration of advances to settlers' legislation. It would not be too much to say that the interests of the Downs selectors were, once again, sacrificed to the propertied group of the east.[66]

Once Downs farmers were able to borrow from the Agricultural Bank it was soon evident that the pattern in other colonies was being re-

[64] Cross, Labour MLA for Clermont, was the Parliamentary pioneer of State banking, mortgage control and cheaper finance for small farmers. The Downs members, particularly the influential Groom and Morgan, do not appear to have taken the lead in these matters. *QPD*, Vol. 78, (1897), pp. 1517-28 and Vol. 80, (1898), pp. 1099-100.

[65] G. S. Griffiths, *The Farmer*, p. 206.

[66] *TC*, 25 May 1893, p. 6, c. 4.

peated.[67] Interest rates were certainly lowered but the farmers who benefited were still the prosperous group with comfortable securities who had usually been able to secure finance from the old sources. It was still hard for the pioneer Stanthorpe apple-grower or Chinchilla dairy farmer to borrow cheaply. The necessary specialized channels and varying types of credit to suit all the farmers on the Downs had not yet been evolved.

67 *QPD*, Vol. 72, (1894), pp. 1037-42; Vol. 78, (1897), pp. 1520-1 and Vol. 86, (1900), pp. 2396-406. For the classic Australian banker's view of the introduction of state-guaranteed credit, *see: AIBR*, Vol. 18, No. 2, 19 February 1894, pp. 69-70.

CHAPTER 9

MIDDLEMEN, MILLERS AND MARKETS

The commission charges and selling practices of the metropolitan and country-town middlemen were a perennial source of farmer discontent. Auctioneers and dealers were accused of 'overwhelming the sense of justice and destroying the confidence between buyer and seller' by encouraging 'unnatural and unwarrantable fluctuations' in the price of produce.[1] By the early 'nineties, Downs farmers who were producing regular surpluses for disposal outside the region, realized that they were in the humiliating position of having absolutely no control over the marketing process. Having achieved commercial production after years of struggle, they now believed that their due rewards were being withheld. While most upheld current thinking that the mainspring regulating prices was the so-called 'natural law of supply and demand' the middlemen, being close and comprehensible, were accused of aggravating the inevitable colonial consequences of the universal agricultural depression. They alone, the farmers maintained, exploited the position of the hard-pressed farmers by duping and charging them at all stages of business transactions:

There's a man who plays a paying game,
    Whatever he may say—
Whose name is a great and mighty name
    Over the world today.
Who stands at ease where others fall,
    Where others sink can swim;
While those who toil and spin—yes, all
    Work, sweat, live, die for him:
He's an absolute ruler, deny it who can,
    Our modern monarch, King Middleman.

... ...

There's a trick to swell each big account,
    And every little bill,
Each item in the grand amount
    Insensibly to fill;
For they charge to buy, and then to sell,
    They charge for charging, too,

[1] M. O'Keefe, 'Queensland Markets for Agricultural Produce', *QAJ*, Vol. 3, Part 1, July 1898, p. 9. Report of the Rockhampton Agricultural and Pastoral Conference.

And then they charge you for me as well,
Then me for charging you.
'Tis a marvellous science, deny it who can,
The double game of the Middleman.[2]

The middleman, whose 'auction rings trap the producers and . . . charge exorbitant prices' was denounced for importing huge consignments of cheap food from the southern colonies and New Zealand and deliberately discouraging the sale and distribution of Downs produce.[3] These were valid charges but the Downs farmers could not guarantee a regular and adequate supply of good quality foodstuffs. Apart from the Germans, many agrarians were often unwilling to take the time and trouble to prepare semi-processed articles of an even quality for the discriminating urban markets. Their rancid butter, mouldy hay and badly-cured bacon were no longer acceptable now that refrigeration and the factory system were revolutionizing processing.[4]

Primitive and haphazard methods of disposal by the Downs farmers in the nineteenth century played into the hands of the middleman. Isolation made dealers such as Marwedel of Toowoomba, Grimes of Brisbane and Barnes, Archibald and Company (whose tentacles reached all over the Downs) indispensable to the pioneers. But once in their grip some found it difficult to escape. Many farmers brought their surplus produce to the nearest country town by wagon, cart or dray and hawked vegetables, butter and eggs from door to door. Others took the produce to dealers who usually fixed their own prices and then resold on an open market. Those without pressing financial commitments and with large surpluses consigned their produce to auctioneers in Warwick, Toowoomba, Ipswich or Brisbane.[5]

Commission charges varied from 5-10 per cent and the consignee was obliged to pay for railage, cartage, bags or bales. With maize at 2s. per bushel and lucerne hay at £4 per ton little wonder that sales often barely covered expenses.[6] Agents were accused of setting high prices in the season so that Downs produce would pour in and glut the market. They could then purchase cheaply and take advantage of later sudden price rises when the farmers' crops had been harvested and sold.[7]

2 *Colonial Couplets*, Christchurch 1889. Quoted by R. Wallace, *The Rural Economy of Australia and New Zealand*, London 1891, p. 82.

3 *WE&T*, 6 May 1891, p. 2, c. 2 and *QVP*, Vol. 3, (1892), 'Evidence Taken Before the Select Committee on Assisted Land Settlement', pp. 185-6.

4 E. B. Rice, 'One Hundred Years of Queensland Dairying', *QAJ*, Vol. 89, 1959, pp. 561-6.

5 *WA*, 24 March 1888, p. 2, c. 4. 'Report on formation of the produce firm of Barnes, Archibald and Company'. Evidence of F. W. Peek, Rockhampton Agricultural and Pastoral Conference, p. 10.

6 ibid., p. 11.

7 ibid. Evidence of J. G. Palethorpe of Toowoomba, p. 21; T. Weedon, *Queensland*, p. 247; J. D. Hicks, *The Populist Revolt*, pp. 57-77 and D. F. Warner, 'The Farmers' Alliance and the Farmers' Union; An American-Canadian Parallelism', *Journal of Agricultural History*, Vol. 23, No. 1, January 1949, pp. 9-19.

Those selectors who were able to market wool and fat-stock for which there was always some external market were in a less exposed position. Yet even graziers were still subjected to the ebb and flow of international commodity prices and the exactions of the middleman. Almost all their problems were the same as those of the squatters whom they had replaced but their marketing expenses were usually proportionately greater. Of all the middlemen 'who would sell their own grandmothers for 5 per cent', the miller-storekeepers, operators of the only significant processing industry on the Downs, were the focus of most agrarian grievances, distrust and envy.[8] Their subsidiary activities as storekeepers and financiers strengthened the tendency of the farmers to regard them as their natural economic enemies. Although this attitude seldom reached the bitter intensity that the persecuting and profiteering of the Minneapolis aggregation engendered, the relationship was never harmonious.[9] From the commencement of the first Warwick mill in 1861 until the compulsory wheat pools were introduced sixty years later, the two interests clashed. Nineteenth-century farmers were slow to connect this aspect of their troubles with political action. Millers even represented them in Parliament. But the latter were adept publicists, astutely creating an image of helpfulness and providing necessary public works in a *laissez-faire* environment where commercial advantage was a virtue and co-operation was a dream.[10]

It is clear that a milling monopoly existed on the Downs which compelled the farmer-debtors to accept for their wheat what the millers offered. Warwick had only one mill until 1877, there was no competition in Allora until 1882 and Toowoomba did not have more than two small mills at any one time after 1873. These local monopolies, created when the selectors were struggling to survive, originated attitudes which festered for years. Pioneer millers such as Clark, McKeachnie and Horwitz of Warwick deliberately set out to use their position to accumulate large profits in the shortest possible time, by ruthlessly operating the closed credit, truck and marketing system.[11]

While Warwick, Allora and Toowoomba each had two flour-mills after 1882 this situation did not altogether stifle the farmers' complaints that a vicious regional monopoly was in operation. The millers did not have the control over wheat and flour transport enjoyed by the Minneapolis Millers' Association of 1879 with their secret railroad agreements.[12] Until 1889, however, the Downs mills were the only pur-

[8] *WE&T*, 10 April 1875, p. 2, c. 4.

[9] C. B. Kuhlmann, *The Development of the Flour Milling Industry in the United States*, Cambridge Mass. 1929, pp. 127-35. For two typical Downs clashes, *see*: *WA*, 22 April 1868, p. 2, c. 1 and 26 September 1876, p. 2, c. 3.

[10] *See* speech of Francis Kates at Warwick Town Hall, 15 August 1887 and *WA*, 16 August 1887, pp. 2-3.

[11] ibid., 23 August 1867, p. 2, c. 3. Not until 1880 was the truck system finally abandoned in Warwick. ibid., 3 July 1880, p. 2, c. 6.

[12] C. B. Kuhlmann, *Flour Milling*, p. 129.

chasers of wheat in Queensland. Even the erection of the large Brisbane mills simply meant that South Australian and Victorian wheat and not flour was imported. The railway rates at first effectively insulated the Downs from this metropolitan market.[13]

Farmers alleged, that while flour and wheat prices were generally fixed by fluctuations on the world (i.e. Liverpool) market, the prices offered by local millers did not follow these external price movements very closely. When South Australian flour prices fell Downs millers were forced to conform as it was difficult for them to compete at first with a cheap and supposedly superior product. But the farmers held that the millers successfully attempted to fix uniform local prices and to make the selectors bear the brunt of falling overseas quotations.[14] In 1880, 1884-5, 1889-90 and 1893 millers' 'rings' were formed in order to keep prices down to 'satisfactory levels'. As Groom declared:

> In 1884 there was a perfect revolution among the farmers on the Darling Downs when the millers combined and fixed a price of only three shillings a bushel for wheat . . . Indignation meetings were held. One miller boasted in Brisbane that he had brought the farmers to their knees and had made £20,000 that season.[15]

Those obligated to Warwick millers resembled 'rats with two terriers worrying them' as they were offered only 2s. 6d. per bushel.[16]

Until 1901 Queensland grain was consistently and deliberately underpriced every season by 4d.-6d. per bushel. This margin also covered the cost of transporting southern wheat to Brisbane. It was not until parity was achieved by press agitation, the intervention of powerful intercolonial mercantile firms and an appeal to Queensland patriotism stamped on every sack of Kennedy's Allora 'White Rose' flour, that the millers admitted their mistake, if not their guilt. 'Low prices', stated Hayes and Crisp, 'had undoubtedly restricted the industry in the past.'[17]

As soon as the first mills appeared the farmers alleged that the proprietors made excess profits at their expense. The first grievance was the gristing charge levied on small quantities of wheat the farmer had ground for his household. Until 1874, when it was reduced to 1s. 3d. per bushel the charge was invariably 3s.[18] Furthermore, the Warwick mill, with its 'system of mere selfishness' consistently refused to grind quantities of less than 150 bushels at a time. English mills were then

[13] *WA*, 24 May 1890, p. 2, c. 6-7.

[14] ibid., 6 November 1880, p. 2, c. 5-6 and *QPD*, Vol. 46, (1885), pp. 540, 606.

[15] *QPD*, Vol. 49, (1886), p. 608. This charge was indignantly denied by Kates in the same debate. Kates stated that he gave 4s. 6d. per bushel in 1884 when Adelaide flour was selling for only £9 per ton in Brisbane, ibid., p. 608. This last statement was untrue, as Kates himself, during his speech to the Swan Creek farmers on 4 February 1885, confirmed that he gave only 3s. 3d. per bushel. *WA*, 7 February 1885, p. 2, c. 1.

[16] ibid., 24 January 1885, p. 2, c. 6 and *TC*, 6 January 1885, p. 3, c. 2.

[17] *BC*, 20 November 1903, Harvest Supplement, p. 7, c. 1-2.

[18] *WA*, 22 April 1868, p. 2, c. 1-2 and *BC*, 28 April 1874, p. 3, c. 5.

charging 6d. per bushel for gristing. By 1890 the uniform Downs levy had been reduced to 1s.[19]

The Downs entrepreneurs, like their Victorian and Riverina counterparts, were indisputably exploiting their rural suppliers.

Apparently, the millers' profit margins fell during the late 'eighties. But the new roller machinery, cheaper labour and more dependable and plentiful wheat supplies substantially reduced milling costs. Selectors could not make corresponding reductions and they, rather than the millers, suffered from falling flour prices.

Average Wheat and Flour Prices—Warwick-Allora, 1874-98[20]

Year	Av. cost price of wheat (per bushel & equivalent ton)	Millers' retail flour prices (per ton)	Bran & pollard retail prices (per ton)	Gross margin between raw & processed product
	£ s. d.	£ s. d.	£ s. d.	£ s. d.
1874	5 0 12 10 0	17 0 0	2 14 0	7 4 0
1877–8	5 0 12 10 0	15 0 0	3 12 0	5 4 0
1884–5	3 3 8 2 6	12 0 0	3 3 0	7 0 6
1890–1	3 9 9 8 4	12 10 0	2 10 0	5 11 6
1897–8	4 3 10 12 6	12 15 0	1 10 0	3 12 6

Yet the farmers' antagonism was not only confined to their well-founded suspicion of millers' profits. The millers usually purchased their wheat direct from the producers who either delivered it in bags by dray or consigned it by railway. Some processors, detested by miller and farmer alike, bought from storekeepers and commission agents who had taken the grain on the truck system and who often indulged in private speculation. No uniform system of inspecting, grading and storing the grain before sale existed, these operations being arbitrarily undertaken

19 *DDG*, 25 March 1865, p. 3, c. 4.

20 These figures are taken from quotations in the two Warwick newspapers. The gross margin of profit should be considered as a guide rather than as an accurate analysis. Actual manufacturing costs are unavailable and, in any case, varied between mill and mill. At most, the cost of production would not exceed £2.10s. per ton and it is likely that the true cost was much lower. £1.2s.6d. per ton was given as a fair cost of production in 1893 for an efficient mill. Even if the higher figure is adopted it will be seen that the millers usually made much more than the £1 per ton profit they considered 'reasonable' in 1914. Furthermore, these figures are calculated on the basis of 50 bushels per ton of flour and 36 bushels of sharps. The real figure was probably lower. *WE&T*, 28 November 1878, p. 2, c. 5. A. Bruce-Suttor, 'Comparative Values of Wheat and Flour, 1893' *Agricultural Gazette of N.S.W.*, Vol. IV, No. 8, August 1893, pp. 627-8. *QVP*, 1898, Vol. 3, p. 1097.

by the millers.[21] Without independent or state-controlled elevators and grading, the farmer who had threshed his crop was entirely at the mercy of the miller. Once sold, the farmer's own wheat was used as a weapon against his fellows. Quotations were always 'wide'—a prevalent device by shrewd buyers to deceive sellers. Not until the inauguration of 'open auction' sales in 1901-2, combined with a rational system of advances, did farmers have some idea of true market prices and urban manipulations. No system of bulk handling had yet been developed. The principle that 'wheat is like water—it can run, it can be poured, it can be pumped' was not yet recognized in Australia.[22]

But the millers were not quite the satanic monopolists that the agrarian radicals portrayed. Hampered by the inability of the farmers to supply sufficient raw material, forced to import southern wheat in order to keep their considerable capital investments employed for most of the year, harassed by total crop failures in alternate years, unable to speculate largely in futures, subjected to stiff competition from the large and efficient mills in the south, and obliged to lend money on poor security, they considered that they had the right to indulge in what were to them perfectly legitimate trading practices.[23]

Even without statistics it was obvious that the millers were better pupils of Samuel Smiles than their clients. As yet, however, the farmers had no desire to interfere with the 'free play of a free market'. But middlemen were at their most oppressive when the selectors were either making the initial adaptation or were feeling the effects of depressed prices.[24] The co-operative mills were a palliative rather than a cure and, although entirely new concepts might have eventually emerged, the better prices after 1897, the diversification of Downs farming and the opening of new wheat areas soon erased any half-formed ideas of state regulation and producer-control from the minds of the graingrowers. What the Downs farmers did clutch at was the illusory panacea of agricultural protection.

The development of agricultural export industries in South Australia, Victoria and New Zealand after 1865, coupled with the recognition that selection did not automatically ensure staples for eastern markets, led to the formulation on the Downs of a policy of colonial agricultural protection.[25] This would nurture the new agriculture and

21 Evidence of R. W. Scholefield (Toowoomba) and W. D. Lamb (Yangan), Rockhampton Agricultural and Pastoral Conference, pp. 35-7. *BC*, 20 November 1903, p. 7.

22 A. J. Thynne, 'The Bulk Handling of Wheat', *QAJ*, Vol. 11, Part 1, 9 June 1902, pp. 13-15. *See also* Kates' plea for railway terminal and siding storage facilities. *QPD*, Vol. 52, (1887), pp. 420-30.

23 *See* Hayes' apologia: *WA*, 10 February 1885, p. 2, c. 5. For a review of the whole question, *see*: *QVP*, First Session, Vol. 1, 1915-16, 'Report of the Royal Commission on the Supply and Distribution of Wheat and Flour in the State of Queensland', pp. 49-152.

24 *TC*, 16 December 1893, p. 2, c. 7 and p. 3, c. 1; *WA*, 1 August 1893, p. 2, c. 3.

25 Both Groom (Drayton-and-Toowoomba) and Morgan (Warwick) advocated agricultural protection during the 1870 election. This was the first time that the tariff had been an issue on the Downs. *TC*, 30 July 1870, p. 2, c. 4 and *WE&T*, 13 August 1870, p. 2, c. 1.

assure it an adequate market. In contrast to other sectional demands, however, the agitation for protection originated with the amateur economists of the towns rather than the working farmers.[26]

On such an issue the Downs representatives and their constituents were at a decided disadvantage. Ranged against them were the influential squatters and the numerous miners, both traditional free-trade adherents. The sugar-growers of the North, the urban artisans of the metropolis (traditional allies of the Downs spokesmen in land matters) and the middlemen and merchants of the town were all prepared to sacrifice what the Downs agrarians thought to be their future interests to reciprocity, the 'poor man's loaf', and the ten per cent cut.[27] Apart from their numerical and political inferiority, however, the agrarians were placed in an ideological dilemma. Free trade was now accepted dogma for most New World rural societies. The old protectionism was irrelevant. Unable to produce an export surplus, the Queensland farmers had to face a rising demand for industrial protection from stronger sections of the community.[28] Only when revenue demands became imperative, as in 1870 and 1888, and when industrial protectionism became politically feasible, were the Downs agrarians conceded some measure of tariff protection.

Until 1870 all agricultural produce was admitted to Queensland ports free of duty. That year, Ramsay, Palmer's treasurer, proposed a new tariff to bolster up the colony's shaky finances. Ramsay totally rejected the arguments of Groom and the few agricultural protectionists and stated that the Government had simply adopted the Gladstonian principle of taxing as many commodities as possible.[29] While the core of the proposals, the flour duty, was defeated when Lilley and other urban 'liberals' refused to consider any alteration in bread prices, this tariff did imply some measure of protection.[30] Similar duties, levied in 1874, had the effect of further protecting basic Downs produce.[31]

26 Groom, 'formerly a disciple of Cobden and Bright', was converted to protection during the slump of 1866. *QPD*, Vol. 11, (1870), pp. 74-5. For the views of Lilley, the leader of the urban radicals, *see*: ibid., pp. 93-4.

27 The willingness of the sugar and mercantile interests in 1877, 1886, and 1890 to sacrifice the Downs farmers by exchanging South Australian wheat and flour for Queensland sugar was strongly opposed on the Downs. *QPD*, Vol. 23, (1877), pp. 276-377, 384-402 and Vol. 49, (1886), pp. 731-2; *TC*, 24 May 1890, pp. 2-3.

28 *QPD*, Vol. 55, (1888), pp. 209-21, 277-356.

29 An income tax was rejected as it was 'expensive to collect and encourages immorality'. *QPD*, Vol. 11, (1870), pp. 55-6.

30 On division, the flour-duty was negatived by 17 votes to 13. The Downs members split, Morgan and Bell voting against and Groom making common cause with Ramsay and Wienholt in favour of the tariff. ibid., p. 191.

31

Commodity	Weight	Duty	Date
Butter	lb.	2d.	28.4.74
Cheese	lb.	2d.	30.11.70
Barley	bush.	£5%	1.10.74

(*Continued on facing page*)

These duties remained current until 1888. Both the Downs farmers and millers were dissatisfied with them although agitation for increased protection did not revive until prices began to fall in the mid-'eighties. By then, produce from the southern colonies was pouring in to the east coast markets:

IMPORTS OF AGRICULTURAL PRODUCE, 1885[32]

Commodity	Amount	Value £
Butter	1,179,910 lbs	64,069
Cheese	1,128,019 lbs	31,467
Barley	6,423 bush.	934
Maize	362,279 bush.	64,590
Malt	107,610 bush.	32,052
Oats	285,678 bush.	33,846
Wheat	10,297 bush.	1,743
Flour	33,819 tons	307,763
Bran and pollard	536,674 bush.	27,609
Chaff	4,881 tons	24,854
Pork	893,092 lbs	30,141
Bacon	376,609 lbs	13,371
Hams	433,130 lbs	16,598
		TOTAL £649,037

As these commodities yielded only £54,008 out of a total customs revenue in 1885 of £990,027 it is plain that the duties were neither protective nor productive.[33] Merely a minor irritation to the southern exporters and urban dealers, the imposts could give the Downs farmers only abstract satisfaction and the hope for more material advantages in the future.

(*Footnote 31 continued from p. 188*)

Commodity	Weight	Duty	Date
Maize	bush.	6d.	30.11.70
Malt	bush.	6d.	30.11.70
Oats	bush.	6d.	30.11.70
Bran and pollard	bush.	2d.	30.11.70
Chaff	tons	10s.	30.11.70
Bacon	lb.	2d.	30.11.70
Hams	lb.	2d.	30.11.70

SR, 1874, Part 2.

32 ibid., 1885, Part 2. The imports of agricultural produce then represented 10 per cent of the total value of Queensland's imports in 1885.

33 ibid., pp. 527-47. The reverse was true of the sugar industry which had developed under the umbrella of a protective tariff of £5 per ton on raw sugar and £6.13.4 on refined. The imposition of this duty in 1870 at the same time as the flour tax was rejected shows the relative strengths of these two antagonistic agricultural interests.

Agricultural protectionism was resuscitated on the Downs in 1884 when the millers, led by Hayes of Warwick, commenced an assault on the wheat duty and proposed a stiff flour tariff in its place.[34] The *Allora Guardian* and the short-lived Darling Downs Farmers' Union regarded the proposals with alarm. Repeal was seen as a device which would not only enable the millers to reduce the price of local wheat by giving them a cheaper alternative source of supply but would actually demolish an existing tariff on a product they felt to be the predestined staple of the region.[35] Once more, faith was invoked rather than good works. Further attempts to remove the wheat duty were made in 1885 and 1886 but the Griffith Government, while sympathetic, were afraid of losing the support of their staunch Downs members and were not prepared to antagonize the Downs farmers.[36]

The 1886 debate disclosed a new and paradoxical development. It was now obvious that the Downs millers feared repeal as its new Ipswich and Brisbane advocates were interested in the establishment of large competing mills on the coast. This would break their monopoly. Farmers and millers on the Downs thus united on this issue as the farmer rightly believed that the inducements of higher prices and new markets would never materialize in the face of free wheat imports from the south.[37]

1888 was the crucial year in the history of agricultural protection in Queensland. After his great electoral success McIlwraith decided to introduce Queensland's first full-scale protective tariff to promote new manufacturing industry and bridge the ever-widening gap between Government expenditure and revenue. Substantial increases made agricultural protection a reality for the first time. The public and Parliamentary debates on these unprecedented proposals revealed that the Downs' millers and farmers combination had disintegrated. The millers were temporarily without representation and the Nationalists had broken the old Liberal stranglehold on the Downs by capturing three of the five grain growing seats. Protection was a great issue of the 1888 election campaign on the Downs. While a few obstinate partisans saw McIlwraith's victory as a triumph for free trade, others were more realistic. Only one convinced free-trader was returned for a Downs agricultural constituency.[38] Moreover, McIlwraith with his strong Northern, Western and mercantile contingent, could afford to treat the Downs as he wished.

Personally in favour of imposing a duty of £1 per ton on imported flour, the Premier was forced to drop the proposal by opposition from

[34] *WA*, 30 August 1884, p. 3, c. 1.

[35] ibid., 7 February 1885, p. 2, c. 1.

[36] *QPD*, Vol. 46, (1885), pp. 539-55, 601-9, 620-1. Five Downs members voted against repeal and only one for.

[37] *QPD*, Vol. 49, (1886), pp. 602-11. On this occasion, six representatives were against repeal and two in favour.

[38] *TC*, 28 January 1888, p. 6, c. 7 and 15 May 1888, p. 2, c. 6-7. *WA*, 28 August 1888, p. 2, c. 2.

all sides of the House. After all, his party had won many votes with its slogan 'The Big Loaf' and a costlier slice would hardly appeal. Groom, Allan and Morgan, prompted by their wheat-growing electors, tried to force the flour duty through once they saw that the Government was determined to foster milling in Brisbane by the abolition of the wheat tariff but this motion fizzled out.[39] Despite Groom's warning that 'there was danger ahead if that tax was taken off' most Downs farmers were satisfied with a tariff which gave them their first significant measure of protection.[40] Furthermore, as prices fell the protective value of the duties rose. A tariff of 8d. per bushel on maize was bound to have some effect when Brisbane prices fell to 1s. 6d. The continuance of free flour and the removal of the wheat duty seemed a small price to pay for a host of valuable concessions.[41]

And the price did not have to be paid for long. In 1892 the long-awaited flour duty of £1 per ton was imposed and a wheat tariff of 4d. per bushel was restored.[42] While some Northern, mining and urban representatives resented these alterations as 'yet another concession to the Darling Downs' the pressing need for revenue and production had converted many former free-traders. As in 1888, however, these welcome and beneficial duties were not the result of basic agrarian agitation from the Downs but were a part of the Coalition's economic expedients to alleviate the ever-worsening depression. McIlwraith also hoped that the tariff would allay growing farmer discontent over the railway rates, assist the railways by increasing traffic, help the friends of the Government who had built the new metropolitan mills and who were now trying to compete with dumped Adelaide flour, and soothe the Downs farmers who had been incensed by the re-introduction of coloured labour.[43]

Queensland was the last of the Australasian colonies to impose heavy protective tariffs on agricultural commodities but they do not appear to have played a direct and critical part in producing the later explosive

39 *QPD*, Vol. 55, (1888), pp. 214-17, 376-7, 496-7.

40 ibid., p. 498.

41

Commodity	Weight	Duty
Butter and cheese	lb.	3d.
Barley	bush.	9d.
Maize and oats	bush.	8d.
Malt	bush.	3s.
Bran and pollard	bush.	4d.
Chaff and hay	ton	15s.
Bacon and hams	lb.	3d.
Pork	lb.	2d.

SR, 1888.

42 *QPD*, Vol. 68, (1892), pp. 1015-16, 1057-112.

43 ibid., pp. 1117-18, 1127-9.

increase in Downs rural production.[44] A strong metropolitan milling industry, which eventually absorbed all the surplus grain the Downs could grow was the direct outcome of 1888. So far as the farmers were concerned, however, technical progress, rising prices and Government assistance were of far more significance. Whether or not the same rate of growth could have been maintained after 1891 without protection is a hypothetical question to which there is no simple answer. Even in Victoria, the real advantages and disadvantages of protection and its precise effect on the economy still await convincing analysis.

Perhaps the main effects of the post-1888 policy were psychological and educative. In the campaign for protection the Downs farmers perceived that stronger elements in the community now accepted their potential ability to make the colony self-sufficient in agricultural products. Protection gave some homesteaders new faith in themselves and in the future possibility of regulation and assistance by legislation when they needed it most. It involved them in an economic argument that concerned a continent rather than a comparatively small strip of grassland between the Great Dividing Range and the Condamine River. Paradoxically, however, this very involvement promoted isolationist thinking, as the long and vocal opposition to Federation disclosed.[45]

Federation, with eventual intercolonial free trade, soon dispelled the fears of the Downs farmers that they would be swamped by the southern producers. Integration did absolve the Downs farmers from having to choose between a high tariff policy for all commodities and reverting to the old free trade fold. Protection may have helped to give the Downs agriculturalists a breathing space before conversion to a larger economy, but during the first decade of the present century they faced much the same tariff, marketing and export problems as all other Australian smallholders.

The Darling Downs, from the first days of selector settlement, had been regarded by its inhabitants and promoters alike as capable of producing all the temperate-zone produce the colony could absorb. Butter, cheese, hay, grain, fruit and fat-stock were expected to pour from the farms in a flood which would overwhelm the importers and doubters

[44] By 1900, 79,304 acres were under wheat in Queensland, compared with a mere 9,602 acres in 1888. *QVP*, Vol. 2, (1901), p. 901.

[45] For rural attitudes to Federation on the Darling Downs, *see* the debates on the Australian Federation Enabling Bill. *QPD*, Vol. 75, (1896), pp. 134-59, 192-245, 263-80 and 287-302. The nine Downs electorates rejected Federation in 1899 by a vote of 4,538 to 3,857. The figures for the six grain-growing electorates are even more striking: 3,888 against and only 2,673 in favour. In Aubigny 974 voted against Federation and only 169 for, while in Cambooya 278 were in favour and 938 against. *QVP*, Vol. 1, (1899), p. 753. For an interpretation favouring the thesis that fear of southern competition played the major part in producing this adverse vote, *see*: R. S. Parker, 'Australian Federation: The influence of economic interests and political pressures', *Historical Studies*, Vol. 4, No. 13, November 1949, pp. 1-24. For a rejoinder pointing out the significance of the German vote, *see*: G. Blainey, 'The Role of Economic Interests in Australian Federation' and Parker, 'Australian Federation', ibid., Vol. 4, No. 15, November 1950, p. 233.

of the eastern seaboard. The reality was somewhat different. Obstacles—physical, human and technological—had to be overcome before the Downs smallholders could exploit the potential market of southern Queensland, let alone the world.[46]

The first markets were the expanding towns within the region itself—Toowoomba, Warwick, Dalby and Allora. After the first phase of settlement between 1868 and 1881, however, even these markets proved incapable of absorbing all local agricultural produce. Although the combined population of these four centres had reached 8,867 by 1871, it was a modest increase to 10,728 by 1881 and ten years later the urban population was still only 13,291. On the Downs as a whole the population trebled between 1861 and 1870 but the rate of increase was much slower over the following two decades. Between 1871 and 1881 total Downs population rose by 48 per cent and by 22 per cent in the next decade. Then there were a mere 40,375 people on the Downs of whom at least one-third were farming families who usually produced their own subsistence requirements.[47] Moreover, as the adaptative process continued, output rose more rapidly than the region's towns and its western pastoral hinterland could absorb. Wheat production only occasionally satisfied the flour needs of the area after 1891 although increasing quantities of other commodities flowed from the farms after the late 'seventies.[48] Some of the increase was absorbed by the large camps of migrant railway workers but this unreliable market depended largely upon external economic and political considerations. Nevertheless, such stimulus was sometimes enough to ensure a successful farming career for a fortunately placed homestead selector.[49] Other temporary markets also sprang up as a result of the Stanthorpe tin discoveries. The 2,000 miners, dependants and suppliers on the field by 1876 were a magnificent market for the Swan Creek, Killarney and Freestone Creek smallholders. Similarly, the Canal Creek and Talgai gold diggings, while ephemeral and unproductive, created local demands for foodstuffs and raised prices at a critical time. So, too, did the steam sawmills of Killarney, Crow's Nest and the Bunya Mountains.[50]

46 *QVP*, Vol. 2, (1867), p. 775, 'Darling Downs Petitions on the Crown Lands Sale Bill'.

47 *SR*, 1861-91. Total Queensland population rose much more rapidly—from 30,059 in 1861 to 120,104 in 1871; 213,525 in 1881; and 393,718 in 1891.

48 In 1872, there were only 15,056 acres cultivated on the Darling Downs but by 1882 there were 46,782 and by 1892, 95,620. In 1892 the combined acreage under wheat and maize almost equalled the entire sugar acreage, whereas a decade earlier these two grains represented only 40 per cent of the area planted in cane. ibid.

49 The Warwick Reserve farmers benefited greatly from the construction of the Stanthorpe railway. 784 men were at work on the line in 1879. Drayton-Toowoomba selectors supplied the contractors for the great Western line reaching out towards Roma and Charleville. *QVP*, Vol. 2, (1879), p. 451, 'Report by the Railways Commissioner' and *BC*, 2 December 1872, p. 3, c. 6.

50 The New South Wales threat to the border markets monopolized by the Downs was always considered to be a very real menace in the region. It certainly influenced

(Continued on next page)

Until refrigeration opened the markets of the Old World to animal products Brisbane, with an 1891 population of 93,657, was the only accessible market capable of absorbing most of the Downs' surplus produce. The gold discoveries at Gympie, Charters Towers and Mount Morgan, the northern sugar plantations and the chain of coastal ports were all open to the cheap producers of the southern colonies with their low ocean freight rates. The growing agricultural economy of the Downs never supplied some of the most rapidly expanding portions of Queensland. Thus, although the population of the colony increased from 30,059 in 1861 to 213,525 in 1881 and 393,718 in 1891, the potential market for Downs produce remained restricted to southern Queensland. Mixed farmers, however, were in a better position as there was always some market for their few bales of wool and surplus sheep, cattle and horses.[51]

The Brisbane market was never the exclusive preserve of the Downs agriculturalists. Despite the apparent advantages of protection, other small farmers also looked towards the metropolis.[52] Though they could not profitably cultivate wheat (and the Downs farmers themselves took thirty years to produce a regional surplus) the Moreton men grew much the same crops as their fellows on the Darling Downs. Furthermore, Brisbane was much closer.[53] In an era in which competing local economies were expanding, the Downs farmers believed that one answer to their marketing problems lay in cheap and efficient transport facilities.

The problem of communications was faced by most Australasian and North American selector communities during the nineteenth century.[54] Agricultural areas, such as south-east South Australia, that had suitable geographical conditions for the development of cheap, rapid and reliable arteries had inestimable advantages over less well-endowed localities.[55] Straddling a limited western market and a growing metropolis, and with physical features encouraging swift development of road and rail, the Downs selectors were in an intermediate position. The squatters made the first trunk roads (which grew from horse and dray tracks) to carry their wool to eastern markets. As the pastoral industry only demanded

---

the construction of railways, and New England competition was a factor in the movement towards agricultural protection. *WA*, 23 May 1885, p. 2, c. 5. Although most soon left for the north, there were about 850 diggers on the Talgai and Canal Creek goldfields in 1865-6. *QVP*, Vol. 1, (1866), pp. 1463-5. 'Report on the Talgai Gold Fields'.

51 *SR*, 1861-91. In 1884, Downs railway-stations handled 6,248 bales of 'selectors' wool; *QVP*, Vol. 3, (1885), 'Report of the Commissioner for Railways'.

52 *BC*, 10 February 1872, p. 4, c. 3-4.

53 *QVP*, Vol. 3, (1885), 'Railways Report'.

54 Areas such as Gippsland, the Northern Rivers of New South Wales and the scattered village settlements of the North Auckland peninsula in New Zealand had irregular, costly and sometimes dangerous communications which hampered the rapid consolidation and expansion of commercial farming based on the family selection. For an examination of these factors in New Zealand, *see:* D. B. Waterson, 'Railways and Politics in New Zealand, 1908-1928', *unpublished thesis*, University of Auckland 1959.

55 E. Dunsdorfs, *Australian Wheat-Growing*, pp. 160-4.

routes that would carry seasonal traffic, secondary roads were unnecessary and non-existent. The main roads themselves were, by 1863, in an atrocious condition and almost completely incapable of sustaining dense traffic.[56] Though railways relieved the situation in the following decade, emphasis on selector settlement demanded a closer road network. Costly, unremunerative and subject to political whim and unreasoned agitation, road development lagged behind railways for most of the period.[57] Roads over the Downs were easily constructed, requiring few earthworks as they mostly followed the gentle natural contours; the numerous small watercourses, however, required expensive timber bridges.[58] Small settlers on the slopes of the Main Range not only had numerous creeks to ford but rugged gullies to cross and scrub and trees to fell before roads suitable for wheeled transport could go through.[59]

The main physical drawback was the impassability of the black and red soils when scarred by wagon wheels and inundated by summer downpours and floods. In 1893, the road between Allora and the nearest siding at Hendon was 'in a terrible condition [with] three breakdowns and drays up to their axles in the ruts'.[60] Furthermore, many of the large freehold estates had no public roads through them and many others existed only on surveyors' tracings and parish maps.[61]

Although the municipalities gradually extended adequate main roads to their boundaries, all other highways could only be formed or improved with the assistance of government money derived from both the loan account and the general revenue. This arrangement was haphazard, arbitrary, wasteful and slow. As the farming communities largely depended on the roads and bridges capabilities of the local member, the state of the roads usually reflected political enthusiasm, horse-trading and influence rather than genuine economic need. Well-roaded Toowoomba and its environs was the shining example of Groom's political adroitness and manipulation.[62]

By 1879 it was recognized that some form of decentralized administration, with local rating powers, was necessary to maintain the highways and to build up the secondary roads as feeders for the new railways. It was now conceded that railway investment was lopsided with-

56 *QVP*, Second Session, (1863), 'Report from the Select Committee on the Main Roads of the Colony', pp. 533-87.

57 For an eye-witness account of the dreadfully muddy state of the Warwick roads, *see*: *BC*, 2 October 1876, p. 3, c. 7 and 28 October 1876, p. 6, c. 6.

58 In 1863 it was estimated that the Toowoomba-Warwick main road alone required six bridges which would cost over £2,500. *QVP*, Second Session, (1863), 'Main Roads Report', p. 571.

59 Many of the Highfields scrub selectors were completely isolated until the late 'seventies. *DDG*, 18 March 1865, p. 3, c. 3 and *BC*, 17 February 1877, p. 4, c. 3.

60 *Allora Guardian*, 22 April 1893, p. 2, c. 6-7.

61 The huge block of 35,000 acres pre-empted on Glengallan was almost roadless. *BC*, 28 April 1874, p. 3, c. 4. As late as 1880, Macansh of Canning Downs 'bullied and threatened' the farmers by closing roads. *WA*, 30 March 1876, p. 2, c. 2.

62 D. B. Waterson, 'The Remarkable Career of W. H. Groom', *Royal Australian Historical Society Journal*, Vol. 49, Part 1, June 1963, p. 38.

out simultaneous construction and maintenance of country roads.[63] At first, most Downs farmers agreed with their spokesmen that the new Divisional Boards Act:

> . . . is unsuited to the wants of the country, will prove almost unworkable, and will be received by the farmers and the majority in the settled districts with great disfavour.[64]

But the ten boards created in 1880 soon removed the fears of most opponents of the measure and the sturdy and self-reliant farmers modified their views of the State's obligation and accepted taxation.[65] 'That most attractive measure' succeeded in improving many of the Downs roads. Though the squatters gained control of key boards such as Glengallan and Clifton, imposed rating on the basis of improvements and the net annual value of the land rather than on the capital value, the control of these bodies gradually passed from the 'wealthy classes' to boss-cockies and small farmers.[66]

Although Brisbane, the Downs' great potential market, was not linked with the railhead at Ipswich till 1875, the Pure Merinos had been quick to initiate railway construction. Toowoomba was linked with Ipswich in 1867, Dalby in 1868, Warwick in 1871 and Stanthorpe in 1881. While this network was perfectly adequate for the squatters it was not of comparable value to those who had selected miles away from the trunk lines. It did, however, make mixed farming on small selections possible by lowering the cost of carriage on small consignments of wool and fat-stock.[67]

Much of the best land near the railways was alienated by dummying and pre-emption and some selectors were forced on to inaccessible areas such as the Highfields scrubs, the Beauaraba Homestead Area and the Emu Creek and Irvingdale resumptions. The railway reserve between Allora and Warwick was virtually confiscated by the pastoralists and the proprietors of Jondaryan secured a ten-mile frontage to both sides of the Western railway. Thus the railways did not inevitably open land for small settlers. The State lost potential revenue, the future settlers lost their chance of accessible land and the squatters gained the unearned increment.[68]

63 *WA*, 7 February 1880, p. 2, c. 1-2 and K. T. Cameron, 'Early Road Transport', *JRQHS*, Vol. 5, No. 1, (1953), p. 841.

64 *WE&T*, 13 September 1879, p. 2, c. 1 and *WA*, 31 July 1879, p. 2, c. 4.

65 ibid., 25 January 1881, p. 2, c. 1-2 and 22 October 1881, p. 2, c. 1-2.

66 *WE&T*, 7 February 1880, p. 2, c. 4. *See* the Canning Downs Valuation Appeal Case, Warwick Police Court, 24 September 1880. Macansh successfully appealed against the valuation of the Glengallan Divisional Board. The original estimate of £8,366 as the net annual value of the estate was reduced to £4,510. The Board thus lost a great deal of revenue. *WA*, 25 September 1880, p. 2, c. 3-4. The Jondaryan Divisional Board had £3,500 on fixed deposit in 1890 which the squatter majority refused to release for secondary roading. *BC*, 7 February 1890, p. 5, c. 6.

67 *TC*, 18 March 1884, pp. 2-3.

68 *See* Gore's charge that Clark of Talgai had dummied much of the Warwick Railway Reserve. *QPD*, Vol. 11, (1870), pp. 36-7.

Shann has postulated that profitable agriculture could not flourish beyond a fifteen-mile radius from a railway and Coghlan has adopted a twelve-mile circle as the limit for viable grain growing.[69] On the Downs, the evidence suggests that smallholders, apart from subsistence selectors and small graziers, could not economically market their produce unless they were within ten miles of a siding. This dictum was not restrictive at first as many selectors were near the towns and engaged in satisfying a regional market. Once surpluses began to appear, however, the demand arose for branch railways to serve farmers rather than squatters.

These demands were usually met. Between 1884 and 1887 three branches were constructed to serve areas of predominantly homestead settlement. The Killarney (1885), Crow's Nest (1886) and Pittsworth (1887) lines were all considered as the main assistance that the State could afford to the selector. While this concept of the railway as an automatic developmental mechanism and wealth-producer for both selector and government was sometimes dubious from the immediate economic point of view, it is indisputable that the Downs farmers, when compared with the rest of Queensland, were well served by the allocation of the flood of British loan money. For once, agrarian ideals and the practical commitment of the State to their realization appeared to coincide.

Yet all railways lagged behind the rate of selection. The selectors on the Agricultural Reserve had to wait for seven years before the line reached Warwick, the '1868 men' on the Highfields road had a ten-year hiatus while others left their farms long before the railways arrived.[70] Year after year, however, these branches returned losses. The great era of Downs branch line construction was immediately followed by the depression of the late 'eighties and the consequences of anticipating revenue by building for settlement and development alone were revealed. The investment was often a very long-term one indeed.[71]

As a group, the Downs selectors were not generally involved with the route squabbles, political scheming and propaganda which occurred before a new line was constructed. These politics of detail they left to the competing country towns and their parliamentary representatives. Nor were they concerned that these concessions to a minor interest were at the expense of the rest of the country. Such economic stiffening was regarded by the agrarian pioneers as being no more than their due. This rationalization, however, did not stop them from speculating with

69 E. Shann, *An Economic History of Australia*, Australian Edition, Melbourne 1948, p. 292. Coghlan is quoted by I. A. Parker, 'The Transport Industries of New South Wales, 1861-1891', *unpublished seminar paper*, ANU, 28 July 1958, p. 24.

70 Some Highfields farmers paid 20 per cent of their total produce receipts for transport to Toowoomba. *QPD*, Vol. 23, (1877), p. 309 and *WA*, 31 July 1879, p. 2, c. 3.

71 For typical speeches 'boosting' Downs railways, *see: QPD*, Vol. 26, (1878), pp. 707-19 (Highfields Railway); Vol. 34, (1881), pp. 157-65 (Killarney branch) and Vol. 46, (1885), pp. 703-19 (Beauaraba line).

the unearned increment and failing to live up to their optimistic promises of support once they had the new lines.

Railways and their politics obscured consideration of more profound grievances in the very community they were designed to serve. In some ways, as the railway rates controversy disclosed, the two hundred miles of Downs railway construction, with its incidental agitations were a form of smoke-screen—an effective form of political bribery—which at first concealed from the selectors that at this time government assistance ended when the champagne flowed and the top-hats opened the lines.[72]

Compared with similar areas of small settlement in Australia, however, the Downs was well served by train, coach and dray. Unlike the North American sod-busters whose Granges and Peoples' Alliances spent most of their time and energies fighting the private railroad monopolies, the selectors had the benefit of a system that was ostensibly devoted to furthering the ideals and interests at the expense of commercial considerations. In Australasia, the railways were deliberately built in advance of revenue by governments whose credit was generally sound and whose personnel were extraordinarily sensitive to the demands of certain rival interests and localities.[73]

Although freight charges were higher than in New South Wales and Victoria, the Downs farmers, in a relatively weaker economic position than their southern brethren, had little grounds for complaint. Queensland railway policy followed the orthodox colonial practice of pegging rates low enough to monopolize all the potential goods traffic. The aim was to encourage settlement and production, while at the same time paying working expenses and obtaining a moderate return on the borrowed capital. Certain classes of goods were always charged more than others. 'Up traffic' from Brisbane to the Downs comprised manufactured goods and equipment that were more valuable per unit of weight, less elastic in demands and always high rated. 'Down traffic' on the other hand was seasonal, had a low value in relation to weight and was generally low rated. Rates, as well as the character of the service, were deliberately weighted in favour of farmers, millers and the south-east Downs.[74]

The Downs was extremely sensitive to any threat to this privileged

[72] *WA*, 19 October 1889, p. 2, c. 1-2. For a typical opening ceremony of an agricultural branch, *see* the description of the inauguration of the Beauaraba line: *TC*, 22 September 1887, p. 3.

[73] W. F. Zornow, *Kansas. A History of the Jayhawk State*, Oklahoma 1957. For an illuminating illustration of the influence of politics upon public works, *see: QPD*, Vol. 37, (1882), pp. 636-44.

[74] *QVP*, 1874-88, 'Annual Reports of the Railways Commissioner', T. A. Coghlan, *A Statistical Account of the Seven Colonies of Australasia*, Sydney 1893, pp. 75-81; I. A. Parker, 'Railway Traffic Policy in New South Wales and Victoria, 1855-88', *unpublished seminar paper*, ANU, September 1959. In 1876 wool sent from Toowoomba to Brisbane was charged 57s. 6d. per ton. Warwick wool was charged 90s. Agricultural produce was carried at one-third of these rates. *QVP*, Vol. 1, (1876), (JLA), p. 244.

position. A move to increase the rates in 1879 was soon squashed by protests from Warwick and Toowoomba and the agitation even resulted in a demand for still lower rates so that the region could compete with Adelaide flour for the western market. Warwick interests complained that as agricultural produce cost nearly £1 per ton if railed from the area to Brisbane, they could not compete with Sydney produce merchants sending freight by steamer at 12s. 6d. per ton.[75] Yet the rates on Adelaide flour from Brisbane to Roma (317 miles) were £7 11s. 8d. per ton while Warwick and Toowoomba flour was charged only £2 14s. 8d. and £1 16s. 2d. per ton respectively.[76]

Farmers consigning from Toowoomba and surrounding areas were in a more favourable position than graingrowers and mixed farmers of the south-east who had to rail produce over an extra 58 miles at an additional cost of 9s. per ton. Thus, in 1879-80, Toowoomba and its satellites dispatched 5,638 tons of produce to the Brisbane market while Warwick sent only 2,006 tons. Here was the seed of the Via Recta agitation when commercial and agricultural interests on the Southern Downs combined to secure a direct route to Brisbane.[77] Largely through the machinations of rival interests and politicians in Toowoomba, the project failed and the Warwick organization now concentrated upon securing discriminatory rates which would enable them to compete on equal terms with the producers and distributors of the Central Downs. This movement, however, was soon submerged in a concerted bitter and prolonged agitation by almost all rural and commercial interests on the Downs to have the whole rating system for agricultural products reviewed.[78]

Beset by falling prices, rust and drought, the farmers were trying to lower fixed costs at the State's expense. That excessive rail charges did bear heavily upon some producers was demonstrated by the experience of J. McDougall of Lyndhurst who sent two and a half tons of chaff to his Brisbane agent in February 1888.

	£	s.	d.
Amount realized	£6	14	7
Railage	£2	9	0
Commission and cartage	£5	6	11
Direct loss	£1	1	4

McDougall's experience, although extreme, was not uncommon. Thomas Allen of 'Woodlawn' estimated that railway freight charges accounted

75 *WA*, 12 June 1880, p. 2, c. 1. These rates had been imposed in 1876 following successful protests by the Warwick farmers and the reduction granted to Victorian farmers. *QVP*, Vol. 2, (1876), p. 815; *QPD*, Vol. 21, (1876), pp. 1170-2 and *WA*, 5 October 1876, p. 2, c. 5.

76 ibid., 6 November 1880, p. 2, c. 7.

77 *QVP*, Vol. 11, (1880), p. 1309; *TC*, 19 February 1887, p. 3, c. 4-5 and *WA*, 21 May 1887, p. 2, c. 2-3.

78 *DDG*, 15 October 1887, p. 2, c. 2-3.

for 20 per cent of the total cost of producing and selling a ton of chaff on the Brisbane market in 1891.[79] Just before the 1888 election, however, a sop was thrown to the Warwick farmers—a 33 per cent rate reduction on Brisbane-bound produce.

The incoming McIlwraith administration, which had little genuine sympathy with the Downs farmers, soon handed over the railways, 'lock, stock and barrel' to an independent Board of Commissioners that was instructed to cease reckless expansionism, 'make the railways pay', halt the burden on the consolidated revenue and stop regional and sectional concessions which:

> . . . were the result of political manoeuvrings . . . to keep a set of wretches in power and . . . were the most offensive mode of protection—protecting a favoured class at the *expense* of the revenue; not the ultimate advantage of the revenue as in Protection proper.[80]

New rates, implementing these directions, were introduced by the Board on 1 January 1891. They aroused nearly as much ill-feeling and bitterness on the Downs as the old squatter-selector feuds in the late 'sixties. Cherished agrarian illusions and assumptions had been ruthlessly violated by these 'businessmen of Brisbane' with their new 'injurious, serious and disastrous imposts'.[81] All agricultural produce rates were increased by 50 per cent and the differential rate of £1 per ton in favour of Downs flour for the west was abolished.[82]

Packed meetings were held at most farming centres on the Downs during 1891. But agitation, resolutions and deputations all met with no response from either the Commissioners or the Government. Morgan's motion for concessions was defeated in the Assembly and the shearing strike diverted attention from the campaign and temporarily drowned it. National issues for a while took precedence over sectional grievances.[83] Some concessions, however, were made to the 'hay and corn' party in May 1892 when 'miserably inadequate' reductions were made on maize and wheat charges. But the farmers, describing themselves as 'a poor class getting poorer', were still not satisfied.[84] These railway rates, declared James Kemp of Yangan, 'were the last straw that broke the camel's back'.[85] Onions rotted at Killarney, 'husbands, wives and children worked in vain in the scrubs to make ends meet', and maize from Emu Vale realized only 1s. per bushel in Brisbane after 6d. freight and 2d. commission had been paid.

79 *WA*, 3 March 1888, p. 2, c. 7 and 31 March 1888, p. 2, c. 7; *TC*, 13 January 1891, p. 3, c. 7.

80 *DDG*, 3 January 1891, p. 4, c. 2-3 and *WE&T*, 25 August 1888, p. 2, c. 2. For similar urban views, *see: BC*, 16 December 1890, p. 4, c. 3-4.

81 *WE&T*, 21 January 1891, p. 2, c. 2.

82 *TC*, 1 January 1891, p. 3, c. 6.

83 *QPD*, Vol. 65, (1891), pp. 1127-48 and *WA*, 13 January 1891, p. 2.

84 ibid., 31 May 1892, p. 2, c. 2; *TC*, 2 June 1892, p. 2, c. 5, 4 June 1892, p. 3, c. 1 and 7 June 1892, p. 3, c. 1-2.

85 *WA*, 21 June 1892, p. 2, c. 5-7 and p. 3, c. 1-2.

The railway rates were the crystallizing agent which transformed incoherent grievances into genuine sectional consciousness and political action. Disgusted and disillusioned with their parliamentary representatives and their economic and ideological associations, a section of the farmers turned to the creation of their own organizations.[86]

[86] ibid. The 1891 increases, which added one penny per mile all round, were as follows:

	Old charge per ton	New charge per ton
Toowoomba-Brisbane	10s. 5d.	13s. 10d.
Warwick-Brisbane	12s. 8d.	18s. 3d.

TC, 1 January 1891, p. 3, c. 6 and *QGG*, Vol. 51, No. 127, 18 December 1890, Supplement, pp. 1353-94.

CHAPTER 10

ASSOCIATIONS AND ALLIANCES

FARMERS' ORGANIZATIONS ON THE DARLING DOWNS

Between 1860 and 1890 the numerous selectors on the Darling Downs failed to create a single exclusive and permanent farmers' organization for any purpose whatsoever. All moves to achieve parity with other economic sections by the formation of marketing, processing and political associations of influence and mutual advantage collapsed. Until the 'nineties the farmers were always eclipsed in this field by the squatters and storekeepers and they were even overtaken by the dynamic, effective and rapid organization of both urban and shearing labour. As in South Australia, Victoria, Canada and the United States, farmers would combine on current issues in order to secure some minor concessions within the existing political and economic framework. Such movements, however, were shortlived as they lacked ideological cohesion and sustained numerical support. Even educational movements such as the American Grange, the New Zealand Farmers' Clubs and the South Australian Mutual Associations were lacking. The earnest Self-improvement Clubs and the Schools of Arts which flourished in the country towns were derided or else half-heartedly supported by the selectors.[1]

Politically interested farmers and sympathetic observers deplored this characteristic failure to combine. Suggestions for solving this weakness were never lacking although the constant flow of admonitions was resented. Pundits such as Angus Mackay of the *Queenslander* and local newspapermen were regarded as dreamers totally incapable of coping with the practical difficulties of farming. Moreover, the transitory nature of the sponsored movements that arose from such theorizing reveals that genuine and permanent farmers' organizations could not be artificially created by well-meaning 'outsiders'. The attitude of E. Boland, a butcher/farmer and candidate for Cambooya in 1893 was typical: 'We are being ruined by Government parasites . . . New Chum Professors of Agriculture must go.'[2] Only after a relatively lengthy period of

[1] Cf. De Witt C. Wing, 'Trends in National Farm Organizations', *United States Yearbook of Agriculture*, Washington 1940, pp. 944-9 and H. S. Patton, *Graingrowers Co-operation in Western Canada*, Cambridge Mass. 1928.

[2] *TC*, 8 April 1893, p. 2, c. 5.

economic, social and political evolution could bodies develop which could truly represent the Downs farmers. It is clear that they alone could originate and control effective movements which owed allegiance to no other personal or sectional interest but this crucial fact took a long time to be accepted.[3]

Certain difficulties, originating amongst the farmers themselves or deliberately imposed by their self-styled friends, crippled all endeavours to alter the existing situation. It was not until a new, vital group of leaders appeared in the 'nineties that progress could be made and the rising discontent be made articulate. Sometimes ill-educated and often uncouth, these new representatives were nevertheless persuasive, able to formulate rural policies and establish and maintain associations to modify the existing order. To be successful and effective, however, such leaders had to be supported by a growing consciousness of mutual solidarity and agrarian separateness. For many would-be leaders their long and indifferently successful public life was arduous and disillusioning. These isolated apostles were long derided as wild theorists. Yet year after year the Downs farmers smarted under real and imaginary injustices, the sources of which they only dimly comprehended and whose remedies remained unapplied or even undiscussed.[4]

Farming on small selections, often taken up at different times and scattered over some two million acres of dissimilar terrain, was not conducive to the creation of strong centralized movements with active committees able to meet regularly and often, implement decisions and apply rapid and effective pressure. Unlike labour, the farmers had no paid delegates or Trades Hall secretariat. A community of interest was usually perverted by sterile parochialism. The Warwick graingrowers held aloof from the graziers of North Branch, the Highfields 'corn shellers' felt little kinship with the Westbrook homesteaders and the Stanthorpe orchardists stood apart from the small Drayton mixed farmers. Such destructive localism was understandable when all districts were openly competing for roads and bridges. Adequate communications reduced isolationism but it was some time before adjustments could be made to wider issues. This fragmentation, which continued well into the present century, was a major characteristic of almost all Australian small farmers' movements.

Squatters and graziers, as the strikes of 1891 and 1894 demonstrated, were quick to realize the overwhelming advantages of colonial-wide organizations. Such speed, determination and effectiveness could not be attained by the small agriculturalists.[5] Harvesting and ploughing difficulties, as well as processing and marketing arrangements, even made simple co-operation impracticable at this time.

Downs farmers in close proximity to the main towns tended to become

[3] W. Deacon, 'Farmers' Organizations', *QAJ*, Vol. 6, Part 1, 1 July 1901, pp. 8-54. Report of the Bundaberg Farmers' Conference, 1901.

[4] *WA*, 5 July 1890, p. 2, c. 1-2.

[5] W. Deacon, 'Farmers' Organizations', p. 11.

absorbed into the political as well as the economic and social life of the municipalities. They accepted the leadership of the storekeepers, publicans, lawyers and journalists who had largely fought and won the battle for cheap land and who seemed keen to assist the agricultural interest. These established leaders, holding so many educational, economic and political advantages, proved difficult to dislodge.[6] Most selectors, lacking formal education, were suspicious of those who had acquired it through some early advantage or by self-teaching. Once again, the contrast with the labour movement with their self-educated leaders and keen, almost reverent attitude towards book learning is apparent.[7] Socially awkward and often inarticulate in strange company, the farmers resented their reliance on the old paternalism and patronage but were unable at first to see how this subservience could be replaced by equally effective modifications of the administrative and organizational structure.

Elements in the rural myth and associated land legislation which fostered the family farm as the ideal agricultural unit also inhibited co-operation. Every Downs farmer, particularly the growing potential leadership group of prospering mixed farmers, considered himself as the one true 'individualist' of the colony. He alone had triumphed over his environment by the exercise of his own judgement and talents. While Protestant fundamentalism was weaker on the Downs than in the United States and Canada, the ethic of predetermined success for those who worked hard and demonstrated the other rural virtues, was extremely strong. The wealthier farmers considered that newcomers, or even their less successful neighbours, had little right or even the need to benefit from new-fangled political devices which might curtail their illusory or otherwise 'freedom of action'. Some boss-cockies had accepted the existing marketing, financial and political organizations and regarded themselves as new and worthy pillars of the local Downs ruling group. These gentry were unwilling to see the current structure modified and their privileged position jeopardized by semi-radical outsiders with dangerous conceptions.

Yet much of this 'individualism' was mythical. Downs farmers had always appealed to the State and the long depression had demonstrated that hard work was not the sole key to success. But the patriarchal family society and the slower circulation of new ideas made these old concepts hard to kill. Disinclined to accept advances in agronomy unless financial rewards were substantial and quick, the farmers were even less enthusiastic for new forms of semi-political activity. The very nature of pioneering with its arduous, grinding drudgery gave little time for logical reflection, attendance at meetings and seminal discussions. The gradual introduction of machinery, however, reduced fatigu-

6 D. B. Waterson, 'The Remarkable Career of W. H. Groom', *Royal Australian Historical Society Journal*, Vol. 49, Part 1, June 1963, pp. 49-50.

7 P. Sorokin and C. C. Zimmerman, *Principles of Rural-Urban Sociology*, New York 1929, pp. 288-300.

ing tasks and some farmers could hand the daily management of their properties over to their growing sons and turn to the consideration of perplexing questions and oppressive activities.[8]

Most farmers lacked ready cash. Even a ten shilling subscription to an agricultural society was often beyond their means. Promising producer organizations started on a wave of enthusiasm but quickly lost impetus when more cash was needed.[9] Successful farmers were notoriously tight-fisted. Frugality and thrift, they reasoned, had been a major factor in their success and they were happy to let the squatter and storekeeper pay for their position and privileges. These farmers failed to realize that this passive acceptance was, in the long run, indirectly harming their own pockets. It can be argued that the rise of independent boss-cockies and working farmers with bank accounts encouraged direct political participation. So did the payment of members. But the farming community as a whole lacked wealthy backers.

Finally, the presence of two large groups of farmers outside the ruling rural *ethos* hindered the evolution of farmers' organizations. The alien Germans, striving to retain their cultural identity, were historically and economically much closer to co-operative and organizational ideals than other national groups but their initial exclusiveness debarred transference to other sections. Co-operation on the producing level was practised among themselves but the energies of their pastors and secular leaders were persistently devoted to the preservation of their Lutheran faith rather than to active political and economic commitment. Involvement, they reasoned, would automatically destroy what the older generation were determined to preserve. We have seen that the retention of German was thought to be the only way in which the Lutheran faith could survive on the Downs. Participation, if it was to be effective, depended upon the destruction of the language barrier, but this was the very thing that the leaders of the German community were determined to avoid.[10]

Many Germans lacked political consciousness and, even more than other farmers, attached themselves to patrons whose aims were sometimes at variance with their economic interests. Nevertheless, social and political assimilation was more rapid on the Downs than in other areas. By 1890, economics had apparently triumphed over old cultural attachments. Several capable leaders had emerged from the Germans' ranks and were taking some share in local government and farmers' politics. Dispersion, economic success and willingness to learn new forms had produced such men as Philip Imhoff, Maas Hinz and Peter Hagenbach.

8 By the mid-'eighties many farmers had been established for twenty years and had families capable of tackling the heaviest and most exacting labour on the farm.

9 For an excellent modern analysis of the difficulties and dilemmas of agricultural co-operation, *see*: L. P. F. Smith, *The Evolution of Agricultural Co-operation*, Oxford 1961.

10 F. O. Theile, *One Hundred Years of the Lutheran Church in Queensland*, Brisbane 1938, pp. 86-9.

These farmers emerged not as spokesmen for a separate ethnic group but as rural leaders concerned with problems which affected all Downs settlers.

Irish farmers, politicians by nature and tradition, were more often swayed by religious issues and social antagonisms than economic logic. Some of the advanced teachings of their Roman Catholic church undoubtedly preached co-operation, but the successful Irish farmer was basically an economic conservative. Educational disabilities were marked among them and once they had acquired their cherished farm and achieved a reasonable standard of living they could see no good reason for fundamental changes.[11] After 1885, however, farmers of Irish birth or descent played an increasingly important part in local body affairs. Ten years later, the election of Thomas McGahan as Independent Farmers' representative for Cunningham marked the complete identification of this group with current Downs politics.

The first organizations on the Downs in which the farmers played any prominent part were the nine agricultural and horticultural societies established between 1860 and 1882.[12] They encouraged the discussion of regional problems and indirectly stimulated individual farm production. The local show, whether it was held at Toowoomba, Allora, Warwick or Stanthorpe, was the major event in the farming families' social calendar. For most, it even eclipsed the bush races. It was there that the selector gossiped, aired his problems and views and was brought into contact with visiting politicians eager to impress and willing to be suitably overwhelmed by the wheat and stock exhibits of the farmers and the preserves, butter and needlework of their wives and daughters.[13]

By 1888 banquets were providing a more formal forum for discussion among both farmers and politicians. Here, pent-up grievances were released and rising leaders seized the opportunity to orate and debate.[14] Moreover, these agricultural societies gave them a rudimentary knowledge of committee management, allocating finance, placating personalities and arranging major events. J. T. Wilson, Henry Roessler and W. J. Peak first convinced others of their talents while serving on such bodies.

Generally, however, Downs farmers took a back seat on these committees (*see* table p. 207).

11 *See* the derogatory views on co-operation expressed by two successful Irish farmers on the Westbrook Homestead area, Pat Ryan and Mickey Hickey, *BC*, 13 June 1893, p. 2, c. 6.

12 For a list of Darling Downs agricultural, pastoral and horticultural societies in 1890, *see* Appendix IX.

13 *WE&T*, 28 February 1885, p. 2, c. 2. The idea of the Farmers' Alliance was first mooted by a group of farmers attending the Toowoomba Show in August 1891.

14 *See* speech of P. Higgins, agricultral selector, at the annual dinner of the Eastern Downs Society, Warwick, 9 February 1883. *WA*, 10 February 1883, p. 3, c. 4 and 11 February 1888, p. 4, c. 3-5.

Occupations of Committee Members, 1878 and 1884[15]

	Central Downs A. & H. Assoc. 1878	Eastern Downs A. & H. Assoc. 1884
Squatters	2 (1 President) (1 Vice-President)	2 (1 President)
Storekeepers	4 (1 Vice-President)	6 (2 Vice-Presidents)
Publicans	2	1
Sawmiller	1	—
Minister of religion	1 (Vice-President)	—
Grazier/miller	1	—
Farmers	7	6
	18	15

Alien participation was inevitable. Only rich squatting patrons such as W. B. Slade of Glengallan could issue substantial cheques to organize the show. The storekeepers and publicans helped with prize-money, publicity and organization, and politicians such as W. H. Groom sometimes managed to extract government subsidies.[16] These donations had their price. It was customary for subscribers to be entitled to a number of votes at the annual general meetings in proportion to the amount subscribed. Members who gave ten shillings had one vote, two pounds entitled them to two votes, and five pounds to three; this gave them complete control of committee even when they did not have a majority.[17] Sometimes special agricultural organizations were founded such as the Drayton and Toowoomba and the Swan and Freestone Creek Associations by farmers and their allies who resented the deliberate exclusiveness of the Pure Merino societies.[18]

Established societies suffered from petty jealousies, shortage of funds and incompetent administrators.[19] These shows helped unite farmers of differing ethnic and occupational backgrounds. They countered enforced isolation and encouraged farmers to regard themselves as part of a wider world and contributors to the progress of the area and the colony.

15 *Pugh*, 1885, p. 154 and *WA*, 12 September 1878, p. 2, c. 2.

16 In 1871 Parliament subsidized the squatters' societies but refused a grant to the agriculturalists. *QVP*, Vol. 1, 1871-2, p. 32; *QPD*, Vol. 24, (1877), pp. 923-8, 967-72, 1102-4 and Vol. 30, (1879), pp. 1597-605, 1668-80.

17 B. M. Sims, *Allora's Past. The Early History of the Allora District*, Allora 1930, p. 54.

18 The leading show society on the Downs, the Royal Agricultural Society of Toowoomba, fixed its first membership fees at £10 per annum for squatters and £2 for 'others'. Only squatters served on the Committee and farmers were prevented from exhibiting stock. *DDG*, 11 October 1860, p. 3, c. 3-4.

19 The Eastern Downs Association was in a 'pitiable plight' in 1880. *WA*, 14 September 1880, p. 2, c. 1-2.

Many went back to their scrub or black-soil selections with renewed heart and stimulated political interests after their annual outings. Giving 'a decided impulse to agriculture' these shows were for long considered to be the most important and influential activities on the Darling Downs. So far as the improvement of stock and grain were concerned, however, the societies had little initial effect. Grain samples, for example, were personally selected by the farmer and the key characteristics of yield and milling quality were disregarded.[20]

Established in 1880, the Divisional Boards were also initially controlled by squatters and storekeepers. The small farmers were well aware of this drawback and by 1890 had managed to alter their composition. It was the election of their own representatives that was the first direct manifestation of the farmers' political power. Glengallan was the first Board to have a selector-majority; a reflection of both the early and successful agricultural settlement of the area and the precocious rural radicalism which developed during the land battles of the mid-'sixties.[21] Where the small farmers were numerically weak or newcomers to the area, however, the boards remained firmly in control of the squatters and their allies. They were determined to keep rates down and their ailing freehold estates intact. Once again they were aided by property qualifications, a subdivisional electoral system weighted in favour of sheep rather than men, and the established concept of rural leadership. As the boards were dependent on government subsidies, effective political influence was regarded as a prerequisite of office. Such services, many farmers at first considered, could be most effectively rendered by the old guard.

The extent of this traditional participation is revealed by the following analysis:

Seven Settled District Divisional Boards, 1890[22]

Occupation	Number
Freehold squatter/managers	12
Storekeepers	4
Storekeeper/farmers	2
Sawmillers	5
Journalist	1
Journalist/farmer	1
Publicans/farmers	2
Farmers	26
Other occupations	3
	56

20 *WE&T*, 12 May 1883, p. 2, c. 7.

21 *WE&T*, 7 February 1880, p. 2, c. 4 and 25 February 1882, p. 2, c. 6.

22 The Boards analysed are Rosalie, Jondaryan, Highfields, Gowrie, Clifton, Glengallan and Rosenthal. *Pugh*, 1891, pp. 150-62.

Like the committees of the agricultural associations, these boards gave such elected farmer members as William Vickers and Donald Mackintosh semi-political and administrative experience. Membership of these local bodies created individual and sectional confidence in their ability to master affairs on the colonial level. After all, colonial politics were considered by many to be local problems writ large. All successful Darling Downs politicians after 1893 had served their apprenticeship with these organizations. But as such leaders tended to be drawn from the more prosperous farmers, a new aspect of rural conservatism emerged rather than radicalism.

Dissatisfaction with prevailing marketing and milling arrangements encouraged attempts, between 1874 and 1890, to create quasi-co-operatives capable of distributing and processing Downs products without the intervention of the middlemen. Only one lone venture succeeded.

The first target was the Warwick milling monopoly. In September 1874 the Darling Downs Farmers' Co-operative Association was formed at Warwick under the aegis of the local pro-selector member, James Morgan, to build and operate a modern flour-mill.[23] Although 2,300 £1 shares were issued 1,111 were forfeited for non-payment of calls within six months. Efforts to raise more capital for the purchase of machinery failed when 'half of those present left the room when it was decided to call for additional shares'.[24] The directors actually made the incredible mistake of mortgaging the mill to the rival miller, Horwitz, for £300 at 8 per cent interest.[25] Wrangling continued throughout 1875 and in September 1876 the imposing but empty building was sold, after heated argument, to a local speculator for £1,000—enough to return shareholders half their original investment.[26]

This project had excellent prospects of success but was dogged from the start by speculative 'eagle-hawks hovering over their prey' who expected to purchase a cheap mill.[27] The farmers' apathy, the incompetence of the inexperienced directors and their inability to raise immediate and cheap finance were serious handicaps. But the established millers and storekeepers sabotaged the project and the shareholders themselves, with their petty jealousies and foolish quarrels were their unwitting allies. This expensive failure demonstrated the farmers' crippling lack of business sense. Competent millers eventually turned the enterprise into a most profitable undertaking.[28] Again, in 1885, further dissatisfaction with the Warwick millers led to the issue of a prospectus for the Darling Downs Farmers' Mutual Co-operative Flour Mill Limited.

23 *WA*, 24 September 1874, p. 2, c. 6.

24 *WA*, 24 September 1874, p. 2, c. 6 and 8 October 1874, p. 2, c. 2.

25 *WA*, 3 February 1876, p. 2, c. 5; 10 August 1876, pp. 2-3 and 7 September 1876, p. 2, c. 3.

26 *WE&T*, 10 April 1875, p. 2, c. 4.

27 ibid., 25 September 1875, p. 2, c. 6 and *WA*, 28 June 1877, p. 2, c. 3.

28 *WA*, 24 January 1885, p. 2, c. 6.

Originating in the minds of farmers of the Glengallan Divisional Board this proposal quietly lapsed through indifference, crop failures and lack of capital.[29]

A third attempt in 1890 was successful. An existing Warwick mill was purchased on 1 January 1891 and profitably operated by the Warwick Farmers' Milling Company. Although several farmers invested in this concern and served on the directorate one critic more correctly labelled the organization as the 'Storekeepers' Milling Company'. Only four of the nine directors in 1891-2 were farmers; two were storekeepers, one a grazier, one a publican and the other a cordial manufacturer.[30] The merchants instigated the project, raised most of the £5,000 capital and managed the concern.[31] Yet this mill, while not a true co-operative, was heartily supported by many farmers as an acceptable alternative to their own company. While the rebates to shareholders benefited the storekeepers as much as the farmers, a more liberal attitude towards prices, advances and storage prevailed amongst the directors. Such competition influenced the policies of the other millers and the success of the Farmers' Company pointed the way to future joint undertakings by the town capitalists and the agriculturalists.[32]

When refrigeration, the cream separator and reliable transport made commercial dairy farming and processing possible on the Downs, much of the old antagonism to technical and institutional innovations disappeared. All farmers had cows. All, boss-cocky and raw selector alike, could see the advantages of a monthly butterfat cheque. Moreover, dairying offered an insurance policy against failure and a more efficient and profitable way of employing female and juvenile labour. These possibilities G. A. Buzacott glimpsed when he opened the first dairy factory at Hampton, Crow's Nest, during 1887. The following year W. R. Robinson brought the first cream separator to his new private plant at Helidon. But the manufacture of butter and cheese was one activity ideally suited to co-operative endeavour. Dairy factories were comparatively cheap to build, simple to operate, capable of turning out a uniform and saleable product and able to yield immediate dividends. But the first attempts at Warwick and Lucky Valley to commence this new industry on a co-operative basis collapsed through the usual personality clashes and site disputes.[33] Once again it was left to the entrepreneur to inaugurate the

29 ibid., 24 November 1891, p. 3, c. 1. Ironically, this mill was the same one which had been sold by the farmers in 1877. ibid., 26 April 1890, p. 3, c. 1.

30 ibid., 18 November 1890, p. 2, c. 3 and 31 December 1892, p. 2, c. 5.

31 ibid., 18 November 1890, p. 2, c. 3. More farmers afterwards joined the directorship. Between 1894 and 1914 the mill returned an average dividend of 4½ per cent. *QPD*, Vol. 120, (1915-16), p. 207.

32 A called-up share capital of only £1,000, 20 per cent of that required for a flour-mill, was needed to commence a dairy factory. *WE&T*, 2 July 1890, p. 3, c. 4 and *WA*, 5 April 1893, p. 2, c. 6-7.

33 Denham and Reid, Brisbane merchants and middlemen, built the first cheese factory in the Warwick area at Yangan in 1893. A small semi-co-operative was also started at Greenmount in the same year.

industry and reap the profits.[34] Co-operation certainly followed later but only in an attenuated form.[35]

Co-operative marketing associations were also failures. Among the objects of the Darling Downs Farmers' Association, formed at Allora on 4 May 1885 on the basis of South Australian and New South Wales mutual associations, was the disposal of produce by co-operative means at reduced commission rates.[36] Branches were formed at Southbrook, Elphinstone, Freestone Creek and Clifton Back Plains but the movement, inspired by the radical Allora journalist and farmer, Edward Harvey, and controlled by all-farmer committees was a total failure.[37] So too was its Toowoomba counterpart, the Darling Downs Farmers' Union. Although commission agents and other outsiders were foolishly allowed to participate they were not wholly to blame for the collapse.[38] Once more, short-sighted indolence, hostility and impecuniousness had defeated their own venture. A similar fate befell the promising Brisbane-based Queensland Farmers' Co-operative Association.[39]

While these co-operative endeavours mostly failed on the Downs, they did instruct the farmers in the complexities of arousing collective action and sustaining and enforcing crucial decisions. Most of all, such minor tragedies convinced the active minority that usually leads, stimulates and rationalizes otherwise incoherent radical currents that the only hope for them, and for their fellow-farmers, lay in direct political action. Pioneers in all Australian colonies and in North America anticipated or paralleled these thoughts. Kansas farmers were advised to 'raise more hell and less corn' and this concept of political action was enthusiastically endorsed.[40] The resemblance between such movements as the Northwestern Farmers' Alliance and the Darling Downs' Queensland Farmers' Alliance, which was the 1891 manifestation of this upsurge, is particularly striking. There does not, however, appear to have been any direct communication between the Middle West and Queensland.[41]

All the accumulated financial, marketing, transport and milling grievances of three decades of Downs selection unerringly supported the conclusion that remedial legislation could only be initiated and passed by the pressure of representatives drawn solely from the ranks of the farmers.[42]

34 *WE&T*, 25 July 1893, p. 7 c. 6.

35 None of the essential conditions for true co-operation—sole shareholding by farmers, voting in accordance with production, and an all-farmer directorate—were obeyed on the Downs. Too many farmers at this time regarded dairying as a sideline and not as their major source of income. F. B. Stephens, 'Co-operation in New Zealand', in H. Belshaw (ed.), *Agricultural Organization in New Zealand*, Melbourne 1936, pp. 745-63.

36 *WA*, 2 May 1885, p. 3, c. 4 and 23 June 1885, p. 2, c. 2; *TC*, 5 May 1885, p. 3, c. 2-3.

37 *TC*, 5 May 1885, p. 3, c. 2-3.

38 *WE&T*, 1 July 1885, p. 2, c. 7 and *TC*, 22 February 1890, p. 2, c. 6.

39 *BC*, 22 September 1890, p. 3, c. 4.

40 *WA*, 23 August 1887, p. 3, c. 2 and 15 January 1889, p. 3, c. 3.

41 D. F. Warner, 'The Farmers' Alliance', p. 28.

42 F. M. Drew, 'The Present Farmers' Movement', *Political Science Quarterly*, Vol. 6, June 1891, pp. 293-4. This article gives the platform of the Northwestern Alliance which so much resembled the Darling Downs proposals.

> The hapless condition of the farming electorates in the matter of Parliamentary representation has attracted general attention . . . the railway tariff showed that the farming electorates are really disenfranchised. It is therefore imperative for the farmers in self-defence to unite and take decisive steps to ensure efficient farming representation . . . and to act in co-operation with kindred bodies.[43]

Even some leaders of the old order recognized the validity and radical possibilities of the farmers' dissatisfaction:

> There is a threat farmers may ultimately send men of a different stamp to Parliament . . . who will perhaps retard legislation instead of assisting it, until they get their wrongs righted.[44]

This threat the Downs farmers were determined to enforce. A thirty-year apprenticeship had been served and the time had now arrived for new men and novel measures.

[43] *BC*, 16 September 1891, p. 5, c. 7. Report of Proceedings at the Clifton Farmers' Conference.

[44] *QPD*, Vol. 65, (1891), p. 1137.

PART THREE

PERSONALITIES, PROPERTY AND PUBLIC WORKS

I'm an eclectic: as to choosin'
'Twixt this and that, I'm plaguey lawth;
I leave a side that looks like losin',
But while there's doubt I stick to both;
I stan' upon the Constitution,
Ex predant (sic) statesmen say, who've planned
A way to git the most profusion
O' chances ex to ware they'll stand.

'Bohemian' quoting an American 'representative':
BC, 21 November 1873, p. 2, c. 3

Parliament is not a congress of ambassadors from different and hostile interests, which interests each must maintain, as an agent and advocate, against other agents and advocates; but Parliament is a *deliberative* assembly of *one* nation, with *one* interest, that of the whole; where, not local purposes, not local prejudices ought to guide; but the general good, resulting from the general reason of the whole.

Speech of Edmund Burke to the electors of Bristol.
Quoted by Arthur Morgan:
WA, 24 September 1895, p. 4

Two candidates . . . are not required to expound any political creed of a national character. The whole question as to whether Mr Morgan is a fit and proper person to be returned to Parliament . . . for Warwick . . . or whether Mr Horwitz should be sent there in his stead, turns on what the late member has done for Warwick, and what he is prepared to do in the future, in comparison to what Mr Horwitz is prepared to do.

The Week, 10 November 1878. Quoted by *WE&T*,
16 November 1878, p. 3, c. 3

CHAPTER 11

THE QUALITY OF REPRESENTATION

He had been sent into the House to advocate the claims of a certain class, but, in doing so, he should be careful not to injure any other interest.

John Watts, MLA, Western Downs,
QPD, Vol. 3 (1866), p. 53

The Government of Queensland at present, as in the past, is a Government of professional politicians, by the politicians, and for the politicians.

DDG, 8 April 1876, p. 5, c. 3

Darling Downs politics between Separation and the crash of 1893 were a microcosm of Queensland politics as a whole. The local feuds, personality clashes, combinations and regional issues which were the stuff of electoral contests and parliamentary performances were repeated, in different settings, all over the colony. Yet, in some respects, early politics on the Downs were unique and possibly more significant than those in other areas. Nowhere else was there such a wide range of antagonistic interests and their champions concentrated in such a small area. Pure Merino fought Pure Merino, freehold pastoralist, selector and storekeeper alike. Storekeepers competed with Brisbane professionals for the votes of farmers and miners. Town disputed with town and district with district. Above all reigned the land question. Dominating all other issues during the first twenty years of Queensland's existence, this issue was largely a battle for the possession of the red and black soil plains between Dalby and Warwick.

While the great political contests for position and power were staged at the colonial capital and although some polarization of individuals and factions around the two dominating leaders, McIlwraith and Griffith, to some extent simplified the national scene after 1878, the representation of the Downs reflected local rather than colonial concerns. The Downs, although it produced many ministers of the second rank, never gave the colony an acknowledged statesman, capable of transcending local affairs, welding diverse factions and regional interests together and enforcing coherent policies on the colonial level. After all, Groom, then considered to be the Downs' most valuable and 'successful' representative, never obtained ministerial office, fell out sooner or later with every dominant faction and was merely renowned as one of the best 'horse-traders' in the colony.

The representation of the Downs was firmly in the hands of property. To win and survive election campaigns, all candidates had to have money, stamina, influence, a political intelligence which would enable them to hold their own in regional and colonial intrigues, and perseverance and negotiating abilities in the field of government expenditure. As there were only 9,500 enrolled electors on the Downs in 1893, suitable men were difficult to find and often mediocre candidates were accepted in lieu of capable, principled and trustworthy applicants. Thus, in practice, the Downs had only a small pool of eligible men from which to draw its representatives until the pool itself was enlarged by the inclusion of rising groups that had hitherto been represented by the 'establishment' or had not been considered at all. Until 1870, the Pure Merinos had a monopoly of Downs representation. They were slowly replaced by a diverse group of country-town entrepreneurs who in turn were challenged in some electorates by the mixed farmers:

PRIMARY OCCUPATIONS OF DOWNS REPRESENTATIVES, 1860-93[1]

Occupation	Total numbers 1860–93	Analysis at certain years				
		1860	1863	1873	1883	1893
Pure Merino	14	6	6	2	1	1
Freehold squatter	6	—	—	1	2	1
Farmer	1	—	—	—	—	1
Farmer/storekeeper	1	—	—	—	—	—
Newspaper proprietors	3	—	—	1	1	2
Auctioneer	1	—	—	—	1	—
Brewer	1	—	—	—	1	—
Publican	1	—	1	1	—	—
Storekeeper/millers	2	—	—	—	2	—
Storekeepers	2	—	—	—	—	—
Sawmill owner	1	—	—	1	—	—
Fellmonger	1	—	—	—	—	1
Brisbane lawyers	6	1	—	1	1	2
TOTAL	40	7	7	7	9	8

[1] Where representatives followed different occupations at different times or possessed more than one interest, the major and most persistent calling is listed. A few members who represented constituencies between the years mentioned above have been disregarded but they do not affect the overall impression. The average tenure of a Parliamentary seat was six years.

The contingent of Brisbane lawyers and opportunists—Pring, Macalister, Douglas, Thornton, Gore Jones, Foxton and J. T. Bell—who represented Downs constituencies were exotic, clever, professional politicians totally unlike the usual 'native sons' sent to Parliament by the region's electors. Furthermore, several representatives with extensive interests on the Downs represented other constituencies at various times. McIlwraith, Morehead, Hodgson and the Thorn family of Ipswich all had property on the Downs. All posed as 'liberals' who were prepared to fight the wicked Pure Merinos in the interests of country-town radical and rural selector. Macalister, Douglas and other candidates successfully contested those electorates where and when the selector-squatter controversy, itself carefully inflamed by these urban gentlemen, was at its peak.[2]

Their brief triumphs on the Southern Downs were partly the result of the absence of acceptable local 'liberals' prepared to pit themselves against what appeared to be impossible odds, their clever, rousing and apparently sincere pro-selector speeches and protestations during the great Land Bill debates between 1867 and 1878, and the belief that from their exalted position they would shower public works and private favours.[3] The trust placed in these men by their Eastern Downs, Warwick and Carnarvon supporters was not rewarded. All committed the worst political crime of all in the eyes of their followers: they failed to satisfy the insatiable material needs of their adopted constituencies. Thornton, who was 'seldom at his post and [who] never spoke or voted to benefit the town' and who was 'void of the smallest amount of influence', was, together with Macalister, castigated and finally rejected:

> What are the fruits for us? Not a single, solitary, and even half-ripe plum! Are we really to imagine that Macalister esteems the importance of his own constituents and of our own representative at the value of the benefits conferred upon us by his Government? If so, then we are all doubly sold; and then—'In the name of the Prophet—FIGS'.[4]

[2] *See* Macalister's manifesto to the Eastern Downs electors, September 1868. *WA*, 2 September 1868, p. 3, c. 3 and 9 September 1868, p. 2, c. 1-2. John Douglas, the disappointed squatter, trenchantly opposed the 'extreme squatting party' when addressing the Eastern Downs electors in 1867. Nevertheless, as Colonial Treasurer, he felt it his duty to 'place as much land as possible on the market' in order to stabilize the colony's finances. 'Nothing could alter,' declared Douglas, 'the natural differences between the rich and poor.' ibid., 5 January 1867, p. 2, c. 2-6.

[3] Macalister promised Warwick that he would have the railway extended to the town, ibid., and 16 September 1868, pp. 2-3 and *WE&T*, 20 February 1869, p. 2, c. 1-2. In 1869 Macalister defeated Davenport; the arch-dummier and land-order manipulator was placed in an impossible position, *WA*, 10 February 1869, p. 4, c. 3.

[4] *WE&T*, 21 August 1869, p. 2, c. 2-3. For the comments on Thornton, the 'absent member', *see*: ibid., 21 July 1871, pp. 2-3. This paper, which now supported Macalister, had described him as 'the arch schemer of his day' two years earlier! ibid., 20 February 1869, p. 3, c. 2. Undercurrents were always present. The *Argus* roundly attacked Thornton in 1869, not so much because of his lack of energy but because he was allegedly pressing the proprietors of the newspaper for arrears of interest on the bill-of-sale he held on the plant. *WE&T*, 26 June 1869, p. 2, c. 3.

Macalister's desertion of the radicals on 15 November 1870 to take up the Speakership under Palmer and his personal involvement in the Yandilla land machinations at a time when he was acting as the champion of the free selector discredited him once and for all on the Downs.[5] Groom and other Downs representatives who had been duped and 'sold' by Macalister were publicly furious at what they regarded as a gross betrayal. The debates gave the impression that such a desertion could only be matched by J. D. Lang turning Roman Catholic. So far as dabbling in Crown land was concerned, however, other consciences were more elastic than Macalister's. Pechey accumulated a modest run of his own by 'wise selection', Davenport, Miles, Simpson, Bell and Thorn all dummied extensively and Groom speculated in township sites along the routes of the branch railways he happened to advocate in Parliament.

Pring, that 'politician whose creed or principles it would not be easy to define, beyond saying that when in Parliament he has always either been struggling to gain or struggling to keep the Attorney-Generalship', was actually hung and burnt in effigy when the radical miners and storekeepers of Stanthorpe heard of his resignation and desertion to Palmer, in 1874, after he had 'pledged himself unconditionally to the radical Opposition'.[6]

The Downs electors were quite prepared to tolerate these shifting factional allegiances on the part of their representatives as part of the political game. They would, however, rather have been used as tools by members domiciled in the region who might throw them a railway or bridge from the public-works estimates, would keep in touch with local opinion, and would calculate the material benefits for their constituency as well as themselves when they changed benches.

A member who held ministerial office was the most valuable representative of all when the material needs of the colony were under consideration. The Downs was fortunate in this respect as its Cabinet representation was largest when the rapid provision of basic nineteenth-century utilities—public buildings, roads, bridges, railways and telegraphs—was indispensable for the continued development of the region. The key post of Colonial Treasurer was held by Downs members between 1862 and 1867 and again from 1871 until 1874, while the Department of Public Works was in Downs hands during 1862, from 1866 until 1870, between 1877-8 and 1883-7.[7] The consequences of regional representatives administering the Lands portfolio were not so beneficial and,

[5] *QPD*, Vol. 11, (1870), pp. 2-3.

[6] *BC*, 8 July 1879, p. 2, c. 3. Pring, with Groom's active support, was elected as 'Liberal' member for Carnarvon in 1874 after pledging himself to give unconditional support to the opposition and stating that there were 'grave private reasons why he could not join Palmer', ibid., 7 January 1874, p. 3, c. 7.

[7] All of these Downs Treasurers were Pure Merinos—Moffatt (Herbert, 1862-4), Bell (1864-6, Herbert and Macalister, and 1871-4, Palmer), McLean (Herbert and Macalister 1866-7) and Ramsay (Palmer 1870-1). Works Ministers St G. R. Gore (Herbert, 1862), Watts (Macalister, 1866-7), Macalister (Lilley 1868-70) and Miles (Douglas, 1877-8 and Griffith, 1883-7). *See also*: M. Birrell, 'The Political Influence of the Squatters 1850-1885', *unpublished thesis*, University of Queensland, 1951.

indeed, were often disastrous from the genuine agricultural selectors' point of view. Watts, Bell, Macalister and Taylor consistently used their administrative powers to favour one group and all recklessly distributed the only exploitable and unique resource of the Downs—the land. Few, if any, great advances in selection legislation ever originated with Downs members during their years of executive power. If anything, the so-called 'liberal' squatters—those who had made social if not intellectual adjustments—were even more dangerous than the diehards. It was not difficult for the former to concede what appeared to be generous selection measures and then circumvent them or manipulate the clauses to their own advantage. Fitz, McDougall, Bell and Wood in the Council were useful foils for the so-called 'liberals' who could contrast their willingness to make concessions with the dogged inflexibility of the pastoral rearguard. The influence of the strong contingent of Downs pastoralists in the Council has often been disregarded or neglected, but their actions were scarcely less significant than those in the Assembly.

In this era of personalities, the careers, opinions and policies of four native Downs politicians illustrate the quality of representation more concisely and realistically than a mere chronological and descriptive account of the tortuous political issues and processes.[8] There was no such person as a typical nineteenth-century Downs representative. Yet Edward Wienholt, James Taylor, William Allan and William Henry Groom, with their differing backgrounds, ideas and actions did signify diverse political positions and attitudes around which others rallied to support or oppose. Edward Wienholt, a brother of Arnold (MLA, Warwick, 1863-7), represented Western Downs in the Legislative Assembly between 1870 and 1873 and Darling Downs from 1873 until his resignation in 1875. Of Austrian descent, Wienholt claimed noble blood, but his father, John Birkett Wienholt, was a successful London merchant and gentleman farmer near the family seat of Llaugharne Castle, Carmarthenshire, South Wales. After his father's death, Edward followed his brother to Queensland and invested his substantial capital in a squatting partnership with William Kent at Fassifern, Jondaryan and Goomburra. Further spectacular western investments made him one of the wealthiest squatters on the Downs. With his 'dash and self-reliance . . . tempered by a native shrewdness which caused him seldom to make a mistake' was combined the advantage of a most fortunate and wealthy marriage.[9] Like other Pure Merinos, Wienholt retired to

8 To attempt to describe the interaction of Darling Downs and Queensland politics is a task for the colonial historian or political scientist rather than the regional analyst. Where colonial issues directly affect Downs politics they have been considered, but the interplay of national personalities such as Griffith and McIlwraith and the influence of such issues as coloured labour, land-grant railways and Separation have been deliberately neglected.

9 M. J. Fox, *The History of Queensland*, 3 vols, Brisbane and Adelaide 1921, pp. 171-2. Wienholt married the only daughter of Daniel Williams, the Victorian, New South Wales and Queensland (Toowoomba-Warwick) railway contractor, mine-owner, iron-founder and pastoral investor. Williams left £500,000 when he died in July 1884. *WE&T*, 26 July 1884, p. 2, c. 5.

England, making frequent visits to inspect the properties of the Wienholt Pastoral Estates Company, formed in 1889 to concentrate the vast holdings of the family.[10]

An Anglican, a member of both the exclusive North Australian Club of Ipswich and the Queensland Club, Wienholt first contested Western Downs in harness with Robert Ramsay of Eton Vale. Nominated by James Taylor and George King, Wienholt was the archetype Pure Merino. Acknowledged 'a true English gentleman', he had played little part in previous contests but that combination of public duty, self-interest and group solidarity which characterized his type propelled him into politics.[11] Most of his neighbours had had a Parliamentary stint and 'Buggins' turn' among these self-styled 'men of ability and integrity [who are] better than a nest of lawyers' was a duty they owed themselves and their fellows.[12] Wienholt, 'one of the most ultra-squatters that ever sat in the Queensland Parliament', was aptly portrayed in a contemporary election jingle:

> And lo! now WIENHOLT to the front advances
> (Midst dubious smiles and interchanging glances),
> The offshoot of the old and storied band
> 'The roost once ruled' in a foreign land;
> And here, in Queensland, he'd revive their glory,
> As ultra Squatter, and a would-be Tory,
> (Though perfect gentleman), this truth he shows:
> 'As doth the old bird, so the young one crows'.
> 'The time for him is out of joint', and 'spite'
> I fear, 'He was not born to set it right'.[13]

His views were 'eccentric, chimerical and wild', although 'advocated with a zeal and earnestness worthy of a better cause'.[14] But Wienholt was more honest than others of his ilk. In 1870 he confessed that 'it was necessary for those who had a stake in the country to take part in its Government', and thereby 'protect themselves from great and unnecessary liabilities'.[15] Wienholt was opposed to all public works likely to benefit towns or selectors, was in favour of drastic retrenchment, was a staunch free-trader, was an advocate of 'complete free-trade in lands' without conditions, and favoured generous compensation for pastoral tenants.[16]

His whole philosophy permeated his speech on the 1872 Education Bill:

[10] In 1888 the Wienholt family had an interest in 289,966 acres of freehold land on the Darling Downs alone. *QVP*, Vol. 3, (1888), pp. 351-8.

[11] *TC*, 7 September 1870, p. 2, c. 4.

[12] ibid.

[13] This verse was a contribution by one 'Shortfellow' of Leyburn. *TC*, 3 September 1870, p. 3, c. 5.

[14] ibid., 13 March 1875, p. 3, c. 1-2.

[15] ibid., 20 August 1870, p. 3, c. 3.

[16] ibid. *See also* his speech on the Homestead Areas Bill of 1872, *QPD*, Vol. 14, (1872), p. 977.

The chimerical scheme . . . proposing to give to the whole of the children of the colony high-class . . . education at the expense of the State, I look upon as too extravagant and visionary an idea to be at present seriously considered.[17]

But Wienholt's brief political career was marked by his temporary withdrawal of support from Palmer whose 'liberal land legislation' failed to satisfy this 'colonial Tory'. Nevertheless, he gave Palmer 'fair and reasonable support' during his Ministry and even after his defeat.[18] His resignation ended, not a promising political career, for only the Legislative Council could have accommodated one whose blatant dummying on Jondaryan, Irvingdale and Rosalie Plains was a colonial scandal, and who 'looked on storekeepers and townspeople near his possessions as simply a nuisance . . . blacksoil settlers [to him] were an unclean thing', but an era in Downs politics where one's wealth and nominees won election. The time was passing when views and actions, however reactionary, could contradict those of the majority of one's constituents and where elections could be contested on personal images and historical loyalties alone.[19]

James Taylor, the 'King of Toowoomba' was a different species of the same genus. The acquisition of wealth and social position activated this Cecil Plains squatter who intrigued, fought and speculated his way from lowly horse-holder at Drayton to Pure Merino at Clifford House—'St James' Palace'. So mean and frugal that he 'filled his pen every morning at the Post Office', Taylor always used his Parliamentary position for the utmost personal advantage. A personal enemy, James Houston of Drayton, stated a widely-held opinion of Taylor which, although malicious, was essentially true:

Taylor was capable of doing anything for gain . . . he was an oily boy, full of soap, [who] ingratiated himself into the favours of Mr Russell, like an Irish Jew, who gave him £100 to pay for 100 acres of land in Toowoomba.[20]

Unlike Wienholt, his personal interests were never subordinated to the interests of the group to which his money gained him admission. Wienholt and the Pure Merinos had usually shown a sense of *noblesse oblige*: Taylor lacked this trait, openly displaying his contempt for those who had failed to prosper as he had.[21] His philosophy of life was essentially

17 *WE&T*, 27 September 1873, p. 3, c. 6-7.

18 At the crucial 1873 division when Palmer's Government was saved by the casting vote of the Speaker, Wienholt, with the other three Downs Pure Merinos, supported Palmer. *QPD*, Vol. 15, (1873), p. 126. Wienholt again adhered to Palmer on 6 January 1874 when Macalister ousted the Government. ibid., Vol. 16, (1872), p. 22.

19 *WE&T*, 25 October 1873, p. 2, c. 6.

20 Little is known of Taylor's origins or early life. His opponents often alleged that his acquisition of Cecil Plains from his partner, Henry Stuart Russell, in 1856 was a rather dubious transaction. de Satgé has a brief sketch of him in his book: O. de Satgé, *Journal*, pp. 67-8. *DDG*, 28 June 1865, p. 2, c. 3-5.

21 During the late 'fifties and early 'sixties Taylor 'shamelessly and profitably' operated the detested calabash system on the Downs. *DDG*, 4 July 1861, p. 3, c. 6 and *BC*, 2 February 1872, p. 2, c. 6.

the crude Darwinism of the 'robber barons' of the United States with whom he had much in common. With his substantial speculative interests in Toowoomba, Taylor supported any Ministry likely to spend money at the right time and in the right place.[22] Whenever expenditure was diverted from the neighbourhood of his investments, Taylor was 'seized with a violent attack of economy'.[23] Taylor was a bluff, crude, ungrammatical 'plebian buffoon'—'a good, sound practical man of action' who boasted that he never read books and derided all 'wild theorists'.[24] He was not the cultivated squatter of Queensland legend but a 'landtaker' in the Penton vein. Yet however much he scorned his 'effete fellows' and their strategic withdrawals in the face of the agrarian threat, Taylor voted and sat with them in the Assembly where he represented Western Downs between 1860 and 1870. On 28 January 1869, however, he joined Lilley's Ministry as part of the price the latter had to pay for Downs support. The cost to the people of Queensland was heavy as Taylor administered the land laws for his own profit and satisfaction.[25] This self-styled 'liberal squatter' committed political suicide at the 1870 elections when he opposed Groom at Toowoomba. His conversion to agricultural protection, loans for Downs railways, and his pledge to vote for repeal of the two-thirds clause was too sudden and too suspect for the commercial interests of the town to accept.[26] Groom, once his political ally in the Assembly and 'the symbol of the revolt of the town against the squatter', toppled the 'King' in an acrimonious, 'red-hot' contest. Taylor had claimed when Groom was first elected that 'he would use him as an old spade—work it while it lasted and throw it aside when it was useless'. The 'old spade' ultimately proved to be more politically durable than the one who had hoped to wield it.[27] Elevated to the squatters'

[22] The 'right place' being Toowoomba, which was really Taylor's creation. With great insight he realized the superior advantages of 'the Swamp' with its key position and abandoned the established settlement at Drayton in favour of the new settlement. *DDG*, 28 June 1865, p. 3, c. 3.

[23] A Government grant of £1,000 in 1863 was nearly all spent on forming Russell Street, Toowoomba, which bisected Taylor's large estate. The railway-station was also sited in a hollow in the same locality. *DDG*, 21 May 1863, p. 3, c. 3 and 25 January 1865, p. 2, c. 5-6.

[24] *WE&T*, 27 November 1867, p. 3, c. 1 and *TC*, 27 July 1870, p. 3, c. 6.

[25] Huge areas of Cecil Plains were put up to auction in vast lots during 1870 with the inevitable result. This was one of the reasons why Groom deserted the unfortunate Lilley in 1870. *QPD*, Vol. 10, (1870), pp. 110-12; *TC*, 26 February 1870, p. 2, c. 5-6 and 23 April 1870, p. 2, c. 5-6. The *Courier* vainly called for an inquiry into the whole affair. *BC*, 1 June 1870, p. 2, c. 4 and 26 May 1870, p. 2, c. 4.

[26] Taylor was elected unopposed for Western Downs in 1867 and again in 1868. His opinions—a continuation of State aid for education, no free selection before survey, long leases for all squatters, and no premature resumptions—made him a strange bedfellow indeed for Groom and Lilley. *TC*, 5 June 1867, p. 2, c. 5. After the election of 1870, Taylor disclosed his true colours when he turned around to support Wienholt for Western Downs, who opposed most measures in Taylor's cynical 1870 platform. *TC*, 27 July 1870, p. 3, c. 6 and 27 August 1870, p. 2, c. 6.

[27] ibid., 24 August 1870, p. 2, c. 3-4 and *DDG*, 28 June 1865, p. 3, c. 3-5.

retreat–the Council–by Palmer in November 1871, his 1881 attempt to capture the second Toowoomba seat in McIlwraith's interest ended in disaster and he devoted his talents to even more obstructive conservatism, financial speculations and pastoralism until his death in 1895.[28]

William Allan, MLA for Darling Downs (1881-3), and Cunningham (1887-96), was a more attractive, popular and politically successful Downs squatter than either Wienholt or Taylor. This Edinburgh attorney's son, with his excellent education and lengthy pastoral experience in N.S.W. and Queensland, purchased 'Braeside' near Warwick in 1879 to use as his headquarters and breeding establishment for his Whyenbah and Woolerina stations on the Balonne and Maranoa Rivers.[29] Widely travelled, a Fellow of the Royal Geographical Society, a member and President of the Queensland Club, and interested in a host of local and colonial organizations, the genial Allan was a trusted and successful local member.[30] Allan first contested the Darling Downs constituency in November 1881 after Kates, goaded and taunted, had resigned in a fit of petulance over the refusal of the Government to repurchase Canning Downs before the Killarney Railway was constructed.[31] Kates' resignation alienated the strong Warwick and Allora commercial interests, then suffering from the effects of drought, the exhaustion of the Stanthorpe tin field and curtailment of Government expenditure. Warwick's feelings of neglect and frustration at the relative decline of the town were strong and sustained:

> The electors . . . could not have been more disregarded had they been a few aboriginals instead of a numerous body of intelligent, enlightened and well-to-do colonists which they are.[32]

Allan, using his wealth, the religious issue and a strong committee of influential supporters, conducted a clever and appealing campaign to

[28] Taylor was defeated by Groom's nominee, Robert Aland. *TC*, 15 January 1881, p. 2, c. 2 and 13 January 1881, p. 2, c. 4-6. During the 'eighties, Taylor sat on the boards of the Queensland Brewing Company, the Land Bank of Queensland and the Queensland Mercantile and Agency Company. W. F. Morrison, *The Aldine History of Queensland*, Vol. 2, Supplement, Sydney 1888.

[29] *Pugh*, 1900, p. 413 and *BC*, 21 October 1901, p. 5, c. 6.

[30] An excellent judge of stock, Allan was a committee member of the National Association (Brisbane), the Royal Agricultural Society (Toowoomba) and the Eastern Downs Pastoral and Agricultural Association (Warwick). He was also a member of the Queensland Club (President, 1891) and an Hon. Major of the Darling Downs Mounted Infantry Regiment. ibid., and *QPD*, Vol. 64 (1891), p. 775.

[31] The 'petulant and impetuous' Kates was deliberately baited in the Assembly by a Ministerialist who foresaw that the Government would have a good chance of capturing his seat with a strong candidate who could expertly dangle the public-works carrot. *The Week*, 19 November 1881, p. 4. Even Kates' supporters admitted that he made a fatal mistake in 'throwing up the sponge' and 'opening the door to a serious danger being inflicted on the party with which he was associated'. *WE&T*, 9 November 1881, p. 2, c. 2 and 12 November 1881, p. 2, c. 7.

[32] *WE&T*, 19 November 1881, p. 2, c. 1-2.

win this seat from the Griffith-liberal Kates.[33] National issues were deliberately neglected. 'My main object,' declared Allan, 'is simply to do my utmost to benefit this electorate' and he pledged himself to secure branch railways, foster local interests and secure Government money for a host of local projects.[34] Underlying his entire campaign was the intimation that this nominally 'independent' candidate had close ties with the ruling McIlwraith administration and that the return of a Government supporter would reverse the stoppage of public expenditure.

The intervention of Griffith and Groom was not enough to counteract these telling declarations. Even the *Warwick Argus* stated that Kates' 'affirmation of faith in Griffith is not enough to secure re-election' when 'a very desirable representative' with a capacity for 'good' works was available:

> Martyrdom is all very well in theory, but we would require stronger reasons . . . before consenting to sacrifice ourselves on the altar of party politics.[35]

Warwick's resentment, combined with the pastoral vote, were decisive and the squatter triumphed over the storekeeper. Nor was the electors' confidence misplaced. When he retired in 1883 Allan could point to a long list of material blessings which he had bestowed on the district, ranging from new cattle-yards at Warwick to a post-office at Allora.[36]

Although rejected for Warwick in 1887, Allan was elected unopposed for Darling Downs in 1887 on the death of Miles and was returned for the new Cunningham constituency in 1888.[37] At this election he narrowly defeated his old rival Kates and in 1893 survived a powerful challenge from the Alliance candidate, Brewer. Both these contests were won by shrewd assessments of local issues in spite of his obvious McIlwraithian affiliations. In 1888, Warwick disillusionment over the Via Recta fiasco, a strong agricultural protection plank and promises of future favours gave Allan victory, while his 1893 success was a triumph for country-

[33] Allan's chief supporters were the rival miller, Charles Hayes, and the Swan Creek grazier George Affleck. He was also supported by the infant *Allora Guardian* and those such as 'Freeholder' who desired 'gentlemen of substance and social weight . . . well positioned . . . men of capital . . . who can drag us out of the slough of despond' to represent them. ibid., 12 November 1881, p. 2, c. 7 and *WA*, 22 November 1881, p. 2, c. 4-7.

[34] *See* the manifesto of Allan, *WA*, 19 November 1881, p. 3, c. 2-3.

[35] *WA*, 19 November 1881, p. 2, c. 2.

[36] Allan's election was considered to be a considerable defeat for Groom whose 'baneful influence' and great power over the small farmers and selectors 'who take the words of the *Toowoomba Chronicle* for gospel' was rankling with Warwick storekeepers who were envious and fearful of Toowoomba's rise to the position of regional 'capital'. ibid., 26 November 1881, p. 2, c. 1. *See* Allan's own testimonial, ibid., 11 August 1883, pp. 2-3. Speech at a farewell banquet to Allan, *DDG*, 10 February 1883, p. 2, c. 6-7.

[37] Allan could not withstand a challenge from the even more popular Arthur Morgan and his *Argus* when he contested Warwick. Morgan, another 'sound local member', had a very wide appeal but Allan gave him a close fight. *WA*, 19 July 1887, p. 2, c. 4. The voting was: Morgan 264; Allan 205; informal 5. ibid. *See also*: B. A. Knox, 'Hon. Sir Arthur Morgan', *unpublished thesis*, University of Queensland 1959, pp. 22-3.

town and rural 'conservatism' over the new radicalism of the small farmers.[38]

Throughout his career Allan denied that he supported any faction, but he never opposed McIlwraith on no-confidence motions (the supreme test) and the key role he played during the shearing strikes showed that his sympathies lay firmly with property and capital.[39] Honest, hospitable and generous—the Downs counterpart of the English squire—Allan by 1893, like Wienholt twenty years earlier, was a survivor from an expiring political age. Once the retrenchment and inertia of the bewildered Coalition faced with unprecedented economic stresses and new radical movements from farm, factory and station had destroyed his ability to satisfy material needs, he could only reaffirm his basic belief in the old 'establishment' and its discredited and irrelevant slogans and programmes.

From his election for Drayton-and-Toowoomba in 1862 until his retirement to enter Federal politics nearly forty years later, William Henry Groom exercised a potent influence upon Downs politics and development. Yet, while acknowledging his paramount authority over Toowoomba's political representation and his effectiveness in securing economic favours for the area from the Government, it is doubtful whether his influence on and control of Darling Downs politics as a whole was as important and as complete as has been asserted. That he often successfully sponsored candidates in adjacent electorates and thus at times controlled more votes than his own is undisputed. But his constitutional inability to retain the loyalty of his protégés and the conflicting claims of districts within the region itself destroyed his later attempts to form a Darling Downs faction under his aegis. Nor do the claims of Groom and his supporters for unyielding consistency in Queensland politics bear detailed examination. Groom was no less avid for place and patronage than other colonial politicians, and, while his then radical views on questions of land policy, protection and electoral reform remained relatively constant, he was prepared to veer and tack as well as the next legislator as long as he could discern some political advantage for himself and solid financial gain for his beloved Toowoomba.[40] That

38 *WA*, 5 May 1888, p. 2. The *Argus* again supported Allan who 'will work hand in hand with Morgan'. ibid., 12 May 1888, p. 2, c. 3. Allan's position as managing partner in the pastoral firm of B. D. Morehead and Company was counter-balanced by his opposition to land-grant railways and his unauthorized pledge to secure the construction of the Thane's Creek and Via Recta lines, ibid., 5 May 1888, p. 2.

39 Allan was the Darling Downs representative on the Council of the United Pastoralists' Association of Queensland, represented the Association in Sydney during September 1890 and in March 1891 became the first President of the Pastoralists' Federal Council of Australia. *Pastoralists' Review*, Vol. 1, No. 4, 16 June 1897, p. 102. Elevated to the Council in 1897, Allan died at Sydney on 19 October 1901.

40 Groom deserted Lilley in 1870 because he disapproved of Taylor's actions, the steamer purchase, the provision of free education and the failure of the redistribution proposals. *QPD*, Vol. 10, (1870), pp. 110-12 and *TC*, 22 June 1870, p. 3, c. 1-2. Again, in 1877, Groom abandoned Douglas for the Opposition, ostensibly because of the former's adherence to the auctioning of Crown lands but more probably because Miles and not he secured office. *The Week*, 21 April 1877, p. 497.

his efforts to trim his sails to fresh political breezes, particularly in 1879 and 1890, met with little success does not invalidate this contention.[41]

Groom was a classic example of a roads-and-bridges politician. His ability in this vital sphere of colonial politics was so marked that he was often the envy of other representatives and the despair of rival Downs factions.[42] So successful was Groom in fulfilling local needs and managing his constituency that he was rewarded with unprecedented loyalty at the poll, a loyalty which persisted among the second generation of electors. After 1866, no rival candidate could stand against him and his chosen running-mate in Drayton and Toowoomba with the remotest chance of success. This fact even his opponents ruefully admitted.

As early memories dimmed, an enduring 'Groom legend' arose in Toowoomba. Past tribulations and feuds were forgotten and an idealistic and expurgated edition of his career concealed the true man with his fascinating combination of virtues and blemishes. Even his uncanny political skill and the way in which he identified himself with the emerging forces on the Downs went unremembered. Groom became a rather dull folk-hero, a pale and respectable Australian version of the *bourgeois* values which Horatio Alger promoted in America. Allsopp adopts Groom's own public estimate of his career which this minor country-town politician so successfully persuaded the locality to accept:

> It is a fact that to write the history of Toowoomba is merely to write the life of Mr Groom . . . His one desire and aim was the betterment of his fellow men and women. His name has been associated with one black mark of which we know little and care less . . . He regarded his seat in Parliament as an opportunity for service. In fact, he was a good democrat, for democracy is not a matter of soap-box, but of spirit.[43]

Perhaps Groom might have been satisfied with this panegyric. Perhaps, with his own self-knowledge and discernment of men and affairs, he really knew better. Certainly, in many ways, for him the end justified the means. Yet he owed his long political survival to other factors as well as his ability to extract loan money from the Government. From first to

[41] In 1879 Groom supported McIlwraith in hope of office and in 1890 his refusal to join the Coalition was mainly activated by his failure to secure a Ministerial position. *QPD*, Vol. 29, (1879), pp. 74-80, 133-45 and *BC*, 22 January 1879, p. 2, c. 5-6. The *Sydney Mail*'s correspondent likened Groom's 1879 refusal of the Chairmanship of Committees and his failure to obtain the coveted Lands portfolio as the action of 'something like a rat with both its holes stopped'. Quoted by: *WA*, 6 February 1870, p. 5, c. 2.

[42] A revealing election pamphlet, published by Groom's own firm, set out Groom's remarkable achievement in fostering the development of Toowoomba: *A Life's Work. What Mr Groom Has Done for Toowoomba*, Toowoomba 1896, (no author stated). The idealized conception of Groom and his work still persists in Toowoomba and has seldom been challenged, even by serious students of the period. *See* the romantic, superficial and rather naïve portrait drawn in J. A. Allsopp, 'The Rise and Development of Toowoomba. The Influence of W. H. Groom', *unpublished thesis*, University of Queensland 1952.

[43] J. A. Allsopp, 'Rise of Toowoomba', p. 1.

last he retained the support of powerful sectional interests and national groups. Even when the old political establishment, based on property, personality and patronage, seemed in imminent danger from western and urban working-class radicalism after 1891, Groom managed to retain this support. Moreover, by involving himself in the rising farmers' movement he was able to maintain his strong position in this sector as well.

Except for his successful tenure of the Speakership (1883-8), Groom never held political office. Thrice thwarted in his bid for an executive position, his direct influence upon the formation of national policy, as opposed to the satisfaction of regional needs, was comparatively minor.[44] In some measure this can be explained by the relative decline of the importance of the Darling Downs in Queensland economic and political life. Ironically, once he had helped to break the power of the Pure Merinos, he found that the claims of the Downs were being swamped by those of the new and steadily expanding areas with their different economies, needs and attitudes. Groom, while reconciling potentially antagonistic elements in his own constituency, became detached from serious political influence. Neither prepared to support the 1890 combination of the old 'ins and outs' which had dominated the Queensland scene or the rising Labour Party, with its 'dangerous notions' of class warfare, he remained in the political wilderness until the turn of the century.[45]

Groom, a native of Plymouth, triumphed over tremendous handicaps in his early political career. Convicted of stealing in 1846, an unpopular ticket-of-leave arrival by the *Hashemy* in 1849, and labouring under the setback of a further conviction for gold-stealing in 1855, Groom arrived on the Downs in 1856 with a tarnished youth, little money and only his storekeeping and agitator's experience on the Sofala diggings to assist him.[46] The contrast with Wienholt and Allan, with their wealthy con-

44 Groom had an indirect influence upon colonial policy through his association with the Royal Commissions on the Sugar Industry (1888) and Crown Lands (1897). *QVP*, Vol. 4, (1889), p. 37f. and Vol. 3, (1897), p. 897f.

45 Groom asserted that the Liberal Party as a party 'were never consulted on the formation of the Coalition' and that they were 'trapped and betrayed' by Griffith who had been 'made a subservient tool in the hands of a certain party and had swallowed the principles of a lifetime'. *TC*, 8 April 1893, p. 2, c. 1-5 and 13 April 1893, p. 3, c. 1-7. On the other hand Campbell, deserted by Groom in 1893, alleged that when Griffith 'did not make him Minister for Lands he deserted the ship and will now do all the harm he can'. ibid., 27 June 1891, p. 3, c. 7. An editorial in the *Chronicle* certainly supports this contention: '. . . the Darling Downs has been passed over with contemptuous indifference in the allocation of portfolios . . . [the Government] has palpably failed to recognize the agricultural interest . . .' ibid., 14 August 1890, p. 3.

46 HO 11/16, *Convict Transportation Register No. 16*, 1849-50, p. 301, (Microfilm copy, ANL). For Groom's life on the Turon diggings, *see*: *Sydney Morning Herald*, 14 December 1854, p. 8, c. 1; 26 December 1854, p. 2, c. 6 and 5 March 1855, p. 4, c. 6. Groom was a correspondent of the *Bathurst Free Press* and an agent for other newspapers. In 1853 this 'self-important orator feeling overcharged with his imagined abilities' was appointed by the diggers to carry their protests to Bathurst and Sydney when the New Gold Act with its obnoxious licence system was introduced. ibid., 5 March 1853, p. 2, c. 5 and 25 June 1853, p. 5, c. 3.

nections, unblemished personal lives and countless acres, is immediately apparent. Yet it can be suspected that Groom and Taylor really had more in common with each other than either of them would have been prepared to admit. But Groom was doubly fortunate. He made a most rewarding marriage, and he arrived on the Downs at a time when the country towns and their agricultural surrounds were beginning to expand and when new forces were clamouring for political expression. Furthermore, either by good judgement or pure chance his business careers, by placing him in constant touch with local opinion, gave him the ideal foundations for success in rural politics.[47]

Although he still retained his auctioneer's licence, he relinquished his Drayton store in 1862 and became landlord of the Royal Hotel, Toowoomba. On the failure of the Bank of Queensland during the 1866 financial crisis, he was compelled to assign his estate and resign his seat in Parliament. This proved only a temporary setback, however, and in 1871 he was able to purchase another hotel.[48] Following the discovery of the Stanthorpe tin field in 1872, he moved to the new township and erected a costly hotel and store.[49] For a time it appeared likely that Groom would abandon his Toowoomba associations in favour of the more remunerative business on the diggings, but his close personal and political affiliations with the town drew him back before his political interests had been damaged.[50] A new phase in Groom's business career opened on 8 June 1874, when he acquired an interest in the *Toowoomba Chronicle*, a liberal journal founded by Darius Hunt in 1861. This purchase was financed by G. H. Davenport, the greatest dummier of the Darling Downs selections, who reaped his reward in 1878 when he successfully contested Toowoomba in double-harness with Groom.[51] On 4 February 1876, after much discord and litigation, Groom became sole proprietor of the newspaper. From then on until his death he wielded a powerful and persuasive weapon with great effect, using its columns to publicize and consolidate his position in local and national affairs. As the district grew and prospered, so did the paper, and with it Groom's fortunes. By 1880, his financial worries appear to have been resolved.

It is impossible to avoid the conclusion that the tribulations of his early life had a deep and lasting impact from Groom's political thought and subsequent actions. From the beginning of his public career until his appointment as Speaker, the snears and jibes of the 'respectable' squatting oligarchy goaded him into an unrelenting opposition to all

47 Groom commenced storekeeping at Drayton in 1856. He was financed by his future father-in-law, John Thomas Littleton, who was already an established merchant. *DDG*, 8 September 1865, p. 1.

48 This was the Commercial Hotel which he sold to the QNB for £2,300 cash. *Queenslander*, 29 June 1872, p. 6.

49 *TC*, 18 October 1873, p. 3.

50 ibid.

51 In 1873 Davenport had stood against Groom but was now rewarded by the latter who asserted that he was 'a socially useful dummier'. *TC*, 12 October 1878, Supplement, pp. 1-2 and *QPD*, Vol. 17, (1874), p. 942.

their works and underpinned his supposed radicalism in land and electoral matters. Groom never forgot nor forgave the gross personal attacks made upon him by his commercial rival, the *Darling Downs Gazette,* organ of the 'Black Soil Dukes', and later by Patrick Perkins, the wayward and outspoken Toowoomba brewer who was Minister for Lands in the first McIlwraith administration.[52] Nevertheless, this mutual antagonism did not prevent him from soliciting the support of the squatters for local improvements. After he had achieved financial independence and became a man of some substance in the community, the bitterness of the attacks made by both sides appreciably diminished.

Such a country-town radical, soaked in the popular 'philosophy' of Samuel Smiles, could count on the support of all the 'lower orders' demanding a place in the sun and an end to the political, economic and social domination of the surrounding squatters. After all, both Groom and his supporters had emigrated to Queensland in search of greater opportunities, a higher standard of living and a more equalitarian social structure. These goals most of the new Downs settlers were failing to achieve. In spite of his 'roads-and-bridges' successes, Groom always had active opposition in Toowoomba. In an era when personalities played such a large part in politics and when 'party' lines were smudged, Groom was never short of rivals. To some, his personal attributes and political manoeuvres were distasteful, while others envied his hold on the Toowoomba electorate. Groom's selection of his running-mate also depended far more upon personalities than upon parties. Aland, whom he had opposed in 1878, won the three subsequent elections under his patronage only to be defeated when he fell out with Groom in 1893. Revealing incidents were sometimes disclosed when politicians fell out. Aland's speech on the declaration of the poll on 9 May 1893 is a case in point. Aland, 'whirling the hatchet aloft in truly scalping fashion' and creating the most 'painful scene ever witnessed on a public platform in Toowoomba', asserted that not only had Groom attempted to replace Davenport before that unfortunate was dead but that, in spite of his liberal land pretensions, he had abstained from voting when squatters' leases were extended to twenty-one years in 1886. This action was in return for a pledge by the pastoralists to help the Toowoomba members defeat the Warwick-St George railway proposal.[53] The full text of Aland's confes-

[52] *DDG*, 2 July 1863, p. 3, c. 1. The editorial in this issue contains the most virulent personal attack ever made upon a Darling Downs politician; 'Groom', the editor stated, 'has a violent addiction to lying . . . [and was] the spawn of crime, born in a barrack land, baptized at Pentonville, and confirmed at Cockatoo . . . he is like the American *skunk*—a decent-looking animal enough when it keeps quiet, but which smells dreadfully when it gets into a frustration.' Perkins' attack, in similar vein, was made on 30 January 1884 after Groom's election to the Speakership. So fiery was this drunken tirade, full of 'disgusting language or direct blasphemy' that it was expunged from *Hansard* by resolution of the House. *QPD*, Vol. 41, (1883-4), p. 181. Groom's conduct on this occasion and during the preceding debate was temperate and dignified. He appears to have made an excellent Speaker and to have completely outlived the jibes of the 'respectable'. ibid., Vol. 41, (1883), pp. 1-9.

[53] *TC*, 11 May 1893, p. 2, c. 5-7.

sion was not published by the *Chronicle* but the Warwick papers gleefully reported the whole proceedings.[54] Apart from the small squatter group, his main opposition seems to have come from certain storekeepers to whom protection was anathema and who relied on the custom of Downs squatters and the credit of the Brisbane merchant. Land speculators and produce middlemen opposed Groom's cheap land and co-operative market plans, some contractors and their pliant workmen favoured the expansionist schemes of McIlwraith, and many personal rivals emerged from his long service in municipal affairs.

Groom was a prime mover in the agitation to have Toowoomba declared a municipality and was its first Mayor during 1861-3. He was re-elected in 1864 and again in 1867, 1883 and 1884, and was a lifelong member of the Municipal Council. Service on the Grammar School Board, the Hospital Board, the Parks Committee and the Drayton and Toowoomba A. and H. Association's Committee gave him strong local connections.[55] He does not appear to have had any permanent political organization but had 'a great friend and intimate adviser', Thomas Trevethen, who managed his electoral campaigns and kept him in close touch with the opinions of the constituency.[56] Electoral committees were formed, but only for each election, until 1883 when the Darling Downs Liberal Association was created to co-ordinate canvassing and to recruit paid agents.[57] Generous financial support was given by his constituents in 1866, 1868, 1876 and 1881, but after the latest date he was apparently affluent enough to finance his own election.[58] By 1892 he was able to imitate the squatters and undertake a European tour. Throughout his career, Groom reported to his constituents at the close of each session, made many speeches in neighbouring electorates and paid great attention to personal grievances.

Between 1879 and 1890 Groom was a loyal supporter of Griffith's Parliamentary Liberal Party. While he was prepared to log-roll with the other Downs members during this period, his record in divisions on confidence motions and matters of party policy was remarkably consistent. This devotion was certainly rewarded by extraordinary Government expenditure whenever the 'Liberals' were in power but it was also responsible for a sharp decline in investment during the years of McIl-

54 *WA*, 13 May 1893, p. 2, c. 6.

55 *A Life's Work*, etc., p. 40.

56 This association, which 'proved themselves past-masters in the systematic management of an election', was largely Groom's creation and tool and was the first successful political organization on the Downs. *TC*, 4 October 1883, p. 2, c. 1-7. *See also*: A. A. Morrison, 'Liberal Party Organizations Before 1900', *JRQHS*, Vol. 15, No. 1, pp. 752-70. Downs organization lagged far behind even the spasmodic metropolitan efforts.

57 In 1866 he received a purse of 100 sovereigns, and one of 250 sovereigns in 1876. His election expenses were invariably paid by his Committee: *A Life's Work*, etc.

58 ibid. In all, during 1874 to 1878, Toowoomba received from Parliament in the form of direct grants, £53,900. The elegant stone post-office, School of Arts, railway-station, court-house and asylum at Toowoomba were all monuments to Groom's lobbying. This was repeated between 1883 and 1888.

wraith's first term of office between 1879 and 1883.[59] Parliamentary party ties were stronger between 1879 and 1890, with several exceptions, than they had been since Separation or were to be in the years following the formation of the coalition. The adherence of the Downs representatives to the two parties, subject to some—albeit loose—party discipline, combined with the relative decline of the Downs' political influence, militated against the old solidarity on developmental issues that had been displayed between 1860 and 1879. Twenty years after Separation, the Downs was well supplied with the basic technical facilities of colonial society: many other areas were not. Henceforth Groom was able to provide for his own electorate but not for the Downs as a whole.

It has been assumed that Groom was for a lengthy period 'the big panjandrum of the Darling Downs bunch' and that his leadership of the band gave him an influence in Queensland politics which had to be taken into account and placated if the political leaders wished to achieve and retain office.[60] This influence does not seem to have been as important as was commonly believed. The original Darling Downs bunch was composed of the Pure Merinos (and their fellows in the Legislative Council) who completely dominated the rural constituencies of the Downs until the redistribution of 1873. This group aimed at retaining their existing privileges in society and their interest in the land. They were also concerned with obtaining, in conjunction with the Ipswich bunch, public works which would lower their cost of production and marketing. The election of Groom as a country-town member introduced a new factor. Diametrically opposed to the first object of the group, he was willing to give general support to their second aim, as he hoped that new railways and roads would assist the growth of agriculture. Although his log-rolling ability was soon recognized, he was never the leader of the group and remained in their eyes a rather disreputable and radical outsider. After the 1873 redistribution, Groom was able to form his own bunch—an amalgam of storekeepers and squatters. This group achieved great success. By common consent they agreed to oppose each other on land questions, while waiting on developmental issues. The political climate between 1874 and 1879 was ideal for such a combination. A period of unstable ministries, factional fighting and personal struggles was the perfect battleground for Groom and his cohorts. During this period, Toowoomba and the Downs received a greater proportion of Government expenditure than either before or since.[61]

By 1877 Groom considered that his influence on the Downs was so

59 C. A. Bernays, *Queensland Politics During Sixty Years, 1859-1919*, Brisbane, n.d. [1919], pp. 17-18.

60 *TC*, 13 September 1873, p. 2, c. 3 and 25 October 1873, p. 2, c. 4-5. Members of this 1873 bunch were Groom, Pring, Pechey, Bell and Morgan. Groom had little control over the group, however, and Pring and Pechey both deserted.

61 Groom attended and spoke at meetings all over the Downs, carefully wet-nursing new candidates and giving them the benefit of his influence and experience. *WA*, 31 October 1878, p. 2, c. 4; *TC*, 5 October 1878, p. 2, c. 1-2; 26 October 1878, p. 2, c. 5 and 21 November 1878, p. 2, c. 7.

great that he could attempt the formation of a bunch which would support his personal advancement as well as that of the region. In return for his assistance at the 1878 elections, the proposed group was pledged to work for his appointment to the Ministry of Lands.[62] At first, Groom's plans went smoothly. Five of his nominees were elected and the cherished dream seemed about to come true. 'I say', declared Groom, 'that the electorates . . . should return six members who will go into the House prepared to vote as one man on all matters connected with the interests of the Darling Downs . . .'[63] Groom's bunch was made up of Perkins (Aubigny), Horwitz (Warwick), Davenport (Toowoomba) and Miles and Kates (Darling Downs). Bell and Simpson (Northern Downs and Dalby—McIlwraith Opposition) were potential members and only Tyrel (Carnarvon—Ministry) appeared to be an intractable outsider.[64] To his chagrin, however, McIlwraith only offered him the Chairmanship of Committees, which he indignantly refused. This was not what he had changed sides for. To add insult to injury, Perkins, one of the bunch, received the coveted portfolio and another, Davenport, refused to follow Groom and the other three into the opposing Liberal camp.[65] Again, during the election of 1883, Groom attempted to re-form the bunch, this time under the Liberal banner. His candidates repeated the victory of 1879, capturing seven of the nine Downs constituencies. Members were: Aland (Toowoomba), Foxton (Carnarvon), Horwitz (Warwick), Campbell (Aubigny—1884), and Kates and Miles (Darling Downs). Jessop (Dalby) and Nelson (Murilla) were the only Nationalists. Groom himself was appointed Speaker after one of the most acrimonious debates in Queensland history. But in 1884 the bunch split neatly into two parts—the northern portion led by Toowoomba and the southern by Warwick—over the proposed Via Recta railway which would bypass Toowoomba and link Warwick and the border areas directly with Brisbane and Ipswich. During the violent five-year controversy, Groom's influence over the southern part of the Downs was irretrievably destroyed. With only three adherents in a House of 72 members, Groom could do little.

62 *TC*, 12 October 1878, Supplement, pp. 1-2 and 21 December 1878, p. 2, c. 6.

63 Perkins' 1883 version of the incident, which the evidence supports, is an example of the stuff of Downs and Queensland politics during the period. Evidently Perkins was the initial mediator between Groom and McIlwraith when the former agreed to join McIlwraith. The price was the chairmanship. After his electoral success, Groom set his sights higher and refused to accept the post, demanding the Lands ministry. McIlwraith called his bluff and the artificial agitation collapsed. *TC*, 22 May 1883, p. 2, c. 1-7. For Groom's highly-coloured, 'principled' version of the incident, *see*: ibid., 21 January 1879, p. 2, c. 5-6 and *QPD*, Vol. 29, (1879), pp. 133-45.

64 *TC*, 8 March 1884, p. 3, c. 3.

65 With 'secret meetings in private rooms' Groom organized Parliamentary opposition to the railway which would have 'lowered property values in Toowoomba by fifty per cent'. *WA*, 23 October 1886, p. 2, c. 2. The 'Toowoomba weathercock' secured the support of Gregory and Taylor, both extreme conservatives with considerable investments in Toowoomba. Groom, Aland and Campbell voted against the Ministry on this question. ibid., 29 November 1884, p. 2; 27 November 1886, p. 2, c. 2 and 21 May 1887, p. 2, c. 2; *QPD*, Vol. 48, (1886), pp. 336-50, 351-2 and Vol. 50, (1886), pp. 1308-32, 1768-72.

Besides, there was a strong feeling throughout Queensland that the Downs had been especially favoured for far too long and that it was time for the balance to be redressed.

The quality of representation was thus decided on a local level by a few small, dominant groups, each representing certain economic interests and social divisions. The membership of such informal bodies fluctuated in both numbers and composition but their individual attitudes were always clear on vital questions affecting the welfare of the sections they were drawn from. However pragmatic their actions and attitudes when involved in the bubble-and-froth of colonial politics, each coterie retained a set of values and allegiances—whether monetary, social or regional—which it was not prepared to sacrifice. Property, its retention or acquisition, was the God all worshipped. Any political expedient which would advance the interests of the group and the locality was adopted.

The political participators on the Downs were drawn from numerically small elements of the area's comparatively small population. It was not difficult for personalities such as Groom, Bell and Morgan to arise from the controlling cliques and either adapt them for their own purposes or create their own electoral organizations to sustain them in power. The key processes of selecting, nominating and eliminating candidates were apt to fall into the hands of the local 'kings' who controlled patronage, finance and organization. Mavericks, without powerful support of their own, who fell out with the all-powerful committees or 'bosses', changed sides at the wrong time or were too 'independent' on matters vitally affecting the welfare of the group as a whole, usually committed political suicide.

The real decisions on Downs representation were not taken by the small electorate or even established local committees but by a few antagonistic 'sets', sometimes in communication with factional leaders in Brisbane, meeting in hotels, clubs, homesteads and newspaper offices. On matters of general policy which did not obviously affect the Downs, regional representatives had a certain freedom of action although, by 1893, the old independence was no longer possible. Those, like Groom, who failed to realize that the basis of representation was expanding and that the old assumptions of property were coming under increasing fire from new groups in both country and town, rapidly became politically impotent. Once the flow of loan money dried up, their *raison d'être* disappeared.

All members were expected to secure as many material benefits for their constituents as possible. If they failed they were discarded, however impressive their contribution to more weighty issues might have been. To desert one faction in expectation of rewards from another was a political virtue and not a crime. Such switches, however, could not be made too often without creating an impression of unreliability and untrustworthiness in both Brisbane and Toowoomba. Downs representatives were all political pragmatists. But to assume that real issues, based on the conflict of sectional interests, did not exist would be entirely misleading. The country-town radicals were certainly as property conscious as their foes the squatters, but the contest for land and the power and influence that went with it was genuine and bitter on both sides, however much either faction might compromise and negotiate. So, too, on questions such as education, electoral reform, constitutional amendments and coloured labour: faint yet discernible divisions were always apparent. Parties in the modern sense hardly existed but by the 'eighties political polarization was much further advanced and the attitudes of Downs representatives to the larger questions of colonial politics were relatively constant, coherent and predictable.

In short, in spite of its geographical unity the Downs in the nineteenth century was a striking example of political diversity, internal strife and sectional pressures. No single interest dominated the scene in 1893 as the Pure Merinos had thirty years before. Even the storekeepers, whose political future had seemed bright indeed after the squatters had been paralysed, were being challenged by both urban and rural radicalism. Queensland was still politically immature in 1893. Basic issues were still being worked out on the Downs in the 'nineties and yet this was the area which had been the first to be settled by free men. The old myths had succumbed to harsh facts and the previously accepted ideals had been warped and changed beyond all recognition by the clash between interest and interest, the fluctuations of uncontrollable world commodity prices and the obvious disparity between prediction and fulfilment in an alien environment. The Pure Merinos' dream of a 'bunyip aristocracy' had been rudely interrupted but those who had disturbed their peace had not yet realized their own alternative aims. But in the sheds of the Western Downs and the workshops of Toowoomba, the colonial myth-makers were once more at work. Queensland's propensities for illusion rather than reality, for palliative rather than cure, were stronger than ever.

CHAPTER 12

THE ELECTORAL SYSTEM IN OPERATION

> . . . there are countless voters on our colonial rolls who do not even know what the word 'franchise' means, and who only value their vote at the price they are able to get for it, whether in beer or spirits, in money or in kind.
>
> *WA*, 25 September 1883, p. 2, c. 3-4

Queensland began her existence as a separate colony in 1859 with one of the most liberal franchises and a set of the most simple and open enrolment procedures of all the Australasian colonies. Grave defects in the electoral system, however, were apparent as soon as the first voters went to the polls in 1860. Many males were not enfranchised, the system was easily manipulated by persons and groups seeking their own advantage, and corruption, fraud and sharp practices were common on the Downs during every election held throughout the nineteenth century. Remedial legislation, pedantic and legalistic, usually confused and prohibited more than it simplified and purified. Without a long history of constitutional and political struggles and attempting to work a political system imposed from above, Queensland was at first rather immature to support and conduct a ready-made and comparatively sophisticated legislative framework.[1] The wonder is that the system worked as well as it did and that it withstood the challenges and stresses produced by a rapidly developing and diversifying economy.

Few Downs inhabitants really fully understood the mechanics of the electoral system. Those who did and could organize accordingly had a tremendous advantage in this age of personal politics. Furthermore, the system was deliberately moulded to favour the interests of certain classes and localities at the expense of other sections. Plural voting, the distribution of electorates throughout the colony, the delineation of boundaries and the siting of polling-stations all affected the political results. Finally, even the manipulation of the infant system by the propertied

1 A. A. Morrison, 'Colonial Society, 1860-1890', *typescript*, 1958, p. 2. Morrison, 'Politics in Early Queensland', *JRQHS*, Vol. 4, No. 3, December 1950, pp. 293-312.

groups was overshadowed by rapid yet fluctuating economic changes and development in an immense, diverse and expanding colony.

The first franchise, based on the New South Wales Electoral Act of 1858, theoretically conferred the right to vote on all natural-born or naturalized adult males who had lived for six months in a particular district or who were in possession of a freehold or leasehold estate of a clear value of £100 or an annual value of £10.[2] Plural voting was allowed but not in the electorate for which the voter held a residential qualification. These conditions remained almost unaltered until 1905. All voting was supposedly by secret ballot and the names of unwanted candidates were struck out.

Governor Bowen and his initial tame politicians were well satisfied that manhood suffrage, as introduced and operated in Queensland, had '. . . a conservative character, and [was] calculated to give increased influence to the landed proprietors and rich settlers in country districts, as opposed to the mixed population of the towns'.[3] Bowen maintained that pauperism and distress were unknown in Queensland. Property was widely distributed and men had every opportunity to acquire it and were thus reluctant to agitate for legislation of a radical nature that might jeopardize their chances. Moreover, pastoral workers 'sensibly' had 'usually exercised their new privileges, when well treated by their employers, as those employers recommended'.[4] The Governor was too sanguine. Many workers were disenfranchised because their wages or board were paid weekly or monthly and not annually as required by the Elections Act,[5] and only the compliant and the intimidated voted on the runs.

The extent of plural voting is difficult to determine, the only reliable figures refer to the 1860 general election (*see* table p. 237).

It is highly unlikely that the proportion of non-resident plural voters afterwards declined and it is possible that, with the development of absentee ownership of Downs freehold and leasehold runs and the steady spread of small urban allotments, this category actually increased.[6] Several close contests on the Downs might well have been decided by this means. Certainly, the one-man-one-vote agitation of the 'nineties which was aimed at the destruction of pluralism and the enfranchisement of the 24,000 or so nomadic pastoral workers and poor urban labourers who had never been enrolled, aroused the ire of the 'respectable and industrious citizens' who valued this privilege of property.

2 C. A. Bernays, *Queensland Politics*, p. 283 and *QPD*, First Series, Vol. 1, (1865), pp. 140-8.

3 Bowen to Newcastle, 6 February 1860. Quoted in S. Lane-Poole, *Bowen Despatches*, Vol. 1, p. 132.

4 ibid., p. 133.

5 *TC*, 23 April 1870, p. 2, c. 3.

6 Many squatters retired to live in Brisbane or Toowoomba during the 'seventies and the Selection Acts made the acquisition of cheap land possible within every electorate in the Settled District.

ENROLLED ELECTORS VOTING FOR DOWNS CANDIDATES, 1860 ELECTION[7]

Electorate	Resident electors	Non-resident electors	Total
Eastern Downs	107	—	107
Northern Downs	256	16	272
Western Downs	168	—	168
Drayton and Toowoomba	187	33	220
Warwick	138	17	155
Maranoa	101	2	103
Darling Downs TOTAL	957	68	1,025
Queensland TOTAL	4,391	399	4,790

As the hysterical *Darling Downs Gazette* declared at the time of the first great shearing strike:

One-man-one-vote would mean the enfranchisement of whole armies of idle or vicious nomads . . . the lazy sundowner, the spieler, would all be enfranchised . . . it would place another weapon in the hands of the plutocracy. Western nomads, like all such people, are essentially venal.[8]

Perkins echoed these views:

One-man-one-vote meant that one man was as good as another and that he unhesitatingly denied . . . it was distinctly stated [in Scripture] that there were different orders . . . was a man's property to represent nothing?[9]

Groom, Morgan and the growing farmers' organizations on the Downs, however, fully supported the principle.[10]

Intricate and easily manipulated enrolment and voting operations, however, made nonsense of the generous statutory franchise on the Downs. Rolls and ballots were subject to local control and influence and the tangled mass of electoral legislation confused rather than clarified what should have been simple procedures. A high degree of mobility, coupled with initially poor communications and a growing agricultural and mining section, did, however, complicate matters. At first, the

7 *Census of Queensland*, 1861, p. 938.

8 *DDG*, 13 June 1891, p. 4, c. 3-4 and 21 February 1891, p. 4, c. 2. *See also* the fears of G. H. Davenport of Headington Hill after visiting the United States and observing 'the unthinking classes ruining the country'. *TC*, 28 August 1877, p. 5, c. 4.

9 *QPD*, Vol. 67, (1892), p. 566. The Pure Merinos, Wienholt and Taylor, had already stated these views—nearly thirty years earlier: 'He would not for a moment believe that population was the proper basis for the interests of the country . . . he did not believe in having too many town members. . . . The country was becoming too democratic.' *QPD*, First Session, Vol. 1, (1865), p. 85. Speech of Wienholt (Warwick).

10 *TC*, 8 April 1893, p. 2, c. 1 and *WE&T*, 18 March 1893, p. 3, c. 1.

Courts of Petty Sessions in the small towns employed collectors to gather names, compiled the rolls and conducted quarterly Revision Courts for the addition or deletion of electors. In 1865 an exorbitant deposit of one pound per objection was instituted to prevent the lodging of wholesale claims. The onus was on the elector to see that his name was on the roll.[11] Frequent and justified complaints alleged that the Police Magistrates, District Returning Officers and local Justices of the Peace were not only political appointees but were often personally engaged in open political activity. These people regarded the Revision Courts as heaven-sent opportunities to help their masters, foster their own concerns, and advance or conserve the interests of their own group.

Warwick was the scene of numerous abuses of this kind. In 1865 a three-man court eliminated 104 of the 189 Eastern Downs electors when no external objections had been received and the necessary notices of intention to revise the rolls had not been served. William Duggan of Allora possessed the same qualifications as the Returning Officer but the Irishman's name was expunged and Dr Aldred's left as 'Duggan was a troublesome person and it was considered advisable to strike his name off the roll.'[12] The Select Committee of Inquiry found that 'a very illegal proceeding had taken place', no rolls had been signed or initialled, and 'that no legal revision of the roll for 1865-66 took place at this revision court'.[13]

Further abuses, for which the 'respectable' perpetrators were never legally tried, occurred at Warwick and Toowoomba before every general election until 1872. All officials constantly displayed a 'disgraceful elasticity of conscience' and one magistrate, Charles Clark of Talgai, openly purged and stuffed the rolls so as to favour his brother's chances at the next Warwick election.[14] This Revision Court was adjourned three times when the Justices refused to attend and hear applications for enrolment from selectors who had travelled very long distances.[15] The Elections Act of 1872 was intended to remedy this situation. Voters' rights, which had to be presented by each elector before polling, were issued to prevent personation and a solemn claim, accompanied by a written declaration, was enough to secure enrolment. The Revision Courts, as established, were replaced by paid officials and the objection fee was reduced to five shillings.[16] Voters' rights were an absolute failure

11 *QPD*, First Series, Vol. 11, (1865), pp. 56-62, 400-1.

12 ibid., p. 469.

13 ibid., p. 643. Thornton, then MLA for Warwick, later alleged that he had sat on the Bench with George Clark when the rolls were being revised. The latter had boasted that 'they had often ridden over the laws of the land on that Bench'. *QPD*, vol. 12, (1871), p. 36.

14 *WA*, 5 February 1868, p. 2, c. 1-2 and *QPD*, Vol. 6, (1867-8), pp. 926-7. *QVP*, Session 1871-2, pp. 307-23. 'Report from the Committee of Elections and Qualifications'. Charles Clark actually sat on the Revision Court Bench just before he contested the election.

15 *QPD*, Vol. 14, (1872), pp. 83-5.

16 ibid., Vol. 13, (1871-2), pp. 146-60 and Vol. 15, (1872), p. 403.

and soon became negotiable currency. Downs squatters and sawmillers sent in for bundles of rights on 'behalf' of their men and used them as they thought fit.[17] The system disqualified many itinerants and illiterates, and others refused to operate such a clumsy device. As the 'packed benches' could erase names who had not applied for a right within twelve months of the poll, many men who had neglected to apply were disenfranchised.[18]

A further Act in 1874 abolished the rights and provided for the police and 'suitable' officials to collect names which the Bench would revise.[19] This system was also a failure. The unpaid police neglected this duty and the benches appointed their own 'hangers-on' as collectors at the rate of one pound per day.[20] Automatic registration by written or personal application was introduced in 1879. The Quarterly Registration Courts revised the lists and Clerks of Petty Sessions had the responsibility for disqualification, although the Returning Officers prepared the actual rolls.[21] This still did not prevent personation or roll-stuffing, at which Groom with his Toowoomba 'scouts and touts' as well as other 'Liberals' were becoming increasingly adept.[22] Increasing power and the ever-present remembrance of past grievances encouraged the radicals to emulate the squatters in the field of electoral manipulation. This they did, and malpractices in the towns soon rivalled those in the country.

Perkins, the Downs' greatest exponent of the fraudulent art, paid a grudging tribute to the new pupil, Groom, when he asserted that:

> If you want to stuff a roll or get into Parliament the proper way is to get associated with a newspaper editor in the country who has nothing to do, who has a story for everyone who passes, who tells lies and makes them appear like the truth, who circulates them in the district, and who has no character.[23]

The Elections Act of 1885 was the last major legislation regulating the electoral system passed until 1897. Electoral divisions were set up within constituencies with Petty Sessions stations as electoral courts. Clerks replaced Returning Officers as roll-keepers and Police Magistrates and Justices—the old unsatisfactory combination—constituted the new courts. Interested outsiders, however, were now able to peruse claims and prevent wholesale disqualifications. Enrolling procedures were changed. Registrars and clerks had to send claim forms and notices to *all* electors three months before an election, and the onus was placed on the elector to return the claim unless he made a solemn declaration

17 ibid., p. 160.

18 *QPD*, Vol. 16, (1874), pp. 263-70.

19 ibid., pp. 277-98.

20 German settlers were disenfranchised by collectors deliberately mis-spelling their names and the returning officers refusing identification. *QPD*, Vol. 28, (1878), pp. 245-6.

21 ibid., Vol. 28, (1879), pp. 121-8, 135-45.

22 ibid., *QPD*, Vol. 29, (1879), pp. 239-46, 259-74 and Vol. 41, (1883-4), pp. 79-99.

23 ibid., p. 100. This statement was made just before Perkins was unseated—an action which he partly attributed to Groom's machinations.

or the registrar had a personal knowledge of the validity of the claim. Clause 122 of the new Act made the stuffing of ballot-boxes a felony for the first time.[24] Impersonation was to be checked by marking the ballot-papers off against the roll, and papers not initialled by the Presiding Officer, without official numbers, possessing additional markings and having too many names struck out, were to be instantly rejected.[25]

This Act did not prevent some repetition of the old abuses, although the Toowoomba case of July 1887 was the last important Downs event of its kind. The Toowoomba Revision Court purged the rolls so drastically on this occasion that the number of electors was reduced from 2,225 to 1,376. Only 50 of the 300 new applications secured by the lively Liberal Association were accepted and discouraged electors soon lost heart.[26] The radical surge on the Downs after 1890, however, soon checked the more flagrant offences of this nature.

The electoral machinery gradually became oiled and adjusted but there was always a wide discrepancy between enrolments and the total number of adult males residing in Downs constituencies.

ADULT MALES AND TOTAL ENROLMENTS ON THE DOWNS, 1876 AND 1886[27]

	1876			1886		
Electorate	Adult males	Registered electors	%	Adult males	Registered electors	%
Aubigny	1,537	1,271	82.5	1,044	844	80.8
Darling Downs (2)	1,258	1,226	97.3	2,212	1,625	73.4
Carnarvon	1,724	1,056	61.2	881	510	57.8
Dalby	731	678	92.6	543	500	92.0
Northern Downs	678	421	61.6	907	438	48.2
Drayton-Toowoomba	1,303	1,244	95.5	1,945	1,362	70.3
Warwick	1,245	1,071	85.4	740	523	70.6
TOTAL	8,476	6,967	—	8,272	5,802	—
Av. per electorate	1,059	871	82.3	1,034	725	70.1

While the Downs seats, with an average registration of 70.1 per cent of all adult males in the area in 1886, were far ahead of the low Queensland average of 54.4 per cent, and while Dalby and Aubigny had the highest figures in the colony, many potential voters, 58 per cent in

24 *QPD*, Vol. 46, (1885), pp. 120-5, 792.

25 ibid., p. 519. This clause was opposed by Griffith and was carried only after pressure from the Opposition and dissenting Liberals.

26 *QPD*, Vol. 52, (1887), pp. 193-8. In 1878 Groom alleged that 300 names—20 per cent of all electors—had been removed from the Aubigny roll. *QPD*, Vol. 29, (1879), p. 243.

27 *Census of Queensland*, 1876 and 1886.

waning Carnarvon and over half in Northern Downs, were not enrolled. Even the 30 per cent spread would have been sufficient to decisively influence results in 1888 and 1893.[28]

Of those enrolled, many did not vote, although once again the percentage exercising the franchise was higher on the Downs than in the rest of Queensland.

PERCENTAGES OF ELECTORS VOTING AT ELECTIONS, 1867-93[29]

General election	Percentage of enrolled Downs electorates	Electors voting Queensland
1867	55·5	41.6
1878	59·5	59·5
1883	66.4	61.4
1888	79·2	73·9
1893	76.2	73·1

Thus, even in 1888, when more Downs males voted than ever before, about 40 per cent of all the adult males in the region either could not or would not take the fundamental political step of any democracy. Warwick, however, with its close interest in election matters, had a constantly high percentage of voters over the period.[30] The superiority of the Downs as a whole was a reflection of increasingly closer settlement by a permanent population, thorough local political organizations and a keen interest in colonial and regional questions which was sometimes lacking in other, less developed and complex, areas.

Only in two contests—Darling Downs in 1875 and Carnarvon in 1883—did informal voting affect the results, although Returning Officers often refused to mark invalid papers as such.[31] Relatively few wasted their votes on the Downs, this fact indicating a fairly high degree of educational and political literacy.[32] Plumping occurred only in the double-electorates of Darling Downs and Drayton-Toowoomba and on no occasion did the process affect the issue.[33] What plumping did decide was the placing of the two successful candidates. Twice, in 1883 and 1893, Groom was deprived of the honorary distinction of becoming

28 ibid.

29 *SR*, 1867, 1878, 1883, 1888 and 1893. Some early general elections are omitted.

30 ibid. 78 per cent of Warwick electors voted in 1867, 73 per cent in 1868, 80 per cent in 1870, 75 per cent in 1871, 74 per cent in 1878, 72 per cent in 1883 and 82 per cent in 1888. The highest figure ever recorded was that of 88.8 per cent in 1893.

31 Many newspaper accounts do not record the numbers of invalid votes.

32 The highest informal vote ever recorded was 67 in a poll of 1,254 at the 1878 Toowoomba election.

33 *TC*, 4 October 1883, p. 3, c. 1 and 9 May 1893, p. 3, c. 6. In 1883, 294 voters plumped for Douglas and only 14 for Groom. In 1893, 359 plumped for Aland, 146 for Fogarty and 56 for Groom.

senior member for Toowoomba by rival candidates and their committees discovering which way the voting was going, conceding the election, and advising their supporters voting later in the day to support the less objectionable alternative.[34] This, however, affected Groom's vanity rather than his political standing and influence.

The contingent vote, originated by A. H. Barlow and created by the Elections Act of 1892 was a device to prevent the rising Labour Party from electing candidates on a split conservative vote. Ironically, the new Farmers' Alliance opposed the measure, little dreaming of its possibilities for such a sectional interest. Their successors in the following century were less obtuse. This modification of a Danish system and the ancestor of the preferential vote was also bitterly condemned by the entrenched 'radical' remnants in Toowoomba and Warwick who were at first unwilling to accept the new polarization in Queensland politics.[35] At first, however, this innovation was but a curiosity on the Downs. In 1893 only the Dalby returns demanded its use and then the ultimate result was no different from the preliminary first-past-the-post returns.[36] The break-up of the old Griffith-McIlwraith factions, Labour's appearance, and the brief flowering of a farmers' group, frightened the propertied element but this novel weapon was now available for use on the Downs during future times of political confusion.

Returning Officers played a major role in all elections. Like the Revision Courts, they were also generally political and personal appointments, a factor which frequently produced bias and sometimes outright favouritism and corruption. Their duties—securing nominations, managing the central booth, deciding voting qualifications, collating the constituency returns, announcing the result and returning the writ—gave them many opportunities to influence or manipulate the voting figures. More often than not, they were the only persons involved who fully understood electoral procedures but some complicated or ambiguous instructions even baffled them on several occasions. These officials were invariably drawn from the 'respectable' elements of the community or else, like Thomas Allen of Cambooya or Thomas Trevethen of Aubigny, were firmly attached to the court of Toowoomba's reigning political personality.[37] During disputes or close contests when mechanics were

[34] *WE&T*, 13 May 1893, p. 3, c. 1.

[35] For Morgan's views, *see*: *WA*, 22 April 1893, p. 2, c. 3. Groom's opposition is stated in, *TC*, 8 April 1893, p. 2, c. 1; *QPD*, Vol. 67, (1892), pp. 576-8. A clear explanation of the new procedure and an open admission that it was intended to hamper the Labour Party is printed in *PR*, Vol. 11, No. 5, 15 July 1892, p. 752.

[36] The voting at the Dalby election was:

Bell	Independent	280
McCarthy	Labour	225
Jessop	Independent	149

Bell received 21 contingent votes and McCarthy 12, giving the former a final majority of 64 over his opponent. *TC*, 4 May 1893, p. 3, c. 4.

[37] For the annual list of Returning Officers, *see: Queensland Blue Book*, Brisbane 1866-94.

all-important, these officers exercised their judgement to help the side of 'progress', 'moderation' or 'safety'. Some, such as William Deacon of Cunningham, William Gunn of Carnarvon, and Thomas Johnson of Warwick convincingly demonstrated their previous political 'neutrality' by indulging in partisan warfare and later standing for Parliament themselves.[38] Of the openly biased, the notorious John Garget of Aubigny fame was the worst and most blatant example but Dr Aldred and James McKeachie of Warwick, George Affleck of Darling Downs and G. B. King of Western Downs ran him pretty close.[39] All helped to swing elections and to elect their favoured candidates. So, too, did the new 'radical' Returning Officers of the towns, but urban abuses were easier to discover and check than in the western pastoral and mixed selector-squatter constituencies.

In addition, these unpaid officials had the duty of selecting their honorary deputies to officiate at each booth. A judicious choice enabled the central officials to control the mechanism at every level and to pander to specific locality loyalties. Thus, in 1870, Western Downs had fifteen booths, each in charge of a station manager, or, in the case of F. N. Isaac of Gowrie, a resident Pure Merino.[40] Deputy Returning Officers were entitled to peruse the list of voters, examine the ballot-papers and then declare the result. No central depot existed to which ballot-boxes from isolated stations had to be sent and the returns were made by telegraph or horsed messenger. The results of contests conducted under these conditions were predictable.[41] The whole system made nonsense of the secret ballot and men were openly informed that an anti-squatter vote meant instant dismissal.[42]

Two further affairs, both involving George Affleck, a Sandy Creek grazier and Returning Officer for Darling Downs, illustrate the ability and desire of such officials to influence elections. On 7 April 1875, Affleck, in a letter to the Speaker of the Legislative Assembly, drew attention to serious informalities which had marred the closely-fought Darling Downs by-election. More ballot-papers than names on the roll (postal voting was unknown) had mysteriously appeared in the boxes at Yandilla and Warwick and these votes could decide the contest. Furthermore, as Presiding Officer at Leyburn, Affleck had compelled voters residing outside the polling district to vote openly without having first proclaimed the areas, as he was required to do under the Elections Act.[43] Affleck refused to endorse the writ declaring Graham elected and, on 4 May, was called before the Bar of the House to explain his refusal to comply with the Speaker's instructions.

38 ibid.

39 James McKeachie was an open partner of Clark in the Warwick Flour Mill. *WE&T*, 2 July 1887, p. 2, c. 6.

40 *BC*, 25 August 1871, p. 3, c. 6.

41 *QPD*, Vol. 13, (1871-2), p. 160.

42 *TC*, 26 August 1871, p. 2, c. 5.

43 *QPD*, Vol. 18, (1875), pp. 8, 53, 82-5.

On Macalister's motion, the House voted along 'party' lines to seat Graham and Affleck was recalled to endorse the writ there and then. This he did, 'at once divesting himself of personal feeling and conscience' and rendering himself 'no longer free to do his duty in that state of life to which he had been called'.[44] No attempt was made by Parliament to investigate the charge that Graham had been 'returned by bribery, intimidation, and every possible evil influence' or the countercharge that Affleck had deliberately tried to obstruct the former's return.[45] Parliament, and not even its semi-judicial Committee of Elections and Qualifications, took all responsibility and it, or rather a small majority within one Chamber, virtually decided the contest.

Affleck was again the centre of debate and controversy in 1878-9 when William Graham charged him with deliberately omitting his name from the nomination list, poll announcement and voting papers for the same electorate. The evidence suggests that Donald McIntosh, to whom Graham's agent G. H. Davenport had entrusted the task of lodging the nomination paper and the £20 deposit, had later withdrawn the absent member's candidature without the authority of either Graham or Davenport and with the full concurrence of Affleck. The latter's defence of his arbitrary action in allowing the withdrawal was unconvincing and it is probable that there was collusion between McIntosh and the Returning Officer to eliminate Graham.[46] Affleck had not forgotten Graham's election by the House three years earlier when he had been 'forced to swallow the leek' and on this occasion he decided to eliminate his personal enemy before the voters went to the polls. At any rate, the Committee of Elections and Qualifications had no hesitation in annulling the election and ordering a fresh bout. It is highly significant that Affleck resigned as soon as the adverse decision and implied censure was published.[47]

While Returning Officers still exercised political influence and were still subject to partisan appointment for many years after these cases and Garget's misdemeanours, the office gradually lost the bias and odium of former days. By the time of the 1893 election, most were personally incorruptible and several were permanent civil servants rather than respectable men of influence tied to area passions and interests.[48] Strict legal controls, such as the central collection of ballot-boxes, provision for effective scrutineering and clearly-defined spheres of responsibility made frauds harder to perpetrate and elections simpler to control. So did better communications and closer settlement. Deputies at the isolated pastoral booths in the Unsettled District, however, still held despotic sway, although Labour successes in 1893 demonstrated that

44 *WE&T*, 8 May 1875, p. 2, c. 1-2 and *QPD*, Vol. 18, (1875), p. 84.

45 ibid.

46 *QVP*, First Session, Vol. 1, (1879), pp. 37-8. 'Petition of William Graham, Esq.'

47 ibid., pp. 524-32.

48 *Queensland Blue Book*, 1894.

even their powers could be challenged and defeated. It was then the turn of the new 'masters' to devise new ways of perpetuating their hard-won position.

Frauds, at which the Returning Officers either connived, or ignored or lacked power to control, were commonplace on the Downs between 1860 and 1893. Each election produced a further crop of allegations of malpractices. These usually took the form of personation, resurrection, patronage, treating, direct bribery and intimidation. The Northern Downs election in 1870 was characterized by the welter of personation practised by Henry Thorn's Ipswich supporters. These, managed by his brother George, arrived by special train at Jondaryan, cut the telegraph wires and swamped the booth. Fred Stanmore of Condamine, by an impossible 'feat of horsemanship' managed to vote at Condamine, Jinghi Jinghi and Dalby.[49] Both sides used these special trains to convey plural voters and 'birds-of-passage' from one electorate to another. Forty voters arrived at Stanthorpe in 1883 to vote for O'Sullivan, while others were driven 120 miles to vote at the isolated booth at Inglewood for the Carnarvon election.[50]

Bribery was rampant, although specific cases were never proved. A vote was worth as little as a few glasses of beer or as much as five pounds if the candidate was wealthy and the contest close. Poor men, who would otherwise be deprived of the franchise, felt that they gained more than they lost by accepting an electoral dividend. They expected to be paid for their services and most did not make the rational calculations necessary to prove that they were harming their own interests by accepting a bonus. A glass in the hand, they argued, was worth more than vague promises, which had little chance of fulfilment, for the future.

Intimidation was rife. On polling-day for the Drayton-and-Toowoomba seat in 1870, eleven men were brought in to vote from Eton Vale station 'guarded on either side from contamination by the radicals of Drayton by men on horseback'. Westbrook employees were similarly shepherded and some who voted independently were discharged and told to 'apply to Mr Groom for sheep to shear'.[51] Sawmillers controlled isolated communities, and railway contractors and even urban aldermen who had jobs and contracts to allocate used this method. In agricultural districts, a more subtle but nevertheless effective form of social pressure exercised by the majority sometimes inhibited the registration of a minority opinion at a small booth. These devices cost money. Candidates with powerful financial resources of their own or shadowy backers were able to influence more votes than poorer farmers or store-

49 *BC*, 8 September 1870, p. 3, c. 3.

50 *WA*, 16 October 1883, p. 2, c. 5. The administration naturally held a great advantage at election times. The resources of the State, particularly the Railways Department, could be pressed into service.

51 *QPD*, Vol. 11, (1870), p. 15 and Vol. 13, (1871-2), p. 160. For an attack on the proprietors of Cecil Plains and Jondaryan and their 'serfs', *see*: *TC*, 27 March 1875, p. 3, c. 1.

keepers, although publicans such as Groom and newspaper proprietors like Morgan had an obvious advantage.

> There was not a single member of the House who had not spent hundreds of pounds to get in . . . it was well known that every candidate had to spend money.[52]

Politicians spent far more ensuring their return than the State did on running an election. The Returning Officer for Western Downs in 1870 boasted that the entire contest had only cost the Government £43.[53] Miles alone was alleged to have paid £800 to secure his return for Darling Downs in 1878 and £600 on a subsequent occasion.[54]

The Aubigny election, held on 17 August 1883, was marked by one candidate's deliberate use of every possible type of fraud, corrupt practice and electoral abuse. This contest marked the climax of over twenty years of political chicanery on the Downs. Previous elections had been marred by direct corruption, but the scale, effrontery and cynicism so blatantly shown on this occasion were so flagrant that the defects in the system could no longer be ignored by any government. Perkins' unseating served notice that '. . . bribery, corruption and nearly all the electioneering sins . . . committed in this contest' would no longer be tolerated on such a scale.[55] After Aubigny, the free-and-easy days were virtually over. At this election, Patrick Perkins, the Toowoomba brewer-speculator, friend of McIlwraith and his clique and Minister for Lands in the latter's administration, was opposed by James Campbell, a Toowoomba butcher and fellmonger and protégé of Groom. When the poll was declared Perkins was found to have a majority of 111 over his opponent. Nearly 82 per cent of all the registered electors voted—15 per cent more than the Downs average and 20 per cent more than the Queensland aggregate.[56] This in itself was an indication that nefarious practices had been employed.

The Committee of Elections and Qualifications which reported on the Toowoomba Petition declared, after the customary party vote, that the Aubigny election was null-and-void. The investigation revealed that personation alone had given Perkins over 97 additional votes. One enthusiast had voted six times, two voted five times and nine voted on four occasions. Altogether, 150 electors had indulged in plural voting, resurrecting the dead, representing the absent and personating the prominent.[57] These men had been procured and instigated by Perkins and his agents. The Returning Officer, John Garget of Toowoomba, was a railway contractor whose 'self interest feeds his political zeal'.[58]

52 *QPD*, Vol. 41, (1883-4), p. 511. Speech of Ferguson, MLA for Rockhampton.

53 *TC*, 26 August 1871, p. 2, c. 5.

54 ibid., 15 October 1887, p. 3, c. 1.

55 ibid., 28 February 1884, p. 2, c. 6.

56 ibid., 18 August 1883, p. 2, c. 1-6.

57 *QVP*, Session of 1883-4, pp. 403-8. 'Report of the Committee of Elections and Qualifications'.

58 *TC*, 9 June 1883, p. 2, c. 2.

An intimate friend of Perkins, who had invested in his undertakings, Garget was also guilty of the most audacious and corrupt practices. Not only did he 'make use of threats and promises to divers electors to support Perkins . . . with the latter's knowledge and consent', but his managers and sub-contractors openly brought in scores of Irish railway navvies and barrel upon barrel of Perkins' famed 'XXXX' ale.[59] Assisted by a judicious blend of ten-shilling notes and threats of dismissal, Ramm's lambs bleated at the right time.[60]

The main breach, however, which cost Perkins the election was Garget's arbitrary removal of the Westbrook Homestead Area polling-booth to the Westbrook head station eight miles away.[61] This placed the booth under squatter control. Free beer flowed in torrents from a tent 150 yards away and the presiding officer closed the door after each voter entered the booth. What went on inside can only be imagined. During the afternoon, a group of docile Germans was turned away by fierce, drunken Irishmen when they attempted to vote. Promised a personal favour by Perkins, the Drayton Police Sergeant refused to attend the disturbance.[62] At Gowrie Junction the hotel next door to the polling-booth dispensed free refreshments all day and 'honest settlers' were again prevented from voting. Perkins later admitted that 'it cost him so much to contest the election that he thought he would retire and occupy his time in another direction'.[63] Certainly the Toowoomba brewery must have had a profitless week.

The *Courier's* conclusion that the 'election [was] a stain on the people concerned and on the electorate as a whole' is a fair summary.[64] The fact that the unsuccessful Liberals had no right to complain because their rivals were greater exponents of fraud than themselves does not excuse the readiness of Perkins and his cohorts to purchase the constituency. After all, matters could be, and afterwards were, arranged in a much more discreet and gentlemanly fashion.

The Amending Act of 1884 and the Elections Act of 1885 owed much to the Aubigny affray. The former was designed to prevent train-loads of unqualified persons in charge of a 'keeper' from flooding booth after booth. In future, no elector could vote unless the residence qualification had been fulfilled. He had to declare that he had been a bona fide resident of the district for at least one full month during the nine months preceding the poll.[65] The 1885 Act incorporated certain provisions of the British Corrupt Practices Act of 1883 and disqualified from voting persons guilty of the Aubigny sins—'treating', 'undue in-

59 *QVP*, Session of 1883-4, p. 408 and *QPD*, Vol. 41, (1884), p. 531.

60 ibid. William Ramm was Garget's manager and the lambs were his workmen or those who wanted employment on the new Highfields railway. ibid., p. 625.

61 ibid.

62 ibid., p. 408.

63 *TC*, 24 December 1892, p. 4, c. 4.

64 *BC*, quoted by *TC*, 28 February 1884, p. 2, c. 6.

65 *QPD*, Vol. 41, (1883-4), p. 79.

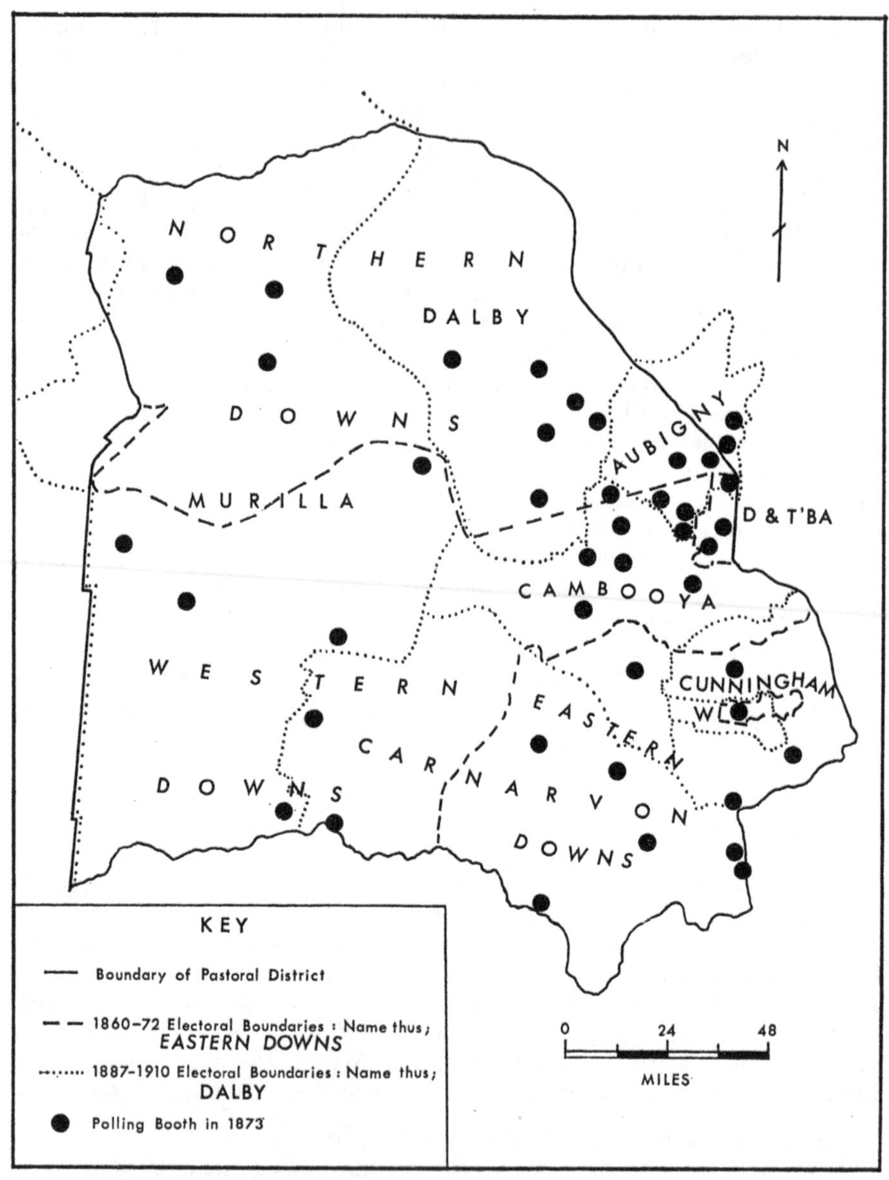

MAP 15 Darling Downs electorates and polling-booths, 1860–93 (after Official Electoral Atlas, 1865 and 1887)

fluence', 'bribery', and 'personation'. Witnesses before the Elections Committee could no longer refuse to testify on the grounds of self-incrimination and it was declared a felony to stuff ballot-boxes.[66]

Darling Downs petitions also re-opened the whole question of the propriety, validity and utility of the dominant Parliamentary faction ensuring a majority on the Elections and Qualifications Committee and brought into question the usefulness of the Committee itself. The Elections Tribunal Act abolished this 1860 body and provided for a trial of petitions by a Supreme Court Judge with a panel of six assessors nominated each year by the Speaker. Although this was not an entirely satisfactory substitute, as the Government always had a majority on the panel, the new system did remove some of the bias and toleration of abuses that had discredited past committees.[67]

Downs elections, then, were colourful and vigorous. In such a small community, politics were of immediate personal concern and most had a keen interest in election results even if they only meant free beer and pound-notes. Land and religion aroused strong passions, and packed meetings and torchlight processions were a welcome relief from drabness and monotony. Thus political participation was widespread even although true political awareness was often absent. In some areas, the emergence of distinct group interests was not yet apparent or else the inhabitants constantly refused to recognize their existence. This pattern was apt to change for a time during relatively brief moments of political upheaval.

On polling-day, decorated carts displaying bunting and placards were used to transport voters to the booths. The Toowoomba Germans marched behind their brass-bands to record a block vote for Groom, while the numerous hotels kept their back doors open and their kegs tapped.[68] Large crowds gathered at Toowoomba, Allora, Warwick and Dalby to hear the declaration of the poll and the candidates' addresses. Cheers and jeers were loud and long but such gatherings were usually good-humoured and the police seldom intervened except to lock up the inevitable crop of drunkards. Nevertheless, egg-throwing was an old Warwick art, while haystacks were sometimes fired and rival headquarters stoned after the poll.[69] Ugly incidents did occur when partisanship and disappointment combined with alcohol to produce assault and riot. The most violent and hotly contested election campaign on the Downs—the Warwick fight in 1871 between Charles Clark of Talgai and James Morgan, the proprietor of the *Warwick Argus*—culminated in an affray more characteristic of eighteenth-century English contests than the rather pedestrian colonial proceedings. The election was fought

66 *QPD*, Vol. 46, (1885), p. 123.

67 ibid., Vol. 41, (1884), pp. 504-12. For instance, it was alleged that Perkins and Foxton had had a violent row during the 1883 election campaign and yet the latter sat on the Committee which judged Perkins' case.

68 *TC*, 4 October 1883, p. 2, c. 1-7.

69 *WA*, 2 October 1883, p. 2, c. 3.

at a time when the selection agitation was at its peak, religious feeling was strong, and uncompromising, and corruption and influence were freely used by both sides. Clark and Morgan were the complete antithesis of one another. So, as it proved, were their respective supporters on the day.[70]

On the evening of 21 July 1871, a large crowd of some 1,800 or more gathered at the Warwick Court House to hear the Pure Merino declared elected by seventeen votes. Bitter hostility towards the winning faction swept through the assembly at this unexpected defeat of the radical candidate. Clark's known adherents were kicked and punched and a whole street block was soon a 'regular mêlée'. The inoffensive English gentleman-farmer, Bertie Parr of Chiverton, was 'stoned and kicked from Horwitz's store to Queen's Park before being dragged to safety in Kingsford's Hotel'.[71] Even the new Member was cuffed and stoned, and waddies and palings were freely employed. It was, remarked an overwrought correspondent, 'worse than street-fighting in Paris'.[72] The five policemen were powerless. At eight-thirty the crowd, now a mob, stormed Bugden's Hotel, the squatters' headquarters. Stones and sticks were thrown through the windows, and some stalwarts attempted to demolish the verandah. Suddenly a shotgun, loaded with birdshot, was fired through the window. When the demonstrators advanced again, four more discharges peppered exposed backsides and dispersed the rioters. There were many sore heads in Warwick next morning.[73]

Between 1860 and 1893 the proportion of Downs representatives to the total number in the Legislative Assembly fell steadily:

THE REPRESENTATION OF THE DARLING DOWNS, 1860-93[74]

Year (Redistribution Acts)	No. Downs members	Total members	% Downs members in Assembly	% Q'land enrolled adult male pop. on Downs
1860	7	26	34	30
1864	7	32	22	21
1872	7	45	15.5	18
1878	9	55	16	17
1887	9	72	12.5	11.6

70 Oddly enough, it was the squatter, Clark, who was an Anglo-Catholic. Morgan was an Irish Anglican who had previously captured the Catholic vote. In retaliation for Clark's successful attacks on him when he was Sheep Inspector, Morgan waged a libellous campaign against Clark's land transactions. *QPD*, Vol. 13, (1871-2), pp. 15, 31.

71 This account is based on reports in: *WE&T*, 22 July 1871 and *BC*, 26 July 1871, p. 3, c. 3.

72 ibid.

73 ibid.

74 *Census of Queensland* and *SR*, 1861-87.

Such a relative decline was inevitable in an age when the pastoral industry was still expanding, the metropolis was growing, sugar plantations were changing the North, and gold-mining was indirectly creating several new constituencies. The effect of this fall, however, was not as serious as the Downs members claimed. The region's numerical strength and influence were at their height when the foundations of closer settlement were being laid and when the district members, acting in concert with each other and with other 'bunches', were able to secure the public funds necessary for essential public works. Although the combination broke up over the land question, for many years 'foreign' representatives complained that the Queensland Land Acts were no more than special measures designed to benefit some elements on the Downs.[75]

The basis of representation was widely debated on the Downs. Three interlocking questions arose whenever this contentious subject was discussed. The first issue arose over whether all electorates should have approximately equal numbers of enrolled voters or whether sheep should count as well as men. Secondly, many Downsmen challenged the principle of determining the number of seats allotted to the region by counting the number of potential voters in the area. Finally, all Downs representatives were determined to impose and retain in a concealed form a 'country quota' in order to counteract Brisbane's rapid increase of population.[76]

Votes were always worth more in some Downs electorates than in others. The northern and western pastoral districts were continually over-represented:

ELECTORS ON THE ROLL, DARLING DOWNS, 1860-71[77]

Electorate	Type	Members	Registered electors at general elections		
			1860	1868	1871
Eastern Downs	Ag/P	1	107	305	325
Northern Downs	P	1	272	407	503
Western Downs	P	2	168	335	601
Drayton-Toowoomba	CT/Ag	1	220	1,000	1,349
Warwick	CT/Ag	1	155	441	729
Maranoa	P	1	103	313	263

75 *QPD*, Vol. 20, (1876), p. 556.

76 ibid., Vol. 52, (1887), pp. 622, 646. With its new communications shrinking distances, it was becoming more difficult for Downs representatives to use the old rural arguments of area and time to justify sparsely populated constituencies.

77 *SR*, 1860-71. For this and the two following tables the abbreviations refer as follows: P—Pastoral; P/CT—Pastoral—country town; P/M—Pastoral—mining; P/M/CT—Pastoral—mining—country town; Ag—Agricultural; Ag/P—Mixed agricultural—pastoral; CT/Ag—Country town—agricultural.

The two urban constituencies, Warwick and Toowoomba, were under-represented. In 1871 there were more enrolments in these seats than in the other five Downs electorates combined. Western Downs with 28.5 per cent of Downs representation had only 16 per cent of the voters.[78]

The compromise Redistribution Act of 1872, passed after the Constitution Act of 1871 had repealed the 'two-thirds clause' formerly used as a conservative device for retaining the old inequalities, created 42 single-member electorates.[79] These were supposedly based on 'natural boundaries' and with 'the member [to be] returned by those belonging to the same class'.[80] While the Downs gained no seats and actually declined in relative strength, the seven new electorates were approximately equal in adult male population when the boundaries were drawn. Yet the three pastoral seats were still over-represented in terms of total enrolments. As the Pure Merinos flatly stated, 'they would be going too far if they ignored the claims of property' and, furthermore, 'colonial towns were not wealth-producers but merely the distributors of wealth produced in the interiors'. Agriculture was beneath their notice.[81]

THE DOWNS ELECTORATES ON REDISTRIBUTION, 1872-3[82]

Electorate	Type	Adult males	Enrolled electors	% of Downs electors per electorate
Northern Downs	P	825	305	6
Dalby	P/CT	761	515	10
Carnarvon	P/M	869	638	13
Darling Downs	Ag/P	907	477	9
Aubigny	Ag/P	992	924	18
Drayton-Toowoomba	CT/Ag	989	1,286	27
Warwick	CT/Ag	953	853	17
TOTAL DOWNS		6,296	4,998	100.0
DOWNS AVERAGE		899	714	14.0

This table reinforces the conclusion that even the adult male basis of representation meant little unless all pastoral workers and tin-miners were enrolled. This the pastoral 'backbone' were determined to frustrate. In addition, the growth of the regional centre, Toowoomba, soon lowered the national value of urban votes. Since 1872 the Downs agricultural population and its dependants also increased faster than the static pastoral population. In March 1878 it was estimated that the four Toowoomba, Aubigny, Warwick and Carnarvon seats held three

78 ibid.

79 *QPD*, Vol. 13, (1871-2), pp. 221-44, 407, 474-6.

80 ibid., Vol. 14, (1872), pp. 41-2.

81 These opinions were expressed by Ramsay and Wienholt. ibid., pp. 331-8.

82 *SR*, 1872-3.

times as many electors as the three squatting constituencies. While this was of little colonial significance, as the Downs members were then split into factions, it was a considerable disadvantage to the Settled District where large-scale public investment was required.[83]

An overdue redistribution in 1878 increased the number of Downs seats to nine but the Assembly was enlarged to 72 members. These figures remained unchanged until 1910. The Act, by which 'the Downs electorates [were] fairly treated and no more' produced little alteration in the degree of representation but, by the creation of the double electorates of Drayton-Toowoomba and Darling Downs, decisively affected regional politics. In the former case, the measure virtually gave Groom and his organization an additional seat and, in Darling Downs, assisted the return of 'liberal squatters' as junior members in place of a possible second storekeeper or farmer.[84]

The 1886 Census revealed that the Downs electorates were again unbalanced although the region as a whole was slightly over-represented. The average adult male population of the constituencies was now 916 but Dalby had only 543, Carnarvon 881 and Warwick 740 potential voters.[85] On the whole, however, the Downs were fortunate that Griffith's administration was not prepared to offend the Darling Downs 'liberals' on this issue, no matter how often the latter might split on other issues. The Downs retained all its seats but now had fewer members than the Brisbane metropolitan area and was completely eclipsed by the momentarily effective sugar, mining and pastoral consortium of Macrossan's 'solid North'.[86]

Inequalities were not slow to appear after 1887:

ELECTORS ENROLLED FOR DOWNS CONSTITUENCIES, 1888 AND 1893[87]

Constituency	Type	1888	Enrolled before general elections		
			Downs %	1893	Downs %
Murilla	P	487	6	622	6
Dalby	P/CT	775	10	909	9
Carnarvon	P/M/CT	700	9	762	8
Aubigny	Ag	850	11	1,213	13
Cambooya	Ag/P	899	12	1,162	12
Cunningham	Ag	1,086	14	1,335	14
Drayton-Toowoomba	CT/Ag (2)	2,014	27	2,395	26
Warwick	CT/Ag	929	13	1,088	12
TOTAL DOWNS		7,740	—	9,486	—
DOWNS AVERAGE		860	11	1,054	11

83 *WA*, 21 March 1878, p. 2, c. 1-2.

84 ibid., 9 May 1878, p. 2, c. 1-2.

85 *Census of Queensland*, 1886, Parts xiv and xvi.

86 *QPD*, Vol. 52, (1887), pp. 450-2, 622-6, 1099, 1113. Brisbane and its suburbs then had fourteen seats and North and Central Queensland twenty-six.

87 *SR*, 1888 and 1893.

By 1893 the Downs was over-represented by about 10 per cent but Murilla, Dalby and Carnarvon were so numerically weak that they were almost in the rotten borough category.[88]

The adult male definition, however, was never approved of by representatives of the growing Downs urban and agricultural constituencies. Closer settlement and the growth of associated towns created support in the east for Lilley's proposal to base representation on the total population of the area.[89] This would give the Downs a decided advantage over both pastoral and northern mining and sugar areas. Family life was the true aim and symbol of all progress, declared Downs radicals, again invoking the agrarian myth. They asserted that those with a landed and corporeal 'stake in the country' were a more productive and stable section than single, migratory bush-workers and miners. Now they possessed property the farmers and businessmen neatly adopted the old arguments of their squatting enemies which they had tried to discredit in the past. But there was one factor which promptly destroyed any attempt to redistribute on the basis of total population. Many Downs inhabitants now believed with Morehead that 'God made the country but the devil made the towns'.[90] Brisbane would gain more than the country towns and the selector belt if this system were enforced. Queensland governments, in practice if not in theory, remained devoted to the principle that a vote in the bush was worth more than one in the city.[91]

Apart from the inequalities produced by the manipulation of population statistics, the delineation of electoral boundaries by political decisions also produced striking inequalities. 'Drawing electoral boundaries is the subtlest form of cartography' and political rather than technical skills were used to satisfy the conflicting claims of property, personality and locality.[92] The first distribution openly favoured the squatters. Warwick and Drayton-Toowoomba each received a seat which included the only major agricultural areas. Until the end of the century, when the enlarged franchise permitted urban workers to swell the rolls, such arguments subordinated the suburban selectors to town storekeepers and artisans. As early as 1871 Warwick farmers petitioning for a separate electorate for each agricultural reserve demanded the elimination of borough and pastoral electors whose 'interests [were] not always identical with those of the agriculturalists'.[93]

Before 1872 pastoral seats penetrated the heart of the eastern Settled District where selection was occurring. Selectors were constantly overwhelmed by the huge western leaseholds.[94] Even the 1887 redistribution was unsatisfactory. The boundaries of two electorates, Cambooya and

88 *Census of Queensland*, 1891. Statement C, p. 803.

89 *QPD*, Vol. 15, (1872), pp. 326-9 and *WA*, 2 June 1877, p. 2, c. 1.

90 *QPD*, Vol. 13, (1871-2), p. 248 and Vol. 52, (1887), pp. 621, 623.

91 ibid., pp. 633-45; *WA*, 2 May 1878, p. 2, c. 2 and 30 May 1878, p. 2, c. 1-2.

92 L. Lipson, *The Politics of Equality*, Chicago 1948, p. 92.

93 *QVP*, 1871, p. 89. 'Petition of 223 Residents of Warwick'.

94 Map 15 shows the Darling Downs electoral boundaries.

Dalby, suspiciously favoured specific individuals and groups. Cambooya, formerly the northern half of the Darling Downs seat, had been dominated by the farmers of Warwick-Allora and the commercial interests of the southern towns. Restless pastoralists and foolish farmers gladly or apathetically endorsed Groom's devious and adroit campaign for a new constituency. Cambooya was a calculated creation of Toowoomba and Groom especially designed to thwart Warwick's railway schemes and provide another Parliamentary minion for the 'father of the swamp'.[95]

For many years Dalby was considered to be a pocket borough under the patronage of the Bells of Jimbour.[96] Yet a proposal to abolish the electorate after the death of J. P. Bell led to effective protests from not only Bell's successor, Jessop, that pliant tool of the Darling Downs and Western Land Company, but a peculiar alliance of pastoralists, Downs politicians and Dalby and Brisbane commercial interests. This association defeated the census returns.[97]

The siting of polling-booths was also of considerable regional importance. Pastoral booths, established at head stations, were openly run by owners and managers and their location was often unsuitable for selectors on the resumptions.[98] In the towns, booths brought business, although there were fewer opportunities for direct manipulation. It was obviously impossible to provide adequate facilities for all voters in an evolving region of such size but more could have been done to ensure that even those eligible to vote could make their decision unhampered by distance and influence.

95 *QPD*, Vol. 52, (1887), pp. 977-81. The election of his ubiquitous enemy, Perkins, in 1888 was a surprise for Groom. For once, he had made a mistake in counting votes before the poll.

96 *The Week*, 24 March 1877, p. 368, c. 2. Groom alleged that the Dalby electorate had originally been gerrymandered so as to include Jondaryan and Cumkillenbar stations and the Oakey Meat Preserving Works—all haunts of the Pure Merinos. *TC*, 18 October 1873, p. 3, c. 2.

97 *QPD*, Vol. 52, (1887), pp. 774-86, 935.

98 The most striking example of this type was Jimbour Head Station. At this polling-booth in the Northern Downs electorate, H. M. Nelson of Loudon received 52 votes on one occasion (1883) and Bashford, his rival, nil. This practically decided the election as Nelson's eventual majority was only 50. *TC*, 8 September 1883, p. 2, c. 5.

CHAPTER 13

VOTING BEHAVIOUR AND GROUP POLITICS ON THE DOWNS

During the first decade of colonial politics, the representation of the Downs was uncomplicated by the presence of several strong, competitive and organized sectional interests. The squatters with their early social cohesiveness, money, influence and control of the electoral machinery dominated the scene. Although they soon lost control of the two country towns, they retained their hold over most outlying constituencies for many years after their numerical strength had waned and new store-keepers and selectors had become established in the Settled District. Apart from the fact that 'subservient feudalism' still survived on selection and station, traditional and local loyalties which the pastoralists had fostered during the pioneer phase gave them a great advantage over newcomers and political apprentices. A freehold squatter usually gathered the votes of his neighbours, be they contractors or farmers, in preference to a distant merchant or Brisbane lawyer. Only in times of acute political crisis, such as the land agitation of 1866-8, were these loyalties likely to be upset. When one squatter challenged another—a common proceeding between 1860 and 1875—personal attitudes and locality support were usually the decisive factors rather than the published address and factional allegiance.[1]

Local sentiment, however, was still strong even when the squatters had been banished from 'mixed' agricultural and pastoral electorates by the storekeepers and manufacturers. The electors of Aubigny voted for Perkins rather than Mackay in 1877 because the latter was not a 'local man' and was therefore unacquainted with the inhabitants and their needs.[2] Douglas, Pring and Macalister all met a similar fate. When several candidates domiciled in an electorate contested the seat, each usually polled well in his home district however limited his appeal to the constituency as a whole.[3] (*see* facing page)

[1] For a typical example, *see* the triangular contest between J. C. White, James Taylor and T. de Lacy Moffatt for the Western Downs electorate in 1863. *DDG*, 9 July 1863, p. 3, c. 2.

[2] 'The result is only what might have been expected between a local man and a Brisbane editor.' *WE&T*, 5 May 1877, p. 2, c. 1.

Shrewd Downs politicians, such as Arthur Morgan and Groom, who 'nursed' their electorates and attempted to be all things to all men, had an immense advantage in this era of personal politics. With their immense number of acquaintances, attention to personal grievances and membership in local organizations, these representatives accumulated a tremendous reserve of goodwill and traditional loyalty which newer candidates could never surmount and which insured them from the effects of colonial crises, factional turmoil and the impact of economic change and development on Downs politics. So strong were the personalities and political adroitness of Groom, Morgan and Bell that they were able to affect the result of contests in neighbouring seats and even influence returns from beyond the grave. Memories gave sons a head-start in Downs politics.[4]

Yet however politically powerful these traditional and local loyalties were, especially when combined with the oblique and often unpredictable effects of religion and nationality, it would be entirely misleading to dismiss the growing influence of sectional economic interests as being worthy of only secondary consideration. However confused and formless the political scene on the Downs usually appeared, and in spite of the frantic counting of heads after each general election, certain groups knew exactly what legislative and administrative action they required and took appropriate action to secure it. All squatters, whatever their 'liberal' or 'conservative' pretensions, wanted to retain their land, income and position. Pastoralists of the former variety such as Miles, Allan and Davenport who replaced Pure Merinos such as Wienholt, Taylor and Ramsay, were prepared to concede piecemeal reforms and innovations as long as their basic interests remained untouched. They were even generous with the distribution of land—as long as somebody else held the lease. These pastoralists worked hard to persuade and satisfy the simple and, to them, harmless initial needs of the selectors and storekeepers who were now cluttering-up the pastoral landscape. Perhaps the Pure Merinos were more honest with themselves and their constituents in their refusal to

---

3 The contest for Darling Downs in 1878 demonstrated the strength of locality loyalties:

Candidate	Domicile and Occupation	Home vote	Total vote
William Miles	Dalby/Brisbane squatter	—	692 (elected)
Francis Kates	Allora storekeeper/miller	120	601 (elected)
H. G. Simpson	Clifton mine-manager	52	214
William Deacon	Allora storekeeper	90	202
J. T. Wilson	Freestone Creek farmer	36	101

WA, 28 November 1878, p. 2, c. 4.

4 Sir Littleton Groom replaced his father as Federal member for Darling Downs and held it from 1901 until his death in 1936 with only one break between 1929-31. Sir Arthur Morgan held Warwick from 1887 until 1896 and again from 1899 until 1906. J. T. Bell successfully retained Dalby from 1893 until his death in 1911.

compromise with the new elements, their outspokenness, and their dislike of change and those who were forcing the pace. Nevertheless, electoral defeat did not mean political oblivion. The Legislative Council invariably beckoned to the rejected Black Soilers.

However devious their political behaviour, the editors and storekeepers of the country towns kept their radical objectives, however pragmatic and limited, firmly in sight. They believed that economic and political opportunities on the Downs should and could be enlarged. The acquisition of private property should, they argued, be the right of all who deserved it and not the prerogative of a few. Their agrarianism and political reformism were limited but sincere, however much they might compromise, intrigue and manoeuvre. Their tragedy, like that of their pastoral predecessors, was that once their promises had been fulfilled they had little else to offer. By 1893, Groom was really a political anachronism. Sooner or later the urban radicals were forced to choose between social-democracy and propertied conservatism. Some found the decision too difficult to make, while others denied the necessity for such a choice at all. While they played the old political games which had served them so well in the past, new interests with new leaders demanding ideological adjustments arose and eventually dominated the political arena. The old Downs politicians were ineffective diprotodons in the new political field where organized sectional groups openly clashed, partly overruled personality and 'independence' meant political suicide.

The impact of religious feeling upon Downs politics was not as marked as it was in Brisbane. Evangelical nonconformity was weak on the Downs and no Brookes, Griffith or Kingsford emerged to deliberately provoke sectarian hostility.[5] The Anglican and Presbyterian squatters held themselves aloof from the petty antagonism displayed by some of the small shopkeepers, although they were often prepared to make political capital out of religious issues. While the strong Masonic lodges on the Downs were controlled by the storekeepers and merchants, such influence as 'the craft' was able to exert was secretive and restrictive.[6] Most Downs squatters felt that they had little to fear from the Irish, many of whom were in their employment. The Protestant Germans were different. Not only did they constantly support the country-town radicals in their efforts to open the Downs to selectors but when they obtained a piece of land they invariably developed and retained it. Furthermore, Irish Catholics had been an indispensable part of station life ever since the Leslies had arrived, forming a rural proletariat and seemingly offering

[5] A. A. Morrison, 'Religion and Politics in Queensland', *JRQHS*, Vol. 4, No. 4, December 1951, pp. 455-70. Unbelievers never proclaimed themselves on the Downs but Vickers was charged with being a freethinker in 1888 and this possibly cost him some Cambooya votes. *TC*, 8 March 1888, p. 4, c. 1.

[6] At least seven Downs representatives between 1873 and 1893 were freemasons—Aland, Tyrel, Pechey, Campbell, Lovejoy, Jessop and James Morgan. E. W. H. Fowlds and E. G. White (editors), *The Jubilee Review of English Freemasonry in Queensland*, Brisbane 1909, (private circulation).

little challenge to the political, economic and social ascendancy and the unique way of life which the squatters had developed.

Sectarian strife was an urban manifestation but most country-town radicals on the Downs publicly discarded this aspect of Lang's teachings and tried to maintain a judicious balance between the various religious groups which made up the towns' population. The extremely strong Catholic vote had to be placated and won on the Downs if most candidates wanted to ensure victory. The squatters secured the votes of this minority by traditional means or else managed to prevent it from becoming vocal or even voting at all. Protestant radicals had to be more subtle, especially when dealing with such inflammatory issues as education and immigration. The large Catholic minority—Toowoomba even had its Irishtown—made the urban politicians wary of organizing this religious group as a political weapon. In an age of personal politics it could easily be turned against them at the next election. Downsmen boasted that the area was a model of religious toleration and that election campaigns were relatively free from bitterness and suspicion. So they were, but this picture is a rather superficial one. At certain times and in certain places the Irish Catholics in particular threw their influence and votes into the scale in an attempt to decide the issue and advance their own interests.

33.6 per cent of the Downs population was Roman Catholic in 1876 and 32 per cent in 1891. These figures were about three per cent higher than the Queensland average.[7] Although there were more Catholics than any single denomination in the census districts of Dalby and Stanthorpe, the most remarkable feature of this religious group is that it was evenly distributed all over the Downs:

TOTAL NUMBERS OF ROMAN CATHOLICS ON THE DARLING DOWNS IN 1876 AND 1891[8]

Census district	1876		1891	
	RC	All denominations	RC	All denominations
Dalby	1,016	2,277	700	1,378
Darling Downs Central	881	2,773	2,420	7,561
Darling Downs East	1,049	3,436	2,068	6,430
Darling Downs North	732	2,163	1,456	4,636
Darling Downs West	247	948	374	1,273
Drayton-Toowoomba	3,070	9,499	2,091	10,759
Warwick	1,390	4,057	1,229	3,402
TOTAL DOWNS	8,385	25,153	10,338	35,439

7 *Census of Queensland*, 1876, pp. 144-5 and 1891, p. 1313.

8 ibid.

III *Personalities, Property and Public Works*

In spite of their numbers, the Downs Catholics produced very few successful politicians:

Religion of Downs Politicians, 1860-93[9]

Church of England (includes two Irish-born)	26
Presbyterian	5
Roman Catholic	3
Baptist	1
Wesleyan	1
Jewish	1
TOTAL	37

Most Irish were rather ill-educated and poor pastoral, urban or railway workers with a considerable sprinkling of small selectors. 'Suitable' Catholic candidates who would be acceptable to the limited electorate were just not available on the Downs. The Irish had just begun to climb the economic ladder and as money, preferably from wool, professional skill or trade, largely determined social status and political opportunity in colonial Queensland, it was left to the second and third generations, working largely through new political groups, to capitalize on their numerical strength and the grievances of the depressed sections to which so many of their faith belonged. Thus the Irish voter in the towns generally supported radicals such as Groom who were tolerant of 'the faith' and were prepared to help realize some at least of their aspirations.

'The Irish vote' appeared on the Downs as soon as politics became live and not just a matter of persuasion, nomination and report. In 1862 Gore Jones defeated St George Gore at the Warwick ministerial election. This unprecedented upset was the direct result of O'Sullivan's rallying of a radical Catholic vote for Jones from among the small farmers around the village.[10] Again, in 1863, Bishop Quinn sent a priest to Toowoomba to campaign for Groom who had declared himself in favour of further Irish immigration to settle the lands which he hoped would be torn from the grasp of the squatters. Quinn's intervention was believed to have cost the squatter the election, although the German vote was probably of greater significance in electing the Downs' second town radical.[11]

The education question cost both Morgan the Warwick election in 1871 and Douglas the Darling Downs seat in 1875. At Warwick, the Catholic selector community apparently cut across their economic interests and social affiliations to vote for Clark, the diehard squatter and one of the few Catholics among that group.[12] William Graham, the

9 This table is constructed from data accumulated for the author's forthcoming *Queensland Political Register, 1859-1929*.

10 *DDG*, 27 March 1862, p. 2, c. 2.

11 ibid., 18 June 1863, p. 3, c. 2. Groom polled 162 votes, F. N. Isaac of Gowrie, 136.

12 *BC*, 26 July 1871, p. 3, c. 3.

Presbyterian freehold pastoralist, secured the Darling Downs Catholic vote when he promised to support the non-vested schools. Morgan alleged that the defeat of the agrarian Douglas was due to 'sneaking opposition' organized by Father S. H. McDonough, the 'fiery little priest' of Warwick.[13] Even Groom suffered from Irish Catholic agitation over the proposal to abolish State aid to church schools. In 1873 his ambivalent attitude cost him many votes and severely reduced his traditionally large majority.[14] Two years later, however, Groom atoned by carrying an amendment to the Education Act of 1875 extending aid to the denominational schools for a further four years. Donavon was crushed in 1878 when he stood again.[15] By this time Groom had even managed to frustrate attempts to defeat the Catholic Perkins when he contested Aubigny for the first time.[16]

With waning of the immigration and education questions and the rise of new sections with economic rather than social and religious grievances, Catholicism apparently ceased to be a decisive factor in a few political contests. Politicians such as Arthur Morgan still deemed it necessary to secure the 'Irish vote' but an election ballad of 1887 demonstrated that he was appealing to a wider audience:

> Morgan helps the Irish cause,
> Then vote for Arthur Morgan.
>
> He'll give old Ireland fairer laws,
> Then shure we'll vote for Morgan.
>
> Let German, Irish, English, Scotch,
> Go vote for Arthur Morgan.
>
> Our truest interests he will watch,
> So vote for Arthur Morgan.[17]

13 *WE&T*, 20 March 1875, p. 2, c. 1 and 3 April 1875, p. 3, c. 1-2. *WA*, 25 March 1875, p. 2, c. 2-3. Morgan was personally attacked from the pulpit by McDonough for this editorial. ibid., 1 April 1875, p. 2, c. 1-2. Allan's promise that he would press for compensation for the withdrawal of State aid secured Roman Catholic support for this Presbyterian squatter in 1881. Many Catholics signed the requisition and he polled heavily in the Catholic outskirts of Warwick, *TC*, 22 November 1881, p. 2, c. 1-3 and 1 December 1881, p. 2, c. 1.

14 Groom polled 329 votes in 1873 to Donavon's 220. It is probable that many of Groom's Irish supporters refrained from voting on this occasion, as only 553 exercised the franchise out of the 1,349 on the roll. *TC*, 15 November 1873, p. 2, c. 5.

15 In 1878 Groom polled 735 votes but Donavon could muster only 208. ibid., 17 October 1878, p. 2, c. 3 and 16 November 1878, p. 2, c. 3.

16 *The Week*, 21 April 1877, p. 488 and *TC*, 5 May 1877, p. 3, c. 3.

17 *WA*, 16 July 1887, p. 1. Knox considers that both the Morgans received the Catholic vote but, in the case of James Morgan, this does not seem to have been the case. Whenever religious issues intruded, they took precedence—in Irish eyes at least—over the land question which was Morgan's over-riding interest. His son was more fortunate as the education question was dormant. Arthur Morgan, however, was the more skilful politician. Not only did he maintain excellent relations with the new priest, Father J. J. Horan, but as a native Queenslander he made a strong appeal to the Australian natives and was most sympathetic towards Home Rule. B. A. Knox, 'Hon. Sir Arthur Morgan', p. 8 and *WA*, 21 December 1916, p. 5, c. 4-5.

In the Warwick election a year later, Patrick Higgins failed in his bid to capture the Catholic vote and, although a Catholic, Fogarty, was elected for Toowoomba in 1893, religion played little part in the campaign although it remained a hidden yet influential agent in Downs politics and administration.

While the Germans were numerically inferior to the Irish Catholics in all electorates, their early concentration in small farming settlements within two constituencies—Drayton-and-Toowoomba and Aubigny—their characteristic block voting gave them virtual control over the electoral fortunes of three representatives. The Germans themselves realized this. In 1877 and again in 1878 they had fully supported the efforts of their great patron, Groom, to secure the election of Perkins for Aubigny.[18] Perkins' repudiation of Groom's plans for his political future and his unwise denunciations of the Germans' wine as 'hogwash', however, alienated his former supporters.[19] Vohland's interjection at Perkins' Oakey Creek meeting on 4 August 1883 summed up the altered situation:

> Hogwash put you in, and hogwash [will] put you out, Mr Perkins. Goodnight, gentlemen![20]

Once their group allegiance had been given to a politician they trusted little could shake it and, while they were loth to part with their 'Deutschtum', they were quick to appreciate the power of their votes even when intensive political activity was not a traditional part of their community life. The Germans accepted their champions and left them to fight their battles. Although there were spasmodic attempts to organize German electoral organizations, these moves came from without rather than from the Teutons themselves.[21]

Economic motives propelled the Germans towards partial participation in Downs politics. The Aliens Act of 1867 granted immediate citizenship to all those taking the oath of allegiance but prevented aliens from holding freehold land.[22] As the acquisition of such property was their main objective, these regulations almost immediately created a large German minority vote without the bitter nostalgia and resentments of the Irish or the sense of political evolution and continuity of the English and Scots.

The Germans were attracted to personalities rather than 'parties' and problems. Most were relatively poor small selectors whose economic aspirations drew them to the side of the country-town radicals who were

[18] *TC*, 12 October 1878, Supplement, pp. 1-2 and 26 October 1878, p. 2, c. 2.

[19] Perkins' new Toowoomba brewery competed with German wine on the Downs. ibid., 7 August 1883, p. 2, c. 3.

[20] ibid.

[21] In 1883 the Griffith Liberals employed two agents, Jaeschke and Berger, to muster the South Queensland German vote. *TC*, 4 October 1883, p. 2, c. 1-7. It was customary for the German settlers to meet before the poll, hear Groom's views and pledge community support. ibid., 11 January 1881, p. 2, c. 1-7.

[22] Queensland Aliens Act 1867 (31 Victoria, No. 28), *Queensland Statutes*, Vol. 1, Brisbane 1889, p. 8.

attempting to redistribute the land.[23] To the Germans, radical 'upstarts' such as Groom had a triple appeal. Like themselves, they had arrived penniless and had prospered by hard work and ingenuity. Groom was a reviled underdog, fighting for position and profit. So were they. Urban agrarianism coincided with the Germans' beliefs, and all successful early radicals on the Downs were Protestants, whereas most of the other 'lower orders' were Catholics. Finally, Groom in particular was the Downs counterpart of the New York immigrant 'boss'. As soon as they arrived on the Downs, he established close ties with the new settlers. Groom negotiated their land orders, transacted their business, and smoothed the difficulties that alien migrants inevitably encountered when dealing with strange institutions. After the wave of German immigration had subsided, the memory of these services remained and was passed to the Australian-born. Few Britons were prepared to take the same trouble and Groom reaped his reward in the form of great majorities and constant support. The German vote elected Groom in 1862 and this he never lost, although several attempts were made, notably in 1878 and 1883, to detach it.[24] Even a German smallholder, Henry Roessler, was completely rejected by his fellow-countrymen in 1878 when he campaigned against Groom. The spectacle of the Middle Ridge Germans, complete with brass-band and flags, marching behind their leaders to vote solidly for Groom and his running-mate was a familiar sight at most Toowoomba elections.[25]

Groom's German affiliations had no counterpart in Downs politics but the two Morgans at Warwick also captured the waning German vote on the Southern Downs.[26] Wherever the Germans were scattered, cultural ties were weak and there was a loss of the powerful group consciousness. Thus a German minority vote cannot be discerned in the areas to the south of Toowoomba where there were many such selectors. It is reasonable to conclude, however, that most Germans voted with other small farmers to return 'liberal squatters' and country storekeepers to Parliament. Many Germans supported the Alliance in the 'nineties—a sign of political maturity and assimilation. The old block voting, however, sometimes did emerge in later times of international crisis or when issues such

[23] The use by some squatters of rash language—'the scum of Europe'—and their attempts to restrict German immigration alienated the Teutons still further.

[24] In 1862 Groom polled 126 votes and J. C. White, the squatters' candidate, 105. Observers estimated that Groom secured 60 German votes which gave him the seat. White had previously sued one Zahn, a German worker, under most harsh and distressing circumstances. *DDG*, 15 August 1862, p. 3, c. 6. The squatters then tried to remove German voters from the electoral rolls. This foolish action consolidated Groom's position. ibid., 12 March 1863, p. 5, c. 6. Ruthning unsuccessfully campaigned for Aland against Groom in 1878 and Douglas and his agents tried to secure the German vote in 1883. *TC*, 14 November 1878, p. 2, c. 1 and 22 September 1883, p. 2, c. 2.

[25] *TC*, 4 October 1883, p. 2, c. 1-7. German-language advertisements were placed in most Downs newspapers throughout the period. Interpreters were provided at some meetings.

[26] It was alleged that the grant of land to the Lutherans in Warwick for a church was the Germans' reward for returning Thornton in 1868. *WE&T*, 31 July 1869, p. 2.

as Federation seemed to threaten the minority's security, faith and agrarianism.

Two German immigrants, both storekeepers and millers, contested and won Downs constituencies between 1878 and 1893. Francis Kates and Jacob Horwitz were both 'assimilated' Germans, outside the general pattern of German faith, occupations and settlement. Both, however, appealed to and won the votes of their fellow-countrymen, although many German tradesmen did not vote with the majority and preferred to follow an 'independent' course.[27]

The 'forgotten men' on the Downs—the urban and country labourers, the poorest selectors and the few miners—had little effective voice in regional politics and no direct representation until the crisis year of 1893. Traditional loyalties to urban leaders and rural masters were strong and generally unquestioned and the towns were small and their social structure relatively simple. Social mobility through the acquisition of property was still the realizable hope of most men, and abundant loan money soon overcame the painful consequences of periodic depressions.

Furthermore, the political mechanism and power were firmly in the hands of squatters, although they, in some eastern areas, had been forced to relinquish control to Downs urban middle-class radicals with boss-cocky support. The latter, with some justification, regarded themselves as advocates for and defenders of 'the lower orders'. W. H. Groom and James Morgan had both been vilified as dangerous radicals stirring up 'class feeling' when all men were 'workers' and no such thing as classes was supposed to exist in the new society. As early as 1870 Groom was recognized by Brisbane artisans as 'a representative of the working classes' and the auctioneer and publican saw nothing incongruous in this.[28] Hard-won property, however, was sacrosanct. Groom's radicalism was of the country rather than the town, and self-improvement was at the core of his philosophy. 'The workers of Queensland', declared Groom in 1892, 'will never support socialist ideas and have aims more consonant with the security of freedom and private property. The interests of employers and employed are identical . . . there is no need for two clear-cut party divisions.'[29]

In the formative years, candidates such as E. L. Thornton of Warwick could appeal without open contradiction for the small working-class vote by stating that they were self-made men who would protect and advance the interests of their former associates. Thornton, who had recently inherited a fortune, saw nothing incongruous in stating as he did in 1868 that he was formerly a pastoral 'worker' but was now able 'to represent the working-classes of Queensland with whom he had long been asso-

27 In 1881 three German tradesmen, D. Beh, R. Rosenstengel and E. B. C. Marwedel, signed James Taylor's nomination paper for the Toowoomba seat. But Taylor's failure to capture the German vote was the decisive factor in his defeat. *TC*, 18 January 1881, p. 3, c. 2.

28 *Queensland Express*, 17 September 1870, p. 3.

29 *TC*, 12 July 1892, p. 3, c. 2.

ciated'.[30] Pechey, in 1871, echoed these remarks when appealing for the bush-worker and selector vote of Western Downs:

Any jackeroo who . . . bought 10,000 scabby sheep and mortgaged them for half as much again as they were worth, was thought far more of than a straightforward and honest working man.[31]

Once Pechey had become a most successful sawmiller, speculator and grazier, however, his radicalism evaporated and his appeal was directed elsewhere.[32]

During the depressions of 1866-7 and 1878-9, definite working-class feeling emerged in the country towns and sporadic outbursts against the existing order occurred on the stations and along the new railway lines.[33] Such discontent never found direct political expression. Even in 1888, Patrick Higgins could stand for the Warwick electorate as a Nationalist and inscribe his placards with the exhortation: 'Vote for Higgins, the Labour Candidate!' Arthur Morgan accepted the fact that Higgins was a 'rough and ready working man' whose 'sympathies were with the artisans and the tiller of the soil' and even conceded that he had some worthwhile radical proposals. The *Argus*' implied sneer that Higgins was without much intelligence or ability except in the procreative sphere, revealed the country-town hierarchy's distrust of such men in politics.[34] Morgan later admitted that working men, of the moderate sort, of course, had a right to a place in Parliament but was at pains to prevent this from being put into practice at Warwick.[35]

By 1891 the position on the Downs had undergone a startling change. Labour was now able to make a strong appeal for electoral support in the region with some promise of success. The worsening economic climate and the real distress which it caused to hundreds who had not known want before, the great shearing strikes of 1889 and 1891, and the collapse of the old political order in 1890, all combined to produce a favourable environment for the new radicalism. Private relief was essential on the Downs after 1889. In June of that year, 68 families in Toowoomba alone were receiving regular outdoor relief and 17 temporary assistance. Unemployed 'callers' wandered all over the area and came to Toowoomba

30 *WA*, 2 September 1868, p. 2, c. 3. Thornton, gaining 179 votes, defeated his squatter rival, Chas. Clark, by 20 votes. *WE&T*, 26 September 1868, p. 2, c. 7.

31 *TC*, 15 July 1871, p. 3, c. 1. Pechey obtained the Drayton and Spring Creek selectors' vote (110) but failed on the stations. (27 votes—his opponent Ramsay received 135 votes from the pastoral districts.) ibid., 26 August 1871, p. 2, c. 5.

32 Between 1886 and 1889 Pechey's income was £915 p.a. and his property was valued at £31,467. Three years later he was technically bankrupt. ibid., 17 July 1890, p. 3, c. 6.

33 For shearers' discontent on the Downs, *see*: *TC*, 28 October 1874, p. 2, c. 6. The Killarney railway navvies staged a quickly crushed strike in 1883. *WE&T*, 29 September 1883, p. 2, c. 7.

34 *WA*, 1 May 1888, p. 2, c. 1. Higgins fathered sixteen children. Morgan annihilated him by 473 votes to 281. ibid., 8 May 1888, p. 2, c. 2.

35 ibid., 22 April 1893, p. 2, c. 3.

from as far west as Goondiwindi in search of work and rations. Others left the towns in search of work and left their families close to starvation.[36] Instead of the situation improving as it had in previous 'bad times', prices, trade and employment declined year after year until there seemed to be no end to the deflationary spiral. Although the Downs with 482 unemployed in 1891 was the least smitten area in Queensland, there was considerable concealed unemployment on the farms and stations where many toiled for rations alone.[37]

The three country towns in 1893 were small centres of misery and despair for many of their inhabitants. At Dalby, large numbers of discharged labourers, station-hands and domestic servants roamed the streets and 'many knew want who never knew it before'.[38] The lower middle-classes—the artisans, small shopkeepers and junior civil servants—felt, for the first time, that their security as a group was threatened as it had never been in the past. Here were new opportunities for the agitators who had so successfully roused and organized the shearers and teamsters on the stations.

The shearing strikes alienated many of the old radical voters who now had property but this reaction was bound to occur sooner or later. Public sympathy for the 'mere beasts of burden, allowed to exist on the verge of starvation' was more widespread than many were prepared to admit.[39] Mere sympathy, however, did not automatically produce Labour votes. Only a long period of disillusionment could change the political habits of three decades. The *Chronicle* conveyed the opinions of the old urban radicals faced with an uncomfortable choice between the supreme rights of property and a militant group, contemptuous of the old order and drawing its basic strength from the underprivileged and disregarded:

> The cause of labour is right, so long as it is identified with the interests of the whole community, but when it resorts to strikes, and seeks to punish the whole people . . . public sympathy will be turned away from it, and the deserted leaders left lamenting.[40]

The shearing strikes and the parallel determination to organize for political action broke the old yoke of the pastoralists in the west. Yet many of these workers were non-voters and all over the Downs the huge station was giving ground before the agriculturalists of the east and the small graziers of the south, north and west. Labour's main hope lay not with the farmers, although its policy had a definite appeal in some districts and the *Boomerang* and *The Worker* were read on the selection

[36] *TC*, 11 June 1889, p. 3, c. 2. Radical 'boosters' and conservative 'wool' newspapers on the Downs made few references to the prevalent distress on the Downs. Presumably it would spoil the 'image' of the region that they were attempting to present.

[37] *Census of Queensland*, 1891, p. 833. For a rare report noting the 'contraction in the purchasing power of the people', *see*: *TC*, 5 December 1891, p. 3, c. 2-3.

[38] *TC*, 17 June 1893, p. 2, c. 6.

[39] ibid., 28 February 1891, p. 3, c. 1-2.

[40] *TC*, 28 January 1891, p. 3, c. 1-2.

as well as in the shearers' huts and in the towns, but with the working-classes of the three small country towns. Here, a few long-suffering idealists such as William Gaisford of Warwick and Joseph Stirling of Toowoomba were already preaching the new doctrines.

13,291 people resided in the five Downs municipalities in 1891. Of these, over half (7,007) lived in Toowoomba and a quarter (3,402) in Warwick.[41] Toowoomba, with its processing, transport and service industries and its large number of public servants, had a long radical tradition and was the most likely field for Labour to plough. The smaller country towns were less promising, lacking a large working-class base and being surrounded by antipathetic farming and grazing districts.

On 18 July 1891, 300 Toowoomba citizens attended the first meeting of the Workers' Political Association on the Downs.[42] This wing of the Labour Party was formed to support Labour candidates for the 1893 elections, popularize the Party programme and allay the fears of specialism and 'red revolution' which the wilder pronouncements of *The Worker* and the actions of the industrial wing engendered. Similar bodies were formed at Warwick and Dalby, and Glassey toured the towns to champion the new cause.[43]

In 1893 Labour on the Downs was prepared to compromise. The true socialists deplored any dilution of the Party's objective but this was the only way in which Labour could make headway in the region. Understandings were reached with the radical rump, with the Farmers' Alliances and with sections of the middle-class who felt that they had little to hope for from the Coalition.[44] The Labour platform, as distinct from the revolutionary socialism of the Australian Labour Federation and *The Worker*, reflected this appeal to sections where support might be available. Electoral reform, a State bank, the repeal of State-aided immigration, the referendum, an eight-hour day and a revision of the railway tariff were planks which found a ready response on the Downs.[45] In fact, there was little difference between this programme and that of the group led by Lilley and Groom. Only the land tax and proposed industrial legislation were greeted with some alarm.[46]

The selection of Downs Labour candidates reflected this moderate attack. Labour left Groom and Morgan alone to avoid splitting the radical vote, Brewer and Lovejoy were supported as Alliance candidates for Cunningham and Aubigny, and Henry Daniels, the Labour candidate for Cambooya, was really closer to the Alliance than to the urban and pastoral radicals. The other three Labour candidates were also a

41 *Census of Queensland*, 1891, p. 42.

42 *TC*, 21 July 1891, p. 3, c. 5-6. 103 new recruits were enrolled at this meeting.

43 *WA*, 6 August 1892, p. 5, c. 6-7.

44 ibid., 8 August 1893, p. 5, c. 6.

45 ibid., 3 January 1893, p. 3, c. 1-3. This issue contains Glassey's Warwick exposition of Labour's policy. For the complete programme, *see: WE&T*, 21 January 1893, p. 3, c. 6.

46 *TC*, 25 August 1892, p. 3, c. 1. Groom expressed wary approval of Labour's new proposals for 'practical reforms'.

curious assortment. Only the Dalby aspirant, Charles McCarthy, was one of the 'new men' of Labour. A union organizer, self-educated and with a working-class background, McCarthy was a product of the new western radicalism.[47] Duncan Cameron, editor of the *Border Herald* and former editor of the agrarian *Allora Guardian*, had been a strong Griffith supporter and was soon to become manager of the huge Welltown station. Cameron stood for Carnarvon.[48]

John Fogarty, the Labour candidate for the second Toowoomba seat, had also had a chequered career. A Roman Catholic storekeeper, Fogarty had been in turn a shop-assistant, carrier, publican and storekeeper. Elected an alderman in 1884, Fogarty had been Mayor of Toowoomba in 1887 and 1892. In 1888 he had contested the constituency as a McIlwraith 'independent' but had come bottom of the poll.[49] Fogarty, although endorsed by Glassey and the WPA, was never really a Labour supporter. In fact, he declared that 'no good had come out of a strike' and that 'extremism', 'confiscation' and 'revolution' were totally unacceptable.[50] He openly asserted 'that he would fight under the banner of Sir Charles Lilley' and his candidature was more the result of Groom's wirepulling and Labour's indecision and willingness to compromise than genuine conviction on both sides.[51]

This mixed bag made a promising start on the Downs in 1893. Fogarty topped the poll for Toowoomba and Daniels won Cambooya. McCarthy and Cameron did well against tremendous odds and the tacitly-supported Groom and Lovejoy were returned.[52] A foundation had been laid but the optimism which these successes generated on the Downs was eventually dissipated. Labour made little headway after 1893.

Unlike the Party in the older colonies, Queensland Labour soon repudiated any alliance with the Opposition rump. Not only did this intransigence eventually result in serious divisions but the Party lost the chance of effecting reform through pressure and combination.[53] As

47 *The Worker*, 14 March 1896, p. 3, c. 3.

48 *WE&T*, 1 April 1893, p. 3, c. 4 and D. Gunn, *Links with the Past*, pp. 109, 158. This mixture was a feature of Labour candidates throughout Australia. Of the 32 Labour aspirants at the 1892 Victorian elections, only 10-12 were genuine 'workingmen'. The rest were solidly middle-class. *Australasian*, 16 April 1892, p. 741 and Mr G. Bartlett, *personal communication*, 10 November 1963.

49 *Pugh*, 1900, p. 423 and *BC*, 9 September 1904, p. 4, c. 7.

50 *TC*, 22 April 1893, p. 3, c. 6-7. Address at the Drayton Court House, 20 April 1893.

51 *The Worker*, 28 March 1896, p. 10, c. 2 and 26 May 1894, p. 2, c. 5. Fogarty never sat with the Labour Party in Parliament, seldom voted with them and actually opposed them several times. ibid., 2 June 1894, p. 2, c. 3.

52 McCarthy was defeated by an immensely strong 'radical' candidate—J. T. Bell, a scion of Jimbour. Nevertheless, he polled more votes than Jessop, the discredited Coalitionist. *TC*, 8 April 1893, p. 5, c. 7. Cameron was defeated (302 votes to 265) by the Coalition Minister J. F. G. Foxton. The Labour candidate carried the Goondiwindi, Wallangarra and Sugarloaf booths by 88 votes to 26 but his failure to win the Stanthorpe storekeeper vote (90 to 149) ruined his chances. *WA*, 9 May 1893, p. 2, c. 5.

53 *See* the attitude of *The Worker* at the time of the Glassey split in 1900. *The Worker*, 7 July 1900, p. 3, c. 1-3. W. P. Reeves states the obvious when he maintains

(Continued on facing page)

prosperity returned to the Downs and as Labour retreated to the citadels of Party doctrine, the sympathy of the old radicals evaporated and the Alliance with the farmers soon disintegrated. The Darling Downs returned to the old order of 'conservative', 'independent' and 'radical', and Labour in Queensland was forced to wait until 1915 for effective Parliamentary power.

While Warwick farmers, as early as 1871, maintained that 'the tillers of the soil' did not necessarily have identical interests with either the pastoralists or the townsfolk and even petitioned for direct representation, their gravest weakness in the political sphere paralleled that of their Manitoba fellows:

> . . . farmers as a class have not in the past and do not even now readily develop the spirit of class-consciousness.[54]

When prices crashed and drought reigned as in 1878-9 and 1882, there were often mutterings for direct political action. Moreover, the successes of the Victorian Farmers' Union, the New South Wales Selectors' Association and the South Australian Farmers' Mutual Association focused attention on possible remedies.[55] But the idea of political participation as a distinct interest grew very slowly. The Farmers' Association of 1885 urged farmers to 'acquire political power and replace their cap-in-hand requests with demands' and to use their new organizations for political purposes.[56] But most Downs farmers were still blind to the correlation between political action and sectional benefits.

The country-town radicals who accepted the credit for the land legislation which had 'provided land for the people' had banked a large deposit of goodwill among the Downs farmers. This political capital lasted a long time and the old slogans and antipathies were still potent long after their justification in terms of the contemporary scene had passed.[57] In 1878 Francis Kates saw no incongruity in describing himself in fatherly terms as 'the friend of the Farmers and Selectors' and the man most fitted in the Darling Downs electorate to be their spokesman.[58] He and his colleagues issued manifestos at every election containing planks which, individually, had considerable appeal to the small selec-

---

that at that time 'Queensland was not prepared to allow a single class to govern it . . . moderation and co-operation was needed . . . they had to have some support from the great colonial middle class if they wanted to succeed'. W. P. Reeves, *State Experiments*, Vol. 1, p. 83.

54 *Graingrowers' Guide*, 12 January 1916, p. 7. Speech of R. C. Hender, President of the Manitoba Graingrowers' Association. Quoted by W. L. Morton, *The Progressive Party in Canada*, Toronto 1950, p. 31.

55 *WA*, 4 November 1879, p. 2, c. 3 and 18 February 1882, p. 2, c. 1; *Australasian*, 21 June 1879, p. 791, 9 August 1879, p. 183 and 11 September 1880, p. 337; *BC*, 24 September 1891, p. 6, c. 6.

56 *TC*, 5 May 1885, p. 3, c. 2-3 and *WA*, 23 June 1885, p. 2, c. 2.

57 D. B. Waterson, 'Remarkable Career of W. H. Groom', pp. 44-7.

58 *WA*, 7 November 1878, p. 5, c. 1.

tors.[59] No candidate, however, had a policy that was designed to alter existing financial, marketing and transport arrangements which were beginning to plague those farmers which had managed to survive. This omission was not seriously regarded until events eventually forced the farmers' hands.

Furthermore, the farm vote was scattered over the Settled District and even where the farmers were numerically strong, old-established and fairly prosperous, they were dominated by nearby country towns. Groom in Toowoomba and Morgan in Warwick had a stranglehold on their constituencies which the farmers could not have broken even if they had wanted to. But both these astute politicians never failed to secure the farm vote. Immediately before the 1878 election, Groom astutely sponsored the Darling Downs Agriculturalists' Association to 'mobilize the political influence of the farmers'. The stated objects were traditional —better communications, electoral organization and assistance to needy selectors—but this Association was really an extension of Groom's personal political machine designed to secure the return of his nominees in farming electorates. The members of the Association were pledged to support only those candidates who would give an undertaking to assist the realization of the platform. Candidates did not have to be farmers—the crucial test—and Groom was determined to avoid any application of such a qualification to his nominees, none of whom ploughed or grazed. The Association quickly disintegrated after the election when its purpose had been achieved.[60]

These short-lived, single-purpose bodies tended to neutralize the most likely sources of farmer political activity. Only Aubigny and the two Darling Downs seats (later Cambooya and Cunningham) offered any hope to farmer candidates as there were more farmers in these areas than any other single occupation.[61] It is significant that when farmer-

[59] ibid. Kates' manifestos invariably included such proposals as a Department of Agriculture, irrigation works, the re-purchase of the freehold estates and specific public works.

[60] *TC*, 17 September 1878, p. 2, c. 4 and 21 September 1878, p. 3, c. 2.

[61] *Census of Queensland*, 1891, pp. 218-19. Unfortunately, the census returns do not correlate occupational statistics with electorates. Only the boundaries of the Drayton-and-Toowoomba constituency and statistical district coincide. The following table is a rough estimate of the number of farmers in each agricultural electorate compared with the total number of adult males:

Electorate	Adult males in 1891	Estimated farming population (male)
Aubigny	1,169	750
Cambooya	1,366	700
Cunningham	1,582	900
Drayton-Toowoomba	2,261	800
Warwick	1,075	350

candidates did appear and win seats, they drew their basic strength from the selector-belt which had been settled in the 'seventies and where rural problems were more acute and settlers more distressed than in other parts of the region.[62]

Between 1878 and 1888 seven Downs farmers contested constituencies. All were unsuccessful and came bottom of the poll. R. F. Walker, a prosperous Gowrie Creek mixed farmer who was nominated for Aubigny in 1873 but later withdrew to avoid splitting the anti-squatter vote, was scorned by the country-town radicals as much as the squatters for his presumptions. His 'only recommendation is that he is a farmer like others in the electorate' trumpeted the *Chronicle*, and Groom castigated the political naivety which would prevent him from obtaining a large public-works allocation.[63] In 1878 Walker put the matter to a vote. During this campaign, a farm vote emerged for the first time on the Downs. Low prices, drought, the temporary eclipse of the land question and the prevailing political atmosphere of confusion and fluidity stimulated discussion of matters outside the traditional fields of soils, squatters and railways. Henry Roessler, a German Middle Ridge smallholder, contested Drayton-and-Toowoomba, James Wilson of 'Ullathorne' stood for Darling Downs, and Walker returned to Aubigny.[64] But Wilson's claim that 'the time had arrived when farmers and selectors would send their own representatives to Parliament' was premature.[65] The new candidates failed to win any support from existing political organizations and did not set up any effective campaign committees of their own. They had no coherent agrarian policies to offer and the rural voters had little confidence in their ability to do a better job than the existing representatives. Nevertheless, these candidates gained some support in small farming localities.

Again, in 1883, John Affleck appealed to the Darling Downs farmers to 'support one of themselves . . . [as it was] high time they were represented in Parliament. They had been too long represented by the big moneyed men and capitalists who trampled them under their feet'.[66] Affleck's adherence to McIlwraith's platform, however, was fatal. Although he polled much better than Wilson had done five years earlier, Miles and Kates still had complete control of the selector vote and the farmer was extinguished as the Liberals swept the Downs. The final result was: Miles, 868; Kates, 863; Affleck, 551. Affleck carried Warwick by 245 votes to 191 (Miles) and 197 (Kates) but lost heavily in the farming areas.[67] (*see* next page)

[62] Aubigny, where many small German selectors were clearing the scrub, was a stronghold of the Farmers' Alliance. In fact, farmers in this electorate felt strong enough to break away from the parent body and form their own alliance. *TC*, 4 February 1893, Supplement, p. 2, c. 1-2.

[63] *TC*, 25 October 1873, p. 2, c. 4-5 and 8 November 1875, p. 2, c. 8.

[64] Wilson only polled 101 votes while Miles gained 692. 36 of Wilson's votes came from his home booth at Freestone Creek. *WA*, 28 November 1878, p. 2, c. 4.

[65] ibid., 10 October 1878, p. 3, c. 7.

[66] *WA*, 25 September 1883, p. 3, c. 1-2.

III *Personalities, Property and Public Works*

Two optimists, Francis McKeon, a Dalby small selector, and William Vickers, a Greenmount mixed farmer, contested the 1888 elections. Both were defeated. Vickers polled better than any previous farmer-candidate but could only carry his two home booths.[68] The return of the discredited Perkins for Cambooya and the colourless Jessop for Dalby indicated that the farmers still responded to the old slogans and were still confident that they could prosper within the existing political milieu.

Between 1889 and 1891, however, the political scene on the Downs underwent an amazing transformation. For the first time, the utterances of those who believed in pressure politics on a sectional basis and conducted by farmer-representatives were taken seriously by the majority of the Downs settlers. The long depression, the disintegration of the old factions and the belief that they were deliberately suffering from the actions of more united and powerful interests, engendered bitter resentment and a determination to emulate the undoubted successes of the new Labour movement which had already demonstrated in the industrial field the advantages of organization and combination.

All these threads were drawn together at Clifton on 15-16 September 1891 when twenty-five delegates and one hundred other farmers from all over the Downs assembled to form an organization to codify 'the wave of public sentiment now passing over the area'.[69] Observers testified to the 'intense earnestness' and thorough debates of the delegates which 'although they sometimes went to extremes', clearly enunciated the farmers' grievances and proposed remedies.[70] The delegates themselves, whether self-appointed or elected by local groups after brief and informal discussion, represented a new element. Most were mixed farmers in com-

---

67

POLLING-BOOTH	MILES	KATES	AFFLECK
Allora	135	139	32
Freestone Creek	42	46	30*
Killarney	67	67	16
Darkey Flat	20	20	22
Clifton	26	33	27
Spring Creek	36	35	9
Cambooya	65	62	24
Clifton Back Plains	31	35	11
Greenmount	46	44	16
Beauaraba	49	42	24
Westbrook HS area	23	20	16
North Branch	16	15	7
TOTAL	556	558	234

*Affleck's home booth.

68 Jessop polled 355 votes to McKeon's 153. *TC*, 12 May 1888, p. 3, c. 7. The latter, however, had no special farming platform. Perkins defeated Vickers by 404 votes to 296. Clifton Back Plains (36/10) and Greenmount (29/20) gave Vickers his only successes. *DDG*, 12 May 1888, p. 3, c. 7.

69 *BC*, 17 September 1891, p. 6, c. 1.

70 *TC*, 17 September 1891, p. 3, c. 7.

fortable circumstances who rejected the old order. In nationality, they were a fair cross-section, five being of German descent, and at least eight from Ireland. Several had had previous political or organizational experience. Nearly all grew some grain and thus represented those who were most distressed by harsh economic disabilities. The poorest selectors, many of whose sympathies secretly lay with Labour, were sparsely represented.

The discussions revealed, and the Covenant stated, that the old assumptions had been discarded:

> We also record our determination to combine for the purpose of considering all political questions affecting the agricultural interests . . . and . . . we are resolved to unite for the purpose of returning men to represent our interests in the Parliament of Queensland.[71]

Although the ubiquitous Groom appeared at the conference, stated that 'he was in perfect harmony with the idea of a farmers' Alliance' and produced material concerning other similar bodies, the conference restricted membership to farmers and their sons over eighteen years old.[72] This action, together with the low subscription of five shillings per annum, was significant and decisive. Together with the resolutions that only bona fide farmers could be endorsed as candidates, that members must pledge themselves to the Covenant and platform, and that electors should have the right of recall on a two-thirds petition, this exclusiveness finally eliminated the dangerous 'sympathisers' and 'termites' who had destroyed past attempts.[73]

While most delegates agreed with such objectives as electoral reform, a State bank, co-operative marketing arrangements, the adoption of scientific methods of agriculture and direct political intervention, a noticeable cleavage occurred between 'right'- and 'left'-wing delegates.[74] Wieck frankly acknowledged the debt to Labour when he considered that 'the last strike was the best thing which had ever occurred here, as it had taught them many lessons', and Anderson rather rashly stated that:

> . . . they would have to call a conference with the labour unions. Their interests were identical [and] must be mutual if they desired their grievances to be redressed.[75]

These views were not universally accepted. The downtrodden farm labourers and the carriers and shearers were prohibited from joining the Alliance although a motion forbidding membership in any other party or interest group was rejected.[76] Furthermore, the shipping and shearing strikes, with accompanying extremist utterances from the Trades Hall, alienated the property conscious who retained the old anti-urban

71 *BC*, 17 September 1891, p. 6, c. 2.

72 *WA*, 19 September 1891, p. 2, c. 7.

73 ibid.

74 The platform of the Alliance is reproduced in Appendix X.

75 *BC*, 17 September 1891, p. 6, c. 2.

76 ibid.

rural myths while adopting new radical action. Nevertheless, a tacit alliance with Labour in 1893, when the farmers first sponsored Parliamentary candidates, was very effective.

This implacable determination to enter politics was derided by the old 'conservative' groups who feared that their hegemony, already under strong radical challenge, was being whittled away by people who had once been amongst their strongest supporters:

Nothing but evil can come of this wretched splitting-up of interest and attempt to settle national questions by their incidence on particular trades . . . as farmers, prosperity will come to them only by shaping their association on the lines of the old motto, *Ne sutor ultra crepidam*.[77]

The *Darling Downs Gazette* anxiously advised that:

Farmers . . . should look to assistance within themselves and not to Parliament. The former resolve is noble, the latter contemptible. The one will land the country in peace and prosperity, the other precipitate it into anarchy and misery.[78]

Fear of a split vote was most pronounced. Now that class-lines were hardening, property felt entitled to expect the adherence of the farmers. It could not grasp the extent of farm bitterness and the lengths to which the new leaders were prepared to go to alleviate disabilities.

Three Alliance candidates contested the 1893 elections, and Henry Daniels, the Pittsworth People's Political Association Labour nominee, received indispensable Alliance support and constantly assured the Cambooya electors that 'labour and farmers' interests are identical'.[79] Cambooya farmers 'had no doubt of the tone in which they desired to speak' and Daniels received a large absolute majority and swept the farming booths. Perkins, even though Boland split the Ministerial vote, was shown to be thoroughly discredited by the poll.[80]

W. T. Lovejoy of Meringandan, the Alliance candidate for Aubigny, sponsored by Groom and the *Chronicle* and standing 'in the interests of

77 *BC*, 25 September 1891, p. 4, c. 5.

78 *DDG*, 3 October 1891, p. 3, c. 1-2.

79 *TC*, 8 April 1893, p. 2, c. 5 and 29 April 1893, p. 4, c. 1-2.

80 *WA*, 9 May 1893, p. 2, c. 6. The final result was: Daniels, 464; Perkins, 198; Boland, 189. The following polling-booth returns illustrate Daniels' appeal to the farmers of the 'selector belt':

Booth	Daniels	Perkins	Boland
Cambooya	30	6	6
Clifton Back Plains	40	6	10
Greenmount	32	14	18
Clifton	19	3	8
Crosshill	24	3	11
Pittsworth	142	53	16
TOTAL FOR FARMING BOOTHS:	287	85	69

WE&T, 10 May 1893, p. 3, c. 1.

the farmers as opposed to the capitalists' was sure that 'conciliation between the rights of labour and those of farming were perfectly practicable'.[81] With an excellent organization, a large core of small, hard-hit selectors to rely on, and a mortgage on the German vote as well as on his farm and hotel, Lovejoy swept every booth and overwhelmed James Campbell, the Toowoomba Ministerialist.[82] Michael Brewer, the highly successful and technically advanced Irish Roman Catholic Mount Sturt farmer, failed to win Cunningham[83] from the wealthy, popular, squatter-Ministerialist William Allan who displayed a novel solicitude for the farmers at this election. In spite of the railway-rates agitation, Brewer was beaten by superior organization and finance, the strength of old

81 *TC*, 11 April 1893, p. 2, c. 7.

82 Lovejoy received 631 votes to Campbell's 231. Again, the Alliance candidate polled best in the poorer small-farming areas:

Booth	Lovejoy	Campbell
Koojarewon	96	14
Plainby	47	1
Emu Creek	24	8
Goombungee	77	14
Glencoe	38	18
Merrit's Creek	25	9
Meringandan	76	3
TOTAL	383	67

TC, 2 May 1893, p. 3, c. 5.

83 *WA*, 11 April 1893, p. 3, c. 5. Once again the Alliance candidate swept the small farming districts:

Booth	Allan	Brewer
Clifton	26	60
Yangan	68	70
Spring Creek	12	32
Freestone	39	57
Darkey Flat	26	20
TOTAL	171	239

The more prosperous, larger farmers of Warwick-Allora returned Allan:

Booth	Allan	Brewer
Allora	205	85
Warwick	94	67
Killarney	84	55
	383	207

TOTAL VOTE:	
Allan	585
Brewer	463
Majority:	122

WE&T, 3 May 1893, p. 3, c. 3.

loyalties, the Warwick absentee vote and the wealthier Warwick-Allora farmers' refusal to follow the new rural radicalism. Brewer polled very well in the small farming areas but these votes were not enough to secure victory.

While the old centrifugal forces gradually reappeared after 1893, these successes were a triumph for the new movement and a practical demonstration of its genuine rural origins.[84] In retrospect, the decline of the Alliance with the return of prosperity and the gradual fulfilment of most of its platform by various administrations can be seen as only a temporary phase in Downs history. One ancestor of the later Country Party, the Alliance was a premature attempt to project a third force into Queensland politics. At the time, its critics were perfectly correct in suggesting that the Downs farmers were not strong enough to act as an effective political engine. Yet when economic conditions deteriorated again thirty years later the same nascent radicalism which had so dramatically emerged in 1891-3 once more appeared in the region.

[84] By April 1892 there were 14 branches of the Alliance on the Downs. *TC*, 7 April 1892, p. 3, c. 7.

Retrospect 1859-93

Few of the forty thousand settlers on the Downs in the nineteenth century ever thought that the problems of pioneering were unsurmountable. Difficulties abounded but to admit defeat in the alien environment would have meant, for squatter, selector and storekeeper alike, the denial of hope itself. For the improvement of their material circumstances through the subjugation of the wilderness was the driving engine of these Queensland Victorians. Some, however, failed. For them the Garden of Queensland remained an intractable desert, a wasteland of deferred hope, blasted youth and futile endeavour. But for many the dreams did not dissolve but crystallized into agreeable reality. Their acres were tilled, a satisfying rural existence attained and, by implication, a richer, more rewarding, apparently self-sufficient life was secured.

Once the political and, above all, economic and technical prerequisites were recognized and then mastered the Downs could join the Canadian prairies, Waikato pastures and Cape vineyards as another agricultural contributor—a minor part of the new colonial yeomanry's tribute to British imperialism and European settlement. By 1900 most Downsmen were integral productive parts of the Australian, if not the Empire's, economy. This role few had consciously sought but most now accepted economic realities. Only a handful questioned the end of a chance to build a new society in an unspoilt wilderness. Their dream had dissolved. Yet in terms of conventional nineteenth-century English values, the agrarian settlement of the Downs, however difficult it may have been within the short context of Queensland history, had been a resounding success. No blood but that of the exterminated 'sub-human' aborigines and slaughtered marsupials marred this settlement. On the Downs, unlike most of Australia, the small man's frontier had eventuated. The family farm was indeed practicable. Even the squatter departed to Britain, bankruptcy, or Brisbane like a wether to the slaughter, surrendering with hardly a bleat to the pressures, customs and mores of the country towns. Agrarian values and justifications may have been destroyed by the pioneering process and the realities of a commercial world but the farmers and shopkeepers, in their own eyes at least, seemed victorious.

By the turn of the century, the classic period of agricultural settlement in Australia was over. A new rural *petit-bourgeois* community with an apparently immutable pattern of society had been created. The landscape now reflected the needs and material satisfactions of this group. Downsmen could now afford to cultivate their comfortable but now irrelevant political myths and enjoy the ancestor-worship which security and conformity alike demands. The period of great, decisive change had ended. It was time to develop and conserve what had been won.

From now on Downs history loses its old flavour and vitality and merges with the complicated eddies of the Australian mass society. Compensations, however, abounded. The virtues and certainties of 'the old pioneers' could now be celebrated. Physical toughness, the need for red blood, strong muscles and thick heads, perseverance, faith in nineteenth-century work-values, religious justification for economic success and the tremendous certainty of most pioneers that progress was desirable, beneficial and necessary saturated the social and mental climate. Indeed they were obvious and necessary virtues to most of the survivors and their children. Larger cream and wheat cheques reinforced this post-selection optimism and the physical landscape—ring-barked trees, ploughed fields, crops of wheat, railways, telegraph wires and small towns—gave it visible confirmation.

But if Downs life was still founded on a belief in economic improvement and personal respectability, the *bourgeois*, on farm or in country town, still retained some sense of social responsibility. However stunted his sensibility, however limited his experience and self-satisfied his bricks and mortar outlook, his eighteenth-century beliefs in reason and the power of man to improve his environment had not yet been submerged. The settlement of the Darling Downs seemed a living monument to such a philosophy.

The hospitals, Schools of Arts, schools and rude attempts at promoting a second-hand English provincial culture testified to this passing phase of middle-class involvement, uplift and improvement. The real and mythical squatting values had been replaced by a suburban and yeoman group ethos. So far, farm and store could appear to reject the implications of the new proletarian values of the eastern urban industrial classes and the western bush-workers while at the same time seeking insulation from the pressures of metropolitan capitalism. Yet for a brief time, and only for a brief time, they glimpsed the same frightening possibility in 1893 as their sons did thirty years later that the demands of a capitalist economy might be a crueller and less endurable fate than that which providence had promised the yeoman farmer. But this nightmare soon passed. The next century, however, was to provide longer and sterner trials.

So the survivors looked over the wheatfields of Allora, the grazing farms of Dalby and the shops and offices of Toowoomba and Warwick and congratulated themselves and their progenitors. The result, they argued, had justified the bodily toil, spiritual stunting, moral disintegration, exploitation of women and children and animal insensibility that seemed inseparable from the pioneering process.

Others were less sure. For some old men, 1893 was the final betrayal, the end of the agrarian dream. Certainly, too, the Downs in the 'nineties exhibited one Queensland characteristic—a rapid decline in the vigour of the pioneering stock and continued need for fresh blood and capital.

The Land Purchase Acts of the 1890s did not so much break up new estates—those were already disintegrating under economic pressures—but it can be argued that they provided the means of reinforcing a spiritually, mentally and technically impoverished yeomanry with new farmers from Victoria and New Zealand. But, in general, men remembered the successful—Groom, Morgan, Taylor, Armstrong, Hinz, Mackintosh, and Slade—and forgot the failures. The tragedies, spiritual and economic, which afflicted ruined squatter, bankrupt storekeeper, alcoholic gentleman-farmer and insane bushworker were stories not now to be taken seriously by the new post-depression optimists. Truth, to some, was unbearable, to most irrelevant. Most Australian born were mute or, like Steele Rudd, refused to, or could not, 'tell the whole truth'. Others, like the poet, Essex Evans, that tragic, gentle romantic who had failed as an Allora selector, never came to terms with the environment that had destroyed them. For them, the Downs was yet another part of Australia which they could not comprehend or even accept.

Evans, in the end, turned his face to the east, to the range below Toowoomba:

> Dark purple chased with sudden gloom and glory
> Like waves in wild unrest,
> Low-wooded billows and steep summits hoary,
> Ridge slope and mountain crest[1]

in the same way that Australians turned once again to old quarrels and old issues of lands they had left behind. But to many these personal tragedies were disagreeable episodes, now concluded. The great clash between those that had landed property and those that contested possession and wanted to cultivate the sheepwalks was finished. The real issues moved back to where perhaps, they had always belonged—the western shed, the eastern factory, the London bank. The Downs settlers in a wider view were but pathetic colonial marionettes dancing on imperial strings, mere extensions of mowing machines cutting the grain to provide Europe with its cheap raw material. The metropolis won in the end—perhaps it always had—but for a time on the Downs, hard work and ambition obscured this fact. But in the 'nineties few questioned themselves or their achievements. They had their land, their businesses and their jobs. With full stomachs and a tamed landscape they were content. Cabbages now grew on the Darling Downs.

[1] From G. E. Evans, 'Toowoomba' in *Collected Verse*, Sydney 1928, p. 49.

APPENDIXES

No doubt all of us would have done the same, had we the same opportunity of those fortunate gentlemen; but it is as well, for the general interest, that the privilege can no longer be exercised . . .

DDG, 23 November 1865, p. 3, c. 1

Appendix I

OWNERSHIP OF THE DARLING DOWNS SETTLED DISTRICT GREAT STATIONS, 1859-93

RUN	HOLDER	DATES	NOTES
Jimbour	Bell & Sons	1859-91	Original lessee 1841
	D.D. & W.L.C.	1881-92	
	Q.N.B.	1892-93	
Cumkillenbar	J. Balfour	1859-62	
	T. de L. Moffatt	1862-66	Brother-in-law of J. P. Bell Deceased 1864
	Bell & Sons	1867-81	Incorp. in Jimbour
Rosalie Plains	Hope & Ramsay	1859-66	
	Kent & Wienholt	1866-69	Bank held lease 1868-72
	J. F. McDougall	1869-89	
	Mercantile Bank	1889-93	McDougall bankrupt
Gowrie }	F. N. Isaac	1859-66	Isaac died
Goombungee }	George King	1866-93	
Irvingdale	R. E. Tooth	1859-67	Bank held lease 1868-72
	Kent & Wienholt	1867-75	Incorp. in Jondaryan
Lagoon Creek	Hodgson & Ramsay	1860-65	Bank held lease 1868-72
	Kent & Wienholt	1866-75	Incorp. in Jondaryan
Jondaryan	R. E. Tooth	1859-67	Bankrupt 1867
	Kent & Wienholt	1867-93	Bank lease 1868-72
Warra Warra	C. J. Mackenzie	1859-61	
	George Thorn	1861-78	Broken up
Greenbank	S. Ross	1859-62	Ross died
	A. H. Richardson	1862-68	Mortgagee
	Janet Ross	1868-70	Forced sale
	Commercial Bank	1870-72	
	E. Vickery	1873-93	
St Ruth }	Buckland & McKay	1859-60	
Sth Toolburra }	N. B. A. Coy	1860-93	
Rosenthal			
Cecil Plains }	Russell & Taylor	1859-63	
West Prairie }	James Taylor	1863-93	
East Prairie	Russell & Taylor	1859-63	
	James Taylor	1863-67	Bank held lease 1868-72

RUN	HOLDER	DATES	NOTES
East Prairie	Kent & Wienholt	1868-75	Incorp. in Jondaryan
Beauaraba } Felton	C. Mallard	1859-65	Bank held lease 1865-67
	J. S. Willis	1865-67	
	Whitchurch & Sandeman	1867-76	Tyson mortgagee 1867-76
	James Tyson	1876-93	
Yandilla Tummaville North Branch }	Gore Family	1859-93	Original lessee 1841
Ellangowan	Peel River Coy	1859-74	
	C. B. Fisher	1874-90	Forced transfer by Fisher
	Aust. T. & L. Coy	1890-93	
Canal Creek } Talgai I	J. Gillespie	1859-65	Talgai: Hood & Douglas 1859-65
	T. H. Hood	1865-68	
	F. A. Stratford	1868-78	
	C. B. Fisher	1878-84	Forced sale 1890
	Q. Inv. & L.M. Coy	1884-93	
Talgai II	Geo. & Chas. Clark	1867-90	'Old Talgai'
	Scott. Aust. Inv. Coy	1890-93	Part
	Geo. Clark	1890-93	Part
Canning Downs	G. F. Leslie	1859-62	Original lessee Mort & McDonald
	G. Davidson	1862-65	L. Smith 1865-75
	F. J. C. Wildash	1865-75	Forced sale 1875
	J. D. Macansh	1875-93	
Glengallan	Marshall & Deuchar	1859-69	Deuchar bankrupt 1869
	C. H. Marshall	1869-73	
	Marshall (execs) & Slade	1873-93	
Goomburra	P. Leslie	1859-60	Original lessee
	R. & E. Tooth	1860-62	
	McLean, Hodgson, Green	1862-78	
	E. Wienholt	1878-93	
Gladfield	P. Leslie	1859-60	Original lessee
	R. and E. Tooth	1860-70	Bank lease 1870-77
	Arnold Wienholt	1877-93	
Maryvale	A. Wienholt	1859-93	
	J. S. Whiting	1859-60	Whiting deceased
Pilton Haldon }	C. H. Marshall	1860-65	
	Fitz & Wilson	1865-90	Bank held lease 1869-78
	W. E. Tooth & Torbeck	1890-91	Bankrupt Run divided
Clifton	W. B. Tooth	1859-76	B.N.S.W. held lease 1875-89
	B.N.S.W.	1876-88	

RUN	HOLDER	DATES	NOTES
Clifton	Gannon Syndicate	1888-91	Tooth deceased 1876
	Q.Inv. & L.M. Coy	1891-93	
Eton Vale	Hodgson & Watts	1859-67	Hodgson original lessee
	Hodgson & Ramsay	1867-93	
Westbrook	McLean & Beit	1859-74	
	Shanahan & Jennings	1874-93	Shanahan deceased 1882
Toolburra	Massie & Walker	1857-65	
	Thomas Coutts	1865-93	

SOURCE: *QGG*, 1859-75, 'Lists of Run Leases' and 'Runs Transferred'. Various sources for freeholds.

Appendix II

CHANGING LEASE OWNERSHIP OF TEN DARLING DOWNS UNSETTLED DISTRICT RUNS, 1860-93

NAME AND AREA (sq. miles)	LEASEHOLDER	
1 Jingi Jingi	J. B. Watts	1857-60
134	W. B. Tooth	1860-63
	G. K. Ingelow	1863-65
	S. Murray	1865-78
	E. Bassingthwaite	1878-93
2 Dunmore	H. Russell & J. Taylor	1857-63
260	J. Taylor	1863-80
	Queensland N. Bank	1880-81
	E. Vickery	1881-93
3 Wongongera	Clark Irving	1857-62
200	Gibson & Buchanan	1865-67
	N.Z. & Aust. Land Coy	1867-84
	G. Sandeman	1884-85
	A.J.S. Bank	1885-86
	G. D. Macansh, jun.	1886-87
	A.J.S. Bank	1887-93
4 Wyaga	D. Gunn	1860-65
163	R. Napier	1865-66
	Wm Turner	1866-70
	Bank of Australasia	1870-72
	E. Knyvett and W. Box	1872-75
	Alex Campbell	1877-79
	R. Y., C. T. and H. Holmes	1879-81
	Lavinia Holmes	1881-93
5 Texas	A. L. & J. F. McDougall	1860-62
234	Morehead & Young	1862-75
	Scott. Aust. Inv. Coy	1875-93
6 Weranga	T. S. Mort & E. Cameron	1848-62
338	Mort and Laidley	1862-71
	Henry Mort	1871-83
	Campbell, Gibson & Matthews	1883-85
	Q.Land and Past. Assoc.	1885
	Scott. Aust. Inv. Coy	1885-87
	Duncan Macneil	1887-93
7 Cooranga	Bell and Sons	1850-93
8 Cobblegum	J. A. and J. P. Bell	1852-73
140	C. F. Crawshaw and A. H. Smith	1873-76
	M. Daisey	1876-87
	Bank of Australasia	1887-93

NAME AND AREA (sq. miles)	LEASEHOLDER	
9 Welltown	T. S. Mort & E. W. Cameron	1850-62
308	Bank of Australasia	1862-65
	Mort, Cameron, Buchanan	1865-73
	Henry Mort	1873-75
	Buchanan and Mort	1875-83
	Loughlin, Leonard and Sinclair	1883-93
10 Dulacca	J. Crowder	1850-60
408	Wm Miles	1860-74
	John Ferrett	1874-78
	C.B.C., Sydney	1878-93

SOURCE: *Votes and Proceedings of the New South Wales Legislative Assembly, NSWVP.* (1859-60), Vol. III, pp. 688-9; *QGG*, 1860-93; 'Annual Pastoral Rent Lists', and 'Quarterly Run Transfers'.

Appendix III

PRE-EMPTIVE SELECTIONS UNDER THE 1847 ORDERS-IN-COUNCIL, DARLING DOWNS SETTLED DISTRICT, 1860-74

Run	Lessee 1874	Acreage Pre-empted in 1865	Total Acreage Pre-empted	Total Area of Run
Westbrook	Shanahan and Jennings	23,197	43,475	83,030
Jondaryan	Kent and Wienholt	15,654	21,281	98,560
Irvingdale	Kent and Wienholt	2,194	5,522	91,520
Canning Downs	McDonald and Smith	—	22,994	258,080
Cecil Plains	J. Taylor	—	8,955	172,800
Clifton	W. B. Tooth	16,124	16,124	89,600
Gowrie	Geo. King	883	10,886	65,920
Goombungee	Geo. King	601	601	58,297
Haldon	Fitz and Wilson	3,966	3,882	43,520
Pilton	Fitz and Wilson	1,259	5,524	34,788
Eton Vale	Hodgson and Ramsay	12,037	34,204	67,200
South Toolburra	Nth British Aust. Coy	1,627	1,947	37,120
Toolburra	Thos. Coutts	4,037	10,765	16,000
Talgai	George and Chas. Clark	14,975	25,263	58,240
Killarney	McDonald and Smith	—	320	21,000
St Ruths	Nth British Aust. Coy	—	1,282	95,360
Glengallan	Marshall and Slade	18,172	31,166	44,800
Cumkillenbar	Bell and Sons	—	1,797	103,680
Jimbour	Bell and Sons	7,442	40,417	266,445
Rosenthal	Nth British Aust. Coy	960	2,595	275,200
Beauaraba	James Tyson	—	3,706	18,470
Felton	James Tyson	1,372	8,444	49,920
Ellangowan	C. B. Fisher	187	187	44,160
Goomburra	Edward Wienholt	5,362	12,205	60,800
Gladfield	Arnold Wienholt	—	2,902	27,520
Maryvale	Arnold Wienholt	—	2,620	21,120
Tummaville	Gore and Coy	161	1,277	129,920
Yandilla	Gore and Coy	1,727	2,047	229,760
Warra Warra	George Thorn	640	1,270	66,120
	TOTAL ACREAGE	132,577	323,658	2,628,950

NOTE: Maps 4, 5 and 6, inserted in the text, should be consulted in conjunction with this appendix. The abnormally high ratio of pre-emption to total acreage on Glengallan (66 per cent), Toolburra (60 per cent), Eton Vale and Westbrook (both 50 per cent), should also be noted.

SOURCE: *QVP*, Vol. 1, (1866), pp. 1417-21, and ibid., Vol. 2, (1874), pp. 562-7.

Appendix IV

'"THE DUMMIES" CHARTER'—FREE SELECTION BEFORE SURVEY, 1867

INSTRUCTIONS TO LAND AGENTS

(Circular)

Surveyor-General's Office,
BRISBANE, 17th August 1867

Sir,

I have the honor to inform you that it has been decided that the *Leasing Act of 1866* is applicable to the selection of unsurveyed lands in agricultural reserves, and to request that you will afford every facility to intending selectors.

Under the instructions to land agents hitherto in operation, selections of unsurveyed lands were restricted to purchases only, and the operation of the *Leasing Act* was confined to lands which had been surveyed and proclaimed for sale.

The instructions now furnished to you will enable persons to select lands in agricultural reserves previous to survey, by paying the annual rent of 2s. 6d. per acre, in the same manner as if the land had been surveyed and proclaimed open for selection under the *Leasing Act*.

It will of course be necessary for applicants, to lease before survey, to comply with the conditions of the fifth and sixth clauses of the *Agricultural Reserves Act*, by furnishing such description of the land they desire to obtain as may enable me to issue the necessary instructions for the survey, especially in reference to the estimated distance and direction from some known point on the office maps, as it might otherwise occur that two persons might select the same land under different descriptions, in which case the prior application must take precedence.

The minimum area to be selected will be eighty acres, as in the case of selections by purchase before survey, and the total holding must not exceed 320 acres in any one reserve, but it is necessary that the leased blocks should be conterminous.

The first year's rent at the rate of two shillings and sixpence per acre must be paid at the time of application, and also the amount of the survey fee, according to the rate paid to licensed surveyors, if the applicant desires to have the survey made by the Government.

The applications should be on the form used for selections by purchase before survey, with the alteration shown on the enclosed schedule.

The operation of the Acts not being very clearly understood in reference to the conditions required to be complied with by selectors in agricultural reserves, you may intimate that the cultivation of one-sixth of the land within one year is the only condition which will have operation, residence and fencing being no longer required.

No applications are to be taken unless accompanied by the full amount of deposit, and the form of application duly signed and declared to by the selector; but the application so signed may be received from an agent's hands, or by post.

I have, &c.,
A. C. GREGORY,
Surveyor-General

The Land Agent, Ipswich, Toowoomba, Warwick, Dalby, Maryborough, Rockhampton, Gladstone, Brisbane

Surveyor-General's Office,
BRISBANE, 24th August 1867

Sir,

A considerable area of land in the Darling Downs District which have been surveyed for sale at auction and lease, under the Leasing Act, as ordinary country lands, having been included within the Darling Downs Agricultural Reserve by the proclamation of the 18th day of April, 1867, and as these allotments are generally of a size unsuited for proclamation as surveyed lots, under the provisions of the *Agricultural Reserves Act,* it has been deemed expedient, pending the subdivision into more convenient portions, to throw the land open to selection as unsurveyed lands under the provisions of the *Agricultural Reserves Act* and the *Leasing Act*. . . .

The lands in the Pilton, Felton, Clifton, King's Creek, and Warwick Agricultural Reserves having been surveyed into suitable portions for proclamation for selection as surveyed lands, are not open to selection under the regulation as unsurveyed lands.

I have, &c.,
A. C. GREGORY,
Surveyor-General

The Land Agents, Toowoomba and Warwick

NOTE: Under these regulations Fisher and Davenport dummied their 36,000 acres at Headington Hill during 1867-8. Kent and Wienholt, Miles and Simpson all took advantage of this regulation—the only instance of free selection before survey on the Darling Downs.

SOURCE: *QVP*, Vol. 2, (1867), p. 797.

Appendix V

REGULATIONS DEALING WITH APPLICATIONS FOR CERTIFICATES OF FULFILMENT OF CONDITIONS ON CONDITIONAL PURCHASES, 1875

REGULATIONS

Application for Certificates of Fulfilment of Conditions on Conditional Purchase

1. Applications for Certificates of fulfilment of conditions on conditional purchases shall be made to the Land Commissioner in *open court* by the selectors *personally*, who will also be required to produce at the time of application credible witnesses, as provided in the Act, in support of their respective applications; and the Land Commissioner having publicly heard any such application, and the evidence in support thereof, by affidavit or otherwise, and all objections thereto, shall give his decision *in open court* as to the granting or refusal of the certificate applied for.

2. Notice in writing of the selector's intention to apply for a certificate of fulfilment of conditions will require to be forwarded to the Land Commissioner of the district, at least four weeks prior to the date of the Land Commissioner's court sitting at which the application will be heard.

3. Applications can only be made at the court sitting of the Land Agent's district in which the selection is situated.

4. The Land Commissioner may postpone the hearing of any application to the next succeeding court sitting, if the evidence in support thereof is insufficient to satisfy him as to the conditions and provisos of the Act being complied with.

5. Notice under the hand of the Land Commissioner of all applications for certificates proposed to be made before him at his court sitting shall be posted in the Land Agent's office and be inserted three times in the local papers. The first notice to appear at least ten clear days before the court sitting.

Lands comprised in selections withdrawn or cancelled before confirmation not available for re-selection until notice is given.

NOTE: This regulation, the key words of which have been underlined, was an attempt to check dummying and speculating by transferring administrative power to the local Land Commissioner and by changing the scene of action from the recesses of the Brisbane Lands Office to a public, regional court.

SOURCE: *QVP*, Vol. 2, (1875), p. 773.

Appendix VI

DARLING DOWNS LAND EXCHANGES, 1877-82

No.	Approved	Vendors	Surrendered (acres)	Received (acres)	Locality
23	24.3.77	Shanahan & Jennings	2,183	4,174	Westbrook
30	16.6.78	Bell and Sons	8,019	8,019	Jimbour
32	10.6.78	E. Wienholt	20,611	41,222	Allora
47	2.7.79	Estate W. B. Tooth	1,333	2,667	Clifton
48	7.5.79	Nth. British Aust. Coy	800	2,220	Darkey Flat
53	24.7.79	James Tyson	657	1,314	Felton
56	2.10.79	J. F. McDougall	2,653	3,434	Rosalie Plains
102	19.7.82	D.D.W.L.C.	8,410	19,574	Jimbour
111	14.10.82	Archibald Munro	1,150	800	Crow's Nest
		TOTAL ACREAGE	49,278	83,424	

SOURCE: *QVP*, (1877-82), 'Report of the Department of Lands'.

Appendix VII

DARLING DOWNS FREEHOLD ESTATES AND STOCK OWNERSHIP, 1888 AND 1892

1 FREEHOLD PROPRIETORS IN THE SETTLED DISTRICT OWNING OVER 25,000 ACRES

A. OVER 100,000 ACRES

NAME	ACRES	ESTATE
Tyson, James	229,748	Felton, Beauaraba, Mt Russell, Cooranga[1]
Kent & Wienholt (Trustees)	162,831	Jondaryan, Irvingdale, Lagoon Creek
Fisher, C. B.	161,947	Headington Hill, O.K., Ellangowan, Condamine Plains
Gore, R. W., G. R., F. A.	159,222	Yandilla, Tummaville, North Branch
Taylor, James	147,310	Cecil Plains and West Prairie
Bank of N.S.W.	128,975	Clifton[2]
Drury, Hart, Palmer (Trustees: D.D.W.L.C.)	124,238	Jimbour, Cumkillenbar
Scottish Australian Investment Co.	118,796	Talgai[2]
Knighton, C. A. D., and Slade, W. B.	103,407	Glengallan
TOTAL ACRES	1,336,474	

B. 50,000-100,000 ACRES

NAME	ACRES	ESTATE
Jennings and Shanahan	85,546	Westbrook
Macansh, J. D.	63,728	Canning Downs
Hodgson and Ramsay	57,825	Eton Vale
Wienholt, Arthur	52,111	Maryvale
McDougall, J. F.	50,406	Rosalie Plains
King, George	50,051	Gowrie
TOTAL ACRES	359,667	

[1] Cooranga not in Settled District.

[2] Downs figures slightly less, as these totals include other holdings.

NAME	ACRES	ESTATE
C. 25,000-50,000 ACRES		
Wienholt Brothers	47,032	Goomburra
Q.Inv. & L. Mort Coy	43,201	Talgai, Canal Creek[2]
Simpson, G. M.	41,939	Bon Accord
Nelson, H. M.	37,157	Loudon
North British Aust. Coy	36,526	Rosenthal, St Ruths
Wilson, W. M.	32,926	Haldon and Pitton
Tooth, W. B.	28,246	Clifton[3]
Wienholt, Edward	27,992	Gladfield
Hogarth, William	26,265	Balgownie
Coutts, Thomas	25,677	North Toolburra
TOTAL ACRES	346,961	
GRAND TOTAL	2,043,102[4]	

2 Downs figures slightly less, as these totals include other holdings.

3 Part of Clifton (one-third) not in hands of BNSW.

4 It is probable that this figure is over-stated—an error of 10 per cent is probable.

SOURCE: Adapted from: *QVP*, Vol. 3, (1888), pp. 351-8 (Estate names added).

2 ANALYSIS OF SHEEP OWNERSHIP DARLING DOWNS PASTORAL DISTRICT 1892

Range	Sheep	Number of owners	% Total sheep
+100,000	520,920	4[1]	22.0
50–100,000	551,796	7[2]	23.3
20– 50,000	537,718	16	22.8
10– 20,000	247,501	18	13.5
5– 10,000	73,342	11	3.2
1– 5,000	268,382	121	14.2
–1,000	24,460	221	1.0
TOTALS	2,224,119	398	100.0

1 Loughlin & Coy (Welltown), 151,347; Kent and Wienholt (Jondaryan) 147,857; Jas. Tyson (Felton, Mt Russell, Wyobie) 112,287; *DDWLC* (Jimbour) 109,429.

2 J. Taylor (Cecil Plains) 97,058; Gore & Coy (Yandilla, Tummaville) 95,980; Fisher & Coy (Headington Hill, etc.) 94,382; Shanahan and Jennings (Westbrook) 69,147; Sth Queensland Past. Coy (Daandine) 66,782; Hodgson and Ramsay (Eton Vale) 64,998; Marshall and Slade (Glengallan) 63,449.

SOURCE: *QVP*, Vol. 4, (1892), pp. 697-720.

Appendix VIII

DARLING DOWNS FREEHOLD ESTATES RE-PURCHASED, 1894-1916

Estate	Acres	Price per acre	Total price
		£ s. d.	£
North Toolburra	10,983	2 0 0	21,966
Glengallan No. 1	6,301	2 15 0	17,328
Westbrook	9,886	2 8 0	23,726
Clifton No. 1	9,208	2 15 6	25,537
Clifton No. 2	7,823	2 12 0	20,340
Clifton No. 3	566	2 0 0	1,132
Headington Hill	36,702	2 4 0	80,745
Glengallan No. 2	9,116	3 13 7	33,553
Glengallan No. 3	21,653	4 0 0	86,612
Pinelands	3,603	2 0 0	7,206
Beauaraba	8,120	1 12 0	12,992
Goomburra	13,120	3 2 3	40,838
Mt Russell	45,144	2 4 0	99,317
Gowrie	43,958	4 0 0	175,834
Jimbour	121,061	3 10 0	423,713
Maryvale	29,155	3 0 0	87,467
Cecil Plains	120,947	2 0 0	241,894
TOTALS	497,346		1,400,200

SOURCE: *QVP*, Vol. 2, (1917), p. 563, 'Agricultural Lands Purchase Act of 1894, Return'.

Appendix IX

DARLING DOWNS AGRICULTURAL AND HORTICULTURAL SOCIETIES, 1890

Name	Formed	Fee p.a.			Value of Property	Nature	Centre
		£	s.	d.			
Central Downs, A.H.A.	1878		10	0	490	Bldgs, stalls, etc.	Allora
Northern Downs Past. A.A.	1882	1	1	0	410	Bldgs, land	Dalby
McIntyre River Past. A. Soc.	1873	1	0	0	312	Fencing, yds	Goondiwindi
Border Ag., Past. & Mining Soc.	1877		10	0	500	Bldgs, etc.	Stanthorpe
Royal Ag. Soc. of Q'land	1860[1]	2	2	0	5,550	Impts.	Toowoomba
Drayton & Toowoomba A. & H.A.	1861[2]		10	0	500	Bldgs, yds	Toowoomba
D.D. Hort. Assoc.	1882		10	0	108	Furniture, land	Toowoomba
Eastern Downs H. & A.A.	1867[3]		10	0	1,072	Land, bldgs, etc.	Warwick
Swan & Freestone Creek A. & H.A.	1879		10	0	626	Land, bldgs, etc.	Warwick

[1] First in colony [2] Second in colony [3] Fourth in colony

SOURCE: *QVP*, Vol. 3, (1890), pp. 801-3.

Appendix X

'COVENANT' AND 'OBJECTS AND PLATFORM' OF THE QUEENSLAND FARMERS' ALLIANCE, 1891

Covenant of the Queensland Farmers' Alliance formulated and adopted at the Clifton Farmers' Conference on 16 September 1891.

> "We, the undersigned, subscribers to the Queensland Farmers' Alliance, do hereby declare our intention to combine for the purpose of promoting the farming interests generally; and we further agree individually to do all that lies in our power, and as far as our knowledge will permit, to cultivate a more friendly and social feeling among the agriculturalists of the colony; and we further jointly agree to aid any movement calculated to conserve the interests of agriculture in Queensland, and the advancement of the interests of the alliance. And we hereby promise to devote our attention and best abilities by attending regularly to meetings, to assist in the solution of difficulties against which the farming interests have to contend, and to give our individual and collective support to the principles of the alliance by advocating the best and most approved methods of scientific and mechanical agriculture. We also record our determination to combine for the purpose of considering all political questions affecting the agricultural interest in accordance with part of the general laws, and also that we are resolved to unite for the purpose of returning men to represent our interests in the Parliament of Queensland."

BC, 17 September 1891, p. 6, c. 2.

Objects and Platform of the Queensland Farmers' Alliance adopted on 16 September 1891:

1. To secure electoral reform by the abolition of plural voting and the adoption of the principle of one-man-one-vote.
2. Protection for agricultural produce and the fostering of native industry.
3. The formation of a State Land Loan Bank to finance struggling selectors at reasonable rates of interest.
4. The formation of Boards of Conciliation for all Industrial Disputes.
5. To oppose Australian Federation on lines laid down by the Sydney Conference.
6. To secure markets in all the large towns for the distribution, exhibition and sale of farm and dairy produce direct to the consumers.
7. To advocate the best and most scientific methods of agriculture.
8. The cultivation of a more friendly and social feeling among agriculturalists.
9. To unite to return farmers' representatives to Parliament. No candidates but farmers to be supported. Elected members to sign the political platform of the Alliance and the electors to have the right of recall.

WA, 19 September 1891, p. 3, c. 1-2.

SELECT BIBLIOGRAPHY

SELECT BIBLIOGRAPHY

Queensland

Alcazar Press, *Queensland 1900. A narrative of her past, together with biographies of her leading men,* Brisbane 1900.
Algar, F., *A handbook to Queensland,* London 1861, (second ed. 1869).
A life's work. Thirty-four years in Parliament. What W. Groom has done for Toowoomba, Toowoomba, n.d. [1896].
Bartley, Nehemiah, *Australian pioneers and reminiscences together with portraits of some of the founders of Australia* (ed. J. J. Knight), Brisbane 1896.
Bernays, C. A., *Queensland politics during sixty years (1859-1919),* Brisbane n.d. [1919].
Boyd, A. J., *Queensland,* London 1882.
—— *Notes on Queensland for the Colonial Exhibition,* 1886.
Coote, William, *A history of the colony of Queensland,* Vol. 1, Brisbane 1882.
Darling Downs Centenary Souvenir, 1840-1940, various authors, Toowoomba 1940.
de Satgé, Oscar, *Pages from the journal of a Queensland squatter,* London 1901.
Evans, G. E., *The garden of Queensland,* Toowoomba 1899.
Fletcher, Price (ed.), *Queensland. Its resources and institutions,* Brisbane 1886.
Fox, M. J., *The history of Queensland,* 3 vols, Brisbane and Adelaide, 1921.
Greenwood, R. H., *The Darling Downs,* Longman's Australian Geographies, No. 6, Melbourne 1956.
Gunn, Donald, *Links with the past,* Brisbane 1937.
Hall, Thomas, *The early history of Warwick District and pioneers of the Darling Downs,* Warwick n.d. [c. 1926].
Holtze, A. L. (ed.), *Toowoomba, 1860-1910,* Brisbane 1911.
Meston, Archibald, *A geographic history of Queensland,* Brisbane 1895.
Morrison, W. F., *The Aldine history of Queensland,* 2 vols, Sydney 1888.
Rudd, Steele (A. H. Davis), *On our selection,* and *Our new selection,* new combined ed., Sydney 1961, (first ed. 1899).
—— *Sandy's selection* and *Back at our selection,* new combined ed., Sydney 1957 (first ed. 1903).
—— *Duncan McClure,* Sydney 1909.
—— *The green grey homestead,* Sydney 1934.
Russell, C. W., *Jimbour. Its history and development, 1840-1953,* Brisbane 1955.

Russell, Henry Stuart, *The genesis of Queensland,* Sydney 1888.
Sims, Bert Munro ('Corbie Dhu'), *Allora's past. The early history of the Allora district, Darling Downs,* Allora 1930.
Thorne, Ebenezer, *An eight years' resident: The queen of the colonies, or, Queensland as I knew it.* London 1876.
Traill, W. H., *A plain explanation of the new Land Act of 1876, and regulations, specially designed for the information and guidance of selectors in every part of the colony,* Toowoomba 1877.
Watts, John, *Pastoral reminiscences* (unpublished autobiography), 1901 [Oxley Library].

AUSTRALIA

Alexander, F., *Moving frontiers: An American theme and its application to Australian history,* Melbourne 1947.
Allen, H. C., *Bush and backwoods. A comparison of the frontier in Australia and the United States,* Michigan 1959.
Barnard, A., *The Australian Wool Market, 1846-1900,* Melbourne 1958.
Borrie, W. D. (assisted by D. R. G. Packer), *Italians and Germans in Australia. A study of assimilation,* Melbourne 1954.
Meinig, D. W., *On the margins of the good earth: the South Australian wheat frontier, 1869-1884,* Chicago 1962.
Penton, Brian, *Landtakers: the story of an epoch,* Sydney 1934.
Perry, T. M., *Australia's first frontier. The spread of settlement in New South Wales, 1788-1829,* Melbourne 1963.
Roberts, S. H., *History of Australian land settlement,* Melbourne 1924.
—— *The squatting age in Australia,* Melbourne 1935.
Ward, Russel, *The Australian legend,* Melbourne 1958.

NOTE: The major primary sources upon which this work is based are:

Official

Queensland Government Gazettes 1860-1900; Queensland Statistical Register 1860-1900; Queensland Parliamentary Debates, and Notes and Proceedings of the Legislative Assembly of Queensland.

Newspapers

Darling Downs Gazette, 1858-1954; *Queenslander,* 1866-1930; *Toowoomba Chronicle,* 1851-1914; *Warwick Argus,* 1864-1914; *Warwick Examiner and Times,* 1867-1914.

INDEX

INDEX